JOSEPH C. LANDIS is currently a professor of English and Director of Jewish Studies at Queens College in New York. He has lectured throughout the United States on English and Yiddish literature. From 1966 to 1969 he was the Jacob D. Berg Visiting Professor of Yiddish Literature at Brandeis University in New York. The plays contained herein have been brilliantly translated by Dr. Landis, one of the foremost authorities on Jewish literature, who also provides an introduction on the moral dimensions of Yiddish literature and theatre, and a historical and literary essay on each dramatist.

THE GREAT
JEWISH PLAYS

In modern translation by
JOSEPH C. LANDIS

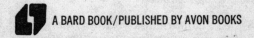 A BARD BOOK/PUBLISHED BY AVON BOOKS

To Laura

AVON BOOKS
A division of
The Hearst Corporation
959 Eighth Avenue
New York, New York 10019

Copyright © 1966, 1972 by Joseph C. Landis
Published by arrangement with
Horizon Press, Publishers, Ltd.
Library of Congress Catalog Card Number: 72-86741
ISBN: 0-380-51573-3

First Equinox Printing, September 1974
First Bard Printing, September, 1980

Printed in the U.S.A.

FOREWORD

The history of the emergence of Yiddish from the status of a vernacular to that of a language of culture parallels, on the whole, the process whereby many another European language displaced the learned Latin tongue and "arrived." The history of Yiddish is, however, unique in that it was embroiled in at least two major ideological conflicts involving its own learned competitor, Hebrew, that left its social status deeply scarred. The first occurred during the eighteenth century. Hebrew had, of course, never been allowed to become the exclusive property of a learned class. It was always the vehicle of the religious education that reached almost every Jewish male and that was, even at its highest levels of learning, fairly widespread. In addition, Hebrew, as the language of Scripture, had a respectability in the Christian world that nearly matched its status in the Jewish world. When, therefore, the Jewish middle class of Central Europe found a possibility of easier access to the Enlightenment of the eighteenth century, it began a parallel movement of Jewish Enlightenment, the Haskala, to modernize Jewish life under the banner of Hebrew, the respected language of religion. Yiddish, as the language of the backward masses of Jews living in the semi-feudal Slavic world and as the vehicle of the pietistic Hassidic movement that stood diametrically opposed to the Haskala, became the object of its scorn. Dubbed a jargon and a bastard offspring of German, Yiddish was derided by this early, Western Haskala, that was as hostile to the concept of a Jewish cultural and ethnic identity as it was apparently indifferent to its egregious error of applying moral concepts to linguistic study. So powerful was the assault upon the respectability of Yiddish, so deep the denigration, that the epithet "jargon" actually became a synonym for Yiddish among the Yiddish-speaking masses, who were, however, mainly ignorant of the opprobrium it conveyed. Even a writer like Sholem Aleichem could still describe himself in the twentieth century as a "zhargonisher shrayber" ("Jargon writer"), when all he meant was that he was a Yiddish writer.

The second great struggle for respectability in which Yiddish was involved grew out of the social upheavals in Eastern Europe a century later. With the emergence of multi-national Russia from its semi-feudal condition amid major social, economic, and political dislocations and with the cracking of that other ponderous multi-national state, the Austro-Hungarian Empire, new ideologies and nationalist sentiments arose among Jews as well as among other minority peoples in central and eastern Europe. The Jewish Socialist movement, which was strongest in Poland, was the Bund, whose ultimate impact was perhaps stronger culturally than politically. The Bund was, for ideological as well as practical reasons, committed to Yiddish. The modern Zionist movement, on the other hand, was profoundly committed to the restoration of Hebrew as the national language of a restored Jewish homeland in Palestine. Once again Yiddish became an object of hostility and scorn, this time on the part of those who, because of their Jewish nationalism, would themselves have been equally unpalatable to the founders of the Jewish Enlightenment. To the Zionist movement, Yiddish became the representative of the despised Diaspora and of the Diaspora mentality.

While Zionism and Jewish socialism were vying for the allegiance of the Jewish masses amidst the break-up of empires and the crumbling of the small-town, isolated, religiously-centered Jewish world, an astonishing Jewish renaissance occurred in Yiddish, led by Yiddish writers at the head of a very numerous intelligentsia throughout the world, where an explosive emigration had carried them. The achievements of these Yiddishist intellectuals during the first four decades of the twentieth century are, in retrospect, breathtaking. Their dream was to effect a transition of Jewish life from its provincial base into a modern, worldwide cultural nationality, with Yiddish as its language of life and creativity. Nearly every modern Yiddish writer was touched by that vision. Nearly every modern Yiddish writer was an activist on its behalf. And in the dedication of two generations of intellectuals, that vision very nearly achieved the illusion of permanence. Throughout the world, Yiddish echoed in urban streets and rural lanes, Yiddish schools at all levels were established, Yiddish scholarship matured, a Yiddish press grew to astonishing circulations, Yiddish theater flourished, and modern Yiddish literature achieved a depth and stature that have not yet been accorded their full recognition.

The destruction of the heartland of Yiddish in Eastern Europe during the Holocaust of the Hitler years, however, effectively ended that vision. The resurgence of Hebrew in Israel and of "Jewish writing" in other languages provided new channels for Jewish creativity, and Yiddish seemed destined for a swift demise. Yet an astonishing phenomenon began to manifest itself in recent years. A movement that had been quietly gathering strength during the sixties suddenly burst upon the American scene with the advent of the seventies. Yiddish became increasingly popular among Jews. A Yiddish revival became evident on the American campus, with dozens of colleges offering courses in Yiddish language or in Yiddish literature in English translation.[1] This revival of interest in Yiddish among the younger generation paralleled a similar revival among the older generation, revealed in such varied phenomena as the record-breaking run of *Fiddler on the Roof,* the best-seller popularity of books about Yiddish such as Leo Rosten's *The Joys of Yiddish,* and the renewed interest in the old Yiddish-speaking Lower East Side of New York, evidenced in the crowds at recent museum exhibits devoted to the Yiddish Theater and to the East Side, and in the sizeable flow of recent volumes devoted to the East Side.

Yiddish has also come to the awareness of non-Jewish America, not only through the increasing numbers of translations of the works of Yiddish writers, but also through the emergence of a number of American Jewish writers of major importance during the post-World War II years. As Julian Moynihan remarked in his lead review of Saul Bellow's *Herzog* in the *New York Times Book Review* some years ago, "Over the past 10 or 15 years, Jewish writers have emerged as a dominant movement in our literature." Whether a movement or not, whether dominant or not, these writers, products, in part, of the world of Yiddish, have entered into the mainstream of American cultural life bearing with them the moral values of that world —or their reaction to them—with which to confront our times.

In a real sense, then, Yiddish is in America, not as a stranger in some private enclave, not as an outsider, but as a participant in a world which has come to see the Jew and his experience as one symbol of contemporary America. There has, indeed, occurred a confluence of two cultures, and a sort of symbiotic

---

[1]Queens College of the City University of New York, with several hundred students enrolled in its Yiddish program, even offers an undergraduate major in Yiddish, apparently the first American College to do so, and publishes a journal in English, titled *Yiddish,* devoted to Yiddish language and literature.

relationship has developed between them. It would hardly be
an exaggeration to say that at no time in its history has Yiddish
been more respected in the Jewish as well as the non-Jewish
world.

What accounts for this Yiddish revival at the very moment
when the latest in a long line of prophets foretelling its doom
were most certain that the end of Yiddish was in sight? Related
questions come pouring forth in profusion. Why should the
second generation of Jews, who had, between the two world
wars, been so eager to escape from the culture of their immigrant parents and be absorbed into the mainstream of American
life, now turn with affection toward the world which they had
in their youth rejected? Why should the old Yiddish-speaking
lower East Side Jewish ghetto of New York now intrigue them?
When did it change from a place to be forgotten to a time to
be remembered? What are they looking for in that bygone
world, destroyed by prosperity as surely as its European counterpart was destroyed by adversity? Is it a historical assessment of
that experience or is it perhaps some sense of a viable past,
some meaning that will inform present identity? Was it an
ordeal and an anguish then and has it become a "fabulous
era," a "magnificent legend" now? Has the old East Side become a Jewish *Our Town,* a halcyon world of the past, a Harry
Golden age when, despite hardships and privations, human
relations were stable and human feelings genuine and spontaneous, when personal identity was clearly definable, and the
world was full of hope? Are so many looking back to see how
far they have come or how much they have lost?

Our time is one in which an "ethnic revival" is blazing among
other minority cultures of America as well as among Jews.
Some of the sources of that revival run three generations deep.
The transition from a rural to an urban America, which was
marked by the end of the frontier, was reinforced by the Great
European Emigration that began almost simultaneously during
the closing decades of the nineteenth century and continued
until the outbreak of the first World War. This period of the
immigrant first generation was followed by the years between
the two great wars, years in which the second generation sought
access to America and to a "native" American culture by re-
pudiating its ethnic heritage and washing itself clean in the
Melting Pot. That movement has been sharply curtailed in
the post-World War II years, the years of the third generation.
This generation is turning back to the culture of its grandparents, reviving the concept of cultural pluralism which Hor-

ace Kallen urged more than half a century ago, proclaiming the end of the Melting Pot, vindicating Marcus Lee Hanson's perception that the third generation returns to the cultural heritage of its immigrant grandparents.

It may be only an accident of history that this return by the third generation to its ethnic roots coincides with a moment in American history when so many have begun to question so much. The prosperity of the middle class has not kept its children from doubting its values. Has it kept the parents themselves from a great malaise? The massive estrangement of people from themselves, from one another, and from their world, that has been one of the commonplace facts of our time, has triggered a restless search for meaning and identity. Since that doubt and that search have coincided with another historic movement, the "return" of the third generation and the accompanying ethnic revival, then the current interest in Yiddish may, indeed, be no mere passing fad. It may well be with us for at least a generation, resulting as it does from historic forces and deep-seated needs. In addition, this Yiddish revival, in its own way a counterpart to the contemporary quest for lost innocence and the search for a simpler and more genuine world, may also reveal unsuspected moral alternatives for a troubled time.

Contents

INTRODUCTION

The Moral Center of Yiddish Literature

The rapid and intense development of modern Yiddish literature is one of the minor wonders of cultural history. Though the dating of periods and eras is often no more than a convenience for the historian, the designation of 1864 as the year inaugurating the modern period of Yiddish literature is less arbitrary than most such designations, for it was the year in which the first major work of its first major writer appeared.

Recent though that date is, however, Yiddish literature was morally rooted in a millennial past. For some nine centuries prior to that, East European or Ashkenazic Jewry, speaking Yiddish and praying Hebrew, had been building a religiously centered world of its own. Though often surrounded by oppressive restrictions from without, it was always reinforced from within by its own spiritual resources. A far-flung world and at times a mobile world, driven and scattered by periodic outbreaks of violent hostility, Ashkenazic Jewry finally settled mainly into the area bounded by the Dnieper River on the east and the Vistula on the west, by the Baltic Sea on the north and the Black Sea on the south. Here, despite incredible hardship and persecution, it grew into a remarkably coherent society of unique characteristics. From its ethical tradition, Ashkenazic Jewry drew and developed all that was humane, life-affirming, and man-revering, and it strove to embody that ethic in the pattern of its life, in the structure of its institutions, in the ceremonial of its customs and rituals, in the celebration of its holidays and holy days, and in the observance of its traditions. It strove to hold continually before its eyes that ideal of conduct and of being.

The phrase "our Judeo-Christian civilization" has become so much a part of our vocabulary that, valid though the words are in emphasizing the continuity which for the Christian world binds the two Testaments together, it yet obscures certain fundamental differences. It obscures the fact that the ethic of the Ashkenazic Jew and his forebears was based on a conception

1

of man and of life that is distinctly different from the Christian view. His conception of what a man ought to be is embodied in the far-reaching implications of the Yiddish word *mentsh*, whose complex meanings suggest far more than the literal denotation "human being" or "person." The frequent admonition "Be a mentsh" was an exhortation to strive for the particular qualities that Ashkenazic Jews valued in a human being— qualities of *mentshlekhkayt* that form a distinct constellation of premises and values.

To the moral vision of *mentshlekhkayt*, the central Christian concept of original sin or innate human depravity is wholly foreign. Counterposed to this view stands the Talmudic sense of man's original innocence, which sees him as unburdened by any sins but his own and capable of responding either to an inclination to good (*yetser tov*) or an inclination to evil (*yetser hara*), a sense of man which sees the victory of evil as temporary, a result either of the outer pressures of circumstances or the inner pressures of sickness and aberration. Though deeply aware of the horrendous power of evil, Jewish tradition is nonetheless convinced of man's ultimate superiority over evil, of the ultimate victory of man's yearning for good. As Maimonides remarks, even if you force a Jew to perform a *mitsva* (commandment, good deed), he still does it voluntarily, because his basic desire is to do it; only error makes him think otherwise. The ultimate victory of good is made possible, however, not by yearning and not by faith, but by the studied application of the moral and intellectual values of mentshlekhkayt.

The Ashkenazic Jew was hardly deluded as to the imminence of the triumph of universal justice. Indeed, his sense of reality was expressed in his use of the phrase "when the Messiah comes" to indicate the remote and improbable; but he was convinced of the ever-present possibility of man's faithfulness to his mentshlekhkayt. For the Jewish ethic, evil, like the snake in Paradise, is an outsider tempting man. And for each man this is the central moral drama, the struggle with the intruding snake, the conflict, within morally free man, between the powers of good and evil. In this struggle, man's inclination to good is capable of conquering without external intervention. By contrast, for the Christian, the central drama involves a struggle against a native taint, a battle with an accomplished, innate, and inevitable evil, a conflict whose ultimate resolution depends on salvation from without.

Central to the conception of humane conduct embodied in the ethic of mentshlekhkayt are obligations and qualities which the Ashkenazic Jew considered so vital and integral to his sense of self that he designated them with the Yiddish phrase *a yidish harts* (a Jewish heart). To have a Jewish heart meant above all to have compassion, to find one's identity among the *rakhmonim bney rakhmonim* (the compassionate sons of the compassionate). It meant to be sensitive to *tsar baaley khayim*, to feel deep distress at inflicting needless pain on man or beast. (Hunting as sport, for example, was regarded as not befitting a mentsh; indeed, merely shaming a man before his fellows was a wrong of greatest magnitude.) It meant to have a great aversion to violence, a deep distrust of its ultimate efficacy, and a suspicious disdain for the violent. To have a Jewish heart meant to admire gentleness and kindliness and modesty. The Ashkenazic Jew's aversion of violence was not based on any sentimental exaltation of weakness or of "the power of powerlessness," but on a principled repudiation of force as bestializing and on a faith in the ultimate victory of reason and morality. The perspective of a millennial history had brought the conviction not only that force proves nothing but that it is ultimately doomed to failure because of its violation of man's mentshlekhkayt.

If Adam's disobedience and fall haunts the Christian imagination, it is Cain's haughty assertion of his irresponsibility that exemplifies the depths of dereliction to the Ashkenazic Jew's moral sense. It is Cain's defiant question, "Am I my brother's keeper?" that is more grievous even than his crime, for with that question he repudiates the sole path to atonement and morality. As compassion is one of the prime qualities of a mentsh, so is responsibility for another, one of his prime obligations. And as one man is responsible for another, so are all men responsible for one another; all are bound together in a responsibility that is social as well as individual. Indeed, the responsibility of the donor is also the right of the recipient, as the derivation of *tsdoko* (philanthropy) from *tsedek* (justice, righteousness) plainly indicates. This sense of mutual responsibility that pervades the Jewish ethic also expresses itself in the Ashkenazic Jew's prizing of family closeness and human relatedness, in his insistence on emotional responsibility, on involvement and social commitment. If the central Christian emphasis is on sin and divine forgiveness, the central Jewish concern is with suffering and its alleviation through mutual aid. From such roots as these grew the Ashkenazic Jew's fundamental respect for ordinary humanity, his trust in its potential, and his commitment to its welfare.

As faith is central to Christianity, so *mitsva* and Torah—good deeds and study—are central to Judaism and its ethic. Indeed, of the three pillars upon which the world rests according to that volume of the Talmud called *The Ethics of the Fathers*, only one relates to the service of God. A second insists on such obligations to man as those that the Ashkenazic Jew conceived of as both shaping the "Jewish heart" and being shaped by it. And a third enjoins the study of Torah, which is, ultimately, the study of morality. Seen in this context, the familiar phrase *a yidisher kop* (a Jewish head), which the Ashkenazic Jew also adopted to express his self-image, is clearly not intended as an assertion of superiority to other heads. It is, rather, a repudiation of unintellectuality, a repudiation of the head that is obtuse to the values of learning and to the respect for learning for its own sake. As *The Ethics of the Fathers* notes, "Whosoever labors in the Torah for its own sake, merits many things. . . ." If to William Blake, heaven is a state of perpetual forgiveness, to the Ashkenazic Jew it was, quite literally, an institution for perpetual study. This unqualified respect for learning, for the study of Torah for the sake of study, this pursuit of learning that is its own reward and its own fulfillment was, like the ideal of a Jewish heart, central to the Ashkenazic Jew's conception of a mentsh. Indeed, if a practical aim had been required for the study of Torah, the Ashkenazic Jew would have identified that aim as the elevation of man to a higher degree of mentshlekhkayt.

To Judaism, the religious embodiment of the ethic of mentshlekhkayt, the concept of a personal redeemer who will liberate from personal sin and guilt, is as foreign as the concept of original sin itself. Redemption, insofar as it involves a Messiah, is entirely a social phenomenon. It posits the liberation of the Jews from exile and the attendant liberation of mankind from injustice and oppression. A "Jewish heart" dreams of a reign of justice "at the end of days" and hopes for the Messianic liberation of mankind that will usher in an age of justice here, in this world. Ultimate faith in the coming of the Messiah is, however, irrelevant to man's obligation to *tsdoko* and righteousness now. The Ashkenazic Jew may even have tempered with irony his faith in an earthly Utopia—"When the Messiah comes . . ." —but he never took other than seriously his obligation to social responsibility and justice now. Individual "redemption" in "the world that is to come" can be achieved only on the basis of living according to the prescriptions and obligations of mentshlekhkayt. But the rewards of heaven were far less vital to the Ashkenazic Jew's consciousness than the necessity for right living here, and they are incidental rather than central to Judaism as a faith. Moral living is itself spiritual salvation. Mentshlekhkayt is its own sufficient reward. And man, however evil his past, is always redeemable, not through faith but through living as a mentsh.

In a world of suffering, the ethic of mentshlekhkayt imposes its own order, a discipline, a Law which makes life significant. The very word "order" continually appears in the terminology of Judaism, whether in the *Seder* (division) of the Talmud or the Passover Seder or the *Sedre* (portion) of the Pentateuch that is read weekly in the synagogue, or the *Siddur* that names the Jewish prayer book. The imposition of this moral order upon behavior is intended less to explain the suffering of life than to affirm the values that enable man to endure his anguish. The morality of mentshlekhkayt becomes a compensation for suffering and a mitigation of it.

The religious expression of the ethic of mentshlekhkayt the Ashkenazic world found in the Torah God had given it; it found its "chosen" religious purpose in bringing the values of that Torah to the world and in enduring—if necessary, dying—on their behalf: and it attempted to implant those values in every individual and in all the social institutions it created. It required everyone to be a mentsh—even God; and it did not hesitate to rebuke Him when it thought He was remiss.

In affirming the necessity for its own vision of moral living, the ethic of mentshlekhkayt affirms life itself, not as something to be endured but as a source of the deep gratification to be derived from the practice and celebration of those humane traditions which the Ashkenazic Jew strove to embody in the pattern of his life, individual and social, secular and religious. Although this ideal of compassionate, socially responsible, intellectually dedicated mentshlekhkayt, man-revering and life-affirming, is not in its separate elements uniquely Jewish, the Ashkenazic Jew felt that as a constellation of values it was distinctively and characteristically Jewish. To his mind, it was wholly different from and greatly superior to both the Christian ideal and that other ideal so often manifest in Western history, the ideal of muscled, aggressive manliness, which admires force and is basically suspicious of man, mistrustful of intellect as "impractical" and of art as "effete" and of social melioration as "visionary." The admonition "Be a man" is very far removed from the exhortation "Be a mentsh."

The Ashkenazic world was certain of the humanizing pow-

ers of Torah and of the capacity of the Torah as ethic to produce men who were more worthy; and the Ashkenazic world
was also certain that the ethic of mentshlekhkayt was an ethic
more worthy of men and of their moral potential.

This ideal of the Jew as mentsh and of man as mentsh, this
ethic of mentshlekhkayt which stood at the heart of Ashkenazic
Jewish life stands also at the moral center of its literature.
From Sholem Yankev Abramovich, who wrote under the
pseudonym of Mendele Mokher Sforim (Mendele the Book-
seller), to Bashevis Singer, the vision of that literature is the
moral vision of mentshlekhkayt. It is the vision of Mendele,
who, however fierce his satire against those who exploit or
betray or delude themselves, never sinks into the misanthropy
of a Swift or a Voltaire, never doubts that the transformation of
a man into a mentsh is a perennial possibility. It is the vision
of Sholem Aleichem (Sholem Rabinowitz), beneath the surface
of whose humor glows in tragic greatness a portrait of the Jew
as mentsh. It is the vision of Yitskhok Leybush Peretz, who turns
from his early satire to a romantic idealization of Hassidic
and folk figures transformed into symbols of Jewish mentshlekhkayt. And it is the vision of Bashevis Singer, the latest of
the great Yiddish prose writers, who, with his acute awareness
of man's capacity for evil, is all the more insistent on the
necessity of mentshlekhkayt.

Out of the moral imperatives and the social and intellectual
values of mentshlekhkayt that nourished the consciousness of
the Yiddish writers of the past hundred years and shaped the
image of man that predominates in Yiddish literature was fashioned also the portrait of the Jewish hero. From the premise
of the native innocence of man grows the sense of the tragic hero
or innocent victim, not of any tragic flaw of his own but of cir-
cumstance or of hostile men. The world which revered most
the multitudes of martyrs who had died for *Kiddush Ha-shem*,
the sanctification of God's name, found in the innocence of
the tragic heroes of its literature a reflection of one of the
prime realities of its life. Though justice may not triumph in
the ordeal of tragedy, though the moral order of the universe
may not be demonstrated in the action of its art, yet man's
capacity for mentshlekhkayt is reaffirmed and the dignity and
joy of man as mentsh towers above the suffering and the cir-
cumstance. In personal qualities the hero embodies the values
of his world: the Jewish hero is the hero as mentsh. The
cathartic experience derives from the vindication of mentshlekhkayt. The Jewish tragic hero is not to be confused with

the anti-hero; that would be to miss his moral stature or to see him only in relation to the premises of an ethic and a world view alien to him. When the Jewish tragic hero is guilty, his guilt lies in his deviation from the values of mentshlekhkayt, not because of an irremediable flaw of character but because of an error of judgment. And the catastrophe that overwhelms him (other than death) need never be irreparable; it can always be mitigated and ultimately transcended by moral conduct. The tragic vision of the Ashkenazic Jew is ultimately less concerned with vindicating God than it is with saving man and affirming morality and life.

It was this ethic that resolved the central paradox of Jewish existence and Jewish faith, the paradox of the God who was, on the one hand, the intimate Father, whose book was a family album, for whom time was irrelevant and place insignificant, and on the other hand, the God who was destiny and history—remote, inscrutable, unanswering; the God who had chosen and the God who ignored. The resolution was achieved through the Torah and its ethic, through the dedication to certain concepts of propriety in conduct which were synonymous with propriety in humanity, through the acceptance of values for living which did not need history either to confirm or vindicate them, whose satisfactions transcended the injustice of things.

It was this ethic that resolved the paradox that a people for whom religion was not merely at the center of life but suffused every action should have produced no devotional poetry; for it was an ethic that was concerned not with individual salvation but with social responsibility and universal liberation. If anything, Yiddish literature produced a flood of what might almost be termed anti-devotional poetry, a genre which, encompassing the poetry of complaint, may seem to have its roots in the Book of Job, but which is distinctly different from Job's questioning that grows out of his personal destiny. Yiddish "anti-devotional" poetry addressed to God is concerned exclusively with the fate of His People, and its range is from such relatively mild complaints as those of Rabbi Levi Yitskhok of Berditchev or Shimon Frug to the indictment and even the conviction of God in Itsik Manger who expels him from the assembly of the true lovers of Israel. That the modern Yiddish poet tended to be a secularist has some small bearing on the absence of devotional poetry and the identification of God with Jewish destiny. The particular relationship of God to His Chosen People makes him answerable for their sufferings. But more important by far is the fact that devotional poetry must have at its heart the individual's personal relationship with God and his concern for his personal salvation. Both of these are relatively unimportant to Judaism and its ethic, for it is the People with whom God made His compact, the People to whom He gave His Torah, and the fate of the individual becomes one with the destiny of the People. This relationship explains the curious fact that men who are essentially secularists write so much about God and that none of this poetry addressed to God can be properly regarded as devotional or even as religious poetry as the non-Jewish mind would conceive it.

The Scope of Yiddish Literature

Although the subject matter of Yiddish literature was at first limited to the world of Eastern European Jewish life, Yiddish writers very quickly enlarged their embrace. It was not only the mass migration of Jews to the United States that enlarged the scope of Yiddish literature; the break-up of the semifeudal economy of Russia also played its role. The railroad whose presence makes itself felt in Chekhov's *The Cherry Orchard* can be heard symbolically hooting through great tracts of Yiddish writing. And the winds of European culture began blowing ever harder over the small-town streets. As a result of pressures from within as well as blows from without, of the emergence of capitalism and a changed political climate, small-town Jewish life during the second half of the nineteenth century felt increasingly the European influences that had hitherto been exercised only on a small body of intellectuals, and the secularization of Jewish life proceeded at a greatly accelerated pace. The intellectual ferment that resulted began to reach even the smallest of communities and yeshivas.[1] By 1900, Yiddish writers in great numbers were creating a literature that takes a worthy place among the literatures of Europe and America. Multitudes of young men who, in other generations, would have become rabbis and Talmudic scholars now gave up their religious studies and became instead writers, artists, critics, philosophers, and secular scholars. Millions worked and fought for freedom and made heroes out of Yiddish writers during those oppressive, hopeful, explosive years till World War I, and other hundreds of thousands rode, walked, swam, or stole by night across roads and towns and borders and seas to

---

[1] Academies for Talmudic and rabbinic studies.

find a new life and freedom and, among other things, to help create a new transatlantic Yiddish literature.

It is customary and proper to date the beginning of modern Yiddish literature with the publication in 1864 of *Dos Kleyne Mentshele* (in English translation *The Parasite*) by Mendele Mokher Sforim, but that date may be misleading. Peretz and Sholem Aleichem, the two writers usually coupled with Mendele as the founding fathers of modern Yiddish literature, did not begin writing Yiddish until the middle to late eighties. And the majority of those who occupy distinguished places in the history of Yiddish literature belong to a still later generation. In a very real sense, then, modern Yiddish literature, with some distinguished forerunners in the nineteenth century, is a literature of the twentieth century, richly varied in its subject matter, universal in its ultimate concerns, confronting—and perhaps disconcerting—the world with the vision of man as mentsh. That it should have achieved what it did in these few decades of our century and in spite of the incineration of the great European Yiddish heartland—this is indeed remarkable.

The Yiddish Theater

Yiddish drama, of course, shares the qualities and the destiny of the rest of Yiddish literature. But the drama always faces special conditions not faced by other literary forms—notably the theater, which is subject to its own pressures and history. Despite the theatrical form of many of the customary Yiddish entertainments, they had little direct effect on the creation of a Yiddish theater. Though a *badkhan* (wedding bard) chanted rhymes at Jewish weddings, though Purim was a regular day for amateur "play" performances, the direct stimulus for a professional theater came from other sources. And it came relatively late; Yiddish plays written before the last quarter of the nineteenth century were written with no hope of performance on a professional stage.

In Europe the professional Yiddish theater grew out of variety entertainment, when a gifted young man with a flair for the dramatic conceived the idea of improving the format of entertainment then popular in the wine-taverns where people gathered after work or business. The usual performer was a singer who, in the manner then popular, sang songs describing the character or plight of various types or occupations in Jewish society and also attempted to impersonate the character in the song. In Jassy, Romania, in 1876, however, Abraham Goldfadden, along with two Brody singers, as these entertainers were called, conceived the idea of adding to the songs an element of plot or continuity, with dialogue improvised in the manner of the *commedia dell'arte*. From this beginning soon came an increasingly widespread musical theater, with a repertoire written almost entirely by Goldfadden himself. Though in later years Goldfadden produced some work of fine quality, notably *Shulamis* and *Bar Kokhba,* the bulk of his early work, as he himself later admitted, was tawdry. The early Goldfadden repertoire was soon brought to America by defecting members of his highly successful company, and the influence of the type was strengthened by Goldfadden imitators.

A second major influence on the Yiddish theater was born in America when Jacob Gordin, with no prior theatrical experience, discovered a talent for writing plays that were vastly superior to the musicals and the melodrama that flooded the Yiddish stage during the eighties and nineties, the first two decades of large-scale Jewish immigration. Gordin scoured European literature for plots and characters, which he reworked into new Jewish plays, but despite the quality of such Gordin plays as *Mirele Efros* and *God, Man and Devil,* his less able imitators, who did the same, produced a constant flow of worthless stuff. It was fed by enterprising businessmen of the theater to an audience of recent immigrants, mainly workers with little education, who found in the Yiddish theater, whatever its fare, a home in a land that was free but strange and hard.

The musical theater, with its melodramatic offshoot, that derived from Goldfadden, and the realistic theater that Gordin introduced from European literature remained the two dominant forces in the Yiddish professional theater until the first World War. But an event occurred in 1908 that heralded as well as stimulated developments a decade later. About the turn of the century, probably under the influence of a revitalized European theater, Yiddish writers began to turn to the drama, though they were fully aware that in the face of Czarist prohibition of Yiddish theater and, later, in the absence of a quality theater their plays had little chance of being produced except in translation. It was, in fact, in translation that some of the early work of Asch and Hirshbein was first seen. The number of young Jewish actors educated and trained for the Russian stage in Russian dramatic schools was, however, growing. With the rescinding of the prohibition of Yiddish theater, new possibilities opened. In 1908, not long after one of Hirsh-

bein's plays, performed in Russian translation in Odessa, had
been enthusiastically received by the Russian critics, a new
Yiddish theatrical enterprise was born. In the cultivated, relatively free atmosphere of favored Odessa, a group of these
trained young actors gathered around Hirshbein and formed
the company that soon came to be known as the Hirshbein
Troupe. Uncompromisingly determined to produce only plays
of literary quality and not to be limited by the realistic form,
the Hirshbein Troupe toured Russia with a repertoire that included, besides Hirshbein's own plays, those of Asch, Pinski,
Sholem Aleichem, and Gordin. When, after two struggling
years, the company was forced to disband as a result of its financial inexperience, it had already demonstrated the commercial
possibilities of an art theater, just as Chekhov and the Moscow
Art Theater had done earlier and as Eugene O'Neill and the
Provincetown Players were to do later.

The first fruit of the Hirshbein Troupe was the famous
Vilna Troupe, which began its career on February 18, 1916
with the performance of a play by Sholem Asch. It attained its
true character and stature some time later when it acquired
the services of David Herman as director. In the course of the
next two decades, the Vilna Troupe and its offshoots, compris-
ing about one hundred trained performers, produced about
one hundred plays, including thirty from other languages, and
toured Europe and America. Its best-known work was its premiere production of Anski's *The Dybbuk* in 1920.

In Poland after the first World War, the art theater movement also included, besides little theater groups like Azazel
and Ararat, such companies as the Vikt (Warsaw Yiddish Art
Theater) and the company that came to be known as Young
Theater, under the direction of Mikhl Veikhert. In 1929
Veikhert reopened the dramatic studio he had headed from
1922 to 1924 and continued on a program of theatrical boldness. In his efforts to break down the separation between stage
and audience, he tried dispensing with curtain and sets, and
he experimented with arena theater.

In Russia the Yiddish theater was reestablished after World
War I with the help—almost at the insistence—of the Soviet
government, which persuaded Alexander Granovski to assume
the direction of a company and provided funds, rehearsal stu-
dios, and a small theater, for which Marc Chagall was commis-
sioned to do the murals. Granovski's style of comic grotesque,
utilizing such elements as buffoonery, grotesque, even acro-
batics, proved most successful with such comedies as those of

Sholem Aleichem or with comic adaptations from Mendele's fiction. When Granovski left the company during its 1928–1929 European tour, the gifted Mikhoels succeeded him. As late as 1940, the State Yiddish Theater in Moscow was among the best in the country, as well as the best of the fifteen Soviet Yiddish theaters.

The Habima, the famous Hebrew company, was also a product of revolutionary Russia. Organized in 1917, it soon succeeded in getting Stanislavsky as advisor and director. He was followed as director by his pupil, the Armenian Eugene Vakhtangov, who worked with the company for three years in preparing its most famous production, Anski's *The Dybbuk*. *The Dybbuk* and H. Leivick's *The Golem* have remained among the most impressive productions in its repertoire.

In the United States as in Europe, the new art theater grew and thrived alongside the tawdry theater of "entertainment." The Jewish immigration of the twentieth century brought large numbers of young men and women who had received a secular education in the Russian or Polish labor and revolutionary movements. Writers also began to turn to a theater whose quality had improved under the influence of Jacob Gordin. Playwrights on both sides of the Atlantic continued to produce; and schooled actors became increasingly available. It awaited only the appearance of a man with the organizational ability of Maurice Schwartz for the professional art theater in America to begin. In 1917 Schwartz made his first efforts. At the suggestion of Jacob ben Ami, an alumnus of the Hirshbein Troupe, he produced three Hirshbein comedies in succession, *Green Fields* among them, and scored a great success. Audience and producer had found each other, and the Maurice Schwartz Yiddish Art Theater was the result. Other companies were formed, though they were less durable than Schwartz's. New playwrights appeared, with dramas in prose and verse, in response to the needs of the new theater, among them H. Leivick. For two decades the Yiddish Art Theater was a major force on the Yiddish stage in America, employing the best actors available in plays of high literary quality.

Of the various other art theater companies in the United States between the two wars, one at least deserves mention, the Artef. Directed by Benno Schneider, formerly of the Habima, who had matured under the influence of Stanislavsky and Vakhtangov, the Artef was for several years a vital group, but it suffered from the disparity between the great talent of its director and the limited capabilities of its largely amateur actors.

So rapid a survey of the Yiddish theater that was available to the dramatists represented in this collection can at best only suggest the similarity between the Yiddish theater and other theaters. Despite its relatively recent—and inauspicious —birth, the Yiddish theater kept pace with the theaters of Europe and America. If it has presented a good deal of commercial dross, it has been no worse than the theater here and abroad, where, as John Gassner observed, "Since the eighteenth century, the bulk of dramatic output . . . consisted of sentimental comedy, transparent farce, and 'thrillers' of murder and crime detection."[2] But it has also, like the other theaters of Europe and America, presented a drama high in quality and varied in form and content. The restless experimentation, the recurrent use of varied techniques that characterizes twentieth century drama as a whole and each of its major practitioners is characteristic of Yiddish drama and dramatists as well. They too probed the possibilities of realism, naturalism, allegory, symbolism, poetic philosophical drama, folk drama, and romantic historical drama; and they evinced the same eagerness for theatrical innovation and change. Like the English theater in the United States, the Yiddish theater here and abroad came to maturity after the first World War. But the blows that began to fall in the thirties and the fate that overwhelmed it in the forties were unique. The destruction of the great Yiddish heartland was an irreparable blow.

The plays in this collection were chosen to suggest the variety of Yiddish drama as well as its quality. Each play is not necessarily the best of its author but is representative of his interests and his talent; and all but one, Pinski's *King David and His Wives*, attained great popularity as well as critical acclaim.

The virtual elimination of Yiddish cultural life in Poland since the War and in Russia since 1952, when almost every Yiddish writer of stature was executed, has not only left the Jewish community of the United States the largest in the world; it has also served to underscore the fact that on the cultural continent within our geographic borders, a large body of non-English writing was created and continues to be created. This body of non-English literature (and it is only one of several) was created in Yiddish, but the writers were Americans. Of the

[2] John Gassner, *The Theatre in Our Times* (New York, 1954), p. 5.

writers in this collection, Peretz Hirshbein and H. Leivick are buried here, each after some forty years of residence; David Pinski lived here for half a century before going off to Israel, where he died; and Sholem Asch, though always a wanderer, was, like the others, a citizen as well as a resident for many years. Anski alone never came to these shores. To list the other Yiddish writers who, having come here as young men, adopted America as their home and lived and wrote here for decades (and continue to live and write here) would involve a sizeable lexicon of Yiddish letters. Only an unfamiliar language has kept these writers from the awareness of a large number of American readers and writers. Of late, the works of Yiddish literature have received increasing attention. Perhaps the time is rapidly approaching when historians and critics will accord them more than silence or passing reference in literary histories of the American people. American-Yiddish literature is the heritage of the American people. And there are relatively few heirs left elsewhere.

JOSEPH C. LANDIS

THE DYBBUK
(Between Two Worlds)

❧

S. Anski[1]
(1863–1920)

❧

The Dybbuk is probably the most famous Yiddish play; it is
certainly so for the non-Yiddish reader and is more frequently
performed in translation than any other Yiddish play. The
total number of performances since Stanislavsky first studied
the 1914 Russian version of the play for the Moscow Art
Theater Studio surely runs into the thousands. Although
Stanislavsky did not stage the play, he did suggest adding the
role of the Messenger, and in revised form *The Dybbuk,* in Yiddish, was first produced by the Vilna Troupe. Unfortunately,
Anski did not live to see it open. The premiere, at the Ely-
seum Theater in Warsaw, did not take place until December
9, 1920, at the end of the traditional thirty-day mourning
period that followed Anski's death on November 8. That
opening began a phenomenal career. Two years later the play
was produced by Maurice Schwartz in New York. In the same
year it was performed in Moscow by the Habima, in Hebrew
translation, under the direction of Stanislavsky's gifted pupil
Eugene Vakhtangov, with music by Joel Engel. (In May,
1928, the Habima celebrated the 600th performance of the
play.) On December 15, 1925, *The Dybbuk,* in English, opened
in New York at the Neighborhood Playhouse, directed, in the
Vakhtangov style, by David Vardi and Henry G. Alsberg. A

[1] The pseudonym of Shloyme Zanvl Rappoport.

national tour followed. It was seen again in New York, this
time in Hebrew, during the visit of the Habima in 1948. In
1954 it was revived by David Ross at the Fourth Street Theater
in New York. The leading members of that cast—Theodore
Bikel, Ludwig Donath, Jack Guilford—with the addition of
Carol Lawrence in the role of Leye (Leah), were again seen
in the television version in 1960–1961 which Sidney Lumet directed for the Play of the Week series. It has had a number of
fine amateur productions, most recently at the University of
Chicago in the summer of 1962, and at Brigham Young University, July 12–14, 1961, under the direction of Mordecai Gore-
lick. It has been performed not only in Yiddish, Hebrew, and
English (in England as well as America), but also in Polish,
Swedish, Bulgarian, Ukrainian, French, Serbian, and Japanese.
It has also been seen as a Yiddish film (produced in Poland
in 1934, music by Henech Kon), and as an opera both by
Ludovico Rocco at La Scala in Milan and by Michael White in
Seattle in the spring of 1963. George Gershwin, in Paris in
1928, also considered the possibility of doing *The Dybbuk* as
an opera.

It comes, therefore, as something of a surprise that none of
Anski's other literary efforts (with the exception of his poem
"The Vow," which became the official anthem of the Jewish
Workers Party of Poland—the Bund, and the unfinished play
Day and Night), achieved any kind of popularity at all. Were
it not for *The Dybbuk*, Anski's reputation would rest almost
entirely on his distinguished achievement as a folklorist, first
in Russian and then in Yiddish. He was for some years a member of the Jewish Historical and Ethnographic Society of St.
Petersburg. He was also the first Jewish folklorist to undertake large-scale fieldwork. With a grant from Baron Horáce
Ginsburg he headed an expedition, begun in 1912 and inter-
rupted by the war, during which he visited nearly seventy
towns and cities in the Ukrainian provinces of Volhyn, Podo-
lia, and Kiev. Indeed, even *The Dybbuk* must be credited to
his interest in folklore, for it followed his return from the field
expedition; what had been merely an idea in 1911, when the
story first began to stir in his mind, became a four-act play in
Russian in 1914. Not only is the play, subtitled in the first
edition "A Dramatic Legend," rich in folklore material, much

of which he gathered during his expedition, but its theme is an illustration of his interpretation of Jewish folklore, in which he sees as the basic motif the primacy of spirit over force:

> From the Old Testament to the present, the central idea of all Jewish creativity is: physical force is not the force that wins. This is the basic idea of the Prophets, of the Aggada, of Jewish folklore. The physically stronger is defeated because he is spiritually weaker. There is no trace of the idealization of physical force in Jewish folk creation and in Jewish folk tales. The motif of physical force is, in fact, met only seldom among Jews, as, for example, in Deborah's Song, in the legends about Bar Kokhba. Even in the cycle of tales about Samson, it is not mere physical force that wins. The Jewish hero does not struggle for power or women or wealth, and his weapons are spiritual rather than physical. The sole motif of the Jewish folk tale is spiritual struggle.[2]

It is in such a moral universe that the action of *The Dybbuk* occurs. A play that on the surface seems to be merely a touching love story set in surroundings strange to Western eyes is something far more than that. Essentially *The Dybbuk* is a play about the ethic of the Ashkenazic Jew, a play about the ways and values of a world, a revelation of the ways of man and the justice of God. The moral universe of *The Dybbuk* is that of the Ashkenazic Jew, in which the interdependence of man is not only a fact; it is an inescapable obligation: man is his brother's keeper. A man is responsible for his fellow men. If not love, at least compassion is the ideal to be translated into conduct. It is a universe in which man is fallible and sins, but never irretrievably. No matter how great the wrong that flows from his having yielded to the inclination to evil, man is always capable of turning to the good, to the *yetser tov*. He may be seduced by temptation, yield to impulse, and be misled by error; he may be weak and mistaken; but he is not evil himself nor is he responsible for any sins but his own. Fallible man, being eternally self-redeemable, may, if he falls, rise again by translating desire into moral action.

[2] S. Anski, "The Jewish Folk Spirit and Its Creations," *Collected Works* (Vilna-Warsaw-New York, Ansk Publishers, 1925), Vol. XV, pp. 23-24 (in Yiddish).

The particular setting of *The Dybbuk* is the world of Hassidic pietism which grew out of one sage's [3] intense sense of the goodness and accessibility of God and out of his profound conviction, therefore, of the necessity for joy and exaltation. The time of the play is well over a century after the death of the Baal Shem Tov. Despite its proximity to the twentieth century, however (one of the deceased Hassidic rabbis mentioned in the play, Reb Dovidl Talner, did not die until 1882), it is still a closed world, remote from modern times. On the one hand it is a world that has not purged itself of faith in magic making, a world tarnished by superstition; on the other hand it is a world pervaded by a mystic sense of the immediacy of divinity, of the omnipresent miraculous, and of the power of man, in Martin Buber's phrase, "to compel the upper world." In such a world the natural and the supernatural, the quick and the dead, commingle in continual relationships, and daily reality is often only a symbol of daily eternity. *The Dybbuk* is not at all a play about the powers of darkness, as Joseph Wood Krutch referred to it in his review of the 1925 Neighborhood Playhouse production; it is a play about the powers of Light and their immediacy in the world of men.

The Dybbuk is a highly complex and meticulously constructed drama. Its motifs are two: the redeemability of man who, though he falls, may always rise by means of his own conduct; and the inevitability of justice in the universe. The first is stated in the words of the chant that opens and closes the play; the second is in the Messenger's last speech, spoken against the background of the chant, each illuminating the other: "Blessed be the True Judge." These words, though they are customary when the Lord takes away, have by the end of the play acquired the larger significance of a statement that in its implications becomes the theme of the play: Blessed be the True Judge whose justice provides the means of man's redemption of himself by his adherence to the values God's Torah provides. Within each act the exposition of the theme and its immediate emphasis is balanced against the illustrative dramatic action. The thread of exposition is spun by the Messenger, who serves both as chorus and as mysterious suggestion

---

[3] Israel ben Eliezer (1700-1760), known as the Bal Shem Tov (the Master of the Good Name), was the founder of the Hassidic movement.

of the interplay of natural and supernatural that constitutes the very texture of the play; he is an awesome figure, prodding conscience, foreshadowing destiny. He speaks at the opening of every act but the last and helps sound the motif that the action will orchestrate. His speeches within each act are rarely without deliberate ambiguity and foreshadowing overtones of meaning, and his pithy comment illuminates the end of every act.

If there is a balance between exposition and action in each act, there is also the counterpoint of a tight plot that rises from calm to climax within each act and continues with mounting tension through all to a crescendo in the fourth, which is, at last, followed by the calm that reflects the reassertion of justice. The very pattern of the acts prepares for the resolution of the last: the first act is Khonnon's, the second is Leye's, the third is Reb Azrielke's, and the fourth is shared by all parties in tense confrontation. Anski conceived of the motive power of the action as the conflict between Khonnon and Leye on the one hand, striving for the fulfillment of their private happiness, and the Tsaddik of Miropolye on the other, concerned for the continuity of the people, intent that a living branch of the eternal tree should not waste away. This conflict is in a sense not really resolved. Both are right. Yet overriding both are the demands of compassionate justice. Had the vow between Nissen and Sender not been made, there would have been no "higher powers" supporting Khonnon's claim. And the vow itself, though not legally binding, is yet regarded as binding by true justice since human lives were affected. Nissen, believing it to be binding, acted in accordance with that belief, and Khonnon's fate was shaped by it. If Khonnon and Leye win in the end it is not because the Tsaddik's aims are less worthy than theirs, but because the case has roots that he was not aware of and because human justice has prior claims. This justice prevails at the end. Khonnon has, of his own free will and by his own action, left the body of Leye. He now begins the slow climb, the rise of a fallen soul, scholarly, gentle, and kind, whose fall plunged the very spheres of divinity into grief. And Sender, also a fallen soul, begins his own climb by his penitential acts of charity and by his acceptance of responsibility for the memory of the deceased. The vow has been fulfilled; the principle of a man's responsibility for his fellow man has been reaffirmed; the fallen have exercised the power that lies "within the fall . . . to rise again." "Blessed be the True Judge."

THE DYBBUK

CHARACTERS

Reb* Sender of Brinnits
Leye, his daughter
Frade, her aged nurse
Gittel ⎱
Bassia ⎰ Leye's friends
Menashe, Leye's bridegroom
Nakhman, his father
Reb Mendel, Menashe's tutor
The Messenger
Reb Azrielke of Miropolye, a *Tsaddik* (a Hassidic master or
    sage)
Mikhol, his *gabbai* (a lay assistant)
Reb Shimshon, the Rabbi of Miropolye
First Judge
Second Judge
Meyer, *Shammes* (caretaker) of the synagogue in Brinnits
Khonnon
Hennakh ⎱ students at the Yeshiva (Talmudical
Asher   ⎰ academy) in Brinnits
First Batlon**
Second Batlon
Third Batlon
First Hassid
Second Hassid
Third Hassid
An Elderly Woman
A Wedding Guest (specially invited, by custom, because he is
    a stranger)
A Hunchback   ⎱
A Man on Crutches ⎰ poor men

---

*A title of respect, not to be confused either with *rebbe* (master,
teacher) or with *rabbi* (clergyman). *Reb* is used always with the first
name.

**Batlon* (pl. *batlonim*): a man with no occupation who devotes
all his time to religious study and synagogue service and lives on the
charity of the community; therefore, also, an impractical man, an
idler, a daydreamer.

21

A Woman with a Limp
A Woman with One Arm
A Blind Woman   } poor women
A Tall Pale Young Woman
A Young Woman Carrying a Child
Hassidim, Yeshiva Students, Prosperous Householders, Shop-
keepers, Wedding Guests, Paupers, Children

*Acts I and II take place in Brinnits, Acts III and IV in Miro-
polye. Three months elapse between the first two acts, three
days between the second and third, half a day between the
third and the fourth.*

ACT I

(Total darkness. Before the curtain rises, a subdued mystic singing is heard, as if from afar.)

> Wherefore, wherefore
> Did the soul
> From its exalted height
> Fall into abysmal depths?
> Within the fall the power lies
> To rise again.

(The curtain rises slowly.

A wooden synagogue, very old, with blackened walls. The ceiling rests on two wooden posts. An old brass chandelier hangs from the middle of the ceiling, over the bima,* which is covered with a dark cloth. High on the rear wall are the small windows looking out of the women's gallery. A long bench stands along the wall, in front of the bench, a long wooden table cluttered with books. On the table, two tallow candle-ends burn in clay candlesticks. The candles are lower than the piles of books. To the left of the bench and table, a narrow door leading to a room for private study. In the corner, a bookcase. Wall right: in the middle, the Holy Ark; to the left of that the cantor's reading stand on which a heavy wax memorial candle is burning. Two windows on either side of the Ark. Benches along the entire wall, in front of them several reading stands. Wall left: a large tile oven. Near it, a bench. In front of the bench, a long table also cluttered with books. A wash basin with a towel on a ring. A wide door to the street. Past the door, a chest, above which a Perpetual Light burns in its niche. HENNAKH, deeply engrossed in a book, sits before a reading stand near the cantor's desk. Around the table at the rear wall, five or six Yeshiva students, slumped over in various attitudes of weariness, sit and chant from the Gemara with a dreamy melody. At the bima, MEYER, bent over, stands sorting the bags containing prayer shawls and phylacteries. Around the table at wall left, FIRST, SECOND and THIRD

---

*Bima (beema): a table on a railed dais in the middle of the synagogue, from which the Torah is read.

BATLONIM *sit singing, gazing into space, wholly lost in dreams. The* MESSENGER *lies on the bench near the oven, with his sack for a pillow. At the bookcase, his hand resting on the top shelf, stands* KHONNON, *deep in thought. Evening. A mystic mood permeates the synagogue. Shadows lurk in the corners.*)

(*The* BATLONIM *finish the song.*)

> Wherefore, wherefore
> Did the soul
> From its exalted height
> Fall into abysmal depths?
> Within the fall the power lies
> To rise again.

(*Long pause. All three sit motionless, lost in dreams.*)

FIRST BATLON (*as though telling a story*). Reb Dovidl of Talna, may his merit protect us, had a golden chair and on it was carved: "David, King of Israel, lives forever." (*Pause.*)

SECOND BATLON (*in the same tone*). Reb Israel of Ruzin, of blessed memory, bore himself like a king. An orchestra of twenty-four musicians always played at his table, and when he travelled, it was never with less than six horses in tandem.

THIRD BATLON (*with enthusiasm*). And Reb Shmuel of Kaminka, they say, used to walk about in golden slippers. (*With wonder.*) In golden slippers!

MESSENGER (*raises himself and remains seated erect. In a calm, soft voice, as from afar*). The holy Reb Zusye of Annipol was a pauper all his life; he begged for alms, and went about in a peasant shirt with a rope for a belt; and yet he achieved no less than the Rebbe of Talna or the Rebbe of Ruzin.

FIRST BATLON (*annoyed*). Please don't be offended, but you really don't know what we're talking about, and yet you intrude. When they speak of the greatness of the Talner or the Ruziner, are they talking about wealth? Aren't there enough rich men in the world? After all, one must realize that in the golden chair, and in the orchestra, and in the golden slippers lay a deep secret, a profound meaning.

THIRD BATLON. Of course! Who doesn't know that?

SECOND BATLON. Anyone with open eyes could see. They say that when the Rabbi of Opt first met the Ruziner on the road, he ran to kiss the very wheels of his carriage. And when they asked him the meaning of his act, he cried out: "Fools! Don't you see that this is the very Chariot of the Lord?"*

THIRD BATLON (*amazed*). Ay, ay, ay!

FIRST BATLON. The point is that the golden chair was no chair, the orchestra was no orchestra, and the horses were no horses. All that was merely a suggestion, a reflection; it was a robe, a sheath for their greatness.

MESSENGER. True greatness needs no rich robes.

FIRST BATLON. You are mistaken! True greatness must have its proper raiment.

SECOND BATLON (*shrugs his shoulders*). Their greatness! Their power! It's beyond comprehension!

FIRST BATLON. The marvel of their might! Have you heard the story about the cat-o-nine-tails of Reb Shmelke of Nickelsberg? It's worth hearing. Two litigants once came before Reb Shmelke, one poor, the other rich and influential, feared by everyone. Reb Shmelke listened to both parties and decided in favor of the poor man. Thereupon, the rich one took offense and announced that he would not abide by the decision. Calmly Reb Shmelke replied: "You will obey. When a rabbi renders a decision, it must be obeyed." Then the rich man grew angry and began to shout: "I laugh at you and your rabbinical authority!" At this, Reb Shmelke arose to his full height and cried out: "Carry out my verdict this very instant! If not, I'll take my cat-o-nine-tails!" This really enraged the rich man, and he began to insult and blaspheme the rabbi. Thereupon Reb Shmelke opened the drawer of his desk a little. Suddenly there burst from it the Primal Snake and wrapped itself around the rich man's neck. Well, well. There was a bit of excitement. The rich man shouted and cried: "Help, Rebbe, forgive me. I'll do whatever you say, but call off the snake." Replied Reb Shmelke, "Indeed you will. And you will even warn your children and grandchildren to obey the rebbe and fear his whip." And he removed the snake.

THIRD BATLON. Ha, ha, ha! A fine whip. (*Pause.*)

SECOND BATLON (*to the first*). There must be some mistake. The story could not have involved the Primal Snake. . . .

THIRD BATLON. No? Why not?

SECOND BATLON. Very simple. It cannot be that Reb Shmelke of Nickelsberg should have called upon the Primal Snake. The Primal Snake is, after all, the Evil One himself, Heaven protect us. (*Spits three times.*)

*The reference is to Ezekiel's vision.

THIRD BATLON. What's the difference! Reb Shmelke must have known what he was doing.

FIRST BATLON (*offended*). I really don't understand you. I tell you a story that occurred before witnesses; dozens of people saw it with their own eyes, and you come along and say that it couldn't have happened—as though I just like to hear myself talk.

SECOND BATLON. Not at all. I merely thought that there are no such names and combinations that can summon the Evil One. (*Spits.*)

MESSENGER. Satan can be summoned only by that great doubly-spoken Name that fuses in its flame the highest peaks with the deepest valleys.

(KHONNON *raises his head and listens attentively.*)

THIRD BATLON (*worried*). Is there no danger in uttering this awesome Divine Name?

MESSENGER (*thoughtfully*). Danger? No. But in the great yearning of the spark for the flame, the vessel could burst.

FIRST BATLON. In my town there is a wonder worker, a real master of miracles. With one spell he starts a fire and with another he immediately puts it out. He can see what is happening a hundred miles away; he can draw wine from a wall with his finger, and things like that. Well, he once told me he knows spells that can create a *golem,* revive the dead, make one invisible, call forth evil spirits, even Satan himself. (*Spits.*) I heard this from his own lips.

KHONNON (*has throughout been standing motionless, listening attentively. He moves toward the table, looks first at* THE MESSENGER, *then at the* FIRST BATLON. *In a distant, thoughtful voice*). Where is he?

(THE MESSENGER *fixes his attention on* KHONNON *and watches him carefully throughout.*)

FIRST BATLON (*surprised*). Who?

KHONNON. The wonder worker.

FIRST BATLON. Where should he be! In my home town, if he's still alive.

KHONNON. Far from here?

FIRST BATLON. The town? Far. A great distance. In deepest Polesia.

KHONNON. How long to walk there?

FIRST BATLON. To walk? A good month. Perhaps even more. (*Pause.*) Why do you ask? Do you want to go to him? (KHONNON *remains silent.*) The name of the town is Krasna. The wonder worker's name is Elkhonnon.

KHONNON (*in surprise, to himself*). Elkhonnon? El Khonnon? The God of Khonnon.

FIRST BATLON. I tell you, he is a master! Once, in broad daylight he tried, with a spell. . . .

SECOND BATLON. Enough talk about such things at nightfall! Especially in a holy place. With a wrong word or phrase one could accidentally cause a disaster. There have, Heaven protect us, been such cases.

(KHONNON *leaves slowly. All watch him. Pause.*)

MESSENGER. Who is that young man?

FIRST BATLON. A student at the Yeshiva.

(MEYER *closes the gate of the bima dais and approaches the table.*)

SECOND BATLON. An excellent student, a genius.

THIRD BATLON. A prodigious memory! He knows five hundred pages of the Gemara by heart and has them at his fingertips.

MESSENGER. Where does he come from?

MEYER. He is from somewhere in Lithuania. Studied here at the Yeshiva and was considered the best scholar in the school. He was ordained as a rabbi. Suddenly he disappeared and was gone a whole year. They said he left to perform the Penance of Exile. He returned only recently. A changed young man. Always deep in meditation, fasts from Sabbath to Sabbath, performs ritual ablutions continually. (*Quietly.*) They say he's mixed up in Cabalistic studies.

SECOND BATLON (*quietly*). There's talk in town, also. People have even come to him for charms, but he refuses.

THIRD BATLON. Who knows who he is? Perhaps one of the great ones. Who can tell? And to look too closely would be dangerous. (*Pause.*)

SECOND BATLON (*yawning*). It's late. Time to go to sleep. (*To the* FIRST BATLON *with a smile.*) Too bad your wall-tapping wonder worker isn't here. I could stand a little drink right now. I haven't had a thing to eat all day.

FIRST BATLON. It's been practically a fast day for me, too. All I had was a muffin after morning prayers.

MEYER (*half whispering; pleased*). Listen to this. I have a feeling we'll be drinking toasts soon enough. Sender drove off to look at a bridegroom for his only daughter. Just let him sign the marriage agreement, and he'll provide a good bottle.

SECOND BATLON. Bah! I don't believe he'll sign any such agreement. Three times he has gone to look at prospective bridegrooms and each time he has returned with nothing. Either he doesn't care for the boy, or the family isn't good enough for him, or the dowry is too small. A man should not be so hard to please.

MEYER. Sender can allow himself that luxury. After all, he is rich—no evil eye—comes from a fine family, and his only daughter is good as well as beautiful.

THIRD BATLON (*with enthusiasm*). I like Sender! A real Hassid; a true Miropolye Hassid. He has real spirit.

FIRST BATLON (*cold*). He is a good Hassid, there is no denying that. But he might have gone about marrying off his daughter in a different way.

THIRD BATLON. Why? What do you mean?

FIRST BATLON. In the old days, when a rich man of good family wanted to make a match he didn't look for money or for social position. He looked for personal qualities. He went to a large yeshiva, gave the headmaster a handsome gift and had him pick the most promising scholar. Sender could have done that too.

MESSENGER. He might even have found a proper bridegroom in the yeshiva here.

FIRST BATLON (*in wonder*). How do you know?

MESSENGER. I'm only supposing.

THIRD BATLON (*hastily*). Well, well, well. Let's not gossip, especially about one of our own. Besides, matches are made by fate.

(*The door is flung open and an* ELDERLY WOMAN *rushes in leading a child in each hand.*)

ELDERLY WOMAN (*runs toward the Ark with the children, crying tearfully*). Ay, ay, God in heaven! Help me! (*Reaches the Ark.*) Children! Let us open the Holy Ark. Let us clasp the Holy Scrolls and not leave until our tears have won back your mother's health. (*Opens the Holy Ark, thrusts her head in and begins a tearful recitative.*) God of Abraham, of Isaac, and of Jacob, behold my woe. Behold the anguish of the little children, and take not their young mother from the world. Holy Scrolls, intercede for a wretched widow! Holy Scrolls, beloved Mothers of Israel, hurry, run to the Almighty, cry out, plead that the lovely sapling be not torn out by the roots, that the young dove be not cast from the nest, that the silent lamb be not taken from the flock! (*Hysterically.*) I will stop at nothing, I will split the heavens with my cries! I will not budge from here until the crown of my head is restored to me!

MEYER (*approaches, touches her gently, speaks calmly*).
Khanna-Esther, should we set a minyan* to reciting Psalms?

ELDERLY WOMAN (*withdraws her head from the Ark. Looks at Meyer uncomprehendingly, and suddenly speaks with haste*).
Yes, of course, set a minyan to saying Psalms. But hurry, hurry.
Every second is precious. For two days she has been lying speechless, struggling with death!

MEYER. Right away. I'll get ten men at once. (*Pleadingly*.)
But they ought to get something for their trouble. They're poor men.

ELDERLY WOMAN (*searching her pocket*). Here's a gilden!
But see that they recite it properly.

MEYER. A gilden. . . . Only three groshen each. . . . Not very much.

ELDERLY WOMAN (*not hearing*). Come children, let us run to other synagogues. (*They leave quickly*.)

MESSENGER (*to the* THIRD BATLON). This morning a woman came to open the Ark on behalf of a daughter who has been in labor for two days and cannot give birth. Now a woman comes to open the Ark on behalf of a daughter who has been struggling with death for two days.

THIRD BATLON. Well, what of it?

MESSENGER (*thoughtfully*). If the soul of one who has not died is to enter a body that has not yet been born, a struggle takes place. If the sick one dies, the child will be born. If she recovers, the child will be born dead.

FIRST BATLON (*surprised*). Ay, ay, how blind a man is! He does not see what is happening around him!

MEYER (*approaches the table*). Well, thank the Lord, we can wet our throats. After we've said the Psalms, we'll have a drink and the Lord will have mercy and send the sick woman a full recovery.

FIRST BATLON (*to the student drowsing at the long table*).
Lads, who wants to recite the Psalms? There a muffin in it for each of you. (*The students get up*.) We'll go into the small prayer room.

(*The three* BATLONIM, MEYER, *and all the students except* HENNAKH *exit into the private room. Soon there is heard the sad chanting of "Blessed is the man. . . ." During the entire time,* THE MESSENGER *remains seated at the smaller table, his eyes fixed on the Ark. A long pause.* KHONNON *enters.*)

KHONNON (*very tired, walks pensively and as though aim-*

*Ten men.

lessly toward the Ark). The Ark open? Who opened it? For whom did it open in the middle of the night? (*Looks into the Ark.*) The Holy Scrolls stand huddled together, calm, silent. And in them are concealed all the secrets, all the veiled allusions, all the mysterious combinations from the six days of creation unto the end of the generations of men. And how hard it is to wrest those hints and secrets from them, how very hard! (*Counts the Scrolls.*) One, two, three, four, five, six, seven, eight, nine Scrolls. The numerical value of the letters in the word "truth." And in every scroll, there are four handles, each called a Tree of Life. Again the number thirty-six. Not an hour passes that I do not come upon that figure—and what it signifies I do not know. Yet I feel that in it lies all the meaning that I seek. Thirty-six is the sum of the letters in the name "Leah." Three times thirty-six is "Khonnon." "Leah" also spells out "not God." Not through God. (*Shudders.*) What a dreadful thought—and how I am drawn to it.

HENNAKH (*raises his head and studies* KHONNON *carefully*). Khonnon! How wrapped in dreams you seem!

KHONNON (*steps back from the Ark. Walks slowly to* HENNAKH. *Pauses thoughtfully*). Secrets, endless hints, but I see no clear road before me. (*Brief pause.*) The town is named Krasna. The wonder worker, Reb Elkhonnon.

HENNAKH. What did you say?

KHONNON (*as if startled from a trance*). I? Nothing. I was thinking.

HENNAKH (*shaking his head*). You have plunged too deeply into the Cabala, Khonnon. Since you came back, you haven't touched a book.

KHONNON (*not comprehending*). Not touched a book? What kind of book?

HENNAKH. What sort of question is that? The Gemara or the other commentaries, of course.

KHONNON (*still not recovered*). Gemara? Commentaries? Not touched? The Gemara is cold and dry. The commentaries are cold and dry. (*Suddenly fully awake. Speaks with animation.*) Within the earth there is exactly such a world as here above. There are fields and forests, seas and deserts, cities and towns. Over the fields and deserts great storms rage. Mighty vessels sail the seas, and in the heavy forests, fear reigns eternally, and thunderbolts crash. Only one thing is missing. There is no tall sky from which the fiery lightning can issue or the sun blaze. Such is the Gemara. It is deep, it is great, and it is glorious. But it chains one to the earth. It keeps one from soaring to the sky. (*Enraptured.*) And Cabala! Cabala tears one's soul from the earth! It raises man to the most exalted holiness; it opens all the heavens to one's sight; it leads straight to Pardes. It reaches out to the infinite! It reveals a hem of the great curtain. . . . (*Collapses.*) I have no strength. I feel faint.

HENNAKH (*very earnestly*). All very true. But you forget that such ecstatic soaring is most dangerous. How easily one can lose his grip and plunge into the abyss! The Gemara elevates the soul, but it does so slowly. It protects a man like a faithful sentinel, who neither sleeps nor drowses. It embraces a man like a harness of steel and prevents him from turning off the proper road either to the right or to the left. But the Cabala? You remember what the Gemara says. (*Recites in the chanting manner of Talmudic study.*) "Four there were who entered into Pardes: Ben Azzay, Ben Zoma, Akhar, and Reb Akiba. Ben Azzay looked and lost his life. Ben Zoma looked and lost his reason. Akhar cut down all that grew; he lost his very faith. Reb Akiba alone entered in peace and departed in peace."

KHONNON. Don't frighten me with them. We do not know how they went or with what they went. Perhaps they stumbled because they went merely to observe, not to elevate themselves. We do see, after all, that others followed them—the holy Ari, the holy Baal Shem Tov—and they did not fall.

HENNAKH. Do you compare yourself to them?

KHONNON. I make no comparisons. I follow my own road.

HENNAKH. What sort of road is that?

KHONNON. You would not understand me.

HENNAKH. I will understand. My soul too yearns for the exalted heights.

KHONNON (*thoughtful a while*). The task of the Tsaddik, the righteous man, is to cleanse human souls, to tear them loose from the incubus of sin and to elevate them to the bright source whence they came. The task is heavy because "sin lurks at the door." One soul cleansed, a second appears, stained with still more sin. One generation brought to repentance, another appears still more stubborn. And the generations grow weaker and the sins ever greater and Tsaddikim—ever fewer.

HENNAKH. Well, what should be done in your view?

KHONNON (*quietly but with great conviction*). There is no need to wage war against sin. Elevate it! As a goldsmith purifies the gold from its dross in a hot flame, as the farmer winnows the chaff from the ripe grain, so must sin be purified of its uncleanness until only holiness remains.

HENNAKH (*surprised*). Holiness in sin? How is that possible?

KHONNON. All that God created has within it a spark of holiness.

HENNAKH. Sin is the creation not of God but of Satan.

KHONNON. And who created Satan? God. Are not the hosts of Satan called "the other side"? And as the other side of God, as a facet of God, they must possess within them sanctity.

HENNAKH (*staggered*). Sanctity in Satan! I can't! I can't conceive it! Let me think! (*His head sinks, pressing on his arms crossed on the reading stand. Pause.*)

KHONNON (*approaches, bends down to him and speaks in a trembling voice*). Which sin is the most powerful of all? Which sin is the hardest to conquer? Is it not the sin of lust for a woman?

HENNAKH (*not raising his head*). Yes.

KHONNON. And if this sin is cleansed in the heat of a great flame, does not the greatest uncleanness turn to highest holiness, to the Song of Songs? (*Breathlessly.*) The Songs of Songs! "Behold, thou art fair, my love; behold, thou art fair; thou hast doves' eyes within thy locks: thy hair is as a flock of goats that appear from Mount Gilead. Thy teeth are like a flock of sheep that are even shorn, which came up from the washing; whereof every one bear twins, and none is barren among them."

(MEYER *emerges from the private prayer room. A soft knock at the door is heard. It opens hesitatingly.* LEYE *enters, leading* FRADE *by the hand.* GITTEL *follows. They pause near the door.*)

MEYER (*hearing them, is very surprised. In a voice of flattery and surprise*). Look! Reb Sender's daughter! Leyele!

LEYE (*shyly*). You remember you promised to show me the old embroidered curtains for the Ark.

(*As soon as her voice is heard,* KHONNON *stops singing. He stares at* LEYE. *Throughout, he is either looking at her or standing ecstatically with his eyes shut.*)

FRADE. Show her the curtains, Meyerke. Show her the old ones, the most beautiful. Leyele has promised to embroider a curtain in time to commemorate the anniversary of her mother's death. She will work the purest gold into the finest velvet, stitching out little lions and eagles, as they did in the old days. And when they hang the curtain on the Holy Ark, her mother's innocent soul will rejoice in heaven.

(LEYE *looks around hesitatingly, notices* KHONNON, *lowers her eyes and remains strained throughout, with eyes to the ground.*)

MEYER. Akh, with the greatest pleasure! Of course! Of course! I'll bring the curtains at once, the handsomest, the oldest. (*Goes to the chest near the door to the street and takes out some curtains.*)

GITTEL (*grasping* LEYE's *hand*). Leyele, aren't you afraid in the synagogue at night?

LEYE. I've never before been in the synagogue at night except on Simkhas Torah,* and then it is bright and festive, but now— and then it is bright and festive, but now—how sad it is here, how sad!

FRADE. Girls, a synagogue must be sad. At midnight the dead come to pray, and they leave their sorrow here.

GITTEL. Granny, don't talk about the dead. I'm frightened.

FRADE (*not hearing*). And every morning, when the Almighty weeps over the destruction of our Temple, his tears fall in the synagogues. That's why the walls in the old synagogues are damp with tears, and they may not be whitewashed. If they are whitened, they grow angry and heave stones.

LEYE. How old this synagogue is, how very old! It doesn't look so from the outside.

FRADE. Old, very old, Child. They even say that it was found fully built below the ground. How many times this town has been destroyed, how many times it has been burnt to the ground, but the synagogue remained unharmed. Only once did the roof catch fire. Then there came doves, doves without number, and they began to beat their wings and they put out the fire.

LEYE (*not hearing, as though to herself*). How sad it feels here and how loving! I don't want to leave. I want to fall against these tear-stained walls, to embrace them and ask why they are so sad and pensive, so silent and so melancholy. I wish . . . I do not really know what I wish, but my heart aches with tenderness and pity.

MEYER (*takes some curtains to the bima, spreads one out*). This is the oldest. More than two hundred years old. It is hung only for Passover.

GITTEL (*delighted*). Look, Leyele, isn't it magnificent! What stiff brown velvet! Look at the heavy gold thread in the lions holding the star of David between them! And those trees on either side, with the doves! Nowadays you can't get such velvet or such gold.

---

*The festival when the annual cycle of Torah reading is concluded and then renewed.

LEYE. The curtain is also kind and sad. (*Caresses and kisses it.*)

GITTEL (*catches* LEYE's *hand and whispers*). Look, Leyele, there stands a young man gazing at you. How strangely he looks at you!

LEYE (*bending her eyes even more to the ground*). He is a student. Khonnon. He used to take his meals at our house.

GITTEL. He stares at you as though he wished to call you with his eyes. He seems to want to come closer but he doesn't dare to.

LEYE. I wonder why he is so pale and sad. He must have been ill.

GITTEL. He is not sad at all. His eyes are sparkling.

LEYE. His eyes always sparkle. Such eyes! And when he speaks with me he grows breathless. And so do I. After all, it's not proper for a girl to speak to a strange boy.

FRADE (*to* MEYER). Would you let us kiss the Holy Scrolls? It is not fitting to visit with God and not kiss his holy Torah.

MEYER. Of course! Of course! Come. (*He leads the way, followed by* GITTEL *and* FRADE *and then* LEYE. MEYER *takes a Scroll from the Ark and holds it for* FRADE *to kiss.*)

LEYE (*passing* KHONNON, *pauses for a moment and speaks quietly*). Good evening, Khonnon. You have come back?

(KHONNON *is breathless, does not reply.*)

FRADE. Come, Leyele, kiss the Scroll. (LEYE *approaches the Ark.* MEYER *holds the Scroll for her to kiss. She embraces it, presses her lips against it. Kisses it passionately.*) Enough, child, enough! Scrolls may not be kissed for long. They are written with black fire upon white fire, you know. (*Suddenly, quite alarmed.*) My, how late it is, how very late! Come home, girls! Come home quickly! (*They leave hastily.* MEYER *closes the Ark and leaves after them.*)

KHONNON (*stands a while with eyes closed. Resumes singing the Song of Songs at the very point at which he broke off*). "Thy lips are like a thread of scarlet, and thy speech is comely: thy temples are like a piece of pomegranate within thy locks."

HENNAKH (*raises his head; looks at* KHONNON). Khonnon, what are you singing? (KHONNON *stops singing, opens his eyes, looks at* HENNAKH.) Your earlocks are wet. Were you at the ritual-bath again?

KHONNON. Yes.

HENNAKH. When you perform your ablutions, do you recite incantations? Do you follow the ritual prescribed by the *Book of Razial?**

KHONNON. Yes.

HENNAKH. And you are not afraid?

KHONNON. No.

HENNAKH. And you fast from Sabbath to Sabbath? Don't you find it hard?

KHONNON. It is harder for me to eat on the Sabbath than it is to fast all week. I have lost all desire for food. (*Pause.*)

HENNAKH (*intimately*). Why do you do all this? What are you trying to do?

KHONNON (*as if to himself*). I want . . . I want to reach a clear and sparkling diamond, to dissolve it in tears and absorb it into my soul. I want to reach the rays of the third holy place, of the third divine emanation, the sphere of beauty. I want. . . . (*Suddenly very distraught.*) Yes! I must get two barrels of gold coins for him who can count only coins.

HENNAKH (*astounded*). Is that it? Look out, Khonnon. Take care. You stand on a slippery road. You will not attain all this by holy means.

KHONNON (*looks at him defiantly*). And if not by holy means, what then? If not by holy means?

HENNAKH (*terrified*). I am afraid to talk to you. I am afraid to stand near you.

(*He hurries out.* KHONNON *remains motionless with a defiant expression on his face.* MEYER *enters from the street, the* FIRST BATLON *from the prayer room.*)

FIRST BATLON. Eighteen** Psalms are quite enough. Should we recite them all for a gildin? But you can't talk to them. Once they get started, they keep going. (ASHER *runs in breathlessly.*)

ASHER. Just met Borukh the tailor. He returned from Klimovka, where Sender met with the prospective in-laws, and he says they did not agree. Sender insisted on ten years' board for the couple, and they refused to go above five. So they broke up.

MEYER. That's the fourth time!

THIRD BATLON. Heartbreaking, isn't it?

MESSENGER (*to the* THIRD BATLON, *smiling*). You said yourself that marriages are arranged by destiny.

---

*A medieval Cabalistic book of magic.
**The numerical value of the word "life."

KHONNON (*straightening up and crying ecstatically*). I have won again! (*Falls back limp upon the bench and remains seated with an expression of joy upon his face.*)

MESSENGER (*picks up his sack and removes a lantern from it*). Time to start on my way.

MEYER. What's your hurry?

MESSENGER. I'm just a messenger. Noblemen employ me to carry important messages, rare valuables. So I must hurry. My time is not my own.

MEYER. Why don't you wait at least until daybreak?

MESSENGER. The dawn is far and my road is long. I'll leave about midnight.

MEYER. It's pitch dark out.

MESSENGER. With my lantern I won't get lost.

(SECOND *and* THIRD BATLONIM *and the students emerge from the prayer room.*)

SECOND BATLON. *Mazel tov.* May the One Above send the sick woman her health again.

ALL. So be it, amen!

FIRST BATLON. Now we should buy some brandy and cake for the gildin.

MEYER. I have already. (*Takes a bottle and some cakes out of the bosom of his coat.*) Let's step into the vestibule and have a drink there.

(*The door opens wide and* SENDER *enters, his coat unbuttoned, his hat perched on the back of his head. He is happy. Three or four men follow him in.*)

MEYER AND BATLONIM. Ah! Reb Sender! Welcome!

SENDER. Happened to be riding by the synagogue, so I thought I'd drop in and see what our people are doing. (*Notices* MEYER *holding the bottle.*) Thought they would be deep in study or discussing some weighty problems. Turns out they're getting ready to have a drink! Ha, ha! Real Mirapolye Hassidim!

FIRST BATLON. You'll have a drop with us, Reb Sender.

SENDER. Fool! I'll provide the bottle myself, and a good bottle, too. Wish me *mazel tov!* Happy be the hour, my daughter is betrothed!

(KHONNON *springs up; he is shattered.*)

ALL. Mazel tov! Mazel tov!

MEYER. And we were just told you couldn't reach an agreement and the whole business was called off.

THIRD BATLON. We were so sorry to hear it.

SENDER. It very nearly did fall through, but at the last moment the groom's father gave in and we signed the agreement.

KHONNON. Betrothed? Betrothed? How is it possible? How could that be? (*In despair.*) So they were useless! All the fasts, all the ablutions, all that harrowing of flesh, all those spells— were wasted! What now? By what road? By what powers? (*Clutches at his breast, straightens up with an ecstatic expression on his face.*) Ah-ah-ah! I see revealed the secret of the great doubly-spoken Name! I . . . see it! I . . . I . . . I have . . . won! (*Falls to the ground.*)

MESSENGER (*opens the lantern*). The candle has burnt out. A new one must be lit.

(*Ominous pause.*)

SENDER. Meyer, why is it so dark here? Light some candles.

(MEYER *does so.*)

MESSENGER (*approaches* SENDER *softly*). Did you come to terms with the groom's father?

SENDER (*looks at him surprised, a little frightened*). Yes.

MESSENGER. It happens that parents promise and then go back on their word. Sometimes it is even brought before a rabbinical court. One should be very careful.

SENDER (*frightened, to* MEYER). Who is this man? I don't know him.

MEYER. He is a stranger, a messenger.

SENDER. What does he want of me?

MEYER. I don't know.

SENDER (*calming himself*). Asher, run over to my house and say that I want them to prepare some liquor, preserves, and a bite. Hurry, now. Be quick about it. (ASHER *runs out.*) While they are getting things ready, we may as well stay here and chat. Has anyone heard of any new saying of our Rebbe's? Some parable? Some new wonder? His every gesture is more precious than pearls.

FIRST BATLON. Save the bottle. We can use it tomorrow.

(MEYER *puts it away.*)

MESSENGER. I'll tell you a parable of his. Once there came to the Rebbe a Hassid, very rich but stingy. The Rebbe took him by the hand, led him over to the window and said, "Look." The rich man looked out into the street. "What do you see?" asked the Rebbe. "I see people," replied the man. Again the Rebbe took him by the hand, led him to the mirror, and said, "Look. What do you see now?" "Now I see myself," he replied. "You see," said the Rebbe, "the window is glass and the mirror is glass. But the glass of the mirror is lightly silvered. And with the addition of silver one no longer sees others. He sees only himself."

THIRD BATLON. Oh, oh, oh! Sweeter than honey.

FIRST BATLON. Holy words!

SENDER (to the MESSENGER). What? Are you trying to needle me?

MESSENGER. Heaven forbid!

SECOND BATLON. Why don't we sing something? (To the THIRD BATLON.) Sing the Rebbe's tune.

(THIRD BATLON begins to sing a quiet, mystic Hassidic melody. All join in.)

SENDER (jumps up). And now a dance. What, is Sender going to marry off his only daughter without a dance? What kind of Miropolye Hassidim would we be? (SENDER, the three BATLONIM, and MEYER form a circle, hands on one another's shoulders, eyes ecstatic. They sing a monotonous mystic tune and circle slowly round the same spot. SENDER breaks out of the circle, happy.) And now a merry dance. Everybody here!

SECOND BATLON. Hey, there, lads, over here! (Some of the young men come over.) Hennakh! Khonnon! Where are you? Join us in a merry dance!

SENDER. Ah-ah! Khonnon! My Khonke is here, is he? Where is he? Bring him right over to me!

MEYER (sees KHONNON on the floor). He is asleep on the floor, of all places.

SENDER. Wake him up! Wake him up!

MEYER (shakes him. Frightened). He won't wake up!

(All approach, bend over, try to wake him.)

FIRST BATLON (with a frightened outcry). He's dead!

THIRD BATLON. A book fell out of his hand. It's The Angel Raziel!

(All are staggered.)

MESSENGER. The harm has been done.

ACT II

(A square in Brinnits. Left—the old wooden synagogue, antique architecture. In front of the synagogue and a little to one side, a mound of earth with an old gravestone bearing the inscription: "Here lie bride and groom, holy and pure, martyred for their faith in the year 5408 [1648]. Peace unto them." Beyond the synagogue, a lane and several small houses that merge into the backdrop. Right—SENDER's house, a large frame house with a porch. Beyond the house, a wide gate leading into the yard, and further back, a lane, a row of small shops that merge into the backdrop. On the backdrop, right, beyond the shops, an inn, a nobleman's mansion and large garden. A broad road leading down to the river. Beyond the river, high on the bank, a cemetery, tombstones visible. To the left, a bridge over the river, a mill. Before that, a bath-house and the town poorhouse. In the distance, a dense forest.

The gate of SENDER's house is wide open. Long tables are set up in the yard and extend out into the square. The tables are laden with food, and seated around them, eating hungrily, are the poor—beggars, cripples, old and young. Waiters carry large platters of food and baskets of bread from the house to the tables.

Women are seated in front of the shops and houses. They knit socks while keeping their eyes glued to SENDER's house. Men of all ages leave the synagogue carrying their prayer shawls and phylacteries. Some go into the shops. Others stand about in groups. From SENDER's yard come the sounds of music, dancing, loud conversation.

It is evening. In the middle of the street, in front of the synagogue, stands the WEDDING GUEST, an elderly man in a satin kaftan, his hands tucked into the belt. Near him, the SECOND BATLON.)

GUEST *(examining the synagogue)*. A majestic synagogue you have here. Handsome, large, the Spirit of God is upon it. Very old, I should say.

SECOND BATLON. Very old. The old men say that even their grandfathers could not remember when it was built.

GUEST (*sees the gravestone*). And what is this? (*Approaches and reads.*) "Here lie bride and groom, holy and pure, martyred for their faith in the year 5408." A bride and groom who died as martyrs?

SECOND BATLON. When that murderer Khmelnicki—may his name be blotted out—attacked our town with his Cossacks and slaughtered half the Jews, he also murdered a bride and groom as they were being led to the wedding canopy. They were buried here, on the very spot where they fell, both in a single grave, and ever since it has been called "the holy grave." (*Whispering, as if telling a secret.*) At every marriage ceremony he performs, our rabbi hears sighs from the grave. And it has long been the custom here to dance around the grave after a wedding and cheer the buried bride and groom.

GUEST. A noble custom!

(MEYER, *emerging from* SENDER's *yard, approaches.*)

MEYER (*excitedly*). What a meal for the poor! In all my born days I've never seen a feast like this one.

GUEST. No wonder. Sender is marrying off his only daughter.

MEYER (*with enthusiasm*). Fish for everyone, then roast fowl, and dessert to top it off! And before the feast, there was honey cake and brandy. It must have cost a fortune. More than you could imagine.

SECOND BATLON. Sender knows what he's doing. If one of the invited guests feels slighted, there's no great harm done. Let him complain all he wants to. But if the poor are not well treated, there's really great danger. You can never tell who is under those pauper's clothes. Maybe just a beggar and maybe someone quite different. A holy man, perhaps, or one of the Thirty-six Just Men.

MEYER. Why not the Prophet Elijah himself? He always appears in beggar's guise.

GUEST. It's not only the poor that must be treated carefully. You can never tell about anyone who he is, or who he was in a previous incarnation, or why he was sent into the world.

(THE MESSENGER, *his sack on his shoulders, emerges from the lane left.*)

MEYER. Sholem aleichem. You have come to us again?

MESSENGER. I have been sent here again.

MEYER. You've come in good season, in time for a rich wedding.

MESSENGER. The wedding is the talk of the entire region.

MEYER. Did you happen to meet up with the groom's party on the way? They're late.

MESSENGER. The bridegroom will arrive in good time.

(*Goes toward the synagogue. The* GUEST, SECOND BATLON, *and* MEYER *go into the yard.* LEYE, *in her wedding gown, appears behind the tables. She dances with one after another of the poor women. Others crowd around her. Those who have had their turn at dancing with her go out into the square and stand about in groups talking.*)

WOMAN WITH A CHILD (*contentedly*). I danced with the bride.

LAME WOMAN. So did I. I took her around and danced. Hee, hee!

HUNCHBACK. Why does the bride dance only with women? I'd like to put my arms around her and dance with her too, he, he, he!

(*Laughter among the poor.* FRADE, GITTEL, *and* BASSIA *come out onto the porch.*)

FRADE (*uneasy*). O dear! Leyele is still dancing with the poor. She'll get dizzy. Girls, bring her here. (*Sits down on a bench.* GITTEL *and* BASSIA *go to* LEYE.)

GITTEL. You've danced enough, Leyele. Come.

BASSIA. You'll get dizzy. (*She and* GITTEL *take* LEYE *under the arms and start to lead her off.*)

POOR WOMEN (*surround* LEYELE, *pleading and whining*). She hasn't danced with me yet. Am I not as good as the next?

I've been waiting for an hour to dance with her.

It's my turn. I'm supposed to dance with her after Elka!

She turned a dozen times with lame Yakhna and not even once with me. I have no luck at anything!

(MEYER *comes out of the yard and climbs up on a bench.*)

MEYER (*in the loud voice and chanting tones of a wedding bard*).

> Sender the Wealthy invites all the poor
> And bids them come to his granary door!
> Hurry, you poor folk, with open palms;
> For each, ten groshen of Reb Sender's alms.

THE POOR (*run into the yard, pushing and shouting*). Ten groshen! Ten groshen!

(*The square empties. Only* LEYE, GITTEL, BASSIA *and a half-blind* OLD WOMAN *remain.*)

OLD WOMAN (*catches hold of* LEYE). I don't need the alms!

Just dance with me. Just one turn with me! It's forty years since I last danced. Oh, how I danced as a girl! How I danced! (LEYE *puts her arms around the old woman, dances with her. The old woman does not let go, begging.*) More! More! (*They turn, the old woman gasping for breath, shouting hysterically.*) More! More!

(GITTEL *pulls the old woman into the yard, returns, and she and* BASSIA *lead* LEYE *to the porch, seat her on a bench. The waiters and servants remove the tables, lock the gate.*)

FRADE. You're as white as a sheet, Leyele. You didn't tire yourself, did you?

LEYE (*eyes shut tight, head thrown back, speaks as though in a dream*). They took me in their arms; they surrounded me, pressed themselves upon me, reached for me with their cold dry fingers. My head swam; I grew faint. Then someone lifted me high into the air and carried me far, far away.

BASSIA (*frightened*). Leyele, look how they've creased and stained your dress! What will you do now?

LEYE (*as before*). If you leave the bride alone before the wedding, demons come and carry her off.

FRADE (*frightened*). What kind of talk is this, Leyele? You mustn't mention those dark spirits by name. They lie hidden and waiting in every nook and cranny. They hear everything; they see everything; and they wait for someone to utter their forbidden name. Then they leap out and hurl themselves upon him. (*Spits three times.*)

LEYE (*opens her eyes*). They are not evil. . . .

FRADE. You must not believe them. If you believe one of that kind, he becomes uncontrollable and may do you some mischief.

LEYE (*with great assurance*). Granny, we are surrounded not by evil spirits but by the souls of people who died before their time. It is they that watch and listen to everything we do and say.

FRADE. God help you, child! What are you saying? Souls? What souls? The untarnished souls of the pure fly up to heaven and repose in the brightness of Paradise.

LEYE. No, granny, they are among us. (*In another tone.*) Granny, a person is born to a very long life. And if he dies before his time, what happens to his unlived life? To his joy and his sorrow? To the thoughts he was not given time to think, to the deeds he was not given time to do? What happens to the children he was not given time to have? Where does all that go to? Where? (*Thoughtfully.*) There lived a young man who had a lofty soul and a deep mind. A long life lay before him. And suddenly, in an instant, his life was cut off, and strangers came to bury him in strange earth. (*In despair.*) What happened to the rest of his life? To his words that were silenced, to his prayers that were cut off? Granny, when a candle blows out, it can be lit again and it burns to the end. How, then, can the unconsumed candle of a life be put out forever? How can that be?

FRADE (*shakes her head*). You must not think about such things, my child! The Lord knows what he is doing. And we are blind. We know nothing.

(THE MESSENGER *approaches unnoticed and remains standing close behind them.*)

LEYE (*not hearing* FRADE. *With conviction*). No, granny. No human life goes to waste. If someone dies before his time, his soul returns to the world to live out the span of his years, to finish the undone deeds, to feel the unfelt joys and sorrows. (*Pause.*) Granny, you once told me that at midnight the dead come to the synagogue to pray. Why do they come, if not to finish the prayers they had no time to say? (*Pause.*) My mother died in her youth. She had no time to live out all that she was destined to. Today I will go to the graveyard and invite her to join my father in leading me to the wedding canopy. And she will come, and afterwards she will dance with me. And so it is with all the souls that left the world before their time. They are among us, but we do not see them; we do not feel them. (*Quietly.*) Granny, if you want to very much, you can see them and hear their voices and understand their thoughts. I know. . . . (*Pause. Points to the grave.*) This holy grave, I've known it since I was a child. I know the bride and groom that are buried there. I have seen them many times in my dreams and in my waking hours, and they are as dear to me as my own kin. Young and handsome they were as they walked to be wed. Before them stretched a long and lovely life. Suddenly evil men appeared swinging their axes, and bride and groom fell dead. Both were buried in a single grave so that they might not be separated for all eternity. And at every wedding, when there is dancing round the grave, they rise up and share the joy of the bride and groom. (*Gets up and walks to the grave.* FRADE, GITTEL, *and* BASSIA *follow her. She spreads her arms high.*) Holy bride and groom! I invite you to my wedding! Come and stand near me under the canopy!

(*A merry musician's march is heard.* LEYE *cries out in fright and nearly falls.*)

GITTEL (*catches her*). Why did you get so frightened? The groom must have arrived just now, and so they are greeting him with music as he comes into town.

BASSIA (*eagerly*). I'm going to run ahead and steal a look at him.

GITTEL. So am I. Then we'll come back and tell you what he looks like. Would you like that?

LEYE (*shakes her head*). No.

BASSIA. She's bashful. Don't be bashful, silly. We won't tell anyone.

(*They leave quickly.* LEYE *and* FRADE *return to the porch.*)

FRADE. A bride always asks her girlfriends to steal a look at the groom and tell her whether he is fair or dark.

MESSENGER (*approaches*). Bride!

LEYE (*shudders, turns*). What is it? (*Looks at him attentively.*)

MESSENGER. The souls of the dead do return to the world, but not as disembodied spirits. Some souls must go through several incarnations before they achieve purification. (LEYE *listens with increasing attention.*) Sinful souls are transformed into birds or beasts or fish or even plants, and they cannot attain to purity by their own efforts alone. They must wait for a Tsaddik, a righteous man, to release them and cleanse them. And there are some souls that enter a new-born body and achieve purification by means of their own deeds.

LEYE (*trembling*). Tell me more! Tell me more!

MESSENGER. And there are wandering souls that find no rest. These enter the living body of another as a dybbuk and thereby attain purity.

(*He disappears.* LEYE *stands astonished.* SENDER *comes out of the house.*)

SENDER. Why are you sitting here, child?

FRADE. She was bringing cheer to the poor who feasted here, dancing with them. She overdid it and is resting up a while.

SENDER. Oh! Bringing cheer to the poor! That's a truly fine thing to do. (*Looks up at the sky.*) Getting late. The bridegroom and his party have arrived. Are you ready?

FRADE. She must still go to the graveyard.

SENDER. Go, child, go to your mother's grave. (*Sighs.*) Shed all your tears there and invite your mother to the wedding. Tell her that I want us both to lead our only daughter to the ceremony. Tell her that I have fulfilled every dying wish of hers. I have devoted my whole life to you alone. I have raised you to be a virtuous Jewish girl. And now I give you in marriage to a young man who is studious and God-fearing and comes of a fine family. (*Wipes away the tears and with bowed head returns to the house. Pause.*)

LEYE. Granny, at the cemetery, may I invite others to my wedding besides my mother?

FRADE. Only the near relations. Invite your grandfather Reb Ephraim, Aunt Mirele.

LEYE. I would like to invite someone . . . who is not related.

FRADE. It is forbidden, child. If you invite a stranger, the other dead might take offense and do you harm.

LEYE. He is not a stranger. In our house, he was like one of us.

FRADE (*in a low voice, frightened*). Oh, child, I am afraid. They say he died an unnatural death. (LEYE *weeps silently.*) There, there, don't cry. Don't cry. Invite him. The sin be on me. (*Reminds herself.*) But I don't know where his grave is, and it's not proper to ask.

LEYE. I know where he is.

FRADE (*surprised*). How do you know?

LEYE. I saw his grave in a dream. (*Closes her eyes thoughtfully.*) And I saw him too, and he told me about himself . . . and asked me to invite him to the wedding.

(GITTEL *and* BASSIA *come running in.*)

BOTH. We saw him! We saw him!

LEYE (*shaken*). Whom? Whom did you see?

GITTEL. The bridegroom! He is dark.

BASSIA. No, he's not. He's fair.

GITTEL. Come, let's go look at him again. (*They leave quickly.*)

LEYE (*stands up*). Granny, come to the cemetery.

FRADE (*sadly*). Come, child. Okh, okh, okh.

(LEYE *throws a black shawl over her shoulders and goes off with* FRADE *into the lane right. The stage remains unoccupied for a while. Music is heard. From the lane at left enter* NAKHMAN, REB MENDEL, *and* MENASHE, *a short, slight youth, frightened, his eyes large and bewildered. After him, his relatives, men and women, in festive dress.* SENDER *comes out to welcome them.*)

SENDER (*shakes hands with* NAKHMAN). Sholem Aleichem and welcome. (*They kiss.* SENDER *shakes hands with* MENASHE *and kisses him. Shakes hands with the others.*) How was the trip, Reb Nakhman?

NAKHMAN. We had a hard and bitter journey. We lost the road and wandered about in the fields for a long time. Then we blundered into a swamp and were nearly swallowed up. We barely escaped. I was even beginning to think that evil spirits, Heaven protect us, were at work to stop us from getting here. Still, in spite of everything, thank God, we arrived in time.

SENDER. You must be tired. You probably want to rest up a while.

NAKHMAN. No time to rest. We still have much to discuss concerning our mutual obligations, depositing the dowry, the expenses of the wedding, and so on.

SENDER. Of course. (*He puts his arm around* NAKHMAN'*s shoulder and they walk up and down the square talking quietly.*)

REB MENDEL (*to* MENASHE). Remember, at the table you are to sit still. Don't move and keep your eyes down. And immediately after the meal, as soon as the wedding bard calls out: "The bridegroom will deliver his oration," you stand up at once, climb up on a bench, and start talking in a loud voice and with a proper chant. The louder you shout, the better. And don't be shy, you hear?

MENASHE (*mechanically*). I hear . . . (*Quietly.*) Rebbe, I'm afraid.

REB MENDEL (*alarmed*). What are you afraid of? You didn't forget your speech, did you?

MENASHE. No, I remember my speech.

REB MENDEL. Well, then, what *are* you afraid of.

MENASHE (*with anguish*). I don't know. As soon as we left home, a great fear possessed me. The places we rode past were all strange to me. I have never seen so many strange people. I'm afraid they're watching me. I'm afraid of their eyes. (*Shudders.*) Rebbe, nothing frightens me so much as the glance of strangers' eyes.

REB MENDEL. I'll charm the evil eye away from you.

MENASHE. Rebbe, I'd rather be alone, hidden somewhere in a corner, and here I'm surrounded by strangers. I have to talk with them, answer them. As though I were being led to the gallows! (*With mystic terror.*) Rebbe! Above all I fear her, the maiden!

REB MENDEL. Pull yourself together! Master your fears, or you might, Heaven forbid, forget your speech. Come, let's go into the inn and you can rehearse it again. (*They start walking.*)

MENASHE (sees *the holy grave in front of him and seizes* REB MENDEL'*s hand in terror*). Rebbe! Look at that! A grave in the middle of the street!

(They stop and silently read the inscription. They stand a while and go off into the lane left with bowed heads. SENDER, NAKHMAN, and the relatives go into the house. The poor come out of SENDER's yard one after another, their sacks on their shoulders, staff in hand; they cross the square sadly and silently and disappear down the lane left. Some stop very briefly.)

TALL PALE YOUNG WOMAN. And now the dinner for the poor has passed too, as though it never happened.

OLD WOMAN WITH A LIMP. Said they'd give a plate of soup, too, but they didn't.

HUNCHBACKED OLD WOMAN. And the pieces of *khale* were so small.

MAN ON CRUTCHES. And he's so rich! It wouldn't have hurt him any to give us each a whole loaf!

TALL PALE YOUNG WOMAN. Could have given us a piece of fowl as well. For the rich guests they prepared chickens and geese and stuffed turkeys.

BLIND OLD WOMAN. What's the difference. When we die the worms will get it all. Okh, okh, okh.

(They leave slowly. The stage remains unoccupied a while. THE MESSENGER crosses slowly and enters the synagogue. It begins to grow dark. The shopkeepers close their shops and leave. Lights appear in the synagogue and in SENDER's house. SENDER, GITTEL and BASSIA appear on the porch and look around.)

SENDER *(uneasy)*. Where is Leye? Where is Frade? What's taking them so long at the cemetery? I hope nothing has happened to them, Heaven forbid.

GITTEL, BASSIA. We'll go to meet them.

(FRADE and LEYE enter hurriedly from the lane at right.)

FRADE. Hurry, hurry, child! My, how late we are! Why did I have to listen to you? I'm afraid something dreadful might happen, Heaven forbid.

SENDER. Well, here they are. What took you so long?

(Women come out of the house.)

WOMEN. Bring in the bride to light the candles and recite the blessing. *(They escort LEYE into the house.)*

FRADE *(quietly to GITTEL and BASSIA)*. She fainted. It was all I could do to revive her. I'm still shaking.

BASSIA. She's fasting and must have grown faint from lack of food.

GITTEL. Did she cry much at her mother's grave?

FRADE (*waves her hand*). Better not ask what happened there! I'm terrified.

(*A chair is set up near the door.* LEYE *is led out and seated to receive the guests. Music plays. From the lane at left come* NAKHMAN, MENASHE, REB MENDEL, *the relatives.* MENASHE *carries a bridal veil in both hands and approaches to throw it over* LEYE's *face.* THE MESSENGER *comes out of the synagogue.*)

LEYE (*tears the veil from her face, jumps out of her seat, pushes* MENASHE *away and cries out*). You are not my bridegroom!

(*A great commotion. Everyone surrounds* LEYE.)

SENDER. (*stunned*). My child, my child! Leye! What's come over you?

LEYE (*tears herself away, dashes over to the grave, spreads her arms*). Holy bride and bridegroom, protect me! Save me! (*She falls. People run over to her, pick her up. She looks around wild-eyed and cries out in a strange, masculine voice.*) A-a! You buried me! But I have come back to my destined bride, and I will not leave her. (NAKHMAN *approaches* LEYE. *She shouts into his face.*) Murderer!

NAKHMAN (*shuddering*). She has gone mad!

MESSENGER. The bride has been possessed by a dybbuk.

(*General consternation and commotion.*)

ACT III

(In Miropolye, at the home of REB AZRIELKE, *the Tsaddik of Miropolye. A large room. Right, a door leading to other rooms. In the middle of the rear wall, a door leading to the street. Benches on either side of the door. Extending almost the whole length of the wall left, a wide table covered with a white cloth. On the table, pieces of khale piled up, to be used for reciting the blessing that begins a meal. At the head of the table, an armchair. In the right wall, past the door, a small Ark and reading stand. In front of these, a table, a sofa, several chairs.*

Saturday evening, soon after sundown. Hassidim in the room. MIKHOL, *the Rabbi's aid, stands at the table and prepares the piles of khale.* THE MESSENGER *is seated near the Ark, surrounded by a group of Hassidim. Others are seated by themselves studying.* FIRST *and* SECOND HASSID *are standing in the middle of the room near the small table. From the rooms within, quiet singing:* "God of Abraham, Isaac, and Jacob.")*

FIRST HASSID. The stranger's tales of wonder are positively frightening. It scares me to listen to them.

SECOND HASSID. What's the matter?

FIRST HASSID. They're full of subtleties beyond my understanding. They sound like the mystic teachings of Rabbi Nakhman of Bratslav. Who knows. . . .

SECOND HASSID. If the older Hassidim are listening, there's probably nothing to worry about. *(They join the group around* THE MESSENGER.)

THIRD HASSID. Tell us another!

MESSENGER. It's late. The time is short.

FOURTH HASSID. Don't worry. The Rebbe won't be out so soon.

MESSENGER *(narrates)*. At the edge of the world stands a tall mountain, and on the mountain lies a great rock, and from the rock flows a clear spring. And at the other edge of the world, there is the heart of the world; for each thing in the world has a heart and the world as a whole has a great heart of its own. And the heart of the world gazes always at the clear

49

spring and cannot have its fill of looking; and it longs and
yearns and thirsts for the clear spring, but it cannot take even
the slightest step toward it. For as soon as the heart of the world
stirs from its place, it loses sight of the mountain top with the
clear spring; and if the heart of the world cannot see the clear
spring even for a single instant, it loses its life. And at that
very moment the world begins to die. And the clear spring has
no time of its own, and it lives with the time that the heart
of the world grants it. And the heart grants it only one day. And
when the day wanes, the clear spring begins to sing to the
heart of the world. And the heart of the world sings to the
clear spring. And their singing spreads over the world and from
it issue gleaming threads that reach to the hearts of all things
in the world and from one heart to another. And there is a
man of righteousness and grace who walks about over the world
and gathers the gleaming threads from the hearts and out of
them weaves time. And when he weaves an entire day, he
gives it to the heart of the world, and the heart of the world
gives it to the clear spring. And the spring lives yet another
day.

THIRD HASSID. The Rebbe is coming! (*All are silent. They
rise.* REB AZRIELKE *enters from the door right, a very old man
in a white kaftan and a shtraymel.**)

REB AZRIELKE (*weary and deep in thought, he walks slowly
to the table, sinks heavily into the sofa.* MIKHOL *stands at his
right hand. The Hassidim seat themselves around the table. The
older ones sit on the benches; the younger ones stand behind
them.* MIKHOL *hands out the* khale *to the Hassidim.* REB
AZRIELKE *raises his head and in a soft quavering voice begins
to chant*). "Here was the feast of King David the Messiah."
(*All respond and each says grace over a piece of* khale. *They begin singing softly a melody without words, mystic and sad.
Pause.* REB AZRIELKE *sighs deeply, rests his head on both hands,
and sits a while deep in meditation. Apprehension pervades the
silence.* REB AZRIELKE *raises his head and begins softly in a
quavering voice.*) They tell about the holy Baal Shem, may
his merits protect us. (*Brief pause.*) Once there came to Mezhi-
buzh some fellows, acrobats they were, that do their tricks in
the street. They stretched a rope across the river and one of
them walked on the rope. And people came running from all
parts of the city to see this marvelous feat. The Baal Shem also
went down to the river and stood there along with everyone
else, watching the man who walked upon the rope. His students

─────────
*A fur-trimmed hat.

were astonished at his presence and they asked him why he had come to watch the tricks. The holy Baal Shem replied: "I came to watch so that I might see how a man crosses a deep abyss. And as I watched, I thought: If Man were to develop his soul as carefully as he has developed his body, what deep abysses might his soul not cross on the slender cord of life!" (*He sighs deeply. Pause. The Hassidim exchange enraptured glances.*)

FIRST HASSID. How lofty!

SECOND HASSID. Wonder of wonders!

THIRD HASSID. How beautiful!

REB AZRIELKE (*softly to* MIKHOL, *who bends down to him*). There is a stranger present.

MIKHOL (*looks around*). He is a messenger and apparently a student of Cabala too.

REB AZRIELKE. What is his mission here?

MIKHOL. I don't know. Shall I ask him to leave?

REB AZRIELKE. Heaven forbid! Quite the contrary, a stranger should be received with honor. Give him a chair. (MIKHOL, *somewhat surprised, gives* THE MESSENGER *a chair. No one takes note of it.* REB AZRIELKE *glances at one of the Hassidim who is singing a mystic melody without words. Pause.* REB AZRIELKE *as before.*) God's world is great and holy. The holiest land in the world is the Land of Israel. In the Land of Israel the holiest city is Jerusalem. In Jerusalem the holiest place was the Temple, and in the Temple the holiest spot was the Holy of Holies. (*Brief pause.*) There are seventy peoples in the world. The holiest among these is the People of Israel. The holiest of the People of Israel is the tribe of Levi. In the tribe of Levi the holiest are the priests. Among the priests the holiest was the High Priest. (*Brief pause.*) There are 354 days in the year. Among these the holidays are holy. Higher than these is the holiness of the Sabbath. Among Sabbaths, the holiest is the Day of Atonement, the Sabbath of Sabbaths. (*Brief pause.*) There are seventy languages in the world. The holiest is Hebrew. Holier than all else in this language is the holy Torah, and in the Torah the holiest part is the Ten Commandments. In the Ten Commandments the holiest of all words is the name of God. (*Brief pause.*) And once during the year, at a certain hour, these four supreme sanctities of the world were joined with one another. That was on the Day of Atonement, when the High Priest would enter the Holy of Holies and there utter the name of God. And because this hour was beyond measure holy and awesome, it was the time of utmost peril

not only for the High Priest but for the whole of Israel. For if
in this hour there had, God forbid, entered the mind of the
High Priest a false or sinful thought, the entire world would
have been destroyed. (*Pause.*) Every spot where a man raises
his eyes to heaven, is a Holy of Holies. Every man, having been
created by God in His own image and likeness, is a High Priest.
Every day of a man's life is a Day of Atonement, and every word
that a man speaks with sincerity is the name of the Lord. Therefore it is that every sin and every wrong that a man commits
brings the destruction of the world. (*In a trembling voice.*) Human souls, through great anguish and pain, through many an
incarnation, strive, like a child reaching for its mother's breast,
to reach their source, the Throne of Glory on high. But it sometimes happens, even after a soul has reached exalted heights,
that evil suddenly overwhelms it, God forbid, and the soul stumbles and falls. And the more exalted it was, the deeper is the
abyss into which it falls. And when such a soul falls, a world is
destroyed, and darkness descends on all the holy places, and the
ten Sephiroth* mourn. (*Pause, as though awakening.*) My children! Today we will cut short our repast of farewell to the Sabbath.

(*All except* MIKHOL *leave silently, deeply impressed by what
they have heard. Brief pause.*)

MIKHOL (*approaches the table with uncertainty*). Rebbe!
(REB AZRIELKE *looks up at him wearily and sadly.*) Rebbe,
Sender of Brinnits has come.

REB AZRIELKE (*as if repeating*). Sender of Brinnits. I know.

MIKHOL. A great misfortune has befallen him. His daughter
is possessed by a dybbuk, God have mercy on us.

REB AZRIELKE. Possessed by a dybbuk. I know.

MIKHOL. He has brought her to you.

REB AZRIELKE (*as if to himself*). To me? To me? How could
he have come to me if the "me" in me is not here.

MIKHOL. Rebbe, all the world comes to you.

REB AZRIELKE. All the world. A blind world. Blind sheep following a blind shepherd. If they were not blind they would
come not to me but to Him who say "I," to the only "I" in the
world.

MIKHOL. Rebbe, you are His messenger.

REB AZRIELKE. So says the world, but I do not know that. For
forty years I have occupied a rebbe's seat, and I am not sure
to this very day whether I am a messenger of God, blessed be
He. There are times when I feel my closeness to the All. Then

*According to Cabalistic doctrine, the emanations of God.

I have no doubts. Then I am firm and I have influence in the worlds above. But there are times when I do not feel sure within. And then I am small and weak as a child. Then I need help myself.

MIKHOL. Rebbe, I remember, once you came at midnight and asked me to recite the Psalms with you. And then we recited them and wept together the whole night through.

REB AZRIELKE. That was once. Now it is even worse. (*With a trembling voice.*) What do they want of me? I am old and weak. My body needs rest; my spirit thirsts for solitude. Yet the misery and the anguish of the world reach out to me. Every plea pierces me as a needle does the flesh. And I have no more strength. I cannot!

MIKHOL (*frightened*). Rebbe! Rebbe!

REB AZRIELKE (*sobbing*). I can go no further! I cannot go on!

MIKHOL. Rebbe! You must not forget that behind you stand long generations of tsaddikim and holy men. Your father, Reb Itchele of blessed memory, your grandfather the renowned scholar Reb Velvele the Great, who was a pupil of the Baal Shem. . . .

REB AZRIELKE (*recovers*). My forebears. . . . My saintly father, who three times had a revelation from Elijah; my uncle Reb Meyer Ber, who used to ascend to heaven in his prayers; my grandfather, the great Reb Velvele, who resurrected the dead. *Turns to* MIKHOL, *his spirits restored.*) Do you know, Mikhol, that my grandfather, the great Reb Velvele, used to exorcise a dybbuk without either holy names or incantations, with merely a command. With a single command! In my times of need I turn to him and he sustains me. He will not forsake me now. Call in Sender.

(MIKHOL *leaves and returns with* SENDER.)

SENDER (*stretching out his arms imploringly*). Rebbe, have pity! Help me! Save my only child!

REB AZRIELKE. How did the misfortune occur?

SENDER. In the midst of veiling the bride, just as. . . .

REB AZRIELKE (*interrupts him*). That's not what I'm asking. What could have caused the misfortune? A worm can penetrate a fruit only when it begins to rot.

SENDER. Rebbe! My child is a God-fearing Jewish daughter. She is modest and obedient.

REB AZRIELKE. Children are sometimes punished for the sins of their parents.

SENDER. If I knew of any sin of mine, I would do penance.

REB AZRIELKE. Has the dybbuk been asked who he is and why he has taken possession of your daughter?

SENDER. He does not answer. But by his voice he was recognized as a student of our yeshiva who some months ago died quite suddenly in the synagogue. He was meddling with Cabala and came to grief.

REB AZRIELKE. By what powers?

SENDER. They say, by evil spirits. Some hours before his death he told a fellow student that one should not wage war against sin and that in evil, heaven protect us, there is a spark of holiness. He even wanted to use magic to get two barrels of gold.

REB AZRIELKE. You knew him?

SENDER. Yes, he ate regularly at my house.

REB AZRIELKE (looks attentively at SENDER.) Did you perhaps in any way cause him grief or shame? Try to remember.

SENDER. I don't know. I don't remember. (In despair.) Rebbe, I'm only human, after all. (Pause.)

REB AZRIELKE. Bring in the girl.

(SENDER leaves and returns immediately with FRADE, both leading LEYE by the hand. She stops stubbornly at the threshold and refuses to enter.)

SENDER (tearfully). Leye dearest, have pity. Don't shame me before the Rebbe. Go in.

FRADE. Go in, Leyele. Go in, my dove.

LEYE. I want to enter but I cannot!

REB AZRIELKE. Maiden! I command you to enter. (LEYE crosses the threshold and goes to the table.) Sit down.

LEYE (sits down obediently. Suddenly she springs up and begins to shout in a voice not hers). Let me go! I refuse! (She tries to run. SENDER and FRADE restrain her.)

REB AZRIELKE. Dybbuk, I command you to say who you are.

LEYE (DYBBUK). Rebbe of Miropolye! You know who I am, but I do not wish to reveal my name before others.

REB AZRIELKE. I do not ask your name. I ask, who are you?

LEYE (DYBBUK) (softly). I am one of those who sought new roads.

REB AZRIELKE. Only he seeks new roads who has lost the right one.

LEYE (DYBBUK). That road is too narrow.

REB AZRIELKE. That was said by one who did not return. (Pause.) Why did you enter into this maiden?

LEYE (DYBBUK). I am her destined bridegroom.

REB AZRIELKE. Our holy Torah forbids the dead to abide among the living.

LEYE (DYBBUK). I am not dead.

REB AZRIELKE. You departed from our world and you are forbidden to return to it until the great ram's horn is sounded. Therefore, I command you to leave the body of this girl so that a living branch of the eternal tree of Israel may not wither and die.

LEYE (DYBBUK) (*shouting*). Rebbe of Miropolye, I know how powerful, how invincible you are. I know that you can command the angels and the seraphim, but you cannot sway me. I have nowhere to go! For me every road is blocked, every gate is shut, and everywhere evil spirits lie in wait to consume me. (*With a trembling voice.*) There are heaven and earth, there are worlds without number, but not in a single one is there a place for me. And now that my anguished and harried soul has found a haven, you wish to drive me forth. Have pity. Do not conjure or compel me.

REB AZRIELKE. Wandering soul, I feel great pity for you, and I will try to release you from the destroying angels. But you must leave the body of this girl.

LEYE (DYBBUK) (*with firmness*). I will not leave.

REB AZRIELKE. Mikhol, summon a *minyan* from the synagogue. (MIKHOL *leaves and soon returns followed by ten Jews, who take their places at one side of the room.*) Sacred congregation, do you give me the authority in your name and with your power to expel from the body of a Jewish maiden a spirit who refuses to leave of his own free will?

ALL TEN MEN. Rebbe, we give you the authority in our name and with our power to expel from the body of a Jewish maiden a spirit who refuses to leave of his own free will.

REB AZRIELKE. (*rising*). Dybbuk! Soul of one who left our world, in the name and with the authority of a holy congregation of Jews, I, Azrielke ben Hadas, command you to leave the body of the maiden Leye bas Khanne and in leaving not to harm her nor any other living creature. If you do not obey my command, I will proceed against you with anathema and excommunication, with all the powers of exorcism and with the whole might of my outstretched arm. If, however, you obey my command, I will do all in my power to reclaim your soul and drive off the spirits of evil and destruction that surround you.

LEYE (DYBBUK) (*shouting*). I do not fear your anathemas and excommunications and I do not believe in your assurances!

There is no power in the world that can help me! There is no more exalted height than my present refuge and there is no darker abyss than that which awaits me. I will not leave!

REB AZRIELKE. In the name of Almighty God I charge you for the last time and command you to leave. If you do not, I excommunicate you and give you over into the hands of the destroying angels.

(*A fearful pause.*)

LEYE (DYBBUK). In the name of Almighty God, I am joined with my destined bride and I will not part from her forever.

REB AZRIELKE. Mikhol, have white robes brought in for all those present. Bring seven ram's horns and seven black candles. Then take from the Holy Ark seven Sacred Scrolls. (*Awesome pause while* MIKHOL *goes out and returns with the ram's horns and black candles. He is followed by* THE MESSENGER *carrying the white robes.*)

MESSENGER (*counts the robes*). There is one extra robe. (*Looks around.*) Perhaps someone is missing here?

REB AZRIELKE (*worried as though reminding himself*). In order to excommunicate a Jewish soul, permission must be obtained from the rabbi of the city. Mikhol, for the present put away the horns, the candles, and the robes. Take my staff, go to Rabbi Shimshon and ask him to come here as quickly as possible. (*MIKHOL gathers up the horns and candles and leaves with* THE MESSENGER, *who is carrying the robes. To the ten men.*) You may go, for the present. (*They leave. Pause.* REB AZRIELKE *raises his head.*) Sender! Where are the groom and his party staying?

SENDER. They remained at my house in Brinnits for the Sabbath.

REB AZRIELKE. Send a rider to inform them in my name that they are to stay there and await my command.

SENDER. I'll send a rider at once.

REB AZRIELKE. In the meantime you may go out and take the girl into the next room.

LEYE (*awakens, in her own voice, trembling*). Granny! I am afraid. What will they do to him? What will they do to me?

FRADE. Don't be afraid, my child. The Rebbe knows what he is doing. He won't harm anyone. The Rebbe cannot do any harm. (*She and* SENDER *lead* LEYE *into the next room.*)

REB AZRIELKE (*sits sunk deep in meditation. As though awakening*). And even if it has been otherwise decided in the worlds above, I will reverse that decision.

(REB SHIMSHON *enters.*)

REB SHIMSHON. May the week ahead be a good one, Rebbe.*

REB AZRIELKE. A good week to you, too, Rabbi, and a good year.* Please sit down. (REB SHIMSHON *sits down*.) I have troubled you because of a most important matter. A Jewish girl has been possessed by a dybbuk, may God have mercy, and nothing will induce him to leave. There remains only the last resort, to expel him by excommunication. I therefore ask your consent, and the good deed of saving a soul will be yours.

REB SHIMSHON. Excommunication is a bitter enough punishment for the living. How much more terrible for the dead. But as long as there is no other way and so godly a man as you considers it necessary, I delegate to you my authority. But I must first reveal to you, Rebbe, a secret that has a bearing on the matter.

REB AZRIELKE. Please do.

REB SHIMSHON. You may remember, Rebbe, a young man from Brinnits, Nissen ben Rivke, a student of Cabala, who was a Hassid of yours about twenty years ago.

REB AZRIELKE. He left for some distant place and died there.

REB SHIMSHON. Yes. Well this very Nissen ben Rivke came to me in my dreams three times last night and demanded that I summon Sender of Brinnits to a trial before a rabbinical court.

REB AZRIELKE. What claims has he against Sender?

REB SHIMSHON. He did not say. He only charged that Sender had spilled his blood.

REB AZRIELKE. If a Jew has a case against another and demands a trial, a rabbi cannot, of course, refuse. Especially when the accuser is deceased and can therefore appeal to the Throne of Glory itself. But does this have a bearing on the matter of the dybbuk?

REB SHIMSHON. It does. I have heard that the deceased young man who entered as a dybbuk into Sender's daughter was the son of Nissen ben Rivke. There is also talk of an obligation that Sender had to Nissen which he did not fulfill.

REB AZRIELKE (*thoughtful a while*). In that case I will postpone the exorcism of the dybbuk until tomorrow noon. In the morning, God willing, right after prayers we will ensure that your dreams are for good, and you will summon the deceased to a trial. Afterwards, with your authority I will drive out the dybbuk.

REB SHIMSHON. Inasmuch as a trial between the living and the dead is difficult and unusual, I would ask you, Rebbe, to consent to be the chief judge and to conduct the trial.

*Exchange of greetings, customary at the end of the Sabbath.

Reb Azrielke. I accept. Mikhol! (Mikhol *enters*.) Have the girl brought in. (Sender *and* Frade *bring in* Leye, *who sits with eyes shut tight*.) Dybbuk, I give you half a day's time, till tomorrow noon. If you will not leave within the designated time and of your own free will, I will, with the authority of the rabbi of the city, expel you by the bitter force of excommunication. (*Pause.* Sender *and* Frade *start to lead* Leye *out*.) Sender! Remain here a while. (Frade *leads* Leye *out*.) Sender! Do you remember your friend of years ago, Nissen ben Rivke?

Sender (*frightened*). Nissen ben Rivke? He died. . . .

Reb Azrielke. Know, then, that last night he appeared three times in dreams before the Rabbi of the City. (*Points to* Reb Shimshon.) And he demanded that you be summoned to trial to answer his charges.

Sender (*staggered*). Me? A trial? Heaven help me! What does he want of me? What should I do, Rebbe?

Reb Azrielke. I do not know what his accusations are, but you must accept the summons.

Sender. I will do as you say.

Reb Azrielke (*with a different tone*). Send the swiftest horses to Brinnits immediately and instruct the bridegroom and his party to be here before noon tomorrow, so that the marriage can take place as soon as the dybbuk leaves.

Sender. Rebbe, what if they no longer approve of the match and refuse to come?

(The Messenger *appears in the doorway*.)

Reb Azrielke (*with authority*). Let them be told that I have commanded it. But see that the bridegroom is here in time.

Messenger. The bridegroom will be here in time.

(*The clock strikes twelve*.)

ACT IV

(Same room as Act III. In place of the long table at left, a smaller one, closer to the footlights. Behind it, in prayer shawl and phylacteries, are REB AZRIELKE, seated in an armchair, and two other judges in ordinary chairs. REB SHIMSHON stands beside the table. MIKHOL stands at a distance. They finish saying a prayer to ensure that a dream is good, not evil.)

REB SHIMSHON. My dream was good. My dream was good.

REB AZRIELKE, FIRST AND SECOND JUDGES *(together)*. Your dream was good. Your dream was good. Your dream was good.

REB AZRIELKE. Rabbi, now that we have turned your dream to good, sit with us as a judge. (REB SHIMSHON *seats himself at the table beside* REB AZRIELKE.) Now we shall notify the deceased to be present at the trial. But first I shall mark a circle beyond whose margin he shall be powerless to pass. Mikhol! Hand me my staff. (MIKHOL *hands him the staff.* REB AZRIELKE *rises from his place and in the left corner of the room he describes a circle with his staff, from left to right. He returns to his seat at the table.*) Mikhol, take my staff and go to the cemetery. And when you pass its gates close your eyes and feel your way with the staff. And stop at the first grave that the staff touches. And striking the grave three times with the staff, speak these words: "Blameless Departed! Azrielke, the son of the great Tsaddik Reb Itchele of Miropolye, sent me to ask your pardon for disturbing your rest, and he commands you to inform the blameless deceased Nissen ben Rivke, by ways known to you, that the just tribunal of Miropolye calls upon him to come at once and with all haste to a trial and asks him to wear the same garb in which he was interred." Say this three times. Then turn about and retrace your steps. And pay no heed, no matter what shouts and cries and calls you hear behind you. And do not let my staff slip from your grasp even for a moment, or you will be in great peril. Go, and may God watch over you, for no harm comes to those who are sent on a virtuous errand. Go, but first send in two men to make a partition for the deceased. (MIKHOL *leaves. Two men enter with a sheet. They screen off, to the*

59

floor, the whole left corner of the room and leave.) Call in Sender. (SENDER *enters.*) Sender, have you done what I told you to? Did you dispatch horses to bring the groom and his party?

SENDER. I sent the swiftest horses, but they have not yet arrived.

REB AZRIELKE. Send a messenger out to meet them and say that they are to drive with utmost speed.

SENDER. I will do so. (*Pause.*)

REB AZRIELKE. Sender! Word has been sent to the blameless deceased Nissen ben Rivke that this court calls him to appear in his case against you. Will you accept our verdict?

SENDER. I will.

REB AZRIELKE. Will you carry out our decision?

SENDER. I will carry it out.

REB AZRIELKE. Step back and stand at the right.

SENDER. Rebbe! I remember now. Nissen must be calling me to trial over a vow we took. But I am not at fault in the matter.

REB AZRIELKE. Tell it later, after the plaintiff has stated his grievances. (*Pause.*) Soon there will appear among us a man from the True World so that we may judge between him and one who is from our world of illusion. (*Pause.*) A trial such as this is proof that the laws of the Holy Torah rule all worlds and all creatures and are obligatory for the dead as for the living. (*Pause.*) A trial such as this is most awful and fearsome. It is watched by all Holy Places. And should this court, Heaven forbid, deviate by a hair from the law, there would be a protest in the Celestial Court itself. We must, therefore, approach such a trial with awe and terror, awe . . . and terror. (*Looks around anxiously, as he speaks. His eye stops at the curtain and he stops talking. A fearful silence.*)

FIRST JUDGE (*to the second, in a frightened whisper*). He is here, I think.

SECOND JUDGE (*in the same tone*). I think he is.

REB SHIMSHON. He is here.

REB AZRIELKE. Blameless deceased Nissen ben Rivke, this just tribunal decrees that you may not step beyond those bounds and that partition that it has assigned to you. (*Pause.*) Blameless deceased Nissen ben Rivke, this just tribunal commands you to state your claims and grievances against Sender ben Henye. (*Terrifying pause. All listen as though petrified.*)

FIRST JUDGE (*as before*). He is answering, I think.

SECOND JUDGE. I think he is.

FIRST JUDGE. I hear a voice, but I hear no words.

SECOND JUDGE. I hear words, but I hear no voice.

REB SHIMSHON (*to* SENDER). Sender ben Henye, the blameless deceased Nissen ben Rivke states his claim saying that in your youth you were students in the same yeshiva and that your souls were bound together in loyal friendship. You were both married in the same week. Later, when you both met at the Rebbe's house during the High Holy Days, each of you pledged that if his wife should conceive and bear a child, the one a girl the other a boy, the children would wed.

SENDER (*in a trembling voice*). Yes, it was so.

REB SHIMSHON. The blameless deceased Nissen ben Rivke states further that soon thereafter he departed for a distant town. There his wife bore a son and at the same time your wife bore a daughter. And soon after that he died. (*Brief pause.*) In the True World he learned that his son was blessed with a lofty soul and was rising to ever greater heights. And the father's heart was joyful and proud. And he saw further that when his son grew older, he went out into the world and travelled from place to place, from country to country, from city to city, for his soul was drawn to her for whom his soul was destined. And he came to the city where you live, and entered your house and sat at your table. And his soul was united with the soul of your daughter. But you were rich and Nissen's son was poor. And you turned your gaze from him and sought other matches for your daughter among families of wealth and station. (*Brief pause.*) And Nissen saw how his son was plunged into despair and went wandering off into the world, seeking new ways. And the father's heart was filled with fear and sorrow. And the Powers of Blackness, perceiving the despairing youth, spread their nets for him and captured him and took him from the world before his time, and his soul wandered homelessly until it entered as a dybbuk into the body of its destined bride. (*Brief pause.*) Nissen ben Rivke declares: with the death of his son he was cut off from both worlds, with none to bear his name or say a prayer for his soul. His light has been put out forever; the crown of his head has rolled down into the abyss. And he asks the just tribunal to judge Sender in accordance with the law of our Holy Torah, for spilling the blood of Nissen's son and of his son's children and their children to the end of time. (*Terrifying silence.* SENDER *sobs.*)

REB AZRIELKE. Sender ben Henye. Did you hear the charges of the blameless deceased Nissen ben Rivke? What have you to say in your defense?

SENDER. I cannot open my mouth and I have no words for my defense. But I beg my old comrade to spare me my child, for I did nothing out of ill will. Soon after our vow, Nissen departed and I did not know whether his wife bore a child nor whether it was a boy or a girl. Then I learned that he had died. Further news of his family I had none, and gradually I forgot.

REB AZRIELKE. Why did you not inquire? Why did you not investigate?

SENDER. It is customary for the boy's family to take the first steps. And so I thought that if a son had been born to Nissen, he would have informed me. (*Pause.*)

REB SHIMSHON. Nissen ben Rivke asks, why, when his son was received into your home and sat at your table, did you never inquire of him who he was and whence he came?

SENDER. I do not know. I do not remember. But I swear that I was always drawn to take the youth for my son-in-law. That is why, whenever a match was proposed, I set such hard conditions that the groom's father would never agree to them. That is how three proposals fell through. But this time the relatives insisted. . . . (*Pause.*)

REB SHIMSHON. Nissen ben Rivke declares that deep in your heart you recognized his son, and therefore you were afraid to ask who he was. You sought for your daughter a life of riches and of ease and therefore you thrust his son into the abyss.

(SENDER *weeps softly hiding his face. Heavy pause.* MIKHOL *comes in and returns the staff to the Rebbe.*)

REB AZRIELKE (*speaks softly with* REB SHIMSHON *and the other two judges. Arises, takes his staff in hand*). This just tribunal has heard both sides and now delivers its verdict as follows: Whereas it is not known whether at the time of the vow between Nissen ben Rivke and Sender ben Henye their wives had conceived; and whereas according to our Holy Torah, an agreement is not binding that pertains to a thing not yet created, we cannot, therefore, conclude that Sender was obliged to fulfill the pledge. Since, however, the pledge was accepted in the Sacred Precincts and the thought was implanted in the heart of Nissen ben Rivke's son that Sender ben Henye's daughter was his destined bride; and since Sender's subsequent actions led to great misfortunes for Nissen ben Rivke and his son, therefore this just tribunal decrees that Sender should give away half his wealth to the poor and that as long as he lives he should, on the anniversary of the death of Nissen ben Rivke and of his son, light a memorial candle and recite the mourner's *Kaddish* for them as though they were his own children. (*Pause.*) This just tribunal asks the blameless deceased Nissen ben Rivke to forgive Sender with full forgiveness. And it further asks him to command with the full authority of a father that his son leave the body of the maiden Leye bas Khanne so that a branch of the fruitful tree of Israel may not wither. And for that the Almighty will manifest his grace to Nissen ben Rivke and to his homeless son.

ALL. Amen! (*Pause.*)

REB AZRIELKE. Blameless deceased Nissen ben Rivke, did you hear our verdict? Do you accept it? (*Terrifying pause.*) Sender ben Henye, did you hear our verdict? Do you accept it?

SENDER. Yes, I accept.

REB AZRIELKE. Blameless deceased Nissen ben Rivke. The trial between you and Sender ben Henye is over. Now you must return to your place of rest. And we decree that on the way you harm neither man nor other living creature. (*Pause.*) Mikhol! Have the partition removed and let water be brought.

(MIKHOL *calls in two men who remove the curtain.* REB AZRIELKE *describes with his staff a circle on the same spot as before only from right to left. A basin and dipper are brought in. All wash.*) Sender! Has the bridegroom's party arrived?

SENDER. There has been no sound of their arrival.

REB AZRIELKE. Send a second rider to meet them and have them drive the horses as hard as possible. Arrange for the wedding and the musicians. Have the bride dressed in her wedding-gown so that as soon as the dybbuk leaves she may be led to the ceremony. What will be done will be finished.

(SENDER *leaves.* REB AZRIELKE *removes his phylacteries and folds up his prayer shawl.*)

REB SHIMSHON (*softly to the judges*). Did you understand that the deceased did not forgive Sender?

FIRST AND SECOND JUDGES (*softly. Frightened*). We did.

REB SHIMSHON. Did you understand that the deceased did not accept the verdict?

JUDGES. We did.

REB SHIMSHON. Did you notice that he did not reply "Amen" to Reb Azrielke's words?

JUDGES. Yes, we noticed that.

REB SHIMSHON. It is a very bad omen.

JUDGES. It is indeed!

REB SHIMSHON. See how agitated Reb Azrielke is. His hands are trembling. (*Pause.*) We have done our part. Now we may leave. (*The judges leave silently and unnoticed.* REB SHIMSHON *prepares to leave too.*)

REB AZRIELKE. Rabbi, remain here till the dybbuk leaves. I should like you to perform the marriage ceremony. (REB SHIMSHON *sighs and, head bent, sits down to a side. Oppressive pause.*) God in Heaven! Hidden and wonderful are your ways. But the way on which I go is illuminated by light from the flame of Your sacred will. And I will not deviate from it, neither to the right nor to the left. (*Raises his head.*) Mikhol, have you prepared everything?

MIKHOL. Yes, Rebbe.

REB AZRIELKE. Have the maiden brought in. (SENDER *and* FRADE *bring in* LEYE, *in a white wedding-gown with a black cape around her shoulders. They seat her on the sofa.* REB SHIMSHON *sits down near* REB AZRIELKE.) Dybbuk, in the name of the rabbi of the city, seated here, in the name of a holy congregation of Jews, in the name of the Great Sanhedrin of Jerusalem, I, Azrielke ben Hadas, command you for the last time to depart from the body of the maiden Leye bas Khanne.

LEYE (DYBBUK) (*determined*). I will not leave!

REB AZRIELKE. Mikhol, call in the men and bring the white robes and the rams' horns and the black candles. (MIKHOL *leaves and returns with fifteen men, among them,* THE MESSENGER. *They bring in the robes, horns, and candles.*) Bring forth the Scrolls! (MIKHOL *removes seven Holy Scrolls and distributes them among seven men. He distributes seven horns.*) Stubborn spirit, since you are not humble unto our command, I give you over into the power of the higher spirits to expel you by force. Blow *tekiah.* (*They blow* tekiah.)

LEYE (DYBBUK) (*tears herself from her place, tosses about, shouting*). Let me go! Do not drag me! I will not! I cannot leave!

REB AZRIELKE. Since the higher spirits cannot conquer you, I give you over into the power of the middle spirits, those who are neither good nor evil. Let them, by whatever cruel means are at their disposal, tear you out. Blow *shvorim.* (*They blow* shvorim.)

LEYE (DYBBUK) (*with failing strength*). My grief is great. All the powers of the world have risen up against me! I am torn by the most terrible of spirits who know no mercy. Against me are arrayed the souls of the great and the just, my father's soul among them, and they command me to leave. But as long as a single spark of strength flickers within me, I will resist them and remain.

REB AZRIELKE (*to himself*). It must be that some mighty

power is aiding him! (*Pause.*) Mikhol! Let the Scrolls be returned to the Ark. (*They do so.*) Cover the Ark with a black curtain. (MIKHOL *does so.*) Light the black candles. (*They do so.*) Let all don the white robes. (*All do so, including* REB AZRIELKE *and* REB SHIMSHON. REB AZRIELKE *rises, raises his hand high. In a loud and terrifying voice.*) Rise up, Oh Lord! And let thine enemies be dispersed and scattered before Thee. Like smoke let them be dispersed! Thou sinful and stubborn spirit, with the power of Almighty God and with the authority of the Holy Torah, I Azrielke ben Hadas, do sunder every thread that binds you to the living world and to the body and soul of the maiden Leye bas Khanne!

LEYE (DYBBUK) (*cries out*). Woe is me!

REB AZRIELKE. And I declare you excommunicated from all of Israel. *Terua!*

MESSENGER. The last spark was fused into the flame.

LEYE (DYBBUK) (*feebly*). I can struggle no more.

(*They start to blow* terua.)

REB AZRIELKE (*quickly silencing the horns. To* LEYE). Do you submit?

LEYE (DYBBUK) (*in a dead voice*). I submit.

REB AZRIELKE. Do you promise of your own free will to depart from the body of the maiden Leye bas Khanne and never to return to it?

LEYE (DYBBUK) (*as before*). I promise.

REB AZRIELKE. By the same power and authority by which I excommunicated you, I now revoke that excommunication. (*To* MIKHOL.) Put out the candles and remove the black curtain. (MIKHOL *does so.*) Remove the horns. (MIKHOL *gathers them up.*) And let those who came to assist remove their robes and leave. (*The fourteen men remove their robes and leave with* THE MESSENGER *and* MIKHOL. REB AZRIELKE *raises his hands high.*) Lord of the Universe! God of compassion and of grace! Behold the great anguish of this tortured and homeless soul whom the sins and errors of others caused to stumble. Avert Thine eyes from its sins and let its previous good deeds, its present torments, and the merits of its forebears rise up to Thee like a vapor. Lord of the Universe, sweep from its path all angels of destruction and in Thy palaces prepare for it eternal rest. Amen.

ALL. Amen.

LEYE (DYBBUK) (*trembling violently*). Recite the *Kaddish* for me. My appointed time runs out!

REB AZRIELKE. Sender! Say *Kaddish* first.

SENDER. *Yisgadal veyiskadash shmey rabo. Bolmo di vro khirusey.* . . .

> (*The clock strikes twelve.*)

LEYE (DYBBUK) (*springs up*). A-ay! (*Falls to the sofa as in a faint.*)

REB AZRIELKE. Lead the bride to the wedding canopy.

> (MIKHOL *runs in.*)

MIKHOL (*very upset*). The second rider just returned. He says the bridegroom's carriage broke a wheel and they are all walking. But they're quite near, on the hill. You can see them from here.

REB AZRIELKE (*astonished*). Let be what must be! (*To* SENDER.) Let the old woman remain here with the bride while the rest of us proceed to welcome the groom. (*With his staff he draws a circle around* LEYE *from left to right. Removes his white robe, hangs it near the door, and leaves, staff in hand, followed by* SENDER *and* MIKHOL. *Long pause.*)

LEYE (*awakens. In a feeble voice*). Who is here with me? Is that you, Granny? Granny? I am so sad. Help me. Rock me to sleep.

FRADE (*caresses her*). Do not be sad, sweet child. Let the Tartar be sad, and the black tom cat, and let your heart be light as a feather of down, as a puff that is blown, as a flake of white snow, and may holy cherubim cradle you in their wings.

> (*A wedding march is heard.*)

LEYE (*trembling, seizes* FRADE'S *hand*). Do you hear? They are going to dance around the holy grave so that the dead bride and groom may rejoice!

FRADE. Do not tremble, child. Don't be afraid. You are guarded by a great watch, a mighty watch. Sixty giants with drawn swords protect you from mishap. Our holy patriarchs and matriarchs protect you from the evil eye. (*Gradually falls into sing-song rhymes.*)

> Soon you will be led to the wedding canopy.
> Happy and blessed will that hour be.
> Your mother, virtuous and wise,
> Walks forth from Paradise,
> From Paradise.
> On her robes are gold and silver.
> Two little angels come to greet her,
> Come to greet her.
> They stand on either side
> To the left and to the right.

"Khannele mine, Khannele fine,
Why on your gown do gold and silver shine?"
And Khannele answers them thus and so:
"My joy is great. Why should my gown not glow?
My only child, the crown of my head,
Is this day to her wedding led."
"Khannele mine, Khannele fine,
Then why is there pain in those eyes of thine?"
And Khannele answers them thus and so:
"Should my heart not grieve, should it not feel woe?
Strangers to the wedding lead the bride,
While I in sadness stand on a side."
Soon to the canopy they will lead her.
Young and old will come to greet her.
Elijah will come and take the great goblet in his hand,
And recite a blessing for the entire land.
Amen and amen.
(*Falls asleep. Long pause.*)

LEYE (*eyes shut tight. Sighs deeply. Opens her eyes*). Who sighs here with such sadness?

KHONNON'S VOICE. I do.

LEYE. I hear your voice, but I cannot see you.

KHONNON'S VOICE. A forbidden circle rings you round.

LEYE. Your voice sounds as sweet to me as the weeping of a violin on a silent night. Tell me, who are you?

KHONNON'S VOICE. I have forgotten. Only in your thoughts can I remember myself.

LEYE. I remember now. My heart was drawn to you as to a bright star. On silent nights I have shed sweet tears, and always in my dreams I saw a figure. Was that you?

KHONNON'S VOICE. It was.

LEYE. I remember now. Your hair was soft, and it glistened as though with tears, and your eyes were sad and gentle. Long and slender were your fingers. Day and night I thought of you. (*Pause. Sadly.*) But you went away and my light was put out and my soul withered. And like a desolate widow was I when a strange man approached. Then you returned and in my heart bloomed a life of death and a joy of sorrow. Why have you forsaken me again?

KHONNON'S VOICE. I broke all barriers, I surmounted death, I defied the laws of the ages and generations. I struggled with the strong, the mighty, the merciless. And when the last spark of my strength was burned out, I departed from your body to return to your soul.

LEYE (*tenderly*). Return to me my bridegroom, my husband. I will carry you, in death, in my heart; and in the dreams of night we will together rock to sleep our unborn babes. (*Weeps.*) We will sew them clothes to wear and sing them lullabies. (*Sings, weeping.*)

> Bayu, bayu, babies dead,
> Without clothes, without a bed,
> Unborn children, never mine
> Lost forever, lost in time.

(*The strains of a wedding march approach.*)

LEYE (*trembling*). They come to lead me to the canopy with a stranger. Come to me, my bridegroom!

KHONNON'S VOICE. I have departed from your body. I come to your soul.

(*He is seen in white upon the wall.*)

LEYE (*joyfully*). The barrier that hems is broken! I see you, my bridegroom! Come to me!

KHONNON (*like an echo*). Come to me!

LEYE (*cries out with joy*). I am coming.

KHONNON (*like an echo*). I am coming.

VOICES (*offstage*). Lead the bride to the canopy!

(*A wedding march. LEYE leaves her black cape on the couch and all in white goes to KHONNON to the strains of the wedding march. She stands in his place and her figure blends with his. REB AZRIELKE enters, staff in hand, followed by THE MESSENGER. They pause near the door. In the doorway, SENDER, FRADE, the others.*)

LEYE (*in a voice as from afar*). A great light flows about me. I am joined with you, my destined bridegroom. Together we will soar higher, higher, higher.

(*It grows gradually darker.*)

REB AZRIELKE (*lowering his head*). Too late.

MESSENGER. Blessed be the True Judge.

(*Total darkness. From afar, very softly is heard:*)

> Wherefore, wherefore
> Did the soul
> From its exalted height
> Fall into abysmal depths?
> Within the fall the power lies
> To rise again.

GOD OF VENGEANCE

❧

Sholem Asch
(1880–1957)

❧

For the non-Yiddish reader, Sholem Asch probably still is, as he was during the 1940's and 1950's, the best-known Yiddish writer. From the very beginning of his career, Asch's works found their way from the Yiddish originals into Polish, Russian, and some twenty other languages. In English alone, seventeen volumes of fiction, mainly novels, have appeared; and it is as a novelist that he is known to the English reader. Not only is he the author of such widely known works as *The Nazarene, Mary, The Prophet, Moses,* and *The Apostle,* but also of *Three Cities, Salvation, In the Beginning, Motke the Thief, The War Goes On, The Mother, Three Novels, Song of the Valley, Kiddush Ha-Shem, Children of Abraham, Sabbatai Zevi, Tales of My People, East River,* and *A Passage in the Night.* Yet, though he wrote nothing for the stage after the late 1920's, he had up to that time authored some twenty plays and had achieved great popularity as a dramatist in the Yiddish theater. In addition, numerous adaptations of his novels were produced, including his own dramatization of *Motke the Thief.*

Asch is a writer of great scope and wide interests. His subjects range from Moses to the present, from Eastern Europe and Israel to America, from the small towns to the world's great cities. He writes of Jews and gentiles, of prophets and peasants; of the respectable middle class, of the tough butchers and draymen without social status, and of the world of thieves and prostitutes. He has an eager eye for externals, for sharp contrasts, dramatic situations, panoramic vistas, and masses in motion; he is less interested in details. Of the themes that run through his works, the most frequent is probably faith; yet it is a faith that is not precisely defined, a faith in miracles, in Judaism, in the reality of a common Judeo-Christian tradition, in the common man and his yearning for morality, in life. It is the drama, the color, the sentiment, the mystical surface of faith that intrigues him rather than its substance, as it was the dramatic situation of the Messiah and the martyr that attracted him all his life—the loyalty and the mystic ecstasy of their ordeal, not the inner struggle or the anguish. Though he admires Jewish—which is more than Stoic—endurance of suffering, he is also intrigued by violence, and he finds a fusion of the two in the violent endurance and the endurance of violence that constitute martyrdom. He has a great enthusiasm for what he admires that leads him to idealize it, to paint it in glowing color and idyllic form. He admires all who have faith or are faithful to a vision of goodness, and these include not only Messiahs and martyrs but virtuous matrons, chaste maidens, young lovers, and harmonious worlds that are past—and owners of brothels. Two types appear in his works with great frequency—one, the traditional pious Jew, who has a disdain for the bestializing and brutalizing effect of violence and an admiration for gentleness, morality, study, and observance; the other, the rough, tough man whose physical work, while it relegates him to a low position in the social scale, endows him with muscle and with the ability to give as well as take a blow. Asch admires them both, but there is no conflict in his admiration, for his men of muscle, though unlearned and unrefined, remain loyal to the ideals and the defense of their people and to the traditions of learning. He met these types early—in his own family. His brothers were tall, brawny fellows who helped their father run his tavern, and took care of the business with the butchers and peasants; his much older half-brothers by a previous marriage were pious and studious Hassidim.

If *Salvation,* a reverent portrait of early nineteenth century Hassidism, is typical of the idyllic vein of Asch's historical fiction, *God of Vengeance* is typical of the hard realism with which he often portrays big-city life and people. The play is dominated by the tough and tragic figure of Yankel Chapchovich, the victim of his delusion that he can raise his only daughter to chaste maidenhood in his home above the brothel that he operates. It is not the brothel owner that the play reveals but the father who is ready to sacrifice himself and his wife as well if only he can save his daughter; the father who clings, foolishly and naively, to the dream of his daughter's innocence; who, in his simple faith in the power of his wish, converts the Torah Scroll into an object of idolatory, a talisman to ward off evil. And it is this very stubborn and desperate naivete that makes Yankel so appealing a figure. Like Jay Gatsby he seems to have remained strangely uncontaminated by the evil of the world in which he moves and with which he deals. And throughout he retains a loyalty to the ideals of Jewish decency and Jewish respect for learning, learned men, and charity. In Gatsby it is the lover who dreams of a love impossibly pure and devoted, symbolic of the unattainable ideals of life; in Yankel it is the Jewish father who cherishes the ideal of a purity in his daughter that his life has long since rendered unattainable. The very tenacity with which he has clung to the illusion is characteristic of him to the last. There is a stubborn nobility about his bitter refusal to be content with mere respectability.

It is, of course, not God who exacts vengeance in the play, but life, which exacts the price of illusion and self-deception. Yet if Yankel pays the price of dreaming, his dream reveals the ugly realities. Not only does the play repudiate any Jewish version of the Victorian compromise that is willing to accept respectability in place of virtue, appearance in place of reality, but it is an indictment of the moral schizophrenia of a free-for-all world, which cherishes the illusion that it can maintain morality in its personal and human relations while it abides by the morality of the marketplace in its business relations. Sinclair Lewis and Arthur Miller both used the salesman as the representative of a world that deals in commodities. Asch, with uncompromising harshness, carries the logic one step further and makes the little world of the brothel, where human flesh is sold, a symbol of the larger world. Yankel is the representative of this, as well as the victim of its moral disease. In his effort to keep the two worlds separate he is reminiscent

of Wemmick in Dickens' *Great Expectations,* who builds a
castle of filial devotion and human relatedness and then surrounds it with a moat to keep it uncontaminated by the world
of business and the accumulation of "portable property"; his
business involves the persons of criminals as Yankel's involves
the persons of prostitutes. Instead of a castle, Chapchovich, as
a Jew, tries to build a kind of chapel, a sanctuary of innocence
and learning. Though Wemmick is successful in keeping one
life undefiled by the other, Asch, with greater fidelity to life,
has Yankel fail, the victim not only of his folly, but also of
an uncompromising honesty and naive integrity that reveal the
true nature of the world's moral disease. If the play bears some
similarity to *Mrs. Warren's Profession,* the resemblance is only
superficial. Where Shaw is interested in prostitution as a social
problem, Asch is interested in the rough-hewn Chapchovich
and his naive honesty, his simplicity, his childlike faith in the
power of his repentance and in the magical power he attrib-
utes to the Torah Scroll. The force of Yankel's raging in the
final action of the play is a fitting expression of the force of
his character and the violence of his downfall.

Although the boldness of its setting in a brothel and its introduction of homosexuality has not given the play a wholly
untroubled career, it was for many years a popular work in the
Yiddish theater. Since its publication in 1907, it has been played
not only in Yiddish, but also in Polish, Russian, French, German, and Italian. Rudolph Schildkraut played it in German,
under Reinhardt's direction, in 1911, as well as in Yiddish and
in English. If the power of the play lies in the forcefulness of
the character of Yankel Chapchovich, some of the credit must
be given to Schildkraut. Asch notes: "I saw Schildkraut for the
first time in 1905, when he played Shylock in Max Reinhardt's
Little Theater. His creation of the role was so deeply moving
that I reworked my *God of Vengeance* and . . . adapted the
character of Yankel Chapchovich especially for Schildkraut
. . . and I can state that no one equalled him in this role." In
the silences as well as the dialogue, in the stage business as well
as the words, Schildkraut apparently succeeded with tragic bril-
liance in projecting the undefiled core of innocence in a deluded, violent, naive man who, though he misunderstood the
nature of morality, never doubted man's need for it.

GOD OF VENGEANCE

CHARACTERS

Yankel Chapchovich, the "Uncle"; proprietor of a brothel
Sore, his wife; a former prostitute
Rivkele, their daughter; a girl of about seventeen
Hindl, first prostitute; in her thirties, the years show
Manke, second prostitute; still young
Reyzl, third prostitute
Basha, a country girl; newly arrived
Shloyme, a pimp; Hindl's bought husband, a handsome fellow
 of twenty-six
Reb Elye, a go-between and a matchmaker for Uncle
Reb Aron, the scribe; a pious Jew
The Stranger, a man interested in a bride for his son
A Woman, blind in one eye; one of the poor

Time: the present
Place: a large provincial town

ACT I

(UNCLE'S *private apartment on the first floor of an old wooden house. The room is above the cellar where the brothel is located. Wooden steps lead up to the apartment from the street. Footsteps on the stairs can be heard inside. The set reveals one large room with a low ceiling. The furniture is new, in the latest Warsaw garish style, which clashes with the age and style of the room itself. The walls are hung with pictures of embroidered canvas, Biblical scenes: "Adam and Eve at the Tree of Knowledge," etc. Girls' work. In the rear wall is the door that leads to the street. At the right, a second door leading into* RIVKELE'S *room. To the right of the rear door, against the wall, two beds, the bedding puffed high under the spreads. To the left, two small windows with shutters on the inside. The windows are hung with curtains; flower-pots are on the sills. Between the windows, a shelf. Beyond one window a chest of drawers. The room is in the final stages of being cleaned up. It appears that company is expected. There are extra benches and tables with baskets of baked goods and other food. An afternoon early in the spring.* SORE *is a tall, graceful woman. Her features are hardened, but there are still traces of her former beauty, which retains a certain measure of impudence. The wig customary for an Orthodox Jewess covers her own coquettish locks, which drop down from time to time. She wears subdued matronly clothes but decorated with too much jewelry. Her movements still betray the world from which she came. She stands near* RIVKELE, *a striking young girl, dressed very neatly and respectably. Her dress is still girlishly short and she wears her hair in two long braids. She is busy tidying up the room.*)

RIVKELE (*attaching paper flowers to the curtains*). There, Mamma. Now to decorate the mirror. Pretty, isn't it, Mamma?

SORE (*busy setting the table*). Hurry, dear, hurry. Father has already gone to arrange for some fine folks to bring the Torah Scroll home.

RIVKELE. How gay it will be! People will come. There will be music, singing, won't there. Mamma?

74

SORE. Yes, my sweet. It's a dedication ceremony, an act of great piety. Not everyone can afford to have a Torah Scroll copied for his own home. Only someone who is well off, a man of prominence.

RIVKELE. And will girls come, too? Will there be dancing? Really, Mamma? (*Pauses.*) Then I must buy a blouse, Mamma dear, and a pair of white slippers. (*Shows her shoes.*) You can't dance in high-button shoes, can you?

SORE. When, with God's help, you become a bride during Passover, I'll have a long dress made for you, buy you shoes; girls will come, fine girls, respectable girls. You can be friends with them.

RIVKELE (*stubbornly*). You're always putting things off till Passover. I'm grown up now. (*Stands before the mirror.*) See, Mamma, I'm grown up now. (*Shows her hair.*) Look how long my braids are. Manke says that. . . . (*Catches herself.*) And Manke will be there too, won't she Mamma?

SORE. No, sweet, only respectable and decent girls. You are a decent and respectable girl.

RIVKELE. Why not Manke, Mamma dear? It was Manke who drew a star for me on the vestment for the Scroll. I'm embroidering it with silk thread and decorating it with leaves and flowers. You'll see how pretty it will be, Mamma. (*She points to the pictures on the wall.*) A hundred times prettier than these.

SORE (*frightened*). Heaven help me, don't tell your father. He'll shout and he'll be very angry.

RIVKELE. Why, Mamma? It's for the Torah Scroll.

SORE. Your father will be angry. (*Steps are heard.*) Hush, Rivkele, here he comes.

UNCLE (*still on the stairs*). You think I'm going to beg them? Who cares! (*Enters. A tall, powerful fellow, about 40, with a pot belly and a thickly bearded face. The beard itself, black, is cut round. His speech is loud and vulgar, accompanied by coarse gestures. When he talks to anyone, he holds him by the lapel. There is, nevertheless, a frankness in his face and about his person.*) So they won't come! Who needs them? I've gotten some of the poor together. I'm not worried. There will be enough customers for the cakes and the geese. (*He sees RIVKELE. Sits down.*) Come over here to your father.

SORE (*angry but she tries not to show it. She serves the food*). You'd think they'd sully their family name if they came here! When they have to borrow a hundred or ask for a contribution

to charity, they're not one bit ashamed of you. You may be
dirty, but your money is clean enough.

UNCLE. Look at how worried she is! There's nothing to be
upset about. Don't be afraid. Nothing will be spoiled. (*He calls*
RIVKELE.) Well, come on over to your father.

RIVKELE (*reluctantly approaches her father. She is afraid*).
What is it, Papa?

UNCLE. Don't be afraid, Rivkele. I won't hurt you. (*Takes
her hand.*) You love your father, don't you?

(RIVKELE *nods her head.*)

UNCLE. Then why are you afraid of me?

RIVKELE. I don't know.

UNCLE. Don't be afraid of your father. I love you. I love you
very much. I'm ordering a Torah Scroll today. It costs a lot of
money. For you, my child, for you.

(RIVKELE *says nothing. Pause.*)

UNCLE. And, with God's help, when you become a bride, I'll
buy your husband a gold watch and a gold chain weighing half
a pound. Your father loves you very much.

(RIVKELE *says nothing, lowers her head in embarrassment.
Pause.*)

UNCLE. Don't be bashful. It's perfectly proper to be a bride.
God said so. (*Pause.*) It's quite all right. Everybody gets
married.

(RIVKELE *says nothing. Pause.*)

UNCLE. Well, do you love your father?

RIVKELE (*nods her head, replies softly*). Yes.

UNCLE. Tell me, Rivkele, what do you want me to buy you?
(RIVKELE *doesn't answer.*) Well, tell me. Don't be afraid. Your
father loves you. Come on. Tell me, what shall I buy you?

(RIVKELE *says nothing.*)

SORE (*busy at the table. To* RIVKELE). Why don't you answer
when your father talks to you?

RIVKELE. I don't know.

SORE (*to* UNCLE). She wants a silk blouse and a pair of white
slippers.

UNCLE. You want a silk blouse and a pair of white slippers?

(RIVKELE *nods her head.*)

UNCLE. You've got it coming to you. (*Takes a gold piece out
of a pocket jingling with coins and gives it to her.*) Here, give
it to Mamma. Let her buy it for you. (RIVKELE *takes the gold
piece and gives it to her mother. A commotion is heard, made
by the poor coming up the steps.*)

UNCLE (*to* SORE). You see? And you thought (*opening the door*) you wouldn't have any guests. (*Calls.*) Well, come in.

(*A crowd of poor people, men and women, enter, at first singly, as though they were stealing into the house, then pushing in. They act impudently, some calling out sarcastically to* UNCLE.) Good morning to you, honorable patron! (*They turn to* SORE.) A good day to you, dear mistress.

(SORE *puts on an apron, fills it with khales, rolls, honey cakes, and other food. She distributes it to the guests.*)

ONE OF THE POOR. Long life to you, mistress. May you be favored to arrange more celebrations.

WOMAN. May the Torah Scroll bring prosperity and blessings to your home.

UNCLE (*tosses pieces of* khale *to the poor, after* SORE.) Give them each a full pound of cake and a bottle of whiskey to take home with them. Let them know that today I'm celebrating. Don't worry. I can afford it.

WOMAN BLIND IN ONE EYE (*praises* UNCLE *and* SORE *to the other poor*). This is some house, so help me. No one ever leaves here empty-handed. A bit of soup if you're sick; a shirt if you're needy. You don't think you'll get anything from the fancy folk, do you? (SORE, *as though she hadn't heard the remark, puts a few extra portions into the* WOMAN'S *apron. The* WOMAN *opens her apron wider and continues talking.*) Here, if they throw a little party, it makes no difference who you are or what business you're in.

OTHER POOR PEOPLE (*to one another*). It's true, so help me!

UNCLE (*takes a handful of change out of his pocket and puts it into* RIVKELE'S *apron*). Here, hand it out among the poor.

(RIVKELE *distributes the coins.*)

WOMAN BLIND IN ONE EYE (*takes heart and points to* RIVKELE). Can you show me another such virtuous girl in the whole town? (*To the other woman.*) Rabbis don't even have such children. (*In a subdued tone but still loud enough for* SORE *and* UNCLE *to hear.*) And God knows how they got such a virtuous child. Brought up in such a house, may God not punish me for my words. (*Loud.*) How they watch over her! How they guard her! Her every step is weighed and measured. It's a joy to look at her. (*She goes over to* UNCLE *and says to him.*) Don't you worry. These things get around. (*Points to* RIVKELE.) If I had a rabbi for a son I'd give her to him for a bride.

THE OTHER WOMEN (*to one another*). Word gets around. It gets around.

UNCLE. You wait and see. Wait till I lead her, with God's help, to her wedding! You'll get a whole goose apiece, a live pike for each of you; and it will ring with rubles, or my name isn't Yankel Chapchovich.

WOMAN BLIND IN ONE EYE. I tell you, as though she'd been raised in a synagogue, forgive the comparison—neat, pretty, more modest than all the respectable girls.

THE OTHER WOMEN. Things get around. Things get around.

UNCLE (*offering glasses of whiskey to the poor, drops a remark as though not noticing*). Even though her father is Yankel Chapchovich.

SORE (*distributing the food*). A fine audience he's found for his boasting!

UNCLE (*expansively. As he talks he fills the whiskey glasses with careless haste*). Rich or poor, it doesn't make a bit of difference to me. Let everybody know it. Let the whole town know it. What I am, I am. (*Points to his wife.*) What she is, she is. It's all true, all of it. But they better not whisper a word against my child. If they do, I'll crack their skulls with this bottle. I don't care if it's the rabbi himself. She's purer than his daughter. (*Points to his throat.*) Or you can cut it right here.

SORE (*stops distributing*). Come on, we've heard it before! Enough of that! (*Brushes off her hands and looks for the broom in a corner.*) I'd better tidy up for the people who are coming. (*Turns to the poor.*) It's a good idea, don't you think?

THE POOR. Sure it is, mistress. How right you are. Bless you. (*They leave one at a time, each offering his good wishes.* UNCLE *tosses them food behind his wife's back.*)

SORE (*to* RIVKELE *so that the departing poor can still hear her*). Go, Rivkele, finish the vestment for the Scroll. Reb Elye will be here soon; so will the scribe. (RIVKELE *exits to her room at right.*)

SORE (*remains alone with* UNCLE. *She sweeps the floor*). Look at the audience he picked to boast to. The cream! Don't you think they would have come anyway? Throw a party every day and they'll be here every day. In decent homes they know how to act so people have respect for them. Not the way you do, letting them become buddies with you right away. What kind of respectability is that, I ask you.

UNCLE. You expect decent people to come here? You must have forgotten who we are.

SORE. "Who we are"? Why, have you robbed anybody? You're in business. Everybody is in business. You don't force anybody

into it. You can be in any business you want to as long as you
don't harm anybody yourself. You just try and give them
money; you'll see how much they'll take from you.

UNCLE. They'll take it from you, but they'll treat you like a
dog. In the synagogue you stand near the door. You're never
called up to bless the reading from Scripture.

SORE. Do you really think they're better than you are? You
don't have to curry favor with them. That's the way the world
is today: if you've got money, even as respectable and pious a
man as Reb Elye will drop in and accept your contribution. He
doesn't ask you where you got it. Steal, rob—as long as you've
got it. That's all that counts.

UNCLE. Don't you go climbing too high, Sore, you hear me?
Not too high! If you do, you may break your neck. (*Shakes his
finger.*) And don't push yourself where you're not wanted.
Don't push, I tell you. You've got a place to live; stay there.
You've got bread; eat it. But don't go where you're not wanted.
Every dog should know his own kennel. (*Leaves the table.
Waves his hand.*) I'm beginning to regret the whole business.
I have a feeling we're in for a fall on account of it.

SORE (*stops walking. Thrusts her arms akimbo*). And you call
yourself a man! You should be ashamed of yourself! I'm a
woman and I can say: What was, is gone, fast, flown away.
You don't have to be ashamed to face anyone. The whole world
is no better. If not for this business, you'd be starving. (*Approaches him.*) But if you like, after you've made your money,
close up shop and there won't be a peep out of anybody. No
one has to know who you were.

UNCLE (*picking up the suggestion*). That might be best.
(*Pause.*) Buy a stable of horses, sell them for export like Ayzikl
Trucker, be somebody, not have people looking into your eyes
all the time as if you were a thief.

SORE (*thinking out loud*). But it's too bad about the business.
Dealing in horses, you won't turn an honest penny so easily.
Here, at least, you can see a ruble in hand.

UNCLE. That's true, too.

SORE (*goes off into the next room, returns with a stack of
dishes, and sets them around the table*). Furthermore, we've
got a daughter who's more decent, thank God, than all the
respectable girls in town. She'll get married, take an honest man
for a husband, have honest children. You see, it's not so bad.

UNCLE (*gets up to admonish her*). Sure she will, the way you
watch over her! (*Angrily.*) Go ahead, let Manke come up to

her from downstairs. Let her stay up here with us, why don't you?

SORE. Listen to him bellow, will you? I brought Manke up here once to show Rivkele how to embroider. She's a girl, after all. You've got to think about her trousseau. Does she have any friends? You don't even let her out into the street. (*Pause.*) But if you object, I won't.

UNCLE. Yes, I object. You hear me? I don't want my home to mix with downstairs. (*Points to the cellar.*) My home must be kept separate, do you hear, the way kosher food is kept separate from forbidden food. Downstairs (*He points to the cellar.*) is a house, and up here lives a pure bride-to-be, you hear? (*Pounds his fists on the table.*) A decent wife for someone lives here! It must be kept separate!

(*Steps are heard ascending the stairs.*)

SORE. All right, all right! But don't shout. (*Listens.*) Sh, someone's coming. It must be Reb Elye. (*She pushes her stray locks under her wig. Takes off her apron. Uncle straightens his beard, adjusts his coat. They both stand near the door, awaiting the guests. The door opens wide and* SHLOYME *and* HINDL *come in.* SHLOYME *is a tall, powerful fellow in his twenties. He is dressed like a good-for-nothing—high boots and a short jacket—and he acts like one. He winks roguishly as he talks.* HINDL *is an older girl. She wears clothes that are too youthful for her. Her face is washed out. They both walk in boldly, thoroughly at home.*)

UNCLE (*to* SORE). Look at my guests, will you. (*To* SHLOYME.) I don't do any business up here. Downstairs, everything downstairs. (*Pointing to the cellar.*) I'll come down.

SHLOYME. What's your rush, huh? Are you ashamed of us?

UNCLE. Well, what's on your mind?

SHLOYME. You're throwing a little party, aren't you? So we dropped in to wish you luck. Old friends, aren't we?

SORE. Look at my "old friends," will you?

UNCLE. That's all in the past. From now on—it's out. You have business? Fine. But downstairs. (*Points to the cellar.*) Up here I don't know you, you don't know me, from now on. You can still get a drink (*he pours them each a glass of whiskey*), but make it fast; somebody might come in.

SHLOYME (*takes the glass of whiskey and says to* HINDL *mockingly*). You see, marriage is a good thing. It makes a somebody out of you, like all the other solid citizens; you order Torah Scrolls to be copied for you. Not like you, hanging around with pimps. (*To* UNCLE.) So you see, I let you set me an example and today—I became engaged to this broad right here. Don't you think she'll make a fine lady of the house? You'll see, once she puts on a married woman's wig, she'll look as pious as a rabbi's wife, so help us both.

UNCLE. Well, may we hear only good news! So you're engaged? And when is the wedding to be?

SORE. Look at whom he has decided to stand around and chat with! Quite an honor, isn't it! Riff-raff, heaven forgive my words. And the scholar and the scribe may be here any minute.

SHLOYME. You want to know when we're going to get married? When do you think one of us boys gets married? If I can get hold of a couple of broads, we'll get hitched and set up a house. What else can a sport like me do? It's too late to become a rabbi. But she'll have to be something extra special, a real sizzler. (*Winks at him.*) Otherwise, it doesn't pay.

UNCLE. And what can I do for you?

SHLOYME. What you can do for me? It's really not much. (*Indicates* HINDL.) She's your tart, right? And she's my bride. She's got a complaint against you. (*Takes out* HINDL's *wage book.*) And from now on you deal with me. Today I don't want much. Ten rubles in advance. (*Slaps the book with his hand.*) She's good for the money, don't worry. (*Indicates* HINDL *with his eyes.*) She wants to buy herself a new hat.

UNCLE. Downstairs, everything downstairs. I'll come down and we'll settle all our business. Here I don't even know you. Here I have no business with you at all.

SHLOYME. It's all the same to me, upstairs or downstairs. The guy upstairs is no stranger and the guy downstairs is no stranger. The devil's the same all over.

UNCLE (*now angry*). Move your carcass out of here! Scram, you hear me? I'm expecting somebody.

SORE. The devil take them! Came up just to spoil our celebration. (*Looks scornfully at* HINDL.) It isn't worth letting a feather-plucker like that upset you.

HINDL (*to* SORE). If Madame doesn't think I'm a good enough tart, she can get down herself.

SHLOYME (*to* HINDL). Tell her she can send her daughter down. (*To* SORE.) So help me, she'll be great for business.

UNCLE (*goes over to* SHLOYME). You can insult me, you hear? (*Points to his wife.*) You can insult her too. We're in the life. But don't let me hear you even mention my daughter's name, you hear? (*Gets closer to him.*) Don't you mention her or I'll cut your insides out. You hear me? She doesn't know you; you don't know her.

SHLOYME. Then I'll get to know her. I'm one of the boys. We're all related.

UNCLE (*grabs* SHLOYME *by the throat*). I'll tear you apart. You can slap my face, kick me, but don't you mention my daugnter's name. (*They struggle.*)

SORE (*runs over*). Good grief! To stand there quarreling with riff-raff. People will be here any minute. Yankel, Reb Elye and the scribe are on their way. Yankel, Yankel, for God's sake! (*She pulls him away.*) What's the matter with you? (*Heavy footsteps are heard ascending the steps.*) Yankel, Yankel, here comes Reb Elye! The Scribe is here! You're disgracing us before decent people!

UNCLE. No, here, on the spot. . . . (*Continues to hold on to* SHLOYME.)

REB ELYE's VOICE (*at the door*). This way, Scribe, this is where he lives. (*Appears in the doorway, first thrusting his large head into the room. He has a pipe in his mouth.*) What's the commotion about? When a man sponsors the copying of a Torah Scroll, there should be rejoicing in his house, not quarreling. (*He withdraws his head into stairway.*) This way, Scribe.

(UNCLE, *on hearing* REB ELYE's *voice, lets go of* SHLOYME. SORE *runs over and, having taken some paper money out of her stocking, she slips a bill into* SHLOYME's *hand. She pushes* SHLOYME *and* HINDL *toward the door. At the door they meet* THE SCRIBE *and* REB ELYE, *who stand back to let the girl and* SHLOYME *pass.*)

SHLOYME (*to* HINDL *as they leave*). You see the kind of people he hangs around with these days? You wait and see, he'll be a councilman before long. (*They leave, the sounds of their voices carrying up the stairs.*)

REB ELYE (*a fat little man. He speaks rapidly and accompanies his remarks with ingratiating gestures. Self-assured and bold, he is immediately at ease*). If you please, Scribe, this way, please. (*Speaks softly to* UNCLE *and* SORE.) It's time you behaved a little more respectably when decent people come.

(THE SCRIBE *enters. A tall elderly man, his thin body wrapped in a large coat. He has a long white wispy beard, wears glasses. He looks about. His manner is aloof and secretive.*)

REB ELYE (*indicates* UNCLE). This is the patron.

THE SCRIBE (*extends his hand, scrutinizing him*). Sholem aleichem.

(UNCLE *extends his hand uncertainly.* SORE *moves away respectfully.*)

REB ELYE (*sits down at the table, pushing over a chair for* THE SCRIBE). Won't you sit down, Scribe. (*To* UNCLE.) Have a seat. (THE SCRIBE *seats himself near* REB ELYE. UNCLE, *uncertain, remains standing.*)

REB ELYE (*to* THE SCRIBE). This is the man for whom I ordered the Torah Scroll. (*He moves the whiskey bottle towards himself and pours a glass for* THE SCRIBE *and then for himself.*) Since he has no son, he wishes to serve God by having a Scroll copied. It is a custom, and if he wishes to observe it, why, that's very nice of him and he should be helped. *Lekhayim*, Scribe. (*Extends his hand to* THE SCRIBE, *then to* UNCLE.) *Lekhayim*, Patron, today you are the host of our celebration. (UNCLE *shakes his hand uncertainly.* REB ELYE *drinks.* SORE *approaches the table and places some preserves near* REB ELYE. UNCLE *tugs at her jacket and motions to her to move away.*)

REB ELYE (*after drinking*). Drink up, Scribe. (*To* UNCLE.) Drink up, Patron. This is your day for rejoicing. God has helped you. And if you can have a Torah Scroll copied, it is a good deed, a very pious act.

THE SCRIBE (*holding his glass in his hand, to* REB ELYE, *concerning* UNCLE). Who is this man?

REB ELYE. What difference does it make? A man. He is not a learned man. Must everyone be a scholar? If a Jew wishes to perform a pious deed, he should be helped. (*To* UNCLE.) Drink the toast, rejoice.

THE SCRIBE. Will he know how to conduct himself with a Torah Scroll?

REB ELYE. Why shouldn't he know? He is a Jew, isn't he, and what Jew does not know what a Torah Scroll is? (*Drinks.*) *Lekhayim, lekhayim*, may God grant Jews better times.

THE SCRIBE (*offers his hand to* UNCLE). *Lekhayim*, Patron. (*To* SORE.) Remember a Torah Scroll is a momentous thing; it supports the entire world, and every Torah Scroll is like the very tablets that were given to Moses our Teacher on Mount Sinai. Every line is copied into a Torah Scroll in purity and holiness. In the house that holds a Torah Scroll, there God resides. That house must therefore be kept clean of every impurity. (*To* UNCLE.) And you should remember that a Torah Scroll. . . .

UNCLE (*frightened, stammers*). Rebbe, Rebbe. . . . I'll tell the Rebbe the whole truth, I will. I am a sinful man. Rebbe, I'm afraid. . . .

REB ELYE (*cuts him off, to* THE SCRIBE). The man is a penitent and therefore he should be helped. The Talmud says so specifically. And how could he not know what a Torah Scroll means? He is, after all, a Jew. (*To* UNCLE.) A Torah Scroll must be respected, revered, just as if a great rabbi were in your house. Where there is a Torah Scroll, there must be no insolent talk, and one must be careful to be modest and pious. (*To* SORE, *looking towards her but not at her.*) A woman must not uncover her hair in the room where the Torah Scroll stands. (SORE *pushes her stray hair back under the wig.*) She may not go near the Torah Scroll with bare arms. For all this, no harm can befall the house that holds a Torah Scroll; it is always blessed with prosperity and good luck, and the Scroll guards its keeper from all misfortune. What do you mean, he doesn't know? They're Jews after all. . . . (SORE *nods her head in assent.*)

THE SCRIBE (*to* UNCLE). Remember, matters of vast importance hang on the fate of a Torah Scroll; within it is the continued life of Judaism. With a single word, heaven forbid, with a single word you could disgrace the Torah Scroll, and, heaven forbid, a great misfortune might descend upon all Jews, may God have mercy on us!

UNCLE (*rises from the table*). Rebbe, I'll tell everything. Rebbe (*approaches closer*), I know you're a holy man. I'm not worthy, Rebbe, that you should be here, under my roof. Rebbe, I am a sinful man. (*Points to his wife.*) She is a sinful woman. We would do wrong even to touch a Torah Scroll. Rebbe, in there (*points to the door at left*), for her, Rebbe. (*Goes into* RIVKELE's *room and leads her out by the hand. She holds a velvet Scroll vestment which she is embroidering with a star of David in gold thread.*) Rebbe, for her it is permissible to care for a Torah Scroll. She is as pure as a Scroll itself. It is for her, Rebbe, that I ordered the Scroll. (*Points to her embroidery.*) You see, Rebbe, she's embroidering a vestment for the holy Scroll. For her it is proper. Her hands are pure hands. I, Rebbe (*taps his heart*), I won't touch your Torah Scroll. She (*points to* SORE), she won't touch your Torah Scroll. She, Rebbe (*places his hands on* RIVKELE's *head*), she will take care of it. I'll put the Scroll in her room. And when she marries—out of my house; take the beloved Scroll with you to your husband.

REB ELYE (*to* UNCLE). That is, you mean that when you marry the girl off, you'll give her the Torah Scroll for a dowry, right?

UNCLE. Reb Elye, when my daughter marries, I'll give her the dowry, and it will be a lot of money, and this is what I'll say to her: Leave your father's house and forget. Forget your father; forget your mother, and have decent children, Jewish children, like every Jewish daughter. That's what I'll say to her.

REB ELYE. In other words, you intend to give the Torah Scroll to your daughter's bridegroom as a wedding present, right? (*To* THE SCRIBE.) You see, Reb Aron, there are still Jews in the world. Here's a man; he's got a daughter; so he has a Torah Scroll copied for her bridegroom. How fine that is! How commendable! I tell you, Reb Aron, that Jewishness . . . that Jewish . . . *akh, akh.* (*Puffs his lips audibly several times.*)

UNCLE (*escorts* RIVKELE *back into her room. Closes the door after her*). Rebbe, I can say it to you. We're alone, after all. My wife can hear it, too. Rebbe, we are sinful people. I know that God will punish us. Let him. Who cares? Let him take my legs away; let him make a cripple out of me. Let me be a beggar. But not her. (*In a lowered voice.*) Rebbe, if you have a son and he disgraces himself, the devil take him. But a daughter, Rebbe, if a daughter sins, it is as though your own mother were sinning. So I went to the holy synagogue, and I went over to this man (*points to* REB ELYE), and I said to him: Get me something that can protect my home from sin. Says he to me: Have a Torah Scroll copied and put it in your house. Rebbe, as far as we are concerned—we've already given our souls over to the devil. It's for her, Rebbe. I'll put the holy Scroll into her room. Let her take care of it. As for us—we're forbidden to.

(REB ELYE *leans over to* THE SCRIBE *and whispers to him, meanwhile gesticulating and pointing to* UNCLE. UNCLE *and* SORE *stand near the table, waiting. Pause.*)

THE SCRIBE (*after thinking it over briefly*). Well, we ought to have some people to celebrate the occasion. Respect for the Torah, you know.

REB ELYE. We'll go over to the synagogue and collect a minyan.* There's no problem about finding Jews to honor the Torah. (*Rises from the table and fills the glasses. He slaps* UNCLE *on the back.*) Well, well, God will help. Be joyful. God helps him who repents. Don't worry. You'll marry off your daughter to a fine scholar. You'll find some poor lad at the yeshiva for her; you'll support him while he studies the holy Torah, and for the sake of the Torah, God will forgive you. (*Pause.*) I've even thought about that, and I've got a young man in mind who's a gem. Fine mind. His father is a very honest man . . . (*Interrupting himself.*) You want to give your daughter a large dowry?

* Quorum of ten Jews.

UNCLE. Rebbe, take everything from me. Even the shirt off my back. Everything, everything. And as for you, my son, don't recognize your father, your mother. . . . I'll take care of everything so that no one will know. Here's your food, your drink. You, my son, just study those holy books of yours, I don't know you; you don't know me.

REB ELYE. It will be all right. For the sake of the holy Torah. . . . Come, Scribe, Patron. Let's go over to the synagogue. We'll find a minyan and rejoice in the Holy Book. (*To* THE SCRIBE.) You see, REB ARON, a Jew, even though he sins—still a Jew, a Jewish soul, wants a scholar for a son-in-law. (*To* UNCLE.) Don't worry, don't worry. God will help. God loves the penitent. But charity to scholars is a must. If you're not one for learning yourself, then you must support a scholar, because *al tora olem omeyd,* "the world rests on the Torah." (*To* THE SCRIBE.) Isn't that so, REB ARON? And, after all, why shouldn't it? (*About* UNCLE.) I knew his father. Quite an honest man he was. He was a teamster. A pretty good Jew. . . . Believe me, God will help, and this man will become as good a Jew as any other. (*To* UNCLE.) But the main thing is, you must be a true penitent. That means to give up one's old ways—and to support scholars.

UNCLE (*bolder, coming closer to* REB ELYE). Reb Elye, just let me salt a little away, so that I can give my daughter a handsome dowry, and my name isn't Yankel Chapchovich if I don't close up shop. I'll deal in horses, I will, just like my father, rest his soul. I'll set up a stable and I'll go to the market in Lovitch to do business. And there, right in that room, my son-in-law will sit and study. And when I come home for the Sabbath, I'll sit down right here and listen to my son-in-law studying the Talmud. My name isn't Yankel Chapchovich if I'm telling a lie!

REB ELYE. Don't worry, don't worry, God will help you. God will help you. Isn't that so, Reb Aron?

THE SCRIBE. Who can tell? Our God is a God of mercy and compassion, but he is also a God of vengeance. (*Leaving.*) Well, it's getting late. Let us go to the synagogue. (*Leaves.*)

UNCLE. What did the Rebbe mean?

REB ELYE. Don't worry, don't worry. God will help. He must help. Come, come get your Torah Scroll and bring it home with rejoicing. (*He starts to leave.* UNCLE *hesitates. Doesn't know what to do.* REB ELYE *notices this.*) What is it? Do you want to tell your wife to prepare something for us all when we get back with the Scroll?

SORE (*to* REB ELYE). It's all prepared, Reb Elye. Everything is ready.

REB ELYE. Then what are you waiting for? The Scribe has gone.

UNCLE (*stands at the door, hesitantly, pointing to* REB ELYE). In the company of the Rebbe on the street?

REB ELYE. Come along, come along. If God forgives you, then we certainly forgive you.

UNCLE (*with enthusiasm*). Reb Elye, you're a fine man (*opens his arms to embrace him, reminds himself, and holds back*), a fine man, as I live and breathe. (*They leave together. It begins to get dark outside.*)

SORE (*starts to tidy up quickly and to set the table. Calls to* RIVKELE *in the next room*). Rivkele, Rivkele, come in here and help me. They'll be here soon with the Torah Scroll.

RIVKELE (*appears in the door. Uncertainly*). Father isn't here?

SORE. No, Rivkele, he's gone to the synagogue with Reb Elye and the Scribe to bring back some people. The Rabbi will be here.

RIVKELE (*shows the vestment for the Scroll*). You see how prettily I've embroidered it?

SORE (*busy*). I see, I see. Comb your hair; get dressed. People will be here soon, the Rabbi. . . .

RIVKELE. I'm going to call Manke up here to comb my hair. I love it, when she does my hair. She combs it so beautifully. She makes it so straight. Her hands are so cool. (*She takes something and knocks on the floor, calling.*) Manke, Manke!

SORE (*frightened*). What are you doing, Rivkele? Stop! Your father will scold you. It's not right for you to be friends with Manke any more. You're old enough to be married; you're a respectable girl with excellent prospects. Fine young men are being proposed for you, good students.

RIVKELE. I love Manke so much.

SORE. It's disgraceful for you to be friends with Manke. You're a respectable girl and you'll be friends with other respectable girls. You have prospects, fine young men. Your father went to look at the young man who'll be your bridegroom. Reb Elye said. . . . (*She goes off into the next room.*) It's time to wash and dress. Our guests will be here soon.

RIVKELE. A bridegroom for me? What kind of young man is he, Mamma dear?

SORE (*from the other room*). He's a gem of a boy, a good student, comes from a fine family.

(MANKE *appears in the opposite door, first pokes her head in, wagging her finger coquettishly to* RIVKELE. RIVKELE *moves stealthily towards her, winking to* MANKE. *It begins to get dark in the room.*)

RIVKELE (*falls into* MANKE's *arms. Talks to her mother in the other room*). Is he good looking, Mamma? (MANKE *kisses her passionately.*)

SORE (*from the other room*). Yes, child, a handsome bridegroom, with black sidelocks and a satin coat and a velvet cap. He dresses like a rabbi, and he is a rabbi's son. Reb Elye said so.

RIVKELE (*in* MANKE's *arms, caressing* MANKE's *cheeks*). Where will he stay, Mamma?

SORE (*from the other room*). Right there, in your room, where the Torah Scroll will be. He'll live there with you and study the holy Torah.

RIVKELE (*in* MANKE's *arms*). Will he love me, Mamma?

SORE (*as before*). Very much, child, very much. And the two of you will have honest children, decent children.

(*During the conversation the curtain descends slowly, leaving* RIVKELE *in* MANKE's *embrace.*)

ACT II

(The room in the cellar, a large room with a high-domed ceiling in an old building. Just below the ceiling level two small windows, deeply-set, with curtains and flower pots, are open. The rain blows in through them. Steps up to a Dutch door, the upper portion of which is open to the night and admits the drizzle outside. To the rear several cubicles separated from each other by thin partitions and curtained in front with heavy black drapes. One curtain is drawn, revealing a bed, a wash stand, a mirror, make-up, etc., a colored night lamp. The furniture of the large room consists of several sofas, a table, benches, card tables. The walls are hung with mirrors, tawdry decorations, and pictures of women in alluring poses. SHLOYME lies stretched out on one of the sofas, his long legs hanging over onto a nearby bench. He is asleep. A spring night. The room is illuminated by a large lamp hanging from the ceiling.)

(HINDL enters, pauses briefly on the steps looking at SHLOYME. She wears a light shawl and is dressed coquettishly in a dress too short for her age. She walks around the room, treading hard to awaken SHLOYME.)

SHLOYME *(wakes up. Looks around)*. Is that you? Why aren't you outside?

HINDL. It started to rain.

SHLOYME *(sitting up on the sofa)*. You talking to me again, Countess? You're not mad at me any more?

HINDL. I wasn't mad at all.

SHLOYME. That so! Well, if you want to, you can stay mad. *(Lies down again.)*

HINDL *(looks around. Runs over to a curtain and listens. Runs over to SHLOYME)*. Shloyme, I'm not leaving this place. Look, we're alone now. There's no one else here. Tell me, in heaven's name, tell me: do you really intend to marry me?

SHLOYME. Go on, Countess, salt your money away and then go complaining to Uncle that I take it all away from you. Tell him you haven't got enough to buy a hat with.

HINDL. Yes, I told him. I was hurt. It kills me, the way you

89

take the shirt off my back and then go alley-catting to that red-headed bitch. I'll let her have a dose right in the face. How can you stand her, anyway? Her mouth stinks. You sure found yourself a bargain!

SHLOYME. Are you backing out? I'll clout you one between the eyes so hard you'll see your great-grandmother!

HINDL. Go ahead, hit me, cut me to ribbons. (*Pushes up the sleeve of one arm and shows him.*) You've already made me black and blue. (*Pushes up the other sleeve.*) Here, cut, pinch if you want to, but tell me right here and now, as you remember your dead father in his grave and recite the *Kaddish* in his memory, will you really marry me?

SHLOYME (*reclining*). Once I wanted to. Now I don't.

HINDL. That's fine too. That's the way I like it. But don't fool me. You want money? Say so. A coat? Here. But why do you have to fool me? (*She moves away from him.*)

SHLOYME. Don't worry. There are plenty of single guys around. You'll catch some sucker.

HINDL (*drawing the curtain of her cubicle*). Why worry your little head about me?

SHLOYME. If you don't want me to, that's all right with me too. (*Pause.*) You still feel like pouring me a glass of tea, at least?

HINDL (*brings him a glass of tea from her cubicle. Sets it on the table. She goes back into her room, sits down near her trunk and searches in it for something. After a short pause, still in her room*). So, you like her. Well, well, now you'll have a job—buying towels to fill out wifey's breasts, having her fitted for teeth, setting her on stilts, and then you'll buy yourself a street organ and lead her around over the streets showing off what you made. You'll make a fine organ grinder, so help me. I'll throw you a couple of pennies out of a window myself.

SHLOYME. Shut your trap, I tell you.

HINDL. And if I don't what will you do?

SHLOYME. I'll slap you around.

HINDL. Ho, ho, there's no more slapping these days. These days slaps are repaid with knives.

SHLOYME (*gets up*). Who's gonna do it? (*Goes into her cubicle.*) Who's gonna do it? (*She quickly hides something in her trunk.*) What have you got there so important that you have to hide it in your silk blouse?

HINDL. What do you care?

SHLOYME. Show it to me, I tell you! (*He struggles with her, tears a red blouse from her hand. He comes out of the cubicle.*)

Well, now, let's have a look. (*He tears the blouse with vigor. A photograph falls out.*) Oho, Moyshele the Locksmith! So he's the lucky fellow! Since when are you two such buddies? (*Goes back into her room.*)

HINDL. What do you care?

SHLOYME. Here's what I care. (*He slaps her a few times. She falls onto her bed, crying.*) So you're palling around with Moyshele the Locksmith, are you, exchanging pictures, a regular bridal pair, and I didn't even know about it. (*Pause. Returns to his table.*) I didn't even know a thing about it. (*Continues to drink his tea, rises, walks up the steps to the door.*) I didn't know a thing about it. (*Stops at the door*). Hindl! (*She doesn't answer.*) Hindl, get over here! (*She doesn't answer.*) Hindl! (*Stamps his foot. Angrily runs down the steps.*) Get over here, I tell you! Do you hear me?

HINDL (*gets up from her bed, goes to him, covering her face with a handkerchief*). What do you want?

SHLOYME. Did you talk to Manke?

HINDL (*crying*). Yes.

SHLOYME. Well, what does she say?

HINDL (*still crying*). When we get our "house" set up, she'll come over to us.

SHLOYME. For sure?

HINDL (*wiping her eyes*). Yes. But she won't go by herself. She wants to bring a friend.

SHLOYME. Of course. Will one tart bring in a living or pay the rent?

HINDL. We really need somebody new.

SHLOYME. That would give us a living, all right, but where are you gonna get her?

HINDL. I've got my eye on a tart—like a tree, still a kid.

SHLOYME (*eagerly*). Can she bring in the money?

HINDL. And how.

SHLOYME. A kid, eh? From a house?

HINDL. No, from a respectable family.

SHLOYME. How do you know her?

HINDL. She comes to Manke every night. Steals out of her father's home. No one sees her. She's drawn to this place. She's so eager.

RIVKELE (*pokes her head in through the open window, signals to* HINDL). Psst, is my father here?

HINDL (*signals back*). No.

(RIVKELE *disappears from the window.*)

SHLOYME (*winks to* HINDL). Her? Uncle's daughter? A gold mine!

HINDL. Quiet. Here she comes.

RIVKELE (*tall and pretty, well dressed, wrapped in a black shawl, glides into the room, runs down the steps in fright, talking more with gestures than with words*). Where's Manke? In there? (*Points to a closed cubicle.*) In there . . . with . . . ?

(HINDL *winks to her in assent.* RIVKELE *walks up to the curtain and listens passionately. Every now and then she looks around in fright.*)

SHLOYME (*quietly to* HINDL). We ought to go look at the place on Pivne Street tomorrow.

HINDL. Where are we going to get married?

SHLOYME. But first you have to have a place to stay.

HINDL. Who knows how much the rabbi's fee will be for marrying us?

SHLOYME. I hope we have enough left for furniture. It's got to look decent.

(*The door opens with a loud noise.* UNCLE *comes in.*)

UNCLE (*his face still retains some of the marks of his wild youth. His dress is now respectable. He shakes the rain from his hat.*) What a business! Who needs the rain? (*Suddenly notices* RIVKELE. *Speaks with anger.*) What? Here? (*Grabs her by the collar and shakes her, gritting his teeth.*) What are you doing here?

RIVKELE. Mamm . . . Mamma sent me to . . . call . . . (*Weeps.*) Father, don't hit me!

UNCLE. Mamma . . . Mamma sent you . . . here. (*Shouting.*) Your mother! (*Pulls her by the collar up the steps.*) She'll lead you to the worst yet! As though a magnet were drawing her! She wants the daughter to be what the mother was.

RIVKELE (*crying*). Father, don't hit me!

UNCLE. I'll teach you to obey your father. (*He leads her out. Her crying can be heard.*)

SHLOYME. Look at Yankel the Bastard; it's below his dignity for his daughter to be a whore. (*Noise is heard from above, stamping of feet, a woman's tearful voice.*) Does he have to split his boots on account of his wife? Oh boy! Oh boy!

HINDL. That's right. A mother should watch her daughter. Whatever you were, you were. But once you're married and have a child, keep an eye on it. You'll see, with God's help, when we have our own children, I'll know how to raise them. My daughter will be as pure as a saint, with beet-red cheeks.

I won't let anyone make eyes at her. She'll get married, yes, to a fine young man, a real wedding. . . .

SHLOYME (*slaps her on the back*). If we live, we'll see. But you talk to Rivkele, work on her, baby, or else it's a lost cause.

HINDL. Don't worry. I'll figure out something.

SHLOYME. We'll see. (*Pause. Softly.*) If you land her, take her right over to my place, you know. . . .

UNCLE (*comes in, angry*). It's time to close up and go to sleep. It's raining. Not even a dog will come in on a night like this. (*Looks at* SHLOYME.) Enough of that, enough of that prenuptial bliss. Let's call it a day. (*Ascends the steps and calls.*) Reyzl, bed-time! Basha, bed-time! (*From without girlish voices:* "Coming," "Coming.")

(HINDL *points to* UNCLE, *signalling to* SHLOYME *to go home.* SHLOYME *walks up the steps. In the doorway he comes face to face with* UNCLE. *They look at each other.*)

UNCLE. Move, move, time to quit. You've been whispering sweet nothings long enough.

SHLOYME (*shoves his hands into his pockets. Looks at him*). When did you become such a pillar of decency?

UNCLE. Scram, scram! I'll tell you some other time.

SHLOYME. Go to hell.

HINDL (*runs up the steps to* SHLOYME). Shloyme, go home! Do you hear me? Go home, I tell you!

SHLOYME (*leaves, glaring at* UNCLE). Jerk!

UNCLE. Who needs him here? (*Points to* HINDL.) You can take the old bag with you and set up shop with her.

HINDL. You don't set up shop with old bags. Old bags let · you sleep. But young dolls. . . .

UNCLE (*calling*). Reyzl! Basha! (*Two girls come running in. Their light, flimsy clothes are soaking wet and water drips from their loosened hair. They are gay, and they laugh as they speak.* UNCLE *slams the door shut as he leaves.*)

BASHA (*a country girl, heavy-set, with red cheeks. Naive. She speaks with a country accent*). How the rain smells! (*Shakes the rain from her.*) Just like the apples at home drying in the attic. It's the first May rain.

HINDL. You're out of your minds to hustle in the rain. You're too ambitious. What fool would you expect to find in this kind of a downpour, anyway? (*She goes off into her cubicle, sits down near her basket and starts to pack her scattered things.*)

REYZL (*shaking off the rain*). I don't need them; the hell with them. I paid my book up yesterday. We were standing under the drainpipe. The rain smells so fresh. It washes the whole winter off your head. (*Goes over to* HINDL. *Shows her wet hair.*) You see how fresh my hair is, how it smells?

BASHA. Back home in my village they're probably having the first schav. You know, when the first rain of May comes down, they're busy cooking the sourgrass soup. And the goats are probably out in the pasture. And the freshly cut logs are floating downstream. And Franek is rounding up the peasant girls for a dance at the inn. And the women are probably baking cheese buns for Shevuoth. (*Pause.*) You know what? I'm going to buy myself a new summer pelerine and I'm going home for a visit this Shevuoth. (*She runs into her cubicle and returns carrying a broad-brimmed summer hat with a long veil. She puts it on her wet head and looks into a mirror to adjust it.*) There, if I were to show up on Shevuoth in this hat and take a walk down to the railroad. Oh, they sure would turn green with envy, wouldn't they? I would go, too, but I'm afraid of my father.

REYZL. Why, would he hit you?

BASHA. He'd kill me on the spot. He's looking for me with an iron bar. Once he found me at the inn dancing with Franek and he hit me so hard across the arm with a stick (*shows her arm*) that I have a scar to this day. (*Pause.*) I come from a respectable family. My father is a butcher. Oh, the matches I could have made! (*In a lowered voice.*) Once they wanted me to marry Notke the meat cleaver. I still have the gold ring he gave me. (*Shows a ring on her finger.*) He gave it to me during Succoth. Oh, how he wanted to marry me, but I didn't want to.

REYZL. Why not?

BASHA. Because I didn't. He stinks from beef. Brr. They call him "Medicine." How could I marry Medicine and every year have another little Medicine. Brr.

REYZL. And what have you got here?

BASHA. Here I'm free. I've got my basket of pretty linens; I'm well dressed, a lot nicer clothes, I'll tell you, than the wife of our local rich man. (*Brings a gaily colored dress out of her cubicle.*) When I walk down Marshalkovska Street in this, you should see their eyes pop. They really sizzle. Oh, if I could only show up in my village wearing this dress (*slips into the dress*), I'd just stroll down to the railroad. (*She walks gaily about the room, lifting her skirt behind her a little, and assuming a big-city air.*) They sure would turn green. They'd have a fit on the spot. (*She walks around the room imitating the grand manner and wearing a haughty expression on her face.*)

REYZL (*straightens the folds of her dress in the back and*

adjusts her hat). That's the way. Now raise your head a little. No one has to know that you were in a house. You can say that you're in business. A count fell in love with you. . . .

HINDL *(from her cubicle)*. And what's the matter with a house? You think we're any different from the girls who go to business? That's the way the whole world is today. That's what our modern world requires. Today, even the respectable girls are no better. This happens to be our business. But if someone like us marries, she's more faithful to her husband than they are. We know what a man is.

BASHA *(continuing to strut up and down)*. Oh, sure! They'd never know the difference! Your heart tells you. That's why my mother died. She couldn't bear it. I've never been to see her grave. *(Stops suddenly in the middle of the room.)* Sometimes she comes to me. . . . I see her at night, in my dreams. She comes in her shroud, covered with thorns and briars because of my sins, and she tears at my hair.

REYZL. Good grief! You actually saw her? What does one's dead mother look like? Is she pale?

HINDL. Quiet! Talking about the dead at night! The dead can't get in here. Our boss has a Torah Scroll standing upstairs, doesn't he? *(Stops abruptly. Pause.)* So his wife was in a house for fifteen years. But when she got married, she made him an honest wife, didn't she? She observes everything that a Jewish woman should, doesn't she? And isn't the boss an honest man? Doesn't he behave decently? He makes the largest contributions to charity. He paid to have a Torah Scroll copied.

REYZL. Yes, but they say you're not even allowed to use such a Torah Scroll, and the daughters of such mothers later become just like their mothers. They're drawn to it. Temptation drags them down into the mud.

HINDL *(frightened)*. Who says so?

REYZL. An old granny, a witch, told me so. It's like sorcery.

HINDL. It's a big lie. Where is she, that gypsy; I'll scratch her eyes out. God's still in his heaven. We still have a great God who rules the world.

MANKE *(glides out from behind the curtain of her room. She is half-dressed in her night clothes. A light shawl is thrown around her. She is wearing brightly colored stockings. Her hair is unkempt. She is very lithe and has an impudently pretty face. She is still young. A lock of her hair hangs down over her forehead. As she speaks, she blinks her eyes. Then her whole body shudders as though her bones were collapsing. She looks around surprised)*. What, nobody here?

REYZL (*cheered at the sight of* MANKE). Is that you, Manke? Good you came in. (*Points to* HINDL.) She's practically made me as pious as a rabbi's wife. Where did you leave your sucker?

MANKE. He fell asleep, so I left.

REYZL. Is he a spender? You think he'll treat us to beer?

MANKE. He's some kind of a nut from up north. This makes the third time he's come to me. He keeps cross-examining me: who's my father; who's my mother. You'd think he wanted to marry me. When he kisses me, he hides his face in my breast, closes his eyes, and smiles like a baby in its mother's arms. (*Looks around, whispers to* HINDL.) Hasn't Rivkele been here yet?

HINDL (*with a flattering laugh*). She was here. She met her father. Boy, did he raise a rumpus.

MANKE. Wow! When did it happen?

HINDL. Quite a while ago. He must be asleep by now. (*Softly.*) She'll probably be right in.

REYZL (*gaily to* MANKE). Come on, Manke, let's go outside. It's raining out—drops like pearls. The first May rain. Who wants to come out with me and stand in the rain?

MANKE (*walks over to the window*). It is raining out. My, how light the rain is! How it smells! Let's go.

BASHA. Back home, when it rains like this, the drains overflow and flood the narrow streets, and we take our shoes and socks off and dance around in the rain. Who wants to go out barefoot? (*She removes her shoes and stockings. To* MANKE.) Take your shoes off, Manke. Let's dance around in the rain.

MANKE (*removes her shoes and stockings, loosens her hair*). Now the rain will soak us from head to toe. You grow taller if you stand in the rain in May, don't you?

BASHA (*runs over*). Come on, let's pour water over each other, handfuls of water. (*She loosens her hair.*) We'll wash our hair as the trees do. Come on.

HINDL. Wait a while. Uncle isn't asleep yet. He'll hear you. (*All listen towards the ceiling.*)

REYZL. Let's go. Can't you hear him snoring?

MANKE. Wait. Let's give Rivkele a signal.

(BASHA *and* REYZL *leave.* MANKE *takes a stick and taps lightly in a corner of the ceiling. From the street come sounds of the girls splashing around in the puddles. They pour handfuls of water through the open window, shouting,* "Come on out! Come on out!")

RIVKELE (*pokes her head through the little window. She is*

wearing her night clothes and is wrapped in a light shawl. She calls softly). Manke, Manke! Did you call me?

MANKE *(takes a chair, puts it under the window, steps up and reaches* RIVKELE's *hands).* Yes, Rivkele, I called you. Come, let's stand under the May rain, and pour water over each other. We'll grow taller.

RIVKELE *(from the window).* Sh, speak softly. I sneaked out of bed so my father wouldn't hear me. He'd beat me if he found out.

MANKE. Don't be afraid of your father. He won't get up so soon. Let's go stand in the rain. I'll undo your hair. *(She undoes* RIVKELE's *braids.)* There, and now I'll wash it for you in the rain.

RIVKELE. I'm only wearing a nightgown. I've been lying in bed all night waiting for my father to fall asleep so I could sneak down to you. I heard you knocking and I slid out of bed. I stole out so quietly, barefoot, so my father wouldn't hear me.

MANKE *(hugs her passionately).* Come, Rivkele, let me wash your eyes in rain water. The night is so sweet, the rain is so warm, and everything is so fragrant. Come.

RIVKELE. Sh, be quiet. I'm afraid of my father. He beat me. He locked the door and hid the key near the Torah Scroll. I was in bed the whole time. I heard you call me. You called so softly. I was drawn to you. I stole the key from the Ark of the Scroll. My heart kept pounding and pounding.

MANKE. Wait, Rivkele, wait. I'm coming out to you. *(She jumps off the chair and leaves the cellar.)* I'm coming. I'm coming to you. *(MANKE leaves. RIVKELE withdraws her face from the window.)*

HINDL *(listened to the entire conversation with great attention, standing at the curtain of her cubicle. Now she walks noisily up and down the room, thinking out loud, talking to herself slowly).* If I could only catch them both at once, with God's help, and tonight. I could bring them both over to Shloyme's. Here, here's bread and butter. Now rent a place, and let's get married. Now you can be somebody, as good as the next fellow. *(She stops in the middle of the room, raises her arms.)* God in heaven, You are the Father of orphans! Mother, help me from beyond the grave! Let me come into a safe harbor! Help me to a settled life! *(Pause.)* If God would grant me this, I would have a Torah Scroll copied for Him for the synagogue. Three pounds of candles for the synagogue every Sabbath! *(A long pause. She is absorbed in her visions of felicity.)*

He is a good God, isn't He? A good God. Father in heaven! Mother, Mother, speak for me, speak for me. Help me. Move heaven and earth for me! (*She returns to her cubicle, begins energetically to pack all her belongings into her basket.*) First of all, I must be ready.

(*A long pause. No one appears on the stage. Then* MANKE *comes in huddling* RIVKELE *against her. Both are wrapped in a single wet shawl. Their hair is dishevelled, having been washed. Their wet clothes drip onto the floor. They are both barefoot.* HINDL *hides behind the curtain of her cubicle and listens.*)

MANKE (*she speaks with a concealed passion and love, softly but deep and ringing*). Do you feel cold, Rivkele? Snuggle up close to me. Let me keep you warm, nice and warm. Come, let's sit on the sofa. (*She leads her to a sofa and sits down next to her.*) That's right, press your face against my breast. Like that, that's the way. And let your body caress me. So cool, like water running between us. (*Pause.*) I uncovered your breasts and washed them with the rain water that ran into my hands. So white and firm, your breasts, and the blood in them cools under the hand like white snow, like ice. And their fragrance is like the smell of grass in the meadows. And I loosened your hair, like this (*she runs her fingers through* RIVKELE's *hair*) and I held it so in the rain and washed it. Its scent is the scent of rain. (*She buries her face in* RIVKELE's *hair.*) The scent of May rain is in it, so light, so soft, so fresh, like the grass in the meadow, like the apple on the bough. Cool me with your hair (*she washes her face in* RIVKELE's *hair*), cool me so. Wait, let me comb you like a bride, hair parted in the middle, with two long black braids. (*Combs her hair.*) Would you like me to, Rivkele? Would you?

RIVKELE (*nodding*). Yes, I would.

MANKE. You will be the bride, a lovely bride. It's Friday night. You're sitting at the Sabbath table with your father and your mother. I'm the bridegroom, your bridegroom come to visit you. Would you like that, Rivkele, would you?

RIVKELE (*nodding*). Yes, I would.

MANKE. Wait, wait. Your father and mother have gone to bed. Bride and groom have met at the table. We're embarrassed. Right?

RIVKELE (*nodding her head*). Yes, Manke.

MANKE. Then we draw close to each other: you're my bride and I'm your bridegroom. We embrace. (*She puts her arms around her.*) We're pressed together, and we kiss very quietly, like this. (*They kiss.*) We blush, we're so embarrassed. It's good, isn't it Rivkele?

RIVKELE. Yes, Manke, it is.

MANKE (*lowers her voice, whispering in her ear*). And then we go to sleep in the same bed. No one sees; no one knows, just the two of us, like this. (*She presses* RIVKELE *to her.*) Would you like to sleep the whole night through with me, Rivkele, in the same bed?

RIVKELE (*embracing her*). I would, I would.

MANKE. Come, come.

RIVKELE (*whispering*). I'm afraid of my father. He may get up.

MANKE. Wait, Rivkele, wait. (*Thinks a while.*) Would you like to go away with me? We'll be together all day and all night. Your father won't be there; your mother won't be there. No one will scold you or hit you. We'll be alone, all day. We'll have such fun. Would you like that, Rivkele?

RIVKELE (*closes her eyes*). My father wouldn't know?

MANKE. No. We'll run off tonight, now, with Hindl, to her house. She has a house with Shloyme. She told me so. You'll see how good it will be. Young men will come, officers. We'll be alone the entire day. We'll dress like officers and ride around on horses. Come, Rivkele. Would you like to? Would you?

RIVKELE (*frightened*). Won't my father hear us?

MANKE. No, no, he won't hear us. He sleeps so soundly. Can't you hear him snoring? (*She runs to* HINDL's *cubicle, seizes her by the hand.*) Do you have a house? Come quickly. Take us there.

HINDL (*agreeing eagerly*). Yes, yes, quickly, to Shloyme's. (*She grabs a dress, throws it to* RIVKELE.) He'll take us there.

MANKE (*quickly dressing* RIVKELE). You'll see how good it will be, how gay it will be. (*They both dress, putting on whatever comes to hand, a shawl, a coat. They slowly ascend the steps. At the door they meet* REYZL *and* BASHA *who have finished washing their hair. The latter look at them in surprise.*)

REYZL, BASHA. Where are you going?

HINDL. Don't make any noise. Don't make a sound. We're going out for some beer, for lemonade. (HINDL, MANKE *and* RIVKELE *leave.* REYZL *and* BASHA *look at each other in surprise.*)

REYZL. I don't like it.

BASHA. Neither do I.

REYZL. There's something fishy going on.

BASHA (*looks at her in alarm*). What could it be?

REYZL. What business is it of ours? Out goes the lamp and we're off to sleep. We don't know from nothin'. (*She turns down the lamp.*)

(*The stage is half dark. The girls go off, each to her room.*)

REYZL (*going off*). Boy, was that fortune-teller right! Boy, could she read the cards! (*Exits. The stage is empty for several seconds. It is dark.*)

(BASHA *runs out of her room, half undressed, with a sobbing outcry.*)

REYZL (*opens the curtain of her room*). What's the matter, Basha?

BASHA. I'm afraid to go to sleep. I keep imagining that my dead mother with the thorns and briars stuck in her is walking around in my room.

REYZL. The Torah Scroll has been defiled, and there's no reason for anyone to keep us from harm.

BASHA. I'm afraid this will be a bad night. My heart is trembling.

(*A commotion is suddenly heard from above, a scraping of benches and tables. The girls listen, their eyes staring in fright. Soon a noise is heard of something heavy falling down the steps.*)

UNCLE (*enters, shouting*). Rivkele, Rivkele, where are you?

REYZL (*to* BASHA). Let's get to bed. We don't know a thing. (*They go to bed and pretend to be fast asleep.*)

UNCLE (*runs in carrying a candle. His hair is dishevelled, a coat over his nightclothes. He shouts wildly*). Rivkele! Is Rivkele here? (*No one answers. He pushes back the curtains of each cubicle.*) Rivkele! Where is she? (*He awakens* REYZL *and* BASHA.) Where is Rivkele? Rivkele, where is she?

REYZL, BASHA (*rubbing their eyes with the sleeves of their kimonos*). What . . . we don't know.

UNCLE. You don't know? You don't know? (*He runs out swiftly. He can be heard bounding up the stairs. Then silence. A noise is heard as of something dashing down the steps. The door bursts open noisily.* UNCLE *tumbles in pulling* SORE *after him by the hair. Both are wearing their night clothes.*)

UNCLE (*drags* SORE *to the floor by her hair. He points to the "house"*). Your daughter! Where is your daughter?

(BASHA, REYZL *both stand pressed against the wall, petrified. The curtain descends swiftly.*)

ACT III

(*The same room as in Act I. Closets and chests of drawers are open and clothes and underwear lie in disorder all over the floor. The door to* RIVKELE's *room is open and the light of a candle can be seen through the open door.* SORE, *her hair dishevelled, her clothes in disarray, keeps picking up the scattered garments and piling them together as though preparing to leave, but she puts most of them back where they were. A gray morning. The gray light seeps in through the closed shutters.*)

SORE (*picking up the clothing*). Yankel, what's the matter with you? Yankel! (*Goes over to the open door to* RIVKELE's *room and looks in.*) Why do you keep sitting there? (*Turns back, picking up some more things.*) What a misfortune! He's fallen apart completely. He's trying to ruin the whole house. (*Goes to the door again.*) Yankel, why do you sit there without a word? What's the matter with you? (*Turns back, with tears.*) The man just sits there in front of the Torah Scroll, thinking and thinking. What's there to think about? If you're in trouble, go down to the police station and talk to the captain. Find the scoundrel by hook or by crook, while there is still time. (*Turns to the door.*) Why don't you say something? Say something! (*She sits down on a bundle near the door, covers her face with her hands, and bursts into tears.*) He sits there all by himself like a madman, looking at the Torah Scroll and muttering to himself. He hears nothing and he sees nothing. What's wrong with him? (*Rises from the bundle, to* UNCLE *from the door.*) It's all the same to me. If you want me to leave, I'll leave. The devil won't take me. I'll manage to earn my bread. (*Begins to pack her things in silence. Pause.*)

UNCLE (*comes in from the next room, without a head covering, without a coat, his hair dishevelled. His eyes have a wild look. His voice is hoarse. His speech is slow*). I'll go . . . you'll go . . . Rivkele will go . . . everything will go. (*Points to the cellar.*) Everything will go down to the house. God does not want. . . .

SORE. Yankel, what is the matter with you! Have you gone

out of your mind? (*Goes over to him.*) Consider what you're doing. Misfortune has struck us. But who doesn't suffer misfortune? Come, let's find Shloyme. Give him two or three hundred rubles. Let him give our child back to us. He'll do it. Why do you sit around doing nothing? What's wrong with you?

UNCLE (*in the same voice, walking aimlessly about the room*). It doesn't matter. I gave my soul to the devil. Nothing will help. God is against it. (*He stops at the window and looks through the slats of the shutters.*)

SORE. "God's against it." You're kidding yourself. You're against it. Do you really love your child? Yankel, Yankel (*she pulls him*), what has come over you? Think carefully while there is still time. He might take her away somewhere while you hesitate. Let's go over to his place. The girl must have taken her there. Why do you just stand there? (*Abruptly.*) I sent for Reb Elye. Let's hear what he has to say! (*Pause.* UNCLE *keeps looking through the window.*) What are you looking at? (*Pause.*) Why don't you answer me? Good heavens, you can go out of your mind. (*Turns away from him weeping audibly.*)

UNCLE (*as before, walking aimlessly*). No more home. No more wife. No more daughter. To the house! Back to the house! We don't need a daughter. We don't need anything. A whore, like her mother. God is against it. Back to the house! Back to the house!

SORE. You want to move down to the house? Go ahead. See if I care! (*Starts packing again.*) Why must he destroy our home? What's the matter with him? (*Thoughtful a while.*) If you're going to sit on your hands, I'm going to do something. (*She removes her diamond earrings from her ears.*) I'm going over to Shloyme's. I'll give him the diamond earrings (*She searches in a package and pulls out a gold chain*), and this gold chain, and if he still doesn't want to, I'll throw in a hundred. (*She puts her hands into* UNCLE's *pockets looking for his wallet. He lets himself be searched.*) And in fifteen minutes Rivkele will be back. (*She throws a shawl around her shoulders and starts to leave.*) He'll do it for me. (*She slams the door behind her.*)

UNCLE (*wanders about the house, his head bowed low*). It's all the same to me. Everything's gone to hell. No more daughter . . . no more Torah Scroll . . . down to the house . . . to the house . . . God says no.

(*A long interval.* REYZL *appears at the door, pokes her head in. Sidles into the house and remains standing at the door.* UNCLE *notices her. He looks at her.*)

REYZL (*stammering*). I've been to Reb Elye's. The mistress sent me. He'll be here soon.

UNCLE (*stares at her for a while*). Gone to the devil anyway. God says no.

KEYZL. She was such a good girl. What a shame!

(UNCLE *looks at her in surprise.*)

REYZL (*apologetically*). The mistress asked me to wait here till she comes back.

UNCLE. Don't be afraid. I haven't gone mad yet. Not yet. God has punished me.

REYZL. Who would have thought it? Such a good girl, she was. It's a shame, so help me!

REB ELYE (*comes in, carrying a lantern*). What happened here anyway? Did you have to call me before daybreak? (*He comes inside, looks out through the shutter.*) Almost time for prayers.

UNCLE (*not looking at* REB ELYE). The Torah Scroll has been defiled, defiled unto death.

REB ELYE (*alarmed*). What are you saying, man? Has anything, heaven forbid, happened to the Torah Scroll? Was it dropped to the ground? The whole city will have to fast. . . .

UNCLE. Worse than that, Reb Elye.

REB ELYE (*angered*). What are you saying! The whole city can be held responsible, heaven forbid! What happened? Say something, man, in heaven's name!

UNCLE. Down into the house. (*Points to the floor and then to* REYZL.) Downstairs with them . . . in the house . . . no more Torah Scroll.

REB ELYE. Man, what are you saying? What's going on here? Talk!

REYZL (*at the door, calms* REB ELYE). No, Rebbe, not the Torah Scroll, the daughter. Rivkele. The Torah Scroll is unharmed. (*Points to* RIVKELE's *room.*) In there.

REB ELYE (*takes a breath of relief*). The Lord be praised! But the Torah Scroll is unharmed?

REYZL. Yes, Rebbe.

REB ELYE (*more calmly; spits*). Thank God it was only a scare. (*To* UNCLE.) What kind of nonsense were you talking? (*Motioning to* REYZL *without looking at her.*) Leave. Isn't she here yet? (*To* UNCLE.) Has anyone gone to look for her?

UNCLE. To me my daughter is holier than a Torah Scroll.

REB ELYE. Stop talking nonsense. Just keep quiet. Just don't make any commotion. Has anyone gone to look for her? To bring her back? Of course not! Why are you standing around?

REYZL. The mistress went after her.

REB ELYE. Does anyone know where she went?

REYZL. Yes, the mistress will bring her home soon.

REB ELYE. Then everything is fine. So why all the noise and excitement? Do you want the whole world to find out? Such things are kept quiet. It's not decent. Let a young man's father find out about it, and it will cost you a couple of hundred extra right off.

UNCLE. It's all the same to me. Let everybody know. No more daughter. No more Torah Scroll. Down to the house! Everything down to the house!

REB ELYE. Say, you're really out of your mind. Supposing misfortune does strike. People do have troubles. May God protect us. Never mind the details. God helps. Troubles pass. The main thing is: nobody knows. Nobody hears anything; nobody sees anything. You wipe your lips and make believe nothing happened. (*To* REYZL.) You've got to watch what you say so that, heaven forbid, it does not get around. Do you hear? (*Turns to* UNCLE *whose gaze is lost in some distant nowhere.*) I saw. . . . (*Looks around to see whether* REYZL *is still present. Noticing her, he stops. After a pause he starts again, more quietly, motioning to* REYZL *to leave. Slowly.*) I saw. . . . (*He looks at* REYZL. REYZL *understands and leaves the room.*) I saw the young man's father in the synagogue between afternoon and evening prayers. I spoke with him. He was close to agreeing. I even gave him to understand, in passing, that the bride did not come from the best of families. Well, another hundred added to the dowry—these days such matters are less important. Saturday, God willing, I'll bring the man up here; then we'll go over and have the rabbi test the young man's learning. But the most important thing is that no one should know; no one must find out about the matter. Heaven forbid. It could do a lot of harm. The man comes from a good family and the son is a fine scholar. Come, come, calm yourself, trust God, and with His help all will turn out for the best. I'm going home to prepare for prayers, and when the girl is back, let me know immediately, you hear? (*Leaving.*) But immediately, without fail. (*Starts to leave.*)

UNCLE (*arises, catches* REB ELYE *by the hand*). Listen, Reb Elye: you take your Torah Scroll with you. I don't need it any more.

REB ELYE (*surprised*). What are you talking about? What do you want? Have you gone crazy? Have you lost your senses?

UNCLE. My daughter went to the house. The Torah Scroll was defiled. God punished me.

REB ELYE (*tries to interrupt him*). What are you talking about?

UNCLE. I am a sinful man. I know that well enough. He should have broken my legs, ruined me, sent me to an early grave. . . . But what did He want of my child, of my poor child?

REB ELYE. Listen, that's no way to talk. You mustn't talk against God.

UNCLE (*angry*). You can say anything, if it's the truth. I may be Yankel Chapchovich, uncle of a house, but I can tell even God the truth. I'm not afraid at all. I came to you in the synagogue. I told you everything. You advised me to have a Torah Scroll copied. I put it in there, in her room. Night after night I stood before it and I said to it: you are a God. You know everything that I do. If you want to punish me, then punish me. Punish my wife. We have sinned. But not my innocent child. Have pity on my poor child.

REB ELYE. But she has suffered no harm. She'll come back. She'll turn out to be a fine Jewish wife.

UNCLE. It makes no difference. She's gone to the devil. She'll be hankering. Once she's made a beginning, she won't rest. If it isn't today, it will be tomorrow. She's given her soul to the devil. I know that. Oh, how I know that.

REB ELYE. You stop talking nonsense. Calm yourself. Ask God's forgiveness in your heart. Give up your business. With God's help, your daughter will still get married like any other Jewish girl, and you will still have much joy in her.

UNCLE. Lost, Rebbe, all is lost. Had she died young, Rebbe, I would have said nothing. Had she died, I would have known that I buried a chaste child, an honorable child. But now what am I worth in this world? You're sinful yourself and you leave behind a sinful generation. And so sin goes on from generation to generation.

REB ELYE. Don't you talk that way; a Jew must not talk that way. You better trust to God and say to yourself: what was done cannot be undone.

UNCLE (*interrupts him*). Don't try to persuade me, Rebbe. I know that it's too late. Sin lies upon me and upon my house like a rope about the neck. God was against it. But I ask you, Rebbe, why was God against it? Why should it have bothered Him if you, Yankel Chapchovich, save yourself from the swamp into which you're sinking? (*Goes into* RIVKELE's *room, returns with the Torah Scroll, holds it aloft, and addresses it.*) You, Torah Scroll! I know—you are a mighty God! And you are our God. I, Yankel Chapchovich, have sinned. (*Beats his breast with his fist.*) The sins are mine! Mine! Go ahead and perform a miracle. Send down a fire to consume me on the spot. Open the earth and let me be swallowed up. But protect my child. Send her back to me as pure, as innocent as she was. I know . . . for you everything is possible. Perform a miracle. You are a mighty God, aren't you? And if you don't—you are no God at all. I, Yankel Chapchovich, say to you, you are no God at all. You are vengeful! You are like a man!

REB ELYE (*rouses himself with a start and tears the Torah Scroll from* UNCLE's *arms*). Do you know whom you are talking to? (*Stares at him, then goes into* RIVKELE's *room with the Torah Scroll.*) Beg the Torah Scroll's forgiveness!

UNCLE. God Himself can be told the truth to His very face. (*Follows* REB ELYE.) If He is a God, let Him here and now perform His miracle.

SORE (*runs in quickly. She is excited. She runs over to the mirror, straightens her hair with her hand, calling*). Come in, Shloyme. Why stand outside?

SHLOYME (*in the doorway*). Where is Yankel? (*Coming in.*) Let him know that I'll do anything for a pal, even though he did insult me.

SORE (*meanwhile she runs over to* RIVKELE's *door and locks it behind* UNCLE *and* REB ELYE). Let him alone in there. Lately, you know, he's got religion. Hangs around with pious Jews. (*Runs over and locks the door behind* SHLOYME.) You sure pick your brides! She's such a pest. You can't shake her off. Chases after you as though you belonged to her already. I'll bet she comes running after you here. (*Smiling.*) Oh, Shloyme, Shloyme, what a bargain you picked up! (*She goes over to the window, opens the shutters with a bang. The room lights up.*) What did they shut themselves in for?

SHLOYME. Don't worry, I tell you. If I promise you I'll do it, I'll do it. I wouldn't do it for everybody, but for you I'll do it, even though you haven't been nice to me lately. But I don't mind. She can drop dead if she wants to; it won't do her a bit of good.

SORE (*walks over to him, takes him by the hand, looks straight into his eyes*). A fellow like you—why do you have to take a girl like that? Who is she, anyway? She's been tossing about from house to house. A fellow like you—you can pick up a pretty penny now; why do you need her? A fellow with a couple of hundred rubles, why can't you take a decent girl? Why not? Aren't you as young as the next fellow? (*Slaps him on the back.*) You talk it over with me, Shloyme. You know I was never mean to you. Even if I did act like that a little lately, still I was always Sore. Wasn't I? Tell me. (*Looks him in the eye.*)

SHLOYME (*brushing his mustache*). Aw, hell. I let that broad turn my head, the devil knows why. It was just temporary. To pick up some change. You didn't think I really intended. . . . My mother would have cursed every bone in my body. My mother is a decent woman. Not to mention my sister.

SORE. Didn't you have anything better to do than to get involved with a nobody like that and set up a house? For the kind of income that you get from a house these days, it certainly doesn't pay to get mixed up with no-goods like that. (*Goes over to him, presses the earrings into his hand.*) Here, you take this, and here's a hundred besides, and you tell me where Rivkele is.

SHLOYME. What's true is true. You were once a good woman. (*Winks to her.*) Lately you got spoiled. But one thing has nothing to with another. Let me tell you, Shloyme is a pal. (*Takes the earrings and puts them into his pocket.*)

SORE. Tell me, Shloyme, where is she now? You can tell me everything even though I am her mother. You know, these things don't scare me. Tell me, have you taken her away somewheres . . . to a. . . .

SHLOYME. She's very near here. If I tell you I'm gonna bring her to you, I'll bring her. But I tell you, what a tart she could be, so help me. Her looks, her class, she's one well-stacked broad, I can tell you that.

SORE. Hey, Sore still knows! Tell me, Shloyme, where have you got her? You can tell me everything. (*She puts one arm around him, slapping him on the back with her other hand and looking him roguishly in the eye.*) Come on, tell me, buddy boy.

SHLOYME. Not far from here, not far. (*The sound of fists pounding on the outside of the door is heard.*)

HINDL (*offstage*). You don't know anything about her! You don't know a thing!

SORE. Let her go jump in the lake. She's really got him in her grimy little paws! Ha ha, he's not even allowed to budge without her! (*Looks at him roguishly.*) Shame on you, running around with girls! (SHLOYME *is thoughtful.* SORE *grabs him by the hand, pulls him aside.*) Talk it over with me. Why do you need her? I'll give you a girl. You'll see. (*Winks at him.*)

HINDL (*bursts open the door, rushes in*). What in blazes have they latched onto him for? The devil take them—their daughter runs off. . . . (*Grabs* SHLOYME *by the hand.*) You don't know where she is. What do they want from you?

SORE (*sits down on a chair, looks roguishly at* SHLOYME, *indicates* HINDL). So that's the dog, eh? Ha, ha, ha.

HINDL (*turns around*). Listen to that vicious cackle. (*To* SHLOYME.) You don't know a thing about her. (*Draws him aside.* '*Quietly.*) We'll go to Lodz, get married there, rent a place. With two tarts like that—think of what you're doing. (*Loud.*) What are they pestering you for? You don't know where she is. (*Draws him by the hand.*) Come, Shloyme. (SHLOYME *is undecided.*)

SORE (*out loud, with a flattering smile*). Well, why don't you go with her, Shloyme? She came for you, didn't she? To go off to Lodz, get married, rent a place. (*Approaches* SHLOYME, *draws him away from* HINDL.) A young fellow like you, with a decent Jewish mother. Your father was a pious man. What does she want from you? Why does she stick to you like a leech?

SHLOYME (*calls*). Come, Sore, let's get Rivkele up here.

HINDL (*clasps her hand over his mouth*). You won't tell! You don't know where she is! (*She runs over to the door, closes it and stands blocking it.*) I won't let you out. (*Rushes to* SHLOYME, *grabs his hand.*) Think, Shloyme, is it all right for them and not for us? Come, Shloyme. Let's go away. We could earn such a good living!

SHLOYME. I've heard all that before. (*Pushes her away.*) We'll talk later. I'm busy now. (*Leaves with* SORE.)

SORE (*comes running back in, bursts open the door to* RIVKELE'S *room, calling*). Rivkele is back!

HINDL (*in the hall*). I won't let you! You won't tell!

SHLOYME (*at the door*). Come, Sore.

SORE (*running out after* SHLOYME). I'm coming, Shloyme. (SORE, SHLOYME, HINDL *leave.*)

REB ELYE (*coming in with* UNCLE). God be praised! God be praised! (*To* UNCLE *who is pacing up and down the room.* REB ELYE *follows him.*) And you see, God did help you. He punishes but he also sends the cure for our ills. Even though you sinned, even though you spoke so blasphemously. (*Warning him.*) From now on you must be careful not to speak such words. You should be respectful. You should know what a Torah Scroll means and what the learning of a Jewish scholar means.

You'll have to go to the synagogue, you will. You'll have to make a substantial contribution for the support of aged scholars. And you'll fast in penance. And God will forgive you. (*Pause. He watches* UNCLE *who is pacing up and down, absorbed in other matters.*) Don't you hear me? With God's help, everything will turn out right. I'll go over for the bridegroom's father soon, and we'll talk the matter over in all the details. But don't haggle. A hundred more, a hundred less—remember who you are and who he is. And pay the dowry right away and don't hem and haw about the wedding so that we don't run into any obstacles, heaven forbid. Such things shouldn't be postponed. (*He looks at* UNCLE.) Don't you hear me? I'm talking to you.

UNCLE (*to himself*). I want to ask her one thing, just one thing. And let her tell me the truth . . . the whole truth—yes or no.

REB ELYE. Don't you multiply your sins. Just thank God that he helped you as much as he did.

UNCLE (*as before*). I won't do a thing to her. Just the truth: yes or no.

REB ELYE. The truth, the truth. God will help and everything will turn out well. I'm going over to see the groom's father. He's in the synagogue, probably waiting for me. (*Looks around.*) Tell your wife to tidy the place up in the meantime. And as for you—shake hands on the matter right away. Don't give him a chance to find out about anything and change his mind. Agree on the wedding arrangements and send the bride off to the groom's family. Just don't jabber. Keep everything quiet. Don't let anyone find out a thing. (*Starts to leave.*) And forget about all that nonsense. Look to God for help. And cheer up a little. Don't let him suspect anything. (*Leaving.*) Tell your wife to put the place in order. (*He leaves.*)

UNCLE (*resumes his pacing*). Just let her tell me the truth, just the truth. (*A long pause.*)

SORE (*at the door*). Come in, come on in. Your father won't beat you. (*Pause.*) Go on in, I tell you. (*Pushes* RIVKELE *in.* RIVKELE *is wrapped in a shawl over her head. She stands at the door, looks in with eyes unabashed and lips set defiantly. She says nothing and does not move from the spot.*)

SORE. Well, why don't you move, darling daughter? All the joy you've given us . . . for our toil . . . for our effort. We'll settle accounts later. (*Stops abruptly.*) Go on in. Comb your hair. Put on a dress. There's someone coming. (*To* UNCLE.) I met Reb Elye. He went for the groom's father. (*Looks around the room*.) Looks like a tornado hit it. (*Begins to clean up hastily*.)

UNCLE (*notices* RIVKELE, *looks at her, approaches her, takes her gently by the hand and leads her to the table*). Don't be afraid. I won't hit you. (*He sits down*.) Sit down here next to me. (*Pushes a chair over for her*.) Sit down.

RIVKELE (*angry. She hides her face in the shawl*). I can stand just as well.

UNCLE. Sit down. (*He sits her down*.) Don't be afraid.

RIVKELE (*from behind the shawl*). Why should I be afraid?

UNCLE (*stammering*). Rivkele, tell me, Rivkele . . . you are my daughter and I am your father. (*Points to* SORE.) There's your mother. Tell me, child, but tell me the whole truth. Don't be afraid of me. And don't be ashamed before me. I know that it was not for your sins, not for your sins but for mine, for mine and your mother's, for our sins. Tell me, child.

SORE. Look at him, sitting down for a heart to heart talk with her. What does he want from her? He could hardly wait! Let her go in and get dressed. People will be here any minute. (*She goes over to take* RIVKELE *away from* UNCLE.)

UNCLE. Let her go, I tell you. (*He pushes* SORE *away from* RIVKELE.)

SORE. He's gone stark raving mad today! What's the matter with him? (*Starts to clean up once more.*)

UNCLE (*seats* RIVKELE *near him*). I won't hit you. (*Puts his fingers around her slender throat*.) Had I twisted your neck off like this before you grew up, it would have been better for you and better for me. But don't be afraid. I won't harm you. It wasn't for your sins that God punished us but for ours. I protected you as one protects the very eyes of his head. I had a Torah Scroll copied for your sake. I put it into your room and I prayed to God the long nights through: Protect my child from evil. Punish me, punish her mother, but protect my child. When you grow up, I thought, I'll make a fine match for you. I'll get you an honorable young man for a husband; I'll support you both; you'll live together . . .

RIVKELE (*from behind the shawl*). I've got plenty of time to get married. I'm not that old.

SORE. She's got the nerve to talk back!

RIVKELE. Trying to make a rabbi's wife out of me! Why didn't Mamma marry as young?

SORE. Shut your trap or I'll shut it for you! She sure learned a lot in one night!

RIVKELE (*misinterpreting*). Yes, now I know. . . .

UNCLE. Let her alone! (*Hastily.*) I just want to ask her one thing, just one thing. And tell me the truth. I won't hit you. I won't touch you. You're not the guilty one. (*Can't get himself to say the word.*) Tell it to me . . . straight. Tell me . . . the truth. I want . . . the truth. . . .

SORE. What's this truth that you want? What do you want from her?

UNCLE. I'm not asking you. (*Rises, takes* RIVKELE *by the hand.*) Don't be embarrassed before me. I'm your father. You can tell me everything. Tell me plainly, are you still . . . are you still as pure as when you left here? Are you still a chaste Jewish girl?

SORE (*pulls* RIVKELE *from* UNCLE's *grasp*). What do you want from her? The child has done nothing wrong. Let her alone.

UNCLE (*holds fast to* RIVKELE's *hand, tries to look her in the eye*). Tell me the truth. I'll believe you. Look me in the eye, straight in the eye. Are you still a chaste Jewish girl. Look me in the eye, straight in the eye! (*He tries to look into her eyes.* RIVKELE *hides her face in the shawl.*)

SORE. Why don't you take the shawl off your head? Do you need a shawl in the house? (*She pulls the shawl off her head.* RIVKELE *resists, hides her face in her coat.*)

UNCLE (*shouting*). Tell me now. Don't be bashful. I won't hurt you. (*He takes her firmly by the hands, draws her towards him, and looks into her eyes.*) Are you still a chaste Jewish girl? Tell me now.

RIVKELE (*tries to hide her face in her coat*). I don't know. . . .

UNCLE (*shouting*). You don't know? You don't know? Well then who does know? You don't know! Tell me the truth: are you still. . . .

RIVKELE (*tearing herself out of her father's grasp*). Was it all right for my mother? Was it all right for my father? Now I know everything. (*She holds her arms up to protect her face.*) Hit me! Go ahead and hit me!

(SORE *runs towards her with hands raised to strike her.* UNCLE *pushes her off with a single blow. He sits down on his chair, pale, breathing heavily.* RIVKELE *drops to the floor, weeping loud. A long pause of silence.* SORE *walks about the room. It is clear that she doesn't know where to begin. After a while she picks up the broom and starts to sweep up silently, almost stealthily. Then she goes over to* RIVKELE, *pulls her up by her hand, and leads her into her room. She does all this in silence.* UNCLE *does not move.* RIVKELE *exits.*)

SORE (*coming back from* RIVKELE's *room, runs over to*

UNCLE, *grasps his hand, pleading*). Yankel, consider what you're doing! Remember God! Why does anyone have to know? (*Pause.*) Calm yourself. (*Pause.*) Rivkele will get married; we'll be proud of her yet.

(UNCLE *says nothing.*)

SORE. Put on your jacket. They'll be here soon. (*Looks at* UNCLE. *Abruptly.*) Why must anyone know?

(UNCLE *says nothing. Stares at the same spot.*)

SORE (*brings* UNCLE's *jacket in. She helps him into it. He lets her*). What a calamity! What a calamity! Who could have expected it? (*She finishes dressing* UNCLE *and begins to straighten her own clothes. She tidies up, runs into* RIVKELE's *room. Sounds of her hiding something. Returns quickly.*) We'll settle with you later. (*Looks around the room to see whether everything is in place, straightens up here and there.*) Raise children these days! (*Sighs audibly.*)

(*Sounds of footsteps coming up the stairs.*)

SORE (*runs over to* UNCLE, *pulling him by the sleeve*). They're coming. Remember God! Yankel . . . it can still turn out right.

(REB ELYE *comes in with a stranger.* SORE *pushes her stray hair underneath her wig, stands near the door to receive the guests.*)

REB ELYE. Good morning.

SORE. Good morning and a good year. Welcome. (*Somewhat confused. She offers them each a chair.*)

REB ELYE (*gaily*). Where's the father of the bride? (*Looks around for* UNCLE.)

SORE (*smiling, to* UNCLE). Yankel, why don't you show yourself? (*She pushes a chair closer to* UNCLE.)

(*The men shake hands with* UNCLE *and sit down.*)

REB ELYE (*gesticulating*). Let's get right down to the matter at hand. (*To the stranger, indicating* UNCLE.) This man wants to arrange a match with you. His daughter is a chaste Jewish maiden and he wants to give her a scholar for a husband, and he'll support them both for the rest of their lives.

THE STRANGER. Good.

UNCLE (*rising*). Yes, my friend, a chaste Jewish maiden, a chaste. . . .

REB ELYE (*to* THE STRANGER). He'll pay five hundred rubles cash at the engagement, support for him to study for the rest of his days; he'll treat him as if he were his own child.

THE STRANGER. There's no need for me to boast about what I've got. Two more years of study and he'll be a rabbi.

REB ELYE. We know that. This man will watch over him as he would the eye of his head. He'll have everything of the best here. And he'll be able to sit and study day and night.

UNCLE (*pointing to* RIVKELE's *room*). Yes, in there, he can sit and study the holy Torah. . . . I have a chaste Jewish daughter. (*He goes into* RIVKELE's *room and drags her out forcibly by the arm. She is still half undressed, her hair dishevelled. Points to her.*) A chaste Jewish maiden will be marrying your son. She'll bear chaste Jewish children, like any other Jewish girl. (*To* SORE.) Isn't that so? (*Laughs wildly to* THE STRANGER.) Yes, indeed, my friend, she'll be a chaste Jewish wife. . . . My wife will lead her to the wedding canopy. . . . Down to the whore house! Downstairs! (*Points to the basement.*) To the house! (*He drags* RIVKELE *by the hair to the door.*) Down to the house!

SORE (*runs over wildly*). Help, everybody, he's gone crazy! (*She tries to pull* RIVKELE *away.* UNCLE *pushes her off and continues to pull* RIVKELE *out by the hair.*)

UNCLE. Down to the house! (*Exits with* RIVKELE. RIVKELE's *crying can be heard offstage.*)

THE STRANGER (*astounded and alarmed*). What's this? (REB ELYE *winks to him. He tugs at his sleeve and nods towards the door.* THE STRANGER *continues to stand there astounded.* REB ELYE *draws him toward the door. They leave. Pause.*)

UNCLE (*returns pulling* REB ELYE *by the arm, having caught him on the stairs*). Take the Torah Scroll with you. I don't need it any more!

GREEN FIELDS

❧

Peretz Hirshbein
(1880–1948)

❧

I see Hirshbein: with peasants floating rafts down a river;
with a company building a Yiddish theater; on ships and
trains, wandering to the corners of the world; at the piano,
picking out his own melodies; with easel and water colors,
painting landscapes; with a collection of rocks accumu-
lated all over the world; beside a dense cobweb, studying
the life and habits of the spider; on a hundred platforms,
speaking an hour and two and three without a drink of
water.[1]

This many-sided man was a rarity among Yiddish writers in
that he was born and raised among farmers. His father, Lippe,
owned a water mill, and for the first dozen years of his life,
Peretz Hirshbein was never far from Lippe's mill, as it was
known. His account of those early years in *Childhood*, a classic
of Yiddish autobiographical writing, recounts their profound
effect upon his imagination. He tells of his mother, who awoke
in him a quick sensitivity to sight and sound; of his hundred-
year-old grandfather, who sang tunes that he designated by
colors—green, yellow, red, blue, and the one young Hirshbein
loved most, the speckled tune; of the ghosts and imps and

---

[1] Menakhem Boraisho, "How I Have Seen Hirshbein," in S. Niger
and M. Elkin, eds., *Peretz Hirshbein* (New York, 1941), p. 148 (in
Yiddish).

shadowy creatures who inhabited the world around the mill and who could be heard in the awful silence of the night, when the mill wheel was not turning.

But the world of farm and field was not the first subject of his literary efforts, which began when he forsook his rabbinical studies for the life of a writer. He turned first to the poverty he saw among the Jews of Vilna, and his first plays were written under the influence of the naturalists, with strong overtones of symbolism and mysticism from Maeterlinck and Andreyev. These early plays, written in Hebrew, were translated into Russian and appeared in a volume entitled *Lonely Worlds*. The book came to the attention of Andreyev, who sought him out and befriended him. And it was in Russian, in Odessa, that Hirshbein first saw a play of his produced. The play, *Across the River*, was well received, though Hirshbein's pleasure must have been marred by a harshly anti-Semitic remark of Ivan Bunin's at a literary party they both attended.

Though plays in Yiddish followed those first efforts in Hebrew, Hirshbein's great contributions to the Yiddish theater did not begin until 1908, when he organized the theatrical company that soon came to be known as the Hirshbein Troupe. In the constant running battle between the drama and the commercial theater, Hirshbein's influence on the modern Yiddish theater is comparable to that of Chekhov on the Moscow Art Theater or O'Neill and the Provincetown Players on the modern American theater. It was both practical and literary. His organization of a company whose members were, for the first time, recruited from among the graduates of Russian dramatic schools in Odessa and other cities laid the groundwork, through its example and the influence of its personnel, for such later companies as the famed Vilna Troupe and Maurice Schwartz's Yiddish Art Theater in New York, of which Jacob ben Ami, a Hirshbein Troupe alumnus, was an early member. But even more important was Hirshbein's contribution as a dramatist. By writing plays that were both artistic and financial successes for art companies, he enabled the movement to flourish for the two decades that were allotted to it after World War I and opened the way for new playwrights.

Of Hirshbein's more than fifty full-length and one-act plays, the ones that are most admired are those written after the dissolution of the Troupe in 1910, when he rediscovered his rural roots—the plays of country life, especially *Green Fields, The Blacksmith's Daughters, The Vacant Inn,* and *Off the Beaten Track.* Perhaps it was a visit to the United States that, in enabling him to see the European Jewish countryside from the perspective of industrialized America, showed him the way to the rediscovery of the ordinary Jew, the *folksmentsh,* in the Jewish farmer. Or perhaps it was another example of a continuing process in Yiddish literature, the discovery of the folksmentsh. Because of his relative lack of education in the intense Jewish world in which education was the highest badge of *yikhes* (social position and family prestige), the ordinary Jew, the worker, whether skilled or unskilled, was often disdainfully regarded. Lowest in the educational scale stood the farmer, whose isolation frequently prevented him from providing for his children even the elementary education that was available in every town. Yet it was the discovery of these ordinary Jews that opened rich veins of ore for many a Yiddish writer. And what they discovered was his mentshlekhkayt, his humane morality, and his stubborn loyalty to a faith that was a way of life and that, in its ways and values, exalted man's obligation to man and hoped for the Messianic liberation of the world from injustice. The valuation of the folk that runs through the stories about the prophet Elijah, who always appears as a pauper, and through the tales about the Thirty-Six Just Men and other secret saints, who are always ordinary men, found another voice in these plays of Hirshbein's that, in their fragile simplicity and naivete, are but a step away from folklore.

Hirshbein's "folk comedies" like *The Blacksmith's Daughters, Off the Beaten Track,* and especially *Green Fields* are more than comedies, or are at least comedies of a very special sort. They are neither satirical, witty, sentimental, nor farcical. They are really pastoral idylls, hymns of praise to bountiful nature and moral man. The morality, unlike the morality of Wordsworth's country folk, results not from the rural setting but from Jewish tradition; nature is merely a warm and kindly provider. *Green Fields* is the most tender of these three plays, with a tenderness unblemished by sentimentality. Its world is the world of the countryside, redolent of green grass and peace and young love, a world suffused with the warm glow of the summer sun and the traditional Jewish values—gentleness, human relatedness, learning. It is a world where quarrels between man and man are always patched up before the High Holy Days, where nature is generous, where young loves do not wither, where yearning for mentshlekhkayt passes on from generation to generation. It is a world of human dignity and human decency. And it is a world in which time and place are irrelevant. There are only the recurrent round of the seasons and of the Jewish holidays and of the generations, and the recurrent, never-absent mentshlekhkayt.

The characters are part of the landscape. Farmers for generations, they belong in it. They are intimate with nature and seem almost isolated in it. An occasional traveler is mentioned and an occasional visit to the surrounding villages or even into town. But in the forefront is the warmth of the sun, the benevolence of nature and of man—"There's always food on a farm"—and the yearning for that moral-intellectual-aesthetic, disciplined fulfillment-responsibility that Jewish tradition is to them. The intimacy of man and nature, of tradition and soil, is reflected in the very names of the characters. On the one hand there is Noyakh (Noah) and Avrom-Yankev (Abraham-Jacob) and Levi-Yitskhok (a name which once belonged to the famed Hassidic rabbi Levi-Yitskhok of Berdichev, called the Compassionate); and on the other hand there are the names that roam the fields and woods, like Hersh-Ber, or that seem to belong to the soil, like Tsine and Stere. Levi-Yitskhok, as the symbol of Jewish tradition, comes both to heighten and to satisfy their hunger for that tradition. Though still a youth, he combines the traditional modesty and gentleness with learning, morality, and the wisdom that stems from both. He reminds Elkone how a mentsh should act. He admonishes Tsine about regard for life: "It's not good to erase a name." And the love he awakens in her causes her to mature from a barefoot country girl to a sedate Jewish young woman who knows how to value a scholar. And he evokes from Avrom-Yankev's imagination that village vision of urban glory: "A synagogue full of [white-bearded] Jews must be really beautiful to see." Levi-Yitskhok's decision to remain on the farm is not merely the result of his love for Tsine, the most winning of Hirshbein's country girls, wild yet shyly modest and guilelessly attractive. It is the result also of his discovery that Jewish tradition and Jewish values can thrive on a farm, even in seeming exile from schools and books; of his discovery of the essential mentshlekh-kayt of farm folk, for even Hersh-Ber, it turns out, can shed a tear.

In this world there is neither greed nor desire under its elms. These are left for other Hirshbein works. In its simplicity and kindliness it is also different from Dickens' stagecoach and Christmas-pudding world of good will, for Hirshbein's reliance is not merely on natural goodness but on morality. And even kindliness, spontaneous or studied, is not enough. There must also be learning and yearning for the Messianic liberation of men. It is a limited world that Hirshbein depicts here, yet it is a real one, a world that once existed, though its skies were not quite so cloudless. It is a world of simple people and simple speech, pervaded by a lyricism that is less in the language than in the mood, in the people, and in the respect for their mentshlekhkayt.

GREEN FIELDS

CHARACTERS
Dovid-Noyakh
Rokhel
Hersh-Ber
Tsine } their children
Avrom-Yankev
Elkone
Gittl
Stere, their daughter
Levi-Yitskhok

ACT I

(On DOVID-NOYAKH's farm. Early spring. About noon. Right
—a farmhouse. Left—a barn. A potato patch stretches into the
background. A few fruit trees are beginning to blossom. A well
stands near the fence of the patch.)

(ROKHEL is seated in front of the house cutting potatoes in
half. DOVID-NOYAKH enters from the garden.)

ROKHEL. Have you planted all of them already?

DOVID-NOYAKH. Ha, Stere showed up. Wanted to race, see
who could finish first.

ROKHEL. Stere? How do you like that!

DOVID-NOYAKH. A fine girl. Handier than Tsine.

ROKHEL. Well, we've yet to see who'll make a better match.

DOVID-NOYAKH. Works like a mule. I couldn't drag a sack
like that around on my back.

ROKHEL. Bless her, blood and milk. You know, she really is
a great help to Elkone.

DOVID-NOYAKH. That's exactly what I've been telling you.
And if she comes here as often as she does, something is up.

ROKHEL. Elkone would like it.

DOVID-NOYAKH. Ha—ha! You really think so?

ROKHEL. You think Elkone would mind having Hersh-Ber
for a son-in-law? He'd even manage to scrape up a dowry somewhere. Speak of the devil—they come! (ELKONE and GITTL
enter.)

DOVID-NOYAKH. Where are you off to, Elkone?

ELKONE. Bless you all. Oh, I don't know, find out what's
going on in the world. I don't know, take a little ride into the
villages.

ROKHEL. How is the cow doing? Still limping?

GITTL. If that were the only thing, it wouldn't be so bad.

ROKHEL. What else is wrong with the poor thing?

GITTL. Lost her appetite.

DOVID-NOYAKH. That's not good.

GITTL. Before Passover I said, let's sell her. I don't like to
have to hand feed a cow. Well, he didn't listen to me. Now
she's started to limp, on top of all her other troubles.

ELKONE. You won't go broke on account of her.

GITTL. As my mother always says, if God's in his heaven, why should I knock myself out?

ELKONE. If my woman takes a dislike to something, nothing will change her mind.

ROKHEL. I'm that way too, may God not punish me for saying so.

GITTL. Why should I deny it?

ELKONE. She took a dislike to the teacher too, and I had to get rid of him. So the children have nothing to keep them busy.

ROKHEL. Have you seen your Stere here?

ELKONE. Oh, she's here, is she?

GITTL. She said she was going over to help Tsine with the potatoes and maybe Hersh-Ber would come over and give Elkone a hand sometimes.

ROKHEL. We were just talking about her.

GITTL. You have no idea what a wonderful child she is. If only Tsine wouldn't spoil her.

ROKHEL. What do you mean?

ELKONE. Ha—ha. Tsine is a little on the wild side.

ROKHEL. You should say a thing like that. . . .

DOVID-NOYAKH. I told you the same thing. You've spoiled her. It's true she's an only daughter, but she's hardly a child any more.

ROKHEL. Oh, please! You don't know what you're talking about. But how do you come to say a thing like that, Gittl dear?

GITTL. I really don't mean anything.

ROKHEL. I'm still not so sure who will make a better match.

ELKONE. Ha—ha—ha. Women. When it comes to their children they're like hens: mine—yours; yours—mine.

DOVID-NOYAKH. No use listening to their chattering.

GITTL. Here Stere came over to help her. No sense fooling ourselves. Tsine wouldn't do it.

DOVID-NOYAKH. Tut, tut! You see, Elkone, now your missus is talking nonsense. A child of Dovid-Noyakh's is, after all—a child of Dovid-Noyakh's.

ROKHEL. And that's why it cut me to the quick.

ELKONE. Come, woman. If you stay any longer you'll just talk more foolishness. Right, Dovid-Noyakh?

GITTL. I really meant no harm, heaven forbid. May all Jews, with God's help, have children like Tsine. Good day.

ELKONE. If I were as worried about my cow as I'm worried about your Tsine. . . . Ekh, if I only had a grown son. . . . Come, woman, come. Good day. (*Both leave.*)

DOVID-NOYAKH. You know what I'll tell you, my dear wife? You have a long tongue.

ROKHEL. How do you like that! I have a long tongue?

DOVID-NOYAKH. So she has a long tongue. What's the difference?

ROKHEL. I know you don't care what people say about your children.

DOVID-NOYAKH. I don't want to quarrel with him.

ROKHEL. What business does she have saying that Tsine spoils her Stere? She should consider it a great honor that Tsine is even friends with her daughter.

DOVID-NOYAKH. For her information, the potatoes would have gotten planted without her.

ROKHEL. That really burns me up. She should not have spoken ill of my child to my face. She knows Stere didn't come to help Tsine but for something else.

DOVID-NOYAKH. I don't understand what you're talking about today.

ROKHEL. Stere came because Hersh-Ber is working the potato patch. Now do you understand?

DOVID-NOYAKH. Really? Are you serious?

ROKHEL. Of course.

DOVID-NOYAKH. She's thinking of Hersh-Ber?

ROKHEL. Well, why not? He's got a heart of gold.

DOVID-NOYAKH. What do you know, and I never suspected. . . . But Elkone really ought to talk with me.

ROKHEL. He will. You saw how quiet he was the whole time. You think they'd let her come here otherwise?

DOVID-NOYAKH. If that's so, then it was really wrong of her to say such things about Tsine.

ROKHEL. Well, we'll see about that. If it comes to anything— I'll refuse. You'll see.

DOVID-NOYAKH. He—he, I had no idea you could get so angry.

ROKHEL. I have a good mind to ask her. Tsine! Tsine!

DOVID-NOYAKH. Oh, don't bother her. Let her finish.

TSINE (*appearing on the other side of the fence*). Did you call me, Mama?

ROKHEL. Come here, child.

TSINE (*climbs over the fence*). You know, we're almost finished.

ROKHEL. I'll be done soon, too.

TSINE. Do you need me?

ROKHEL. Have some bread and butter. You must be hungry.

TSINE. Fix the ribbon in my hair. My hands are muddy.

(ROKHEL *kisses her as she plaits the ribbon into her hair.*)

DOVID-NOYAKH. You wanted to ask her something, didn't you?

ROKHEL. If you're standing around, I can't talk to her.

TSINE. Oh, what is it?

ROKHEL. Nothing. I just had words with Gittl.

TSINE. Why?

ROKHEL. Nothing. It was about you.

TSINE. About me?

ROKHEL. Dovid-Noyakh, go on into the garden.

TSINE. Oh, Mama, what's the matter?

ROKHEL. Nothing, child. What's that look on your face? I haven't said anything.

DOVID-NOYAKH. He—he. First she quarrels and now she's sorry. (*Leaves.*)

ROKHEL. Where is Hersh-Ber?

TSINE. He's helping me with the planting.

ROKHEL. What were you telling Stere?

TSINE. Me? Nothing.

ROKHEL. Did you ask her to come and help you? What is she doing now?

TSINE. She's planting potatoes.

ROKHEL. Did you ask her or did Hersh-Ber?

TSINE. She came herself. I told her I would help her too. And what if she came to help Hersh-Ber? (*Suddenly bursts out laughing.*)

ROKHEL. What are you laughing at?

(TSINE *hugs her mother, kisses her and laughs.*)

ROKHEL. And I thought you needed me to defend you!

TSINE. So that's how it is! You've been peeking at things you shouldn't!

ROKHEL. Oh, go away. Take your hands off me. You know, Gittl is really right when she says you're spoiling Stere.

TSINE. I spoil her? It's too bad I wasn't here. I could have told her a thing or two. She thinks Stere is a little lamb. Well, I'm a lamb in comparison to her. (*Laughs again.*)

ROKHEL. What now?

TSINE. It's funny that you're annoyed and asking about such odd things.

ROKHEL. Why not. I'm a mother and I want to know.

TSINE. I asked her to come over because I knew she wanted to.

ROKHEL. And I thought it was her idea.

TSINE. What's the difference? As long as she kissed him.

ROKHEL. Who?

TSINE. She thought I wasn't looking.

ROKHEL. What?

TSINE. They were both bent over the row, side by side. I pretended I wasn't looking.

ROKHEL. Well, what did he do?

TSINE. He was embarrassed. He looked around to see whether I was watching.

ROKHEL. I would never believe it of her.

TSINE. Oh-ho, she can still teach me plenty.

ROKHEL. I hope to heaven Avrom-Yankev didn't see it.

TSINE. He wasn't in the garden.

ROKHEL. All I need is for him to see such goings-on.

TSINE. Don't tell Papa, because. . . .

STERE (*enters*). What are you hiding from, Tsine? Do you want me to plant your garden by myself?

TSINE. Come here. There's not much left to plant, anyway.

ROKHEL. Thanks very much, Sterele, for coming over to help. When haying time comes, with God's help, we'll all come over to your place to help.

STERE. You know, I'm almost as strong as Hersh-Ber.

TSINE. Did you wrestle with him?

STERE. I rolled that big stone out of the patch all by myself.

ROKHEL. You shouldn't have dragged such a heavy load. If anything had happened, heaven forbid, your mother would have blamed me for it.

STERE. It won't do me a bit of harm.

ROKHEL. I'll plant these few potatoes myself. (*Takes a small sackful of potatoes over her shoulder and leaves.*)

TSINE. Look me straight in the eye, Sterele.

STERE. What?

TSINE. What are you blushing about?

STERE. What?

TSINE. Oh, Sterele, I saw everything.

STERE. What did you see?

TSINE (*embraces her and kisses her*). Silly, what's the difference. I told my mother too.

STERE. So help me, I don't know what you're talking about.

TSINE. You told everyone I asked you to come help me.

STERE. Who told you that? My mother asked me to go herself.

TSINE. Your mother had words here with mine.

STERE. You don't say!

TSINE. What are you so upset about? What do you care if my mother and your mother are angry at each other?

STERE. But what did you mean, you saw everything?

TSINE. I mean I saw you kiss Hersh-Ber.

STERE. It's not true!

TSINE. Silly, I saw you myself. If you had a big brother I would probably do the same thing.

STERE. You're lying!

TSINE. Sterele, silly, why are you so scared?

STERE. You're cruel, Tsine, so help me, you are.

TSINE. But he's my brother, silly.

STERE. I'll be angry with you as long as I live.

TSINE. I can call Hersh-Ber and ask him.

STERE. You just try.

TSINE. I even told Mother.

STERE. Whose mother?

TSINE. My mother. You don't think I'm fool enough to tell your mother? I'm not that fond of your mother to tell her such things.

STERE. No, you're lying.

TSINE. What's the matter with you, Sterele? I saw you myself.

STERE. It's a lie that you told your mother.

TSINE. On my word of honor, I told her.

STERE (*wipes her tears*). I won't talk to you as long as I live.

TSINE. Sterele, silly, what are you crying about? I love you so much, why are you crying? (*Puts her arm around her and wipes the tears from her cheeks with her apron.*)

STERE. You shouldn't have done such a thing to me.

TSINE. I shouldn't have watched you kiss him? Only because he's a fool and waited for you to do it.

STERE (*suddenly explodes into laughter*). He got so red!
     (TSINE *laughs out loud too.*)

STERE. But I still say you're an envious brat.

TSINE. Oh, you don't know what you're talking about.

STERE. How could you do such a thing? I'll be ashamed to look your mother in the eye.

TSINE. Maybe I shouldn't have told her.

STERE. There, you see.

TSINE. Don't look at me that way, Sterele. I really don't know why I did it. When I heard that your mother had quarreled with mine, I wanted. . . . Oh, I really have no idea why I did it. Do you forgive me, Sterele?

STERE. I'm angry.

TSINE. Silly, sooner or later.

STERE (*laughs and weeps*). I wouldn't have cared if he had done it. . . . No, I ought to be angry with you forever. Forever.

TSINE. If you had a big brother I would let the whole world know that I loved him. What is there to be ashamed of?

STERE. No, Tsinele, it's better if no one knows. I would be so happy if no one knew. Now I'll be ashamed even with him.

TSINE. I'll tell him what you said.

STERE. Please don't tease me, Tsinele.

TSINE. I'll tell him what a big jackass he is.

STERE. If you do, I might even drown myself. No one was supposed to know.

TSINE. I would never have believed it of you.

(STERE *weeps quietly.*)

TSINE. Maybe I did act foolishly—you know, Sterele?

STERE. I wouldn't mind the whole thing, if your mother didn't dislike me.

TSINE. There you're wrong.

STERE. I know your mother can't bear to look at me.

TSINE. Oh, go on. You know, I really do envy you. What do I care if you cry? As long as you're really happy.

STERE (*laughing through her tears*). Oh, I'll be so ashamed.

TSINE. Shush! Look. Who is Avrom-Yankev bringing here? There, in the garden.

STERE. A stranger? I'm leaving.

TSINE. What do you know, really a stranger.

(AVROM-YANKEV *and a strange young man enter from the garden and approach the fence. The stranger is dressed in Orthodox fashion and has a pious face. He carries a small bundle on his back and climbs awkwardly over the fence.*)

(TSINE *tries hard to keep from laughing.* STERE *bursts out with a quickly stifled laugh.*)

AVROM-YANKEV. Mother asked you to go into the house. Come in. (*They both enter.*)

(TSINE *and* STERE *throw their arms around each other trying to stifle their laughter.*)

STERE. It may be wrong to laugh at a stranger.

TSINE. Who could he be? He didn't even look at us.

STERE. Too bashful.

TSINE. What a pale face he has!

STERE. Probably a wanderer.

TSINE. Begging, you think?

STERE. I'd love to peek through the window. (*Steals over to the window.*)

TSINE. Well?

STERE. He's put his bundle down.

TSINE. Is he talking to Avrom-Yankev?

STERE. He's looking around.

TSINE. Stay where you are and I'll sneak around behind you.

STERE. You see him? Look at Avrom-Yankev! He's not the least bit afraid of him.

ROKHEL (*arriving*). What are you standing at the window for?

TSINE. Who is he, Mama?

ROKHEL. A stranger. He asked for a night's lodging.

STERE. You hear?

ROKHEL. He looks as though he hasn't eaten today. (TSINE *laughs*.) And what makes you take it into your head to laugh at a stranger?

TSINE. He looks so odd. He's still a boy. I'm ashamed to go into the house.

DOVID-NOYAKH (*enters*). Where is the stranger?

ROKHEL. He's in the house.

DOVID-NOYAKH. Make him welcome. Maybe he wants a bite to eat. (*Goes into the house.*)

TSINE. There are such odd people in the world. They look quite different from us. He had black hair, didn't he?

STERE. And dark eyes, too.

TSINE. He kept looking at the ground.

STERE. He probably has dark eyes.

TSINE. And such a pale face.

STERE. It's a refined face. That's how city folks are.

TSINE. And he wanders over the world on foot.

STERE. Maybe he's not even poor. He might even be. . . . What are you thinking, Tsine?

TSINE. Who could the stranger really be? Maybe he heard me laughing.

STERE. Of course he heard. But he wouldn't think we were laughing at him.

(HERSH-BER *arrives*.)

STERE. I beg you, Tsinele, don't tell him anything.

TSINE. Did you see the stranger?

HERSH-BER. That's what I came to see.

STERE. I'm mad at you.

HERSH-BER. You'll get glad.

TSINE. Hersh-Ber, you're a ninny.

HERSH-BER. What am I?

STERE. Remember, Tsine.

HERSH-BER. You're going to catch it from me. (*He chases* TSINE *playfully. She runs away.*)

TSINE. You're a ninny!

STERE. I'll help you catch her. I'll block her at the well.

(TSINE *jumps over the fence and disappears.*)

HERSH-BER. She'll catch hers from me yet. Tell me, what did ᴉe mean?

STERE. Who knows what she meant!

HERSH-BER. Will your father be here today?

STERE. I don't know. If you want to see him, you can come ⱱer to our place.

HERSH-BER. Your father is very uppish, see? It's just like him ᴐ say it's below his dignity.

STERE. What do you mean?

HERSH-BER. I mean whatever I mean. What's the point of my ⱱalking around doing nothing, and you too, with our eyes ᴐpping.

STERE. So you really think I want to marry you? Just because ⱱou bent down practically under my nose—well, what could I ᴉo?

HERSH-BER. I know. Come on over here.

STERE. Tsine must be hiding around here eavesdropping. She ɑw us before, too, and told your mother.

HERSH-BER. Aw, tell me another.

STERE. My word of honor! She said so herself.

HERSH-BER. Aw, quit bothering me. She fooled you. You ⱱught to know her by now.

STERE. Will you come over to our place later?

HERSH-BER. I thought it's below your dignity.

STERE. Just move away from the window a little. That's ᴉight. . . . (*She throws her arms around his neck.*)

TSINE (*her voice comes from behind the fence*). Hersh-Ber, ⱱou're a ninny.

STERE. Oh, Tsinele, I'll be angry at you forever. (*Embarrassed and confused, she jumps over the fence and runs off.*)

(TSINE *enters.*)

HERSH-BER. What right have you got to spy on us?

TSINE. You *should* be ashamed of yourself. She loves you so ᴉnuch and you act like a ninny. You'd have to wait a long time ᴐr me to kiss you. If it were me, you'd really have to run after ᴉe, don't you worry.

HERSH-BER. Look at her! When did you get so smart?

TSINE. I told Mama you gave her a kiss.

HERSH-BER. But it was she that did it to me.

TSINE. You see, you really are a ninny.

HERSH-BER. But why do you have to go around lying?

TSINE. Oh, you know it's true.

HERSH-BER. If you really told Mama, I'll fix your wagon.

TSINE. We'll see.

HERSH-BER. You have no business spying on me.

TSINE. You can't stop me. If you make her run after you and cry even though you're in love with her, aren't you a ninny?

HERSH-BER. Who cries? (TSINE *laughs out loud.*) You're crazy and there is no use talking to you.

ROKHEL (*coming out of the house*). He's a wonder! You can see he's still a child, but pearls drop from his lips.

TSINE. Really? I want to go inside.

ROKHEL. If you behave yourself. You might burst out laughing.

TSINE. I promise, Mama. I just want to walk through into the next room. (*Goes inside as though on tip-toes.*)

ROKHEL. Why are you standing around, Hersh-Ber?

HERSH-BER. It's her luck you came out. I was really going to let her have it.

ROKHEL. Where is Stere?

HERSH-BER. She must have gone home.

ROKHEL. Is it really true what Tsine says?

HERSH-BER (*at a loss*). What?

ROKHEL. She probably made it up.

HERSH-BER. Made what up?

ROKHEL. Ha, I really didn't mean anything.

HERSH-BER. Then why are you talking as though goodness knows what?

AVROM-YANKEV (*coming out*). You know what his name is, Mama? Levi-Yitskhok.

ROKHEL. That is a beautiful name.

AVROM-YANKEV. Father asked him his name—and he told him.

DOVID-NOYAKH (*coming out*). Where are you, Rokhel? You know what I'll tell you? I like this stranger.

ROKHEL. His mother's milk is still on his lips.

DOVID-NOYAKH. I spoke with him. He might remain here.

ROKHEL. What'll he do here?

DOVID-NOYAKH. You know, he's quite educated. The children will pick something up from him. You should have heard him talk.

HERSH-BER. I'll struggle along just as I am.

AVROM-YANKEV. I'd like to study with him.

HERSH-BER. He's probably as much of a ninny as the last tutor, who didn't know one end of a horse from the other.

DOVID-NOYAKH. If you weren't such a blockhead, you could have learned something from the other tutor, too.

ROKHEL. Well, what's to be done?

DOVID-NOYAKH. Meanwhile we'll have him stay overnight.

AVROM-YANKEV. That's right, Mama, let him stay here.

ELKONE (*arriving*). God bless you all. What are standing around for?

DOVID-NOYAKH. A stranger came by here. Talks like the real thing—brilliant head on his shoulders. We were thinking, it might be a good idea to keep him on as a tutor.

ELKONE. Where is he? I'll contribute!

DOVID-NOYAKH. A youngster, but mature.

ELKONE. I'll contribute!

 (LEVI-YITSKHOK *comes out.*)

ELKONE. Is this him? He's still a kid!

ROKHEL. Godliness itself.

ELKONE. I beg your pardon. Sholem aleichem.

LEVI-YITSKHOK. Aleichem sholem.

ELKONE. You come from far?

LEVI-YITSKHOK. Not from these parts.

DOVID-NOYAKH. That's not hard to tell.

ELKONE. Where are you going?

LEVI-YITSKHOK. No place in particular. Just seeing the world. When I come to a town of learned Jews, I'll stay there.

ELKONE. Why not stay here in the country?

DOVID-NOYAKH. Exactly what I say.

LEVI-YITSKHOK. What would I do on a farm?

DOVID-NOYAKH. There are other Jews in the neighborhood, thank God. We have our quorum of ten men for Sabbath service.

ELKONE. Fine Jewish folk here. You can teach my children and this man's children. You'll be treated with respect. You'll get your clothing and your board and at the end of the term —some money too.

ROKHEL. There's no shortage of food in my house, thank the Lord.

ELKONE. There's always food on a farm. Our children, fine youngsters, but we've never had a tutor whom they could really respect.

DOVID-NOYAKH. Think about it. Take this son of mine. He's a big boy but he's got a good head. If he wants to, he can still learn a lot.

LEVI-YITSKHOK. The children are grown and I'm . . .

DOVID-NOYAKH. If they have respect for you, it doesn't matter. They won't hit a tutor back. Will you respect your teacher, Avrom-Yankev, huh?

ROKHEL. Have you forgotten that he always loved to study?

ELKONE. You can teach the girls to say their prayers.

LEVI-YITSKHOK. I have nothing to teach them.

ROKHEL. Poor sinful creatures, we women, perish the thought.

ELKONE. I'll give you my whip, and if my bunch doesn't behave, let 'em have it. Ha-ha-ha.

HERSH-BER. He sure wouldn't use it on me more than once.

AVROM-YANKEV. You won't need a whip for me.

LEVI-YITSKHOK. Are there really more Jews in these parts?

DOVID-NOYAKH. Of course there are. Where is there a place without Jews?

ELKONE. Good Jews, too. Quite a crowd for Sabbath services.

DOVID-NOYAKH. There's always enough to eat on a farm—milk, butter, cheese.

ELKONE. And potatoes aren't poison either.

ROKHEL. The left-overs we throw out are enough to feed a person.

ELKONE. My woman would want him at our place every Sabbath.

DOVID-NOYAKH. As far as that's concerned, he stays here for the Sabbath.

LEVI-YITSKHOK. I would want some time for myself, for my own studies.

ELKONE. I swear, some day he'll be a rabbi!

DOVID-NOYAKH. The day is long. If you don't mind getting up around daybreak, you can do everything. The children, here, have planted the whole potato patch and it's hardly midday.

ELKONE. I'll tell you what: I'm going home now, and in the evening I'll come back with my bunch so he can test them. You talk it over with him yourself. I'll contribute whatever is needed. Good day. (*He leaves.*)

DOVID-NOYAKH. Go, Rokhel, prepare some food. Maybe he'll have a bite.

LEVI-YITSKHOK (*looking around*). It's a beautiful day you have here.

DOVID-NOYAKH. Of course. Our farm folk are good Jews.

HERSH-BER. Let's eat. Nothing will come of talk.

AVROM-YANKEV (*to* LEVI-YITSKHOK). Would you like to see the potato patch we planted today?

ROKHEL. Go ahead and show the teacher the calves in the barn. (*She goes toward the house.*)

HERSH-BER (*walking toward the house. To his mother*). It'll take you a long while to fatten him up, Mama.

ROKHEL. You don't think I'll stint on his food, do you? (*She goes into the house.*)

LEVI-YITSKHOK. Who was your tutor till now?

AVROM-YANKEV. We haven't had a teacher here for a long time.

LEVI-YITSKHOK. But who was the last one?

AVROM-YANKEV. An old man.

LEVI-YITSKHOK. You didn't behave respectfully.

AVROM-YANKEV. We were very young then. We had no sense.

LEVI-YITSKHOK. I like you.

AVROM-YANKEV. Come, let's look at the calves and then we'll go in to eat. (*They both head for the barn.*)

(TSINE *comes out of the house, steals over to the barn and looks in through a crack.* LEVI-YITSKHOK *comes out of the barn followed by* AVROM-YANKEV.)

AVROM-YANKEV. We have another calf, a bigger one, that's out in the pasture.

LEVI-YITSKHOK. A fine day you have here. (*He does not notice* TSINE, *who hides behind the barn as they pass on their way in to the house.*)

TSINE (*comes out. Calls softly*). Avrom-Yankev! Avrom-Yankev! (*He doesn't hear her. She remains alone. Suddenly she rushes toward the house. Near the threshold she stops and stands thoughtfully a while. She takes a basket of potatoes and goes into the garden.*)

ROKHEL (*her voice is heard calling from the house*). Tsine; Tsi-ne . . .

ACT II

(*In* DOVID-NOYAKH'S *house. Early summer. Midday.*)

(LEVI-YITSKHOK *sits thoughtfully over a book. Rises from his seat; walks back and forth.*)

AVROM-YANKEV (*enters*). Here I am. I thought we wouldn't be studying today.

LEVI-YITSKHOK. Why should today be different from other days?

AVROM-YANKEV. It's haying time.

LEVI-YITSKHOK. But the hired men are doing that.

AVROM-YANKEV. Still, it's good to be out in the meadow. Why don't you ever walk around barefoot?

LEVI-YITSKHOK. There is a time for everything.

AVROM-YANKEV. Are we really going to study today?

LEVI-YITSKHOK. If your father doesn't mind and you don't want to . . .

AVROM-YANKEV. Father doesn't know.

LEVI-YITSKHOK. I know what a fine day it is, too. Do you think I don't know?

AVROM-YANKEV. Let's not study. Let's just talk. Talk to me about something, Rebbe.

LEVI-YITSKHOK. Call me by my name. After all, you're bigger than I am. . . . Do you want me just to chatter away?

AVROM-YANKEV. You want to become a rabbi. It's good to be a rabbi. Is it hard?

LEVI-YITSKHOK. That depends.

AVROM-YANKEV. Could I become a rabbi?

LEVI-YITSKHOK. It's not hard for anyone. But you prefer to be out in the fields; and that's good, too.

AVROM-YANKEV. It isn't that I prefer it. But summertime it's hard to stay in the house when it's so good out there. You're like an old man already.

LEVI-YITSKHOK. If you want to become a rabbi, you have to turn your mind from that, because it disturbs your thoughts.

AVROM-YANKEV. Talk to me about God.

Levi-Yitskhok. What do you mean? Don't you know that God is everywhere?

Avrom-Yankev. Yes, He is in heaven and on earth. I think it would be bad without God. It's He that makes the grass to grow. It's very good that there is a God in the world. If not for God, people might be cut-throats.

Levi-Yitskhok. Like wild beasts.

Avrom-Yankev. Have you ever seen a wolf?

Levi-Yitskhok. It is written: "A wolf devours."

Avrom-Yankev. Last year a wolf mangled one of our horses.

Levi-Yitskhok. Really, a horse!

Avrom-Yankev. He was in the pasture, hobbled. It happened at night. The next morning we found him dead. His throat was ripped open. They recognized the wolf's teethmarks.

Levi-Yitskhok. There, you see?

Avrom-Yankev. Wolves don't know there is a God. Man is really a clever creature.

Levi-Yitskhok. It is written: God created man in His own image. God gave man something of His own greatness.

Avrom-Yankev. But a man couldn't create the world.

Levi-Yitskhok. But a man can destroy a world.

Avrom-Yankev. Really!

Levi-Yitskhok. You know, Avrom-Yankev, I may be leaving here.

Avrom-Yankev. Don't you like it here?

Levi-Yitskhok. What good is it? I have no books here. I lack everything I need. I need the voices of the Torah scholars in the synagogue at daybreak. I need the pure countenances of the pious Jews because of whose merit the world continues to exist.

Avrom-Yankev. I want so much to go with you. I'll get up at dawn to study.

Levi-Yitskhok. You just said you were drawn to the fields.

Avrom-Yankev. That's true. But the world seems an odd place. It sometimes happens that a stranger passes through here, and he looks so different. Last year a rabbi passed through. He had such a long white beard! I've never seen Jews like that in the country. A synagogue full of Jews like that must be really beautiful to see.

Levi-Yitskhok. Of course it's beautiful.

Avrom-Yankev. Teach me to write my name.

Levi-Yitskhok. You must learn the alphabet first.

Avrom-Yankev. I'll bring back a board and a piece of chalk and you'll show me how. (*Runs out.*)

(LEVI-YITSKHOK *gazes through the window as though he noticed someone. He hurries back to the table and buries himself in a book.*)

TSINE (*enters. Barefoot. Her dress hitched up at the side. She straightens it as she comes in. Busies herself making a fire in the oven. She addresses him*). My mother wants to know whether you want anything to eat.

LEVI-YITSKHOK. I'm all right as I am.

TSINE. Do you intend to fast?

LEVI-YITSKHOK. A person should not get too accustomed to food.

TSINE. If you ate as much as I do, you would have more strength.

LEVI-YITSKHOK. Why does anyone need strength?

TSINE. It's bad if you're not strong. You couldn't wrestle with Hersh-Ber.

LEVI-YITSKHOK. A Jew ought not to wrestle.

TSINE. Why not? A Jew should be as strong as the peasants. (*She tries to break a branch over her knee, but she cannot. She turns to him.*) If it's too long, it knocks the soot from the chimney. Maybe you can break it.

LEVI-YITSKHOK. Why break it over your knee, if you can do it with an axe?

TSINE. If you do everything as it should be done . . . I'm not a city girl.

LEVI-YITSKHOK. A person should do things right in the country too.

TSINE (*a little embarrassed*). My mother does say that I'm a little wild. Stere is really better than I am.

LEVI-YITSKHOK. Who?

TSINE. Stere. Elkone's girl. She told me she spoke with you. My brother wants her for his bride.

LEVI-YITSKHOK. Which brother?

TSINE. The older one. Hersh-Ber.

LEVI-YITSKHOK. Have the parents reached an agreement?

TSINE. Why, do you like her?

LEVI-YITSKHOK. What?

TSINE. Do you like Stere?

LEVI-YITSKHOK. It's not proper to ask such questions.

TSINE. Why isn't it proper? I don't understand why it's not proper.

LEVI-YITSKHOK. Actually, I'm thinking of leaving.

TSINE. Don't you like it here?

LEVI-YITSKHOK. I like it very much, but my staying here is of no use. The children don't want to learn.

TSINE. Teach me. I'll study like a boy.

LEVI-YITSKHOK. It's not right. Wives are not obliged to study. Their husbands study for both.

TSINE. Huh?

LEVI-YITSKHOK. What?

TSINE. I'll tell you what, teach me secretly. Of course. No one needs to know. You'll see; it will work out fine.

LEVI-YITSKHOK. It isn't right.

TSINE. Why isn't it right? Is it right for my brother and Stere?

LEVI-YITSKHOK. Why, is he teaching her?

TSINE. No. They love each other. They love each other very much. It's very nice when people are in love. . . . No one will know that you're teaching me. We can hide in the fields or even in the attic.

LEVI-YITSKHOK. I may even leave here today.

TSINE. I won't let you.

LEVI-YITSKHOK. I can't be kept here by force.

TSINE. Please tell me why you're not satisfied here. Maybe your bed isn't comfortable? Tell me, is it? I can let you have mine instead. Tell me, why do you want to leave us?

LEVI-YITSKHOK. I'll tell that to your father. It was he who asked me to stay.

TSINE. But I beg you not to go away. I beg you very much . . .

LEVI-YITSKHOK. I'm not teaching you, so what difference could it make?

TSINE. Oh, if I could only make it so that you would be happy here! You know what? After you eat, come out to the meadow with me and I'll show you how I sweep the hay together. I carry such a big sheaf of hay on my head that only my legs show. Tell me, what's your favorite food? (LEVI-YITSKHOK *smiles in confusion.*) Pretend that you are my husband and I am your wife and I love you very much and I want you to tell me what you like to eat.

LEVI-YITSKHOK. But it's not so.

TSINE. What do you mean, "not so"? Just imagine that we're a married couple; I'm standing at the stove, and I want to know what my husband likes. Oh, that's so beautiful . . . Oh, I'm talking foolishness. I see my talk embarrasses you. Stay here, please.

AVROM-YANKEV (*enters*). Here's a board and some chalk. Let the Rebbe teach me how to write my name.

TSINE. Teach me too, Rebbe. Write my name. I want to see what my name looks like in writing.

(LEVI-YITSKHOK *writes in large letters* "Avrom-Yankev.")

TSINE. Is my name as long as that?

LEVI-YITSKHOK. That spells "Avrom-Yankev."

TSINE. Please, write my name—Tsine.

(LEVI-YITSKHOK *writes.*)

TSINE. Glory be! Let me erase it and you write it again.

AVROM-YANKEV. You're a nut.

TSINE. Write it, please.

(LEVI-YITSKHOK *writes.*)

TSINE (*erases it again*). Now do it again. I love to watch you write.

LEVI-YITSKHOK. You're being silly.

TSINE. I can see you won't leave. I . . .

ELKONE (*enters*). God bless you, Rebbe. I've come to take you to my place.

TSINE. Why?

ELKONE. That's my business.

LEVI-YITSKHOK. I'm leaving the countryside.

ELKONE. My children have nothing to do. I can't let you leave.

LEVI-YITSKHOK. They don't obey their elders.

ELKONE. I'll stand by and I'll let them have it with my whip if they don't obey. . . . What can I do? There's so much work and there is no time even to whip a child.

LEVI-YITSKHOK. There is no need to whip children.

ELKONE. Now, there I disagree with you. I was whipped too; if I hadn't been, there would have been trouble.

(TSINE *whispers something to* AVROM-YANKEV. *He leaves quietly. She is very uneasy as she listens to the conversation.*)

LEVI-YITSKHOK. You need an older person for the children. Then they would have more respect for him.

ELKONE. But, bless you, I like you. As my wife says, why should I fool myself? Our farm folk are plain people but they're good Jews. You can find a bride here—a fine Jewish girl. Ha-ha-ha, no one gets lost in the country. Say, what's that on the board? You're teaching the lad to write? Wrote it himself, did he? (*Examines the board.*) Too bad I don't have my glasses with me.

(TSINE *looks angrily at him from the side.*)

ELKONE. Splendid letters. The writing is so clear.

(DOVID-NOYAKH *enters.*)

TSINE. Father, you know that. . . .

ELKONE. God bless you, Dovid-Noyakh. I've come to take our guest away from here.

DOVID-NOYAKH. My boy just told me. What for?

ELKONE. He certainly ran to tell you fast enough.

DOVID-NOYAKH. What's wrong with my place? Is his bed too hard? Do we stint on his food? And what I promised to do, I'll do; trust me. When the holidays come—what for?

ELKONE. But you don't understand what we're talking about. I say it's better for him to be at my place.

DOVID-NOYAKH. That's what I mean—I don't want to let him go.

ELKONE. My children are like the peasant boys, and if the teacher is around, they'll have more respect.

DOVID-NOYAKH. What do you mean "respect"? How can they not have respect?

(AVROM-YANKEV *enters.*)

DOVID-NOYAKH. You there, tell me. Is it on account of you that our guest is leaving! I'll take a stick and break your bones!

LEVI-YITSKHOK. No, not on account of him. If only all children were like him!

ROKHEL (*enters*). Good heavens, is the Rebbe really leaving?

DOVID-NOYAKH. Don't you hear—Elkone wants to take him to his place.

ROKHEL. You must not do such a thing.

ELKONE. Let's ask the guest: What do you say, Rebbe?

LEVI-YITSKHOK. I think it would be wiser for me to go where I should have gone in the first place. I've been here a month already, maybe even more than a month—enough.

ROKHEL. Why? What for?

LEVI-YITSKHOK. I'll send you an older man.

DOVID-NOYAKH. It's you we want. You're the talk of the whole countryside.

ELKONE. That's what I say, too.

ROKHEL. Go over to him, Avrom-Yankev. Ask the Rebbe to stay with us.

DOVID-NOYAKH. Bah, nonsense. Let things be. Don't shame us country people.

ROKHEL. Unfortunately, in the country you forget God and his commandments. I was in seventh heaven that in my very house there was a—who knows what.

DOVID-NOYAKH. You see! You didn't feed him well and now he's leaving.

ROKHEL. What are you talking about? Did I serve myself before him? Or the children?

ELKONE. That's what I say. Let him come to my place if he doesn't like it here.

DOVID-NOYAKH. You're doing wrong, Elkone.

ROKHEL. If Elkone wants to quarrel with us—let him.

LEVI-YITSKHOK. Don't quarrel over me, good people, you have denied me nothing. I live here only too well. I have food and drink without earning them. I don't want that.

DOVID-NOYAKH. Let things remain as they are. You're shaming us country people. If I lived in town, I could occasionally have the honor of receiving a scholar in my home for a while. I would go to the synagogue and look for one, so help me. In the country, if a Jew wants to be a Jew, he can't. I tried to stuff something into my older one's head. It didn't work.

ELKONE. His mind is on horses, fodder, potatoes.

ROKHEL. Why now? Maybe wait for the holidays. . . .

ELKONE. I have no time—what's the answer?

DOVID-NOYAKH. It's wrong to dismiss country people so lightly. Why don't you take a stroll in the meadow? See what country people do. They don't sit around doing nothing. They may not study Torah, but they're not idle. Go on, Avrom-Yankev. Take the Rebbe out to the meadow.

ROKHEL. Go, child.

AVROM-YANKEV. Will you come, Rebbe?

LEVI-YITSKHOK. We can stroll a little. (*Both leave.*)

ROKHEL (*shouting after them*). Show him, child, how beautiful the corn is when it grows.

ELKONE. Why are you so quiet, Tsine? Have you seen Stere?

TSINE. No.

ELKONE. They're both fine baggages.

TSINE. As long as my mother likes me.

ELKONE. You hear, Dovid-Noyakh, how it's learning to talk back to its elders? If Stere answered me that way, she'd catch her share from me. Modern children. . . . Come, Dovid-Noyakh.

(TSINE *looks out the window, her face turned away from her mother, and wipes her tears.*)

ROKHEL. I thought he liked it here. Turns out. . . . Dear me, why are you crying? (TSINE *sobs.*) Why are you crying, silly? Don't pay any attention to what Elkone says. It's a good thing I controlled myself. He doesn't seem to be the same Elkone lately. He's become so envious. I can still wish to be as well off as he is.

(TSINE *is seated at the window, her head bent, wiping her tears.*)

ROKHEL. I really don't understand why you're crying. Look at her, will you? What's wrong?

TSINE. Didn't you hear what Elkone said?

ROKHEL. Well, where in the world were you? Don't you have a mouth? You could have given him an answer that he would remember.

TSINE. Don't let him go away.

ROKHEL. Is that a reason to cry? I'm sorry for Avrom-Yankev's sake.

TSINE (*hides her face in her mother's lap*). I want him to stay with us. Mama, he's such a fine person.

ROKHEL. You were the one that laughed at him.

TSINE. I didn't understand.

ROKHEL. Well, what can I do?

TSINE. But you don't understand, Mama.

ROKHEL. What is there to understand?

TSINE. When he talks, I could die.

ROKHEL. Is that what you mean, child?

TSINE. I'm not a child any longer. I understand everything. I have never seen such a person.

ROKHEL. I'm afraid to think so high.

TSINE. Then what can we do? What can we do?

ROKHEL. Some day he will be a rabbi somewhere. And what do the likes of us amount to in the world?

TSINE. But why can't I be his wife?

ROKHEL. What?

TSINE. I may die if he leaves this house.

ROKHEL. Child, my heart trembles. Alas, I hear what you're saying.

TSINE. As I not good enough to have such a husband?

ROKHEL. No, that's not it. But after all, what are country people?

TSINE. Well, what if I am a country girl? I'll do as I'm told. If I'm taught to be strictly observant, I will be.

ROKHEL. In town a Jewish girl knows how to pray, but here. . . .

TSINE. Then I'll know, too. I wanted him to talk to me, so I picked some currants, but I was too ashamed to give them to him. I asked him what he liked so I could cook it for him.

ROKHEL. Oh, so that's it! That's where the trouble lies. Now I understand why he wants to leave us. What ever made you do that? And you went to him barefoot, did you?

TSINE. What should I do? What can I do? Why can't I be to him as Stere is to Hersh-Ber?

ROKHEL. That's not the way among Jews. I won't sleep nights since you told me. I didn't even see your father till just before the wedding.

(TSINE *sobs, wiping her tears.*)

ROKHEL. Heaven help me, you've made me dizzy. Maybe I should tell your father. Maybe he will know how to talk to him.

TSINE. No, not Father. I'm afraid for him to know. I couldn't stand it if he went away.

ROKHEL. First of all, child, you shouldn't walk around barefoot when he's around. It's not proper to do a thing like that.

TSINE. Maybe I should change my dress?

ROKHEL. I don't know. Maybe you should.

TSINE (*gaily*). Now I know what to do. I know. . . .

ROKHEL. What's the matter with you? Why the celebration all of a sudden?

TSINE. Now I know exactly what to do.

ROKHEL. If you act like a hussy, he won't even want to look at you.

TSINE. Go, Mama; see where everybody is. I'll be able to cook dinner myself.

ROKHEL. Should I say anything to your father?

TSINE. No, Mama, please don't.

(ROKHEL *wipes away a tear. Goes over to* TSINE, *kisses her, and blows over her three times. She leaves.*)

(TSINE *washes her face and rebraids her hair. She puts a kerchief on her head so that her hair does not show and looks at her reflection in the water bucket. She removes the kerchief and looks again. She throws her braids over her shoulders and looks again. She rebraids her hair into a single braid and puts it up into a bun. Finally she lets the braid hang down her back. She puts on shoes and stockings. She wipes her tears.*)

HERSH-BER (*comes in*). Food ready?

TSINE. It will be ready soon.

HERSH-BER. I have no time to wait.

TSINE. What are you doing?

HERSH-BER. I've got plenty to do. You don't think I'm loafing, do you?

TSINE. You're a bad brother.

HERSH-BER. Then I'll be back later.

TSINE. I really have something to tell you.

HERSH-BER. I know your stories.

TSINE. No you don't. You wait and see. You'll beg me to tell you.

HERSH-BER. Don't tell, if you don't want to. Who cares?

TSINE. You didn't see Stere yesterday, did you?

HERSH-BER. Did you see her?

TSINE. I spoke to her.

HERSH-BER. Did she say anything?

TSINE (*puts her arms around his neck and looks into his eyes*). She weeps; she wails. She can't live without you.

HERSH-BER. Ha-ha, what a girl!

TSINE. She says she may go out of her mind.

HERSH-BER. Now you're lying. How could you have seen her yesterday?

TSINE. Of course I saw her. I was there.

HERSH-BER. You're lying. She asked me last night why you're giving her the cold shoulder.

TSINE. I really didn't talk with her.

HERSH-BER. Ha-ha, see? You're just trying to pull the wool over my eyes.

TSINE. Go ahead and marry Stere. You'll be happy.

HERSH-BER. Are you trying to be a matchmaker? You won't get a thing out of it.

TSINE. You're my brother, aren't you?

HERSH-BER. Then go ahead and talk to her. Why talk to me?

TSINE. She's pining away for you.

HERSH-BER. We should have been married already. But she suddenly became huffy.

TSINE. Her father must have mixed in.

HERSH-BER. Say, how do you know?

TSINE. I know, all right.

HERSH-BER. How come you're talking like this today? Did you make up something with Stere? Tell me. You just get in my way, and I tell you, you'll get what's coming to you.

TSINE. You ninny, how you talk! You're my brother; would I try to hurt you?

HERSH-BER. I know you wouldn't hurt me. That's why I'm asking you why she's so huffy. I said to her, after haying we'll ride into town and I'll buy her some cloth for a dress. Well, she started to stare at me as though she didn't know who I was. And you say you talked to her.

TSINE. I wanted you to feel good.

HERSH-BER. Who cares! Does she think I'm really going to run after her? There are plenty of girls around here.

TSINE. But a fine housekeeper like Stere. . . .

HERSH-BER. Big deal!

TSINE. Have you ever seen her wash laundry? When she beats the wash down by the river, you can hear her all the way up here. It's only because she's ashamed to show it now, but when she's your wife, you'll really find out how much she loves you. She's probably twice as strong as I am. Have you seen her hands? They're probably twice as big as mine.

HERSH-BER. If you're such a good sister, why don't you talk to her?

TSINE. I should talk to her? Shame on you! Why do you hang around the house every evening? Can't you eat your dinner and go over there? Why should she have to sit around by herself on pins and needles, waiting and then nothing happens?

HERSH-BER. Say, how do you know so much?

TSINE. How do I know? I figured it out.

HERSH-BER. You're a fine friend. I'll tell her what you told me to do.

TSINE. You should be ashamed to tell her anything like that. Do you want her to know that I told you to go to her?

HERSH-BER. She's quite a girl, I know that.

TSINE. Make up with her to meet you tonight in our hay field.

HERSH-BER. Will you come too?

TSINE. What do you need me for?

HERSH-BER. She won't want to come if you're not there.

TSINE. Then tell her I'll be there too.

HERSH-BER. But will you?

TSINE. Maybe I won't be there. You can work everything out with her. And you can get married this winter.

HERSH-BER. As I live and breathe, you're a genius! And I thought you were trying to get in my way. Just for that, when I go to the fair, I'll bring back some beads for you.

TSINE. You better bring them for her.

HERSH-BER. I've got time with her. Why bring anything for no good reason? When there's a reason, I'll bring something.

TSINE. Tell her not to listen to her father if he mixes in.

HERSH-BER. Ha-ha, you're really teaching me how to act!

TSINE. You tell her to come out to our hay field. Say, there she is.

STERE (*comes in*). Bless you all. Is my father here?

TSINE. He was here and he left.

STERE. Long ago?

TSINE. Do you really need him so badly?

STERE. I saw Avrom-Yankev strolling with the Rebbe in the meadow.

TSINE. Do you like him?

STERE. I didn't look at him.

TSINE. Swear.

HERSH-BER. Ho, ho! Look how red she got! (*He catches her in his arms. She struggles free.*)

TSINE. Let me; I'll catch her.

STERE (*dodges away*). Why do you want to catch me?

TSINE. Come here, Hersh-Ber. Don't let her get away!

STERE. We'll see about that. (*She struggles loose and, with a ringing laugh, runs out of the house.*)

TSINE. You're a ninny. Go out and tell her to meet you in the hay.

HERSH-BER. I don't need her. She's ill-natured. I tell you, she's ill-natured. Give me something to eat; that'll be the best thing.

(DOVID-NOYAKH *and* ROKHEL *enter.*)

TSINE. Dinner's ready.

DOVID-NOYAKH. He really is no fool.

TSINE. Who do you mean, Papa?

ROKHEL. He means Elkone.

TSINE. What's the matter, Mama? Tell me.

ROKHEL. Oh, leave me alone. What did the girl want here?

TSINE. She came to look for her father.

DOVID-NOYAKH. You could have told her he went home. Such a thing. . . . You see, that's not right. I thought he was a good friend of mine.

ROKHEL. He's smarter than you are.

TSINE. What is it, Mama? What are you talking about?

ROKHEL. It's just as well you don't know.

DOVID-NOYAKH. Make up a new bed for him tonight. Stuff his mattress with fresh hay. Let him have a soft bed to sleep in.

TSINE. Maybe he should take my bed?

DOVID-NOYAKH. That's not a bad idea. Just stuff it with fresh hay.

TSINE. Where will I sleep? Maybe I'll go back to sleeping with Mama.

HERSH-BER. Look at the big fuss they're making over him.

DOVID-NOYAKH. You've got a head like a peasant's and don't realize what an honor we have.

HERSH-BER. What are you cooking?

TSINE. Buckwheat groats and milk.

DOVID-NOYAKH. Rokhel, go see whether there is enough milk in the pot.

TSINE. Enough, enough. I can do it myself.

ROKHEL. You put your shoes on? You did well, child.

TSINE. I'll serve the food.

(LEVI-YITSKHOK *and* AVROM-YANKEV *enter.*)

ROKHEL. It's time to wash up. (*She sets the table. She sets it with dark bread and white bread.*)

AVROM-YANKEV. The Rebbe says he likes it here.

ROKHEL. Thank the Lord.

LEVI-YITSKHOK. Since you're so eager, I'll stay till after the holidays.

DOVID-NOYAKH. You won't regret it. (*They all wash; the men take their places at the table, say the blessing over a piece of bread.*)

(ROKHEL *pours each one a portion of groats in an earthenware bowl.* TSINE *serves with great eagerness.*)

HERSH-BER. We're sitting at the table as we do on the Sabbath.

ROKHEL. Praised be the Lord above.

(*She pours a bowl for* LEVI-YITSKHOK. *Just as* TSINE *is about half-way over, she motions her back and adds a little more milk to the bowl.* TSINE, *as she holds the bowl, bends over and kisses her mother. Then she walks carefully and reverently to the table.*)

ACT III

(In front of DOVID-NOYAKH'S *house. It is late summer. Evening.* LEVI-YITSKHOK'S *voice is heard from inside the house. He is studying.)*

*(*TSINE *seated in front of the door churning butter. Every now and then she pauses and listens to the chanting from the house. She reminds herself of something and runs off into the garden.* LEVI-YITSKHOK *comes out. Examines the butter churn. Tries to work the rod. He notices the globules of butter stuck to the rod. From the garden* TSINE'S *anxious outcry is heard, followed by a noise among the branches of a tree. He stops for a moment, frightened. He takes several steps toward the garden, climbs quickly over the fence but soon returns and hurries back into the house.* TSINE *enters. She is pale and holds her side. She climbs over the fence and approaches her previous place near the door. She examines a bleeding scratch on her arm.)*

LEVI-YITSKHOK *(comes out, carrying a dipper of water).* Here's a drink of water. Did you hurt yourself?

*(*TSINE *takes the dipper from his hand and drinks.)*

LEVI-YITSKHOK. You gave me a start.

TSINE. I fell down from the top of the tree.

LEVI-YITSKHOK. You should thank the Lord.

TSINE. I got frightened and I fell.

LEVI-YITSKHOK. There's blood on your hand.

TSINE. My heart is really pounding.

LEVI-YITSKHOK. Did you really have to go climbing trees?

TSINE. I heard you studying and I went to pick some apples for you.

LEVI-YITSKHOK. For whom?

TSINE. For you. Do you think I didn't pick any? *(Takes two red apples out of her apron pocket.)* You see, as red as the apples for Simchas Torah. It was on account of you that I fell out of the tree. I could have gotten killed.

LEVI-YITSKHOK. God forbid.

TSINE. Why should you care if I get killed?

LEVI-YITSKHOK. I have a Jewish heart, don't I?

TSINE. Take the two apples.

147

LEVI-YITSKHOK. To recite the blessing just before Rosh Hashonna—it's not proper.

TSINE. What if you want an apple and can't resist?

LEVI-YITSKHOK. One must be able to conquer the *yetser hara*, the inclination to do wrong.

TSINE. But the apples grow summertime. How can one resist so long? I eat about ten apples every day, and nothing happens. I didn't even know you weren't allowed to eat them.

LEVI-YITSKHOK. Well, I just told you that you're not allowed to.

TSINE. Who is the yetser hara?

LEVI-YITSKHOK. He lurks within people. You see how he just sent you to climb the tall tree for apples, and you were quickly punished.

TSINE. Oh, you don't know why I fell out of the tree.

LEVI-YITSKHOK. What makes you think I don't know?

TSINE. You don't know. You really don't know at all. If you only knew how I've become a new Tsine. . . . Well, why did I fall out of the tree?

LEVI-YITSKHOK. Certainly not on purpose. Nobody cuts his hand up on purpose.

TSINE. I want to show you something. (*She runs into the house.*)

(LEVI-YITSKHOK *examines the two apples that are lying on the ground near him. He smells them.* TSINE *comes out. She brings a board with letters written in chalk.*)

LEVI-YITSKHOK. What's that?

TSINE. Read what's written here.

LEVI-YITSKHOK. But it's not Avrom-Yankev's handwriting.

TSINE. It's mine.

LEVI-YITSKHOK (*looks at the letters with surprise. He reads*). "Tsine, daughter of Reb Noyakh."

TSINE. Well, who wrote it?

LEVI-YITSKHOK. Not Avrom-Yankev.

TSINE. Erase it.

LEVI-YITSKHOK. Why do you want me to do that? It's not good to erase a name.

TSINE. Please erase it. Wipe it off, like this. . . .

LEVI-YITSKHOK. He—he—so childish. Well, there, I've erased it.

TSINE. Now close your eyes.

(LEVI-YITSKHOK *does so.* TSINE *takes a piece of chalk out of her pocket and writes.*)

LEVI-YITSKHOK. Now?

TSINE. Keep them closed just a little longer. There we are. Now, what does it say?

LEVI-YITSKHOK. My name . . . "Levi-Yitskhok" . . . Who wrote it?

TSINE. I did.

LEVI-YITSKHOK. That's impossible.

TSINE. It certainly is possible.

LEVI-YITSKHOK. I'll erase it and you write it again.

TSINE. Then close your eyes again.

(LEVI-YITSKHOK *closes his eyes.* TSINE *writes his name again in large letters, and as he stands there with his eyes shut, she steals close to him and gives him a kiss. Then she runs into the house.* LEVI-YITSKHOK *is surprised by what has happened. He starts to go into the house but at the door he realizes that he should not go in. He takes the board, wipes his name off, and throws it away. He sits down on the same bench where she sat before. He sits thoughtfully with his head bent.*)

ELKONE (*enters*). God bless you, Rebbe. Alone, are you?

(LEVI-YITSKHOK *looks at him, very upset.*)

ELKONE. What's this? Have you been put to work churning butter? That's a fine state of affairs.

(LEVI-YITSKHOK *looks at him uncomprehending.*)

ELKONE. Are you churning butter?

LEVI-YITSKHOK. There's no reason why I can't churn butter too. What's so remarkable?

ELKONE. I came to ask you to resolve a problem of religious procedure.

LEVI-YITSKHOK. I have no authority to deal with such problems.

ELKONE. What's the difference. As long as we know. Besides, this sort of question is one you can answer for me.

LEVI-YITSKHOK. For instance?

ELKONE. My older daughter took something into her head, and nothing helps.

LEVI-YITSKHOK. Maybe she's right.

ELKONE. What do you mean, a child being right if her father says no?

LEVI-YITSKHOK. It sometimes happens that an older person is wrong, too.

ELKONE. But supposing one is impudent enough to defy a father? That's what I'm asking.

LEVI-YITSKHOK. Sometimes parents should hear what an older child has to say.

ELKONE. No, there I disagree with you. The Torah says that one should honor one's parents. It does say so, doesn't it?

LEVI-YITSKHOK. Who doesn't know that?

ELKONE. That's why I say, a girl ought to obey her father. Say, isn't Dovid-Noyakh here?

LEVI-YITSKHOK. No, he's not.

ELKONE. I can't stand an ignoramus. What's the use of kidding myself? I may not be educated myself, but I can still tell the difference between a man and a swine.

LEVI-YITSKHOK. One must not talk that way about a Jew.

ELKONE. Why be ashamed to say so? Dovid-Noyakh is a nobody and his son is a nobody.

LEVI-YITSKHOK. They're fine people. I have nothing against them.

ELKONE. It's you that I'm really talking about. They don't show you enough respect. This is no way to treat a stranger.

LEVI-YITSKHOK. They certainly don't treat me with disrespect.

ELKONE. The boy doesn't really take after him, that's true. I mean Avrom-Yankev. But he himself is a nobody. Lets his daughter run wild. I wouldn't let her run around like a hussy.

LEVI-YITSKHOK. That's not my business. That's gossip.

ELKONE. You may be learned and pious, but you don't see what they're doing with you. •

LEVI-YITSKHOK. What is there to see? They're Jews like any other Jews.

ELKONE. Well, what am I to do if my daughter latches on to that oaf of a son of his? If I beat her, she talks back to me. That's what I came to talk to you about.

LEVI-YITSKHOK. He's a decent fellow. He'll be a pious Jew.

ELKONE. Ha-ha, I really wanted you to stay at my house. They'd have looked after you better at my place. Maybe the children would have learned something. Well, they got to you first. That's luck.

LEVI-YITSKHOK. You're angry, Reb Elkone, and that's why you're saying things you'll regret. You're a fine man. Dovid-Noyakh wishes you no ill; and the children get along well together. Why do you do such a thing?

ELKONE. Perhaps you're right. A Jew should not act this way. But what can I do? My heart aches. And just because I am an ignoramus. My sons—they'll be nobodies. Well, then, why shouldn't I try to get for my daughter someone, an outsider, who can bring honor to a house? There are the holidays. There is the Sabbath. And especially when you come into town for

...e High Holy Days. What's the use of talking? I wouldn't ...re about the cost—down to my last shirt.

LEVI-YITSKHOK. Well, what's the problem? All you need to do ... ride into town and make inquiries. There are many fine ...oung scholars in town.

ELKONE. Who knows how? Who can turn the trick? Who even ...ought of it? My eyes were just recently opened.

LEVI-YITSKHOK. I don't know what you mean.

ELKONE. You don't follow me? I say, you be my son-in-law. ...ly Stere, the older one; with a good heart. I wanted to hit ...er today, but I felt sorry for her. It isn't even my idea; it's my ...ife. She sent me over here. Why deny it, ha-ha. If you tell ...e where your parents live, I wouldn't mind hitching up and ...king a ride over to see them. Maybe you can tell me where ...ey live?

LEVI-YITSKHOK. They're dead.

ELKONE. Really?

LEVI-YITSKHOK. Died long ago.

ELKONE. An orphan! Isn't that something! It would be a pity ... I let you get away.

DOVID-NOYAKH (*enters*). God bless you, Elkone. What brings ...ou here at this hour?

ELKONE. Nothing much. Just chatting.

DOVID-NOYAKH. Who's churning the butter? My wife is at ...ome, I see.

ELKONE. I thought you people had given the Rebbe the honor ...f churning the butter.

DOVID-NOYAKH. Ha, ha. My wife still knows how to treat ...omeone with respect.

(LEVI-YITSKHOK *goes off behind the house.*)

DOVID-NOYAKH. Isn't there anyone in the house? Let me have ... look. (*He looks through the window*).

ELKONE. I think your girl is inside.

DOVID-NOYAKH. Come on in. Why stand outside?

ELKONE. I'll be getting ready to leave.

DOVID-NOYAKH. Where were you going, anyway?

ELKONE. I was coming here. I wanted to talk to the teacher.

DOVID-NOYAKH. What's the trouble? Don't the children listen ...o him?

ELKONE. I had something else in mind. You know, he's a full ...rphan. Now you tell me, who needs parents?

DOVID-NOYAKH. In town, everything is possible.

ELKONE. He might get the idea that I was trying to malign ...ou.

DOVID-NOYAKH. What might give him that idea?

ELKONE. Where did he go to? He's a big fool. I was talkin
with him, and he probably misunderstood me.

ROKHEL (*enters*). A guest. It's nearly a week since we saw
you last. How is Gittl?

ELKONE. She's a little under the weather.

ROKHEL. Does she still have pains in her side? She ought t
see someone in town. She works too hard.

(GITTL *enters*.)

ROKHEL. Ah, we have a guest. We were just talking about yot

GITTL. As my mother always says, if God's in His heaven
why should I worry. Did my daughter give me a hard time!

ROKHEL. Nothing wrong, heaven forbid.

GITTL. Nothing wrong, you say.

ELKONE. Too bad I wasn't home. She'd have caught it from
me.

ROKHEL. She's as fine a child as anyone would want.

GITTL. I know you like her.

ROKHEL. Of course I like her. If Tsine had at least three
sisters like Stere, what more could I ask for?

GITTL. You hear, Elkone?

DOVID-NOYAKH. A real handy girl; what's there to complain
about? She's a year younger than Tsine and, bless her, she'
twice as big.

GITTL (*to* ELKONE). Why are you afraid to talk? I don't know
what there is to be afraid of. I left the house to come over here
because I don't want it to drag out.

ROKHEL. Gittl, I really don't understand what you're talking about.

GITTL. I want Hersh-Ber to stop annoying her.

DOVID-NOYAKH. What do you mean *annoying* her? What have
you got against him anyway—I mean Hersh-Ber?

ELKONE. I've got nothing against him. To you, he's your son
You like him. I don't.

ROKHEL. And I don't care if you don't like him. Did you ever

GITTL. Then let him stop putting ideas into Stere's head.

DOVID-NOYAKH. What's the matter, Elkone? Is it beneath yot
to be related to me?

ELKONE. It's beneath me for your son to be my son-in-law

DOVID-NOYAKH. Then why come to tell me about it? I don'
know a thing. You can keep Hersh-Ber out of your house. It'
your business.

ROKHEL. I don't even see that he's running after her. I don'
know what you have against my child.

ELKONE. I'll speak plainly.

GITTL. What have you got to be ashamed of?

ELKONE. I want the young stranger, the children's teacher. Y'understand, he's right for Stere.

GITTL. And you packed him off to your house.

ELKONE. Your daughter is spoiling him

DOVID-NOYAKH. What do you mean?

ELKONE. I found him sitting outside.

ROKHEL. What outside? When outside? Whatever I dreamt this night and the other night. . . . What do you want here? Why did you come here to malign my children?

DOVID-NOYAKH. Take it easy. Don't shout. We can discuss it calmly, like reasonable people. I still don't understand the whole thing. He's talking about Hersh-Ber, I thought, not about the girl. What in the world can he have against her?

ROKHEL. Don't you hear what they're saying? I have a good mind to ask. . . . Tsinele? Come on out here for a minute!

(TSINE *comes out, a little confused.*)

ELKONE. Aw, what are you making a fuss about? Go back into the house, Tsine. It won't do you a bit of harm even if I did, heaven forbid, say something against you. Your mother won't put up with it.

TSINE. What do you want me for?

ROKHEL. Where were you when Elkone arrived?

TSINE. In the house.

ROKHEL. I wouldn't have believed it of you, Elkone.

GITTL. So what? Who cares?

DOVID-NOYAKH. But what is there to quarrel about? I say, let's ask the children.

ELKONE. I have nothing to ask anybody. My daughter will do as I say.

DOVID-NOYAKH. Have it your own way.

ROKHEL. Go, child, go into the house.

TSINE. What did you want me for?

GITTL. Tell me, Tsine, what does Stere talk to you about?

TSINE. She talks to me about—she talks to me about everything. How can I keep track?

ELKONE. Do you hear, my wife, how clever some people are? That's the one that's misleading my little one. I'll teach her to come here. I'm going home and I'll give her a piece of my mind. (*Starts off.*)

DOVID-NOYAKH. That's not right, Elkone. I thought you were a better father. Where did he run off to?

TSINE. Do go home, Gittl. Don't let him do anything to her, because she hasn't done anything wrong.

GITTL. I'd rather not say anything to you, Tsinele, since your mother is present, but if she weren't. . . .

ROKHEL. Feel free to leave any time. I didn't send for you. I really thought you were our good friends. Come inside, Dovid-Noyakh; I have nothing to say to her. (*Both go into the house.*)

GITTL. Listen to me, Tsine. Your mother thinks that I wish her ill. I'm not an enemy of yours. I only want to tell you, without your mother's hearing it, that I know everything you spoke about to Stere.

TSINE. I'm not afraid. I said nothing to be afraid about.

GITTL. Here comes Hersh-Ber. I want to talk to him plainly.

HERSH-BER (*enters*). What's Elkone mad about? I called him, but he wouldn't turn around.

GITTL. He knows why he's angry.

HERSH-BER. What are you in a huff about? I didn't throw any rocks into your garden.

GITTL. Let me tell you, you certainly are throwing rocks.

HERSH-BER. What are you making a fuss about? Let me ask you, have you got a better husband for Stere? Why did you start making trouble? What do you want me to do, pay you for her? I love Stere and Stere loves me. So why are you mixing in, tell me?

GITTL. So that's how it is? Has it gone that far?

TSINE. Yes, of course.

GITTL. Look at them, will you! What sort of plague is this?

HERSH-BER. If you don't want to, that's all right with me too. Whatever you say. And tell Elkone that if he raises a hand to her, I'll show him how to be a father.

GITTL. Listen to him! Listen to him, will you!

HERSH-BER. Then don't listen if you don't want to. Come on inside, Tsine. (*He goes inside.*)

GITTL. I can't believe my ears! I must tell this to Elkone. (*She leaves.*)

(AVROM-YANKEV *enters.*)

TSINE. Good thing you came, Avrom-Yankev. I've been looking for you everywhere. Here's a kiss and don't tell the Rebbe that you taught me to write his name and my name.

AVROM-YANKEV. What? What did you say?

TSINE. Please, here's another kiss; all right? Here he comes. Don't tell him anything. (*She runs into the house.*)

LEVI-YITSKHOK (*enters*). Where have you been, Avrom-Yankev?

AVROM-YANKEV. I went to check whether the horse didn't wander off into the mire.

LEVI-YITSKHOK. Why did your sister learn to write my name?

AVROM-YANKEV. Ha-ha—she told me she envied my studying with you. She says she wants to study, too.

LEVI-YITSKHOK. So you taught her, it seems.

AVROM-YANKEV. Is it forbidden? She wanted me to teach her how to say the prayers, but I was afraid. Maybe you're not allowed to.

LEVI-YITSKHOK. Women are allowed to study the prayers. Women have to know how to pray, too.

AVROM-YANKEV. I'll go tell her.

LEVI-YITSKHOK. Wait a bit.

AVROM-YANKEV. She'll be very happy. (*Runs into the house.*)

HERSH-BER (*comes out*). Good you're here, Rebbe. I want to ask you something. Don't take offense.

LEVI-YITSKHOK. Of course.

HERSH-BER. You know the Torah; tell me, what does the law say, if I've picked a wife for myself and her parents get ideas and refuse?

LEVI-YITSKHOK. What do you mean, they refuse? There must be a reason.

HERSH-BER. They don't want to, that's all. What can you do?

LEVI-YITSKHOK. You have to do things so that they are pleased.

HERSH-BER. They've gone daffy and there's nothing you can do.

LEVI-YITSKHOK. Jews can talk things over. There's probably a reason for their actions.

HERSH-BER. What do you mean reason? There's no reason at all. Her father is a stubborn mule and her mother is a jackass and that's all. There's no reason at all. Just plain stubbornness.

LEVI-YITSKHOK. You ought to approach them with kindliness. Explain things to them.

HERSH-BER. Maybe you're right, there. Maybe my words were a little rough. But how can you know what you're doing? Maybe you'd like to mix in, Rebbe; maybe he'd have respect for you, Rebbe. I mean Elkone. I want to take his daughter for my wife. So he messed things up.

LEVI-YITSKHOK. How could I be of any help?

HERSH-BER. He'll respect you. You know her. You've seen her. Grew up together. I want to take her just as she is. But how can you do anything with them?

LEVI-YITSKHOK. It's best to do it yourself. You should speak for yourself; and be kindly and reasonable.

HERSH-BER. I could manage with him. But her mother has turned up her nose.

LEVI-YITSKHOK. Let your mother speak with her.

HERSH-BER. The mothers have quarreled.

LEVI-YITSKHOK. Wait till Rosh Hashonna; they'll make up, as the custom is. During the ten days of penitence, people regret any wrongs they've done.

HERSH-BER. Rebbe, you talk like a tsaddik. But I can't wait that long. I want to go to their house, but they told me not to. I know why, Rebbe; I know the real reason, but I can't tell you. It doesn't matter if you don't know.

LEVI-YITSKHOK. What could I know?

HERSH-BER. I know, Rebbe, that you don't know a thing about it. That's why I say that she doesn't know anything about it either. They're the ones that are after her. She won't hear of it. You can mix in.

LEVI-YITSKHOK. I really don't see how I can be of any help.

HERSH-BER. I wouldn't want my father to hear this. You know, he wants you for a son-in-law.

LEVI-YITSKHOK. Whom?

HERSH-BER. Elkone wants you for his son-in-law.

LEVI-YITSKHOK. What do you mean?

HERSH-BER. He's got a daughter Stere, doesn't he? You know her, Rebbe.

LEVI-YITSKHOK. I don't understand it.

HERSH-BER. So you don't. He comes here to hang around you. Why do you think he manages to come just when there's no one else around? That's the whole story.

LEVI-YITSKHOK. He probably has something else in mind.

HERSH-BER. You tell him that you don't want his daughter.

LEVI-YITSKHOK. The whole thing comes as a complete surprise to me.

HERSH-BER. I told my father and mother that you didn't know the first thing about it.

LEVI-YITSKHOK. I'm simply amazed.

(TSINE *appears in the doorway and listens quietly to the conversation.*)

HERSH-BER. I agree that something like that shouldn't be

done without the parents. But what's the use? What can you do
with them?

LEVI-YITSKHOK. Simply amazing!

HERSH-BER. Don't take it amiss, Rebbe. . . .

(DOVID-NOYAKH *comes out. He catches* TSINE *eavesdropping. She is embarrassed and hides behind the door.* HERSH-
BER *would like to say something more, but gives up and with
a gesture of his hand goes into the house.*)

DOVID-NOYAKH. An obstinate man, this Elkone. It's hard to
believe that a man can be so stubborn. We've had many a
quarrel. The wives too. If not for Yom Kippur, we'd never
talk to each other. My question is: why? Isn't it possible to live
together in peace? Why should Jews quarrel for no good reason
at all? What do you say, Rebbe?

LEVI-YITSKHOK. The world rests only on unity and peace.

DOVID-NOYAKH. I heard that once. The Rabbi in town said it
in a sermon. But, thank God, I don't have to be reminded of
it. I'm a man who knows how little value one has in the world.
My wife does feel like kicking over the traces every now and
again, but I don't let her. If you live way out in the country,
what does it take to become, heaven forbid, like the gentiles?
Gentiles quarrel and Jews—quarrel. . . . I know what I mean.

LEVI-YITSKHOK. Any town should be glad to have Jews like
you.

DOVID-NOYAKH. He-he, you get a little uncouth in the country. But when it comes to wronging someone—you remind
yourself. Thank the Lord, we know up from down. Although in
town they don't have too much respect for country people.
Well, after all, we can't compare ourselves to city folk. The
town Jew is really a Jew. He can exchange a few words with a
rabbi, attend synagogue when he's supposed to, and he can
donate to charity, if heaven helps him.

LEVI-YITSKHOK. You are a fine Jew. No one need be ashamed
of Jews like you.

DOVID-NOYAKH. My father, may he rest in heaven, was a
farmer too. Didn't know how to teach his children. What could
you do? Barely managed to teach us to read. He died right here
in my house. I brought him to town, and when I got there, I
didn't feel like leaving. Well, I suppose the Lord wants us to
live far from Jews and at least to find Jewish burial among
Jews. What can you do? As far as my older one is concerned, it's
too late. But the younger one could still amount to something.
I figured, if Elkone were willing to chip in. . . . So I hear that

his boys get out of hand. Still, let me say this to you: don't leave us. Let things be as they are.

LEVI-YITSKHOK. I'm not leaving, Reb Dovid-Noyakh. I was going to ask you to think it over, maybe. . . .

DOVID-NOYAKH. Let's not discuss it any further. If Elkone won't, I'll do it myself—with everything in my power. After all. . . .

LEVI-YITSKHOK. Maybe you should think it over.

DOVID-NOYAKH. I have nothing to think over.

LEVI-YITSKHOK. I mean, I want to be your son-in-law. That's what I mean.

DOVID-NOYAKH (*somewhat confused*). Wha . . . ?

LEVI-YITSKHOK. My parents are dead, or I would have had them speak for me.

DOVID-NOYAKH. Yes. Tsine. My child.

LEVI-YITSKHOK. You understand . . . that if . . . you have to agree.

DOVID-NOYAKH. Agreed! Agreed! We don't have to ask her anything.

LEVI-YITSKHOK. Her mother must be asked.

DOVID-NOYAKH. I mean, ask her mother, he-he . . . I mean, my child will obey, a fine girl. . . . Rokhel! Rokhel! Come out here for a moment!

LEVI-YITSKHOK. Still. . . .

DOVID-NOYAKH (*calls*). Rokhel, Rokhel, if you please.

ROKHEL (*coming out*). We have a God in heaven, what's all the excitement about?

DOVID-NOYAKH. Here's her mother. He wants to know whether you agree.

ROKHEL. God in heaven, what more could I ask for my child? (*Wipes her tears.*)

DOVID-NOYAKH. You don't understand what we're talking about. . . .

ROKHEL. You think I don't know? How could a mother not know? I know everything. . . . (*Embraces* LEVI-YITSKHOK *and kisses him.*) I'll be like a mother to you. What more could I ask God to bless me with? How should I tell her? Dear me, she may faint when she hears it.

(ELKONE, GITTL, STERE *arrive.*)

ELKONE. Where's your son, Dovid-Noyakh?

DOVID-NOYAKH. I beg you, Elkone, don't quarrel with me now.

ELKONE. Where is your son? I want Stere to tell him in my presence that she doesn't want to know him.

STERE (*with eyes red from weeping*). I wish I knew what you want of me.

(HERSH-BER *comes out.*)

GITTL. There he is in person.

ROKHEL. Don't spoil my happiness, Gittlshe.

GITTL. You're rejoicing but we're suffering.

HERSH-BER. Stere, I'm glad you came. Tell the truth!

ELKONE. She has nothing to say.

HERSH-BER. Let the whole world hear the truth, Stere! I'm not afraid!

ROKHEL. Hush, child, don't shout so loud.

HERSH-BER. Now I'm mad! I laugh at such parents. Stere and I grew up together right here! We grew in the same field, and she's mine! Say it, Stere. Say it. Don't be afraid.

ELKONE. How do you like that head on him, Gittl? He couldn't put two and two together, but what a tongue he's got now! Listen to him talk! Ha-ha-ha.

HERSH-BER. I don't know whether I'm talking properly or not. I asked the Rebbe. I told him I didn't want to oppose her parents. The Rebbe advised kindliness. I wanted to do it tonight, so why did you come now, dragging her here with her eyes full of tears. Why do you want to make her cry, anyway, for no good reason?

ROKHEL. So help me, he's right.

HERSH-BER (*choking back the tears*). You have no reason to make her life miserable. I can't stand to see her cry. . . .

(STERE *bursts out in loud crying.*)

GITTL. Hush, foolish child. He delivered a speech and she. . . .

ELKONE. Ha-ha-ha. Look at me, just standing and listening. What's the matter with you, Elkone?

HERSH-BER. We grew up in the same field. Why do you want to stand in our way? Why? I'll take her as she is. What more do you want? Let's get it over with, once and for all.

ELKONE. I'll give you a dowry, too, Hersh-Ber. When you talk like that, I like you. I thought, maybe. . . . But that's out. Treat her well. Enough, stop crying. Who would have dreamed that Hersh-Ber could shed a tear? It's even made me. . . . (*All wipe their eyes.*) Give me your hand, Dovid-Noyakh. (*They embrace, sobbing. The women weep out loud.*)

(TSINE *and* AVROM-YANKEV *come out, look around in surprise, and start to wipe their eyes too.*)

ROKHEL (*embraces* TSINE. *Kisses her*). My child, you've become a bride.

(TSINE *and* STERE *throw their arms about each other and kiss repeatedly.*)

ELKONE (*goes over to* LEVI-YITSKHOK *and takes his hand*). The best of luck to you You'll have a fine Jewish girl, even though she did grow up among the peasants, out in the fields.

GITTL. You see, even in the country, God provides. . . . (*She embraces* ROKHEL.)

KING DAVID AND
HIS WIVES

❦

David Pinski
(1872–1959)

❦

David Pinski was the first Yiddish writer to become widely known to an American as well as to a world audience. By 1930 a score of his works had been translated into English, his plays had been produced by the Theatre Guild and the Provincetown Players, and his admirers included Martin Buber, Ludwig Lewisohn, Franz Werfel, Rabindranath Tagore, Edith Wharton, George F. Baker, Max Reinhardt, and Stanislavsky. Some of Pinski's popularity derived, no doubt, from his greater accessibility. He was the first major Yiddish writer whose subject matter took him beyond the limits of East European Jewish life and beyond the confines of the small town. The list of his works includes such titles as *Nina Marden's Loves, The Pretty Nun, Mary Magdalene, Alexander and Diogenes.* He was also the first major Yiddish writer whose associations were more with German literature than with Russian or Polish. Indeed, had not the accident of his immersion in writing *The Zvi Family* in the spring of 1904 kept him from a doctoral examination at Columbia University, he might have gone on to teach German at some American university.

Caught up in the intellectual ferment of his generation, Pinski became deeply involved in the social and cultural movements in Jewish life. He also became the dramatist of ideas, the writer of problem plays, who built his dramas around the ideas that were agitating a Jewish world in the process of upheaval, who like O'Neill restlessly tried numerous forms from realistic to symbolist, from one-act to three-act. But behind the ideas that he explored and the forms that he tried lay the distinctive Pinski note that reverberates through the seven decades of his writing, the note of hope and faith and love of life. His characters yearn for life and hunger for love. "Sheyn vi di velt," says the Yiddish expression, "as lovely as the world"; and Pinski's characters sense the world's loveliness and joy and are drawn to it, whether they are peddler-women in the market-place or gravediggers' daughters or kings. Like his High Priest Jochanan, Pinski knew that "He who creates such a wealth of beauty and splendor cannot be merely austere and harsh." It is as though he had been told, as was his Beruriah: "Go and rejoice the hearts of the wretched and exiled. Go and bring gladness to the sad and mournful. Let him that beholds you know that life is worth living. . . ." Or can be. "We need happiness," says the heroine of his symbolist play *The Mountain Climbers,* "but not the happiness of the victor who strides over the corpses of his victims. We need the inner happiness that warms and irradiates and that only goodness can confer upon us." That vision in turn irradiates Pinski's more than sixty plays, his novels and short stories and articles. His subjects were varied: love and sex, greed, hunger for power, the conflict of generations, the awakening of the little Jewish town and its passing, the awakening of the working class—the multifarious impact of new times and worlds on an old culture. Yet his conviction that life is worth the living never faltered. Even when his satire was bitter he never lost the faith that man could alter himself and his fate, and never confused excoriation of folly with hatred of man. Whether he was writing of the defeated, insulted, deprived, or degraded or of the dynamic, the strong and the vigorous whom he admired, he never doubted that "goodness" was profoundly gratifying or that force was innately self-defeating.

In turning to King David, Pinski was treating a figure not only revered in Jewish tradition but a complex character as well: a saviour of his people, a great king, a progenitor of the Messiah, a musician, a poet of a God of love and grandeur, and yet a fighter and lover whose less admirable deeds are also recounted in the two books of Samuel. It is Pinski's achievement that he was able to create a coherent and understandable figure from these materials. In the five scenes of the play he traces the changes in David. In "Mikhal" David is the youthful idealist who will not confuse his love of God with his love of Mikhal, who insists that "my deed must be as blameless in the sight of man as it is in the sight of God." The David of "Abigail," matured by suffering and experience to a wise leader and warrior, is still the just man of God and His commandments. Yet his desire for Abigail betrays the weakness of the later king. For if David the hunted does not take Abigail until "the wickedness of Nabal has fallen on his own head," David the king has no such compunctions. His growing cynicism and sardonic humor betray the man whom power has begun to corrupt, whose hunger for life and experience is unfettered. The David of "In the Harem" has become the frank hedonist, fighting off awareness that age has taken its toll of him as it has of his wives. But it is David the old man of "Abishag" who realizes that achievement is a riddle solved; that it is aspiration which exalts. After a lifetime David learns what David knew: that the unheard melodies are sweeter than the heard, that in pursuit of the ideal lie the exhilarations of life.

If the Biblical suggestions from which one can construct the character of David are plentiful, those for his wives are merely fleeting. Yet it is in the individuality of the wives and in the other secondary characters that Pinski's dramatic skill is revealed as much as it is in the character of David.

In a symbolic sense this play, written in the fifth decade of David Pinski's life, was autobiographical. David the dramatist like David the king hungered for experience, was an artist as well as a man of action, and in his old age was benumbed (but by a stroke, far worse than was the king). Yet with this difference, the dramatist all his life remained true to his ideals of art and life.

MIKHAL

(*Among the flower beds of* KING SAUL'*s garden. Left and right, paths winding among thickly growing trees. In the middle of the densely overgrown, rocky background, a narrow path approached by many steps hewn out of the rock. Dawn of a spring morning.*)

DAVID (*stands on the topmost step, as though framed in greenery, leaning on his harp, gazing with enthusiasm, joy, and exaltation at the gradually brightening sky. His fingers find the strings of the harp and pluck, between pauses, several firm, warm chords, and soon he begins slowly to recite*). The heavens declare the glory of God; and the firmament showeth his handiwork. Day unto day uttereth speech, and night unto night showeth knowledge. There is no speech nor language where their voice is not heard. Their line is gone out through all the earth, and their words to the end of the world. In them hath He set a tabernacle for the sun.

(MIKHAL *appears at right. She hides behind a tree and listens with bated breath, eyes shut and hands clenched in passionate ecstasy.*)

DAVID (*does not notice her and continues to recite with increasing enthusiasm*). Which is as a bridegroom coming out of his chamber and rejoiceth as a strong man to run a race. His going forth is from the end of the heaven, and his circuit unto the ends of it: and there is nothing hid from the heat thereof.

(MIKHAL, *her eyes still shut, has edged out from behind the tree, quite pale and breathing heavily.* DAVID *senses her presence before he sees her. His hand trembles and a false, weak chord terminates his playing. He closes his eyes and stands rigid.* MIKHAL, *at the last chord, opens her eyes. Her face turns hard and cold, and she starts to withdraw.*)

DAVID (*softly*). Mikhal?

MIKHAL (*proud and cold*). I was taking my morning walk.

DAVID (*opens his eyes and looks at her. Calmly*). The king's daughter, all alone?

MIKHAL. Does Mikhal need an armed watch? Must she be guarded at every turn? I like to be alone and undisturbed.

DAVID (*slowly picks up his harp and starts to move up the narrow path behind him*). I take your hint. Your meaning is plain enough. Farewell, Daughter of the King.

MIKHAL (*quickly*). It was not you I meant. I am the intruder. Let me be the one to leave.

DAVID. Since you are mistress, I must go. (*Bows and is about to leave.*)

MIKHAL. You broke off your song in the middle? Will you not sing it to the end?

DAVID (*sadly, his eyes closed*). I cannot.

MIKHAL. I will leave. I will not disturb you any more.

DAVID. My heart is no longer in my song.

MIKHAL. You were singing the splendor of the day and of the sun, the greatness of God and His glory.

DAVID. That was freedom, if only for a moment.

MIKHAL. Freedom?

DAVID (*hastily*). Dwell in peace, Mikhal. (*Turns and is about to go.*)

MIKHAL (*with an outcry*). David!

(DAVID *stops, turns. For a while they look at each other in silence. As though hypnotized, without removing his glance from her,* DAVID *slowly descends the steps and approaches her. They stand close and look at each other piercingly.*)

MIKHAL (*finally breaks the silence softly and with embarrassment*). You said—freedom.

DAVID (*very sadly*). I lay awake all night, despondent.

MIKHAL. Despondent?

DAVID. Till at last, resolve came with the first touch of gray.

MIKHAL. Resolve?

DAVID. And I sought out my harp and silently stole from my room in the king's castle.

MIKHAL (*with an embarrassed laugh*). Not silently enough.

DAVID. Did I wake you?

MIKHAL. My sleep was—restless—too. (*Hastily.*) But tell me of your despair and your resolve and your liberation.

DAVID. It was still dark when I came out, and my eyes and my steps were turned to the west, where all was dipped in deepest blackness. It was as though I had stepped into a sea of shadow where dark waves were washing over me. But it was darker still within me. Heavily and bitterly my spirit wept, and heavily and bitterly my harp echoed, as the darkness brushed its strings.

(MIKHAL *turns her head, eyes brimming with tears.*)

DAVID. But when I had mounted to the topmost step and

was about to plunge into the gloom of that narrow walk, I turned my face to the east, to the path that I had travelled, to your father's palace, and what I saw made me forget my sorrow.

MIKHAL *(curious and eager)*. Oh!

DAVID. I had expected to see the same heavy darkness, but my eyes were met by a stream of early morning light. I was surprised, astonished, and my thoughts were roused from their sadness. I turned my glance to the sky, and a dark cloud tipped with red caught my eye. At first I did not quite grasp what I saw, and the reddened darkness puzzled me. I looked more carefully and soon I broke into a smile of sweet forgetfulness and sweet delight: it was the first touch of the rising sun that lay upon that cloud. My eyes darted across the distant sky like joyful dancers and sought out the red flecks that were heralds of the rising sun. With every passing moment they increased in number. With every winking of my eye the dark red turned bright and brighter still. And soon, from behind the king's palace, appeared the sun itself in all its gold-red fire-splendor. My heart overflowed and the song began to pour from my lips . . .

MIKHAL. And then I came.

(DAVID *bows his head.*)

MIKHAL *(after a short silence)*. What did you resolve?

DAVID. To leave the king's palace forever.

MIKHAL. Ah, I suspected that!

DAVID. I can stay no longer.

MIKHAL. I know it is the king's hatred that is driving you away.

(DAVID *looks away.*)

MIKHAL. But David does not need to steal away from the king. Let him go like a man!

DAVID. Saul will be content if I never show my face again.

MIKHAL *(meaningfully)*. I believe the king is your debtor. You have a claim upon him.

DAVID. The king owes me nothing.

MIKHAL. Owes you nothing? *(Laughs with embarrassment.)* Did he not offer great wealth to the slayer of Goliath?

DAVID. I did not slay Goliath for money.

MIKHAL. Not for money?

DAVID. Not for the greatest treasures nor for the utmost freedom for my father's house.

MIKHAL *(her face brightening)*. Then you—then you slew→ *(Suddenly hard.)* Why don't you claim me of the king?

DAVID *(falls on his knees before her and hides his face in her robes)*. Mikhal!

MIKHAL (*her face brightening again triumphantly*). Ahhh! It was not the King's reward you wanted but my love! Oh, why have you been silent? Why have you avoided me? I have loved you long, from the moment I first saw you. I was in the king's camp when he took the field against Goliath and the Philistines, and of all the king's daughters he offered only me as the prize for Goliath's head. Is another of the king's daughters more beautiful than I? Am I not the youngest? Am I not more beloved of the king than any of the others? Am I not worth the head of Goliath the Philistine? How deeply pained I was when, of all the heroes of Israel, not one stood forth against Goliath! How insulted I was when not one could find the courage within him though *I* was the prize! And then you appeared, young and handsome, with blond hair and apple-red cheeks. How wildly my heart began to beat! And I was filled with rejoicing. I thanked God that no one had come before you. And when you stood forth against the giant, I fell upon my knees and prayed for you. Oh, how I prayed! And I grew certain that you would conquer because you fought for me as prize and that you would come and claim me of my father. Oh, you should have done so! You should have done so! But you did not come. You did not claim me of my father. And I waited for you!

DAVID (*as before*). Mikhal!

MIKHAL (*drops to her knees and takes his face in her hands*). I waited for you and I could not understand what held you back. How frightened I was when the king offered you my sister Merab, and how I rejoiced when you refused. And it grew harder for me to understand why you did not come to claim me as your rightful prize. Oh, David, how I suffered over you. You robbed me of my rest by day and of my sleep by night. But it was good that I did not sleep and listened for you. For that is how I heard you leave your room and the palace, and I followed you at once by the tracks of your feet. Oh, why did you want to run away? Why did you want to leave me? Well, now you know. I love you. Oh, how I love you! Body and soul, I am yours. And now let us go to the king and demand your prize. Come, my warrior hero!

DAVID (*with an outburst, burying his face in his hands*). I cannot, Mikhal! I cannot!

MIKHAL (*recoiling in fright*). You—can—not?

JONATHAN (*running in*). Oh, here you are! The king is looking for you! (*Looks at both in surprise.*) What has come over both of you? What has happened between you? Haven't you heard? The king is looking for you, and he is in one of his rages! He was told that you both arose early and stole away from the palace. He fell into that raging madness that the evil spirit sends him so often now. He began to insult the servants and to curse them. With wild oaths he shook me from my sleep. Surely I must know where you are, where you fled, what secret was between you. And when he could learn nothing from me simply because I knew nothing, yet quite convinced that I would not tell, he dispatched his servants in all directions to find you and bring you back to him dead or alive. Don't you hear me? Why do you stand like that?

(MIKHAL *stands quite motionless in great fright, staring at* DAVID *as though still waiting for him to explain his words. It is as though she had not heard* JONATHAN *and was not even aware of his presence.* DAVID *having arisen slowly at* JONATHAN'S *appearance, nevertheless remains with head bowed, as though he has either not heard* JONATHAN'S *words or has made no sense out of them.*)

JONATHAN. In God's name, what has happened between you?

DAVID (*quietly, with eyes lowered*). I have just told your sister that I cannot take her to wife.

JONATHAN. You cannot?

DAVID (*with a deep sigh*). No.

JONATHAN. But you must marry the king's daughter. She was promised to him who slew Goliath the Philistine. Perhaps you are not he who freed us from Goliath and the Philistines? Perhaps it was not *your* stone that felled the giant? The king's daughter belongs to you.

DAVID. It was not for her sake that I went out against Goliath. Not for the sake of becoming the king's son-in-law did I kill the giant. I did it because he blasphemed God and God's people. I fought only for God and for the name of God.

(MIKHAL *breathes heavily, clenches her fists, and utters a cry of great anguish.*)

JONATHAN. Still, your reward is the king's daughter.

DAVID. I dare not accept the reward. For the scoffers will come and say: David declared that he fought only for God, but he really meant the king's daughter and the king's wealth.

JONATHAN. Why should that trouble you? God sees your heart and knows the truth.

(MIKHAL *laughs.*)

DAVID. My deed must be as blameless in the sight of man as it is in the sight of God. All must know and none must doubt. Only the love of God gave strength to my arm, not the love of the king's daughter nor the pursuit of gold and honor. How will they know that, if I become the king's son-in-law?

JONATHAN. Will you sacrifice your love for fear of evil tongues?

DAVID. I will sacrifice it to God's name, as I was ready to sacrifice my life to Him.

(MIKHAL *groans in fear.*)

JONATHAN (*after a brief pause, looks at* DAVID *searchingly*). Then why are you so sad? Why do you look so unhappy?

(DAVID *turns away.*)

JONATHAN. You risked your life with rejoicing. You went out against Goliath light-footed, as to a dance. Then why does the sacrifice of your love make you so sad? Since you do it for God, you should be filled with gladness.

DAVID (*bitterly*). Oh, don't scoff at me and add mockery to my sorrows!

JONATHAN. Is what I say not true?

DAVID. You have never loved.

JONATHAN. Then hear me and take Mikhal for a wife. Give me your hand. Both of you give me your hands. I will unite you and I will speak for you to the king. I will tell him that his first-born son paid the debt which he refused to pay. (*To* DAVID.) Come and receive my blessing. The tongues of men will not dare to speak against you. The whole people heard the king's proclamation, and still no one dared to arm against Goliath. Only he who was armed with the love of God could dare and to him God also gave the strength. Surely everyone will see this and understand it.

DAVID. You have not loved.

JONATHAN. What does that mean?

DAVID. Those who love would have found the courage too.

JONATHAN. You think so?

DAVID. I know it for certain. Let another Goliath appear to-day and let the King again proclaim Mikhal as the prize; I will accept his offer and say to him before all the people: "My King, I love your daughter Mikhal and for her I risk my life."

JONATHAN. So you need a second Goliath to make you happy! Ha-ha! Still, I love you too much to want to see you in that danger again. Come. Don't be obstinate. Look at Mikhal. You should not let her suffer so.

MIKHAL. Don't speak of my sorrows, Jonathan. I will suffer no more.

JONATHAN. It is Mikhal's pride that speaks so. Be patient, Sister, and say nothing more against your love.

MIKHAL. Mikhal, daughter of King Saul, does not wish to share her love even with God.

JONATHAN. Those are proud words, but what does your heart say to that? Oh, I have not loved, yet I know the ways of love better by far than you. Don't let the flower wither that God has planted in your hearts. Come. I am the eldest and you should both obey me. Give me your hand, David, and let the wagging tongues wag on. Come, Sister, and do not let pride wound your heart. Or should our father's pledge stay unfulfilled? The king gave his word and the king's children will keep it for him.

SAUL (*suddenly steals out from behind the trees at right with several retainers*). Oh-ho! You rebellious son of a rebellious mother! First you lie to me about not knowing where they are or what they plan to do, and now you lie in your throat again when you say I have not kept my word.

JONATHAN. Revile me and my mother if you wish. You are father and husband, and king and ruler too. But I told no lies. I met them here by chance and only here did I find out what was between them. And did you keep the promise made before all the people? Does Goliath's conqueror have your daughter for a wife?

SAUL. Unworthy son! May your lie choke your throat like boiling lead! Did I not offer your Goliath-toppler my daughter Merab? He refused her and I am quit of my pledge.

JONATHAN. Did you offer Merab as the reward for Goliath's head? You offered a daughter: if he does not want the one, you must give him the other.

SAUL (*wildly, clenching his fists at him*). Ahhhh!

MIKHAL (*quickly*). The king is quit of his pledge! (*General consternation.*)

SAUL (*restrains himself in his anger and turns his head slowly to* MIKHAL). What?

MIKHAL. Goliath's conqueror did not even accept the king's conditions.

JONATHAN. Sister!

SAUL (*looking angrily from one to the other*). He did not accept my conditions?

MIKHAL. He fought only for God and stood forth against Goliath only to cleanse God's name.

SAUL (*wildly*). You lying shepherd! That was not your answer when I offered you Merab! You crawled like an abject worm and made nought of yourself. Then you were too lowly and humble and the match far too exalted. How I despise you, you worthless slayer of ten thousands, with all your lying and duplicity.

DAVID. Since Saul does not believe me, I gave him whatever answer would please his ears. But God is my witness that though I love your daughter Mikhal with a burning, holy love, I did not claim her of you. I have her love too, and still I cannot take her for my wife. Rather would I have left your house, so that the beloved sight of your daughter might no longer torture me. I slew Goliath only for God.

MIKHAL. Give him another Goliath and he will slay him for me.

JONATHAN (*with great fright*). Sister!

SAUL. What?

MIKHAL. He said so himself.

JONATHAN. Sister, what are you doing?

DAVID. Yes, I said so myself. Were there an army of Goliaths, I would oppose them for my love of your daughter.

JONATHAN. David, what words are these? The king owes you his daughter.

SAUL. Silence or I'll remind you of what you owe the king and shut your mouth forever. (*To* DAVID.) Do I owe you anything, harp-twanger?

DAVID. Nothing.

SAUL. Have I promised you anything and not kept my word, stone-slinger?

DAVID. You promised me nothing in private, and what you promised in your proclamation was not for me.

SAUL (*to* JONATHAN). Do you hear what the shepherd says? Don't you claim from me what he does not! Ha-ha-ha. (*To* MIKHAL.) And you love this Goliath-killer?

MIKHAL (*breathing heavily*). No, not the Goliath-killer.

SAUL. Oh-ho! The proud princess! Come to my arms. You are truly of my blood. No wonder Saul loves you best of all his children. The others are not like him. See that spineless wretch! His father and the throne are less to him than that shepherd! Ha-ha! "No, not the Goliath-killer!" Ha-ha! Yet you do love him! Him? That harp-twanger with his blond locks and red cheeks and tall figure, that handsome—that glorious—that worm —that viper? Him? You love him? Yes, you love! You do love! Don't bite your lips. Don't ask your pride. Don't toss your head. You love, I can see that. I am old and wild and angry, yet I remember well how love comes, how love drives the heart. You love. You love him. You are no better than your brother.

Leave me! Ha-ha-ha. And he loves you? "Passionate and holy" he said. Ha-ha. Do you love her, sheep-driver? Do you love her, flea?

MIKHAL. Father!

SAUL. Ha-ha! That struck home! Do you love her, bear-fighter?

DAVID. You have heard my answer. And as to your insults, King, you and our people have more than once heard my answer.

SAUL. How proud! The women's hero! The champion in the songs of old, wasted harlots! Yet we shall soon see your courage and the worth of your word. Now all of you hear my word, and King Saul *keeps* his word: Jesse's son shall have my daughter for a wife when he brings me the heads of a hundred Philistines as a dowry.

JONATHAN (*in terror*). Father! (*He covers his head.*)

MIKHAL. Ahhh! (*Looks at* DAVID *with great suspense.*)

    (*A murmur of consternation and fear sweeps through the* KING'S *retinue.*)

DAVID (*with exaltation*). I accept your challenge, my King!
    (MIKHAL *laughs, her face beaming.*)

SAUL. And I will keep my word. A hundred Philistine heads and you shall have her.

DAVID. God bless you, my King. You have given me back my peace of mind. Now I shall be well again. Must I leave at once?

SAUL. At once.

DAVID. Then I go now, and may God restore your spirit as you have restored mine. Farewell, my King! Uncover your head, my Jonathan! See how every fiber in your David sings and rejoices! Your David is filled with courage and strength. Embrace me and rejoice with me. Do you not believe in me? I will be the victor. Do you believe in me, Mikhal? Farewell, my bride. Let me press your hand, but I will long for your lips, and the Philistines will have to pay for my longing. Ha-ha! My love has been liberated and has won Samson's strength. I go! Tremble, ye Philistines! (*Turns to go.*)

MIKHAL (*frightened*). David! Father!
    (DAVID *stops and turns.* JONATHAN *raises his head.*)

SAUL. What tone is this? I do not recognize the voice.

MIKHAL (*composed*). Nothing—I thought a hundred Philistines were too many.

SAUL. For you?

DAVID. A hundred Philistines for my Mikhal? It shall be two hundred! My Mikhal, I love you! (*Goes off with eyes half-*

closed, breathing audibly, arms outstretched as for an embrace.)

SAUL. Ha-ha-ha! That liar! Ha-ha-ha! He'll never be back!

JONATHAN (*despair in his voice*). Sister, what did you do?

MIKHAL (*a joyful expression on her face, intense, exalted, breathing heavily*). He—loves—me. He will conquer!

ABIGAIL

(DAVID's *camp on a rocky spot in the wilderness of Paran.*
DAVID, *his sword across his knees, is seated on a large stone in
the center. On the ground in front of him are seated* JOAB,
ABIATHAR, *and* AHIMELECH. ASAHEL *lies stretched out at his
feet, his head almost touching* DAVID's *knees. All around, in various postures, are* DAVID's *men, exhausted and hungry. Over-
head, the burning midday sun. All eyes are turned left, as
though they were expecting someone from that direction.*)

ASAHEL (*to* AHIMELECH, *extending his clenched hands*).
Guess which hand holds the stone. If you guess right, then
Nabal has granted our request. If not, then he has ignored
David's words.

AHIMELECH (*ill-tempered*). Will that still my hunger?

ASAHEL. It's just to while the time away, and if your stom-
ach's angry, calm it with a game. If you don't want to— Hmm—
How about you, Abiathar! Priest! You're a guesser.

ABIATHAR. Hold bread in your hand and I'll guess right.

ASAHEL. A mouse could do that better. Bah! You're an ill-
tempered lot, not fit for games. (*Moves his head toward* DAVID.)
Why so thoughtful, Uncle? What are you thinking about now?
Where are your thoughts? Are you looking at the past? Can
you see into the future now? I like to see you thoughtful. I have
no thoughts of my own, and so I like to guess at yours and to
think and think . . .

(DAVID *laughs softly.*)

ASAHEL. Were you just thinking of Saul? Or of Jonathan?
Or of your wife Mikhal? Oh, I've caused you sorrow!—Would
you like your harp? (*Derisive laughter all around.* ASAHEL *mim-
ics the laughter.*) He-he-he. (*To* DAVID.) Sing us something.
(*More laughter.*)

(DAVID *lays his hand on* ASAHEL's *head with great kindness.*)

JOAB. Better ask him to gird his sword. He should have taken
my advice in the first place. Instead of sending ten of us, we
should all have gone, and instead of sending Nabal politely

worded requests, we should have made our point with our spears. Then we wouldn't be sitting here now listening to the music of our empty stomachs.

MURMURING. Of course! Naturally! And how!

JOAB. I know nothing of asking. One should never ask for anything.

AHIMELECH. We should have gone to his wife. They say her kindness matches her beauty. He's a no-good.

ASAHEL. He won't dare to refuse us, after all we've done for him.

JOAB. Ha, ha! Look at what we did for Saul! We always helped him. And here we are, wandering all over the Paran Wilderness, suffering hunger and thirst. If we had once or twice suspended our benevolence, we would now be serving the king of Judah.

DAVID (*sternly*). Joab!

MURMURING. The king of Judah! Yes, the king of Judah!

DAVID. Do not utter that word! As long as Saul lives, he is our king, and neither I nor anyone who is loyal to me will harm a hair of his head. He is the anointed of the Lord. Zeruiah's son thinks he loves me and serves me well when he speaks of kingship. He does not know how he offends me.

JOAB. We'll never understand each other.

DAVID. Then hold your tongue and learn to understand me.

JOAB. Very well, explain to me why ten messengers to Nabal. He isn't Saul, God's anointed. Why the soft words and the prayerful language? "Peace unto you and unto your house and unto all that is yours!" And that ending! "Your son, David." Bah!

DAVID. You want me to become king of Judah and yet you ask me to act like a cut-throat.

JOAB. Act like a king. Rule! Command! Order!

DAVID (*sternly*). Then I order you to be quiet! Don't make these lads impatient.

ASAHEL. *I* should have gone. You should have sent me. I'm swift of foot. I would have come back long ago.

VOICES (*left*). Here they come! Here they come!—They're empty-handed! They've got nothing!

JOAB. Ha-ha-ha!

DAVID. Empty-han—(*grasps his sword, rises from the stone and calls to the returning messengers*). Come quickly. I must know the answer.

VOICES. Move! Faster! David wants the answer!

(ABISHAI *and his followers arrive left.*)

DAVID. You've brought nothing?

ABISHAI. As you see.

DAVID. Maybe he sent something after you.

ABISHAI. His scorn.

DAVID. You must have offended him in some fashion. You probably couldn't restrain that sharp tongue of yours, and lost your patience even before you opened your mouth. After all, you are Joab's brother.

ABISHAI. They are all my witnesses. I delivered your request word for word as you instructed me. I rehearsed it all the way there. I even practiced the proper tone for begging favors. Not a word of yours did I omit—they are my witnesses—and not a word did I add. They can tell you. I didn't even lose my patience when he insulted you as well ás us. Do I tell the truth, Friends?

COMPANIONS. Unfortunately! You do!

ABISHAI. We didn't have our swords with us, you know. After all, you took them from us.

DAVID (*impatiently*). Go on!

ABISHAI. We came to Nabal in Carmel. . . .

MURMURING. Nabal! Nabal! Nabal the Noble!

DAVID. Silence!

ABISHAI. And I said to him: "We come to you bearing greetings of peace from our master, David the son of Jesse." His sour face turned sourer still, but I remembered your instructions and my voice showed no trace of anger as I continued: "Thus did David bid us say to you—long life to you (*angry murmuring*) and peace to you and to your house and to all that is yours."

(JOAB *laughs derisively*.)

ABISHAI. "I have heard that you now shear your sheep. Know, then, that your shepherds were with us, and we did not offend them nor was there anything of theirs missing all the while they were in Carmel. Ask your young men and they will tell you. Therefore let my young men find favor in your eyes, for we come in a good day. Give whatever comes to your hand to your servants and to your son David."

JOAB. "Your son David!" "Your son David!"

ABISHAI. Thus I spoke to him, word for word, and in a tone of most humble petitioning. (*To his companions.*) Isn't this true?

COMPANION. We were ashamed, his manner was so beggarly.

ABISHAI (*between clenched teeth*). And how I boiled inside!

DAVID. (*impatiently*). And then?

ABISHAI. He turned from us and, with an angry grimace, walked scornfully away.

(DAVID *raises his sword*.)

ABISHAI. Wait, there is worse still to come. We sat down on the ground and decided to wait for a clearer reply, one with words in it. And behold! This answer came too. We had rested well from our journey by the time he could no longer endure the sight of us, and coming toward us with great wrath he cried out: "Who is David and who is the son of Jesse? There are many servants nowadays that break away from their masters!"

JOAB. What? He said that?

ABISHAI. "Shall I then take my bread and my water and my flesh that I have killed for my shearers and give it to men, whom I know not whence they come?" (*Stops talking*.)

DAVID (*hoarsely*). Well, go on!

ABISHAI. That's all. He left and we—we obeyed you. We left without punishing him. After all, our swords were. . . .

DAVID (*cries out as loud as he can*). Gird your swords! (*Great commotion in the camp. Sound of the command being repeated, of swords clanging as they are girded*.) Four hundred go with me. Two hundred stay to guard the camp. Pick the strongest, the least weary to remain.

JOAB. What's the meaning of this? Your command is completely reversed.

DAVID. You will never understand me. Should not the weariest and hungriest be fed first?

JOAB (*striking his forehead*). I get it! (*Turns to* ABISHAI, AHIMELECH, *and* ABIATHAR.) Come on. Let's pick out the fighters and the resters. (*They mix among the crowd*.)

DAVID. The dog! The dog! The dog!

ASAHEL. He won't bark at you much longer.

DAVID. No living thing shall remain of him or his. Death to all! Death to all!

ASAHEL. Even his beautiful wife?

DAVID. Death! Death! No vestige of him shall remain. The very place where the insult to me was uttered must be laid waste and devastated! Death! Death! To each and to all!

VOICES. Here comes a caravan! Here comes a caravan!

JOAB (*rushes over*). It's a caravan of donkeys loaded with food.

DAVID. Let it through! Let it pass! Touch no one! We will eat our fill this day with Nabal's goods and blood.

(*Several servants run up and prostrate themselves before* DAVID.)

DAVID. Who are these?

ABIATHAR. Forerunners of the caravan.

DAVID. Arise. Go on your way in peace.

YOUNG MAN. We ran ahead to announce that our mistress comes.

DAVID. Your mistress? Who is your mistress? Does she come to me?

YOUNG MAN. To you. She is Abigail, the wife of Nabal.

DAVID. What? Away with them! Take them away from me! Give them what they deserve! (*Turns his head away.*)

(YOUNG MEN *fall on their knees before him and, wailing, grasp his garments.* DAVID's *men try to drag them away.*)

DAVID (*turns to the* YOUNG MEN). In vain I guarded what this fellow had in the wilderness so that nothing was missed of all that belonged to him. And he has repaid me evil for good.

(ABIGAIL *arrives, riding on a donkey.*)

DAVID (*does not notice her as he speaks in a loud voice to the servants prostrate before him*). Let God do this and more to David's enemies if till morning I leave, of all that belong to him, a single living . . . (*suddenly notices* ABIGAIL, *stops, as if struck by her beauty, and ends in a low voice and quite confused*) a single male being.

(*The bystanders notice his look and his confusion. They look at one another, notice* ABIGAIL, *step back releasing her servants, who rush to her for protection. Silence.* ABIGAIL *dismounts from her donkey and prostrates herself before* DAVID. DAVID *withdraws from her.* ABIGAIL *draws closer. Awkward silence.*)

JOAB (*suddenly shouts out a command*) On to Nabal! (*Activity.*)

ABIGAIL (*rises quickly to her knees; with hands outstretched to* DAVID). Oh, my Lord! The offense is mine.

DAVID (*with ironic anger*). Ha-ha.

ABIGAIL. Oh, let your handmaid speak to your hearing. Oh, hear the words of your handmaid.

DAVID. Nabal must die!

ABIGAIL. Oh, let my lord disregard this evil man, this Nabal. As his name is, so is he. As his name means "evil," so are his ways. Could you have expected anything else of him? Could you have hoped for anything but to be refused? But I. . . .

DAVID. Did you too insult my men and send them away empty-handed?

ABIGAIL. I, your handmaid, did not see the men you sent.

DAVID. Is *that* your offense?

ABIGAIL. Oh, my lord! As God lives and as your soul lives, you have more than once been kept from shedding blood and from avenging yourself with your own hand. Was not Saul in your hand?

DAVID. The king?

ABIGAIL. Your greatest enemy, yet you did not slay him. Then let all your other enemies and all who wish you ill have no greater worth than Nabal.

DAVID. I must crush that vermin.

ABIGAIL. See the gift your handmaid brought for her lord. Let it be given to the young men that serve you.

DAVID. You want to buy me? You want to wipe away the insult to me with your gift?

ABIGAIL. Oh, forgive the sins of your handmaid! For God will make my lord a strong house. Since my lord fights God's battles, no evil should be found in you in all your days.

DAVID. I do no evil when I punish.

ABIGAIL. Leave that to God. And should a man arise to pursue you and to take your life, the soul of my lord will be bound in a bond of life with the Lord his God, and the souls of your enemies will be hurled into hell.

DAVID. Woman, what kind of talk is this?

ABIGAIL. And it shall be, when God has done to my lord all the good that he has promised you, to make you ruler over Israel, that then my lord will surely not regret that he did not shed blood without cause or avenge himself with his own hand. And God will deal well with you and you will remember your handmaid. (*Falls prostrate before David with arms spread wide. Her servants edge close to her with quiet moaning and in great fright.* DAVID *moves to raise her.* ASAHEL *anticipates him, raises her to her knees and putting her arm around his neck, helps her to her feet.*)

JOAB. The men are waiting, David. I go with them.

(DAVID *does not answer. He does not take his eyes off* ABIGAIL. ABIGAIL *trembles at* JOAB's *words, opens her eyes wide and looks at* DAVID *with mute pleading.*)

DAVID (*after regarding her in silence for a while*). You— were not sent— (ABIGAIL *raises her arms to him in terror.*) You say that you would have me . . . (ABIGAIL *tries to fall on her knees again.* ASAHEL *restrains her.* DAVID *regards her in silence.*) Blessed be the Lord God of Israel who sent you to me this day. And blessed are your words and blessed are you, who kept me this day from shedding blood and from avenging myself with my own hand.

ABIGAIL (*overjoyed, breathing freely*). Oh, my lord!

DAVID. But as the Lord God of Israel lives, who kept me back from hurting you, had you not hastened and come to me, there would not have been left to Nabal by morning a single . . . a single male being.

ABIGAIL (*lowers her eyes with a sigh of relief*). Blessed is the Lord! (*Raises her eyes to* DAVID.) Will you now receive my gift?

DAVID. With thanks.

ABIGAIL. Two hundred loaves of bread have I brought. Will they suffice? I did not know how great was the number of your men. And two pitchers of wine. These will surely not be enough. Five sheep ready dressed, five measures of meal, a hundred raisin cakes and two hundred cakes of figs. In my haste, that is all I could load on the donkeys.

DAVID. It will suffice. (*Shouts.*) Men, food! Prepare your meal. (*With cries of* "Food!" "Food!" *they crowd left to* ABIGAIL'S *donkeys.*)

JOAB (*angry*). Shrewd Nabal! With this trifle he hopes to save everything.

ABIGAIL (*frightened*). Oh, my lord, I swear to you that Nabal does not know of even a single loaf of bread nor does he suspect that I am here with you.

DAVID. I believe you. Have no fear. Joab is disgruntled only because the business passed without bloodshed. (*To* JOAB.) Go still your thirst with wine. Have my share, too.

JOAB (*leaving*). And what has satisfied you?

ASAHEL (*following* JOAB). I've had quite enough myself.

DAVID (*looks intensely at* ABIGAIL. *She lowers her eyes in embarrassment*). I have no chair to offer you and no carpet. I sat on that stone before. Won't you sit there now?

ABIGAIL. Let my lord sit. Your handmaid will stand before him. Yet, you are hungry. Say what you want and I will serve you.

DAVID. My hunger is stilled when my men have food, and my hunger is stilled, when—do sit down and I will sit at your feet. Sit or I shall have to keep standing. Wait, let me remove my cloak and spread it for you on the stone.

ABIGAIL. Oh, no. There is no need. I shall return home.

DAVID. But—but—but you are not leaving now. You will wait till your donkeys are unloaded. And you need some rest yourself. Or do I displease and frighten you?

ABIGAIL. Oh, my lord, I only want to return home quickly so that Nabal may. .

DAVID. Do not remind me of Nabal, lest I be reminded of my anger. Come. Sit down. (*Takes her by the hand and seats her on the stone. He stretches out at her feet, looks up her, probes her with his eyes.* ABIGAIL *is embarrassed, at a loss. She looks around with quick glances, pausing briefly on* DAVID *as though she wanted to look at him but did not dare to.*)

DAVID (*breaks the awkward silence. Speaks slowly*). Your name is Abigail?

ABIGAIL. Yes, my lord.

DAVID (*as though to himself, lingering on the syllables*). A–bi–gail. (*Pause.*) Abigail!

ABIGAIL. Yes, my lord?

DAVID. Your name sounds sweet to me.

ABIGAIL (*smiling*). I am glad that my name pleases you.

DAVID. Your name and— (*Gazes at her penetratingly.* ABIGAIL *lowers her eyes.* DAVID *speaks suddenly.*) Tell me, do you love your husband? (ABIGAIL *is completely at a loss. She starts to rise.* DAVID *stops her with a motion of his hand. Pause.*) Do you love him?

ABIGAIL (*at last, scarcely audible*). He is my husband.

DAVID. You said before he was an evil man.

ABIGAIL. My parents gave me to him for a wife.

DAVID. And you don't love him. Really, why should I not punish him? He deserves to die.

ABIGAIL (*frightened*). Oh!

DAVID. Well, you do love him.

ABIGAIL. He is my husband.

DAVID. Ha-ha.

ABIGAIL. And my lord should not deign to heed such enemies.

DAVID. A worm should be crushed.

ABIGAIL. No! Do not kill him! Do not kill him!

DAVID. Ha-ha! Tell me, how did you dare to come to me?

ABIGAIL. I knew that you could forgive your enemies.

DAVID. And what if I don't let you go?

ABIGAIL (*jumps up, quite frightened*). Oh, my lord!

DAVID. Why should Nabal have such a precious jewel? How did that scoundrel get such a wife?

ABIGAIL. Oh, you will let me go!

DAVID. To your evil husband?

ABIGAIL. To my husband. Surely you will not go against the Lord or break his commandments. (DAVID *buries his face in his hands.*) You are God's faithful servant and will do no violence to the wife of a stranger.

DAVID (*gets up*). You are right. Go home in peace. (ABIGAIL *bows low.* DAVID *smiles sadly.*) You see, I obey you in all things and treat you honorably.

ABIGAIL (*bows low again*). I will never forget it. (*They look at each other with sadness and longing. Pause.*)

DAVID. And will you not forget me either?

(ABIGAIL *lowers her head, blushes, and starts to leave. A commotion at left. One of* NABAL'S SERVANTS *runs in followed by* ASAHEL *and several others.*)

SERVANT. Oh, mistress, your husband Nabal is on his way here.

ABIGAIL (*trembling*). My God!

DAVID. You are under my protection.

ABIGAIL. He must not find me here!

DAVID. Is that how much you fear him?

ABIGAIL. No, I fear for his health and I fear for his life. He is fat and florid, and should he see me here and discover what I have done with his possessions, it might make him ill or even kill him.

DAVID. He must know, if he is coming here.

ABIGAIL. Oh, where can I hide? Don't let him see me! Deny my gift! Hide it!

DAVID (*to the* SERVANT). How far away is Nabal? I don't see him on the road.

SERVANT. Quite far. I ran ahead.

DAVID (*to* ASAHEL). Run among the ranks and tell our men to stop eating and drinking. Hide the food. Conceal Nabal's servants among the ranks and when Nabal arrives let every man look exhausted. And let Nabal through in peace. I don't want a hair of his head disturbed.

ASAHEL. Leave it to me. We'll play it right. (*Leaves with the servants and the others.*)

DAVID (*to* ABIGAIL). Hide behind the stone. He won't see you.

ABIGAIL (*retreating behind the stone*). I see him now. Do you? The stout one riding at the head of that whole crowd of servants.

DAVID (*sitting down on the stone*). He sits unsteadily on his mount. I could swear he's drunk.

ABIGAIL. And well you might. He is, often enough.

DAVID (*leaning over to her*). And he is your husband?

ABIGAIL. It was God's wish.

DAVID. And it is for his life that you tremble?

ABIGAIL. I have always guarded his life.

DAVID. You faithful soul! And how lovely you are. Don't

hide yet. He is still far. Let me look at you. Stand still. Don't be so frightened. Let me look into your eyes. Don't move. Don't move. How beautiful you are!

ABIGAIL (*cries out*). Oh!

DAVID (*catches her*). No, don't hide yet. He is still far away, as you can see. Or do you want to hide your beauty from me? (*Looks at her intensely.* ABIGAIL *hides her face against the stone.*) Abigail, let Nabal die.

ABIGAIL (*frightened*). No!

DAVID. Abigail, look at me.

ABIGAIL (*with downcast eyes*). I do not wish to be guilty of his death. Oh, he is near. Swear to me that you will not harm him.

DAVID (*after a lengthy pause*). I swear it.

ABIGAIL. How I thank you! If only he will not discover me here.

DAVID. He will not discover you.

ABIGAIL (*cries out suddenly*). He has fallen off! They pulled him down! Your men—

DAVID (*leaps from the stone*). They will pay for this!

(NABAL *enters, scarcely able to stand, surrounded by* ASAHEL, ABIATHAR, AHIMELECH *and others who bow to him in mockery.* ABIGAIL *hides quickly behind the stone.*)

NABAL. Beggars! Hungry dogs! Locusts on the fields of others!

DAVID (*sternly*). Did you drag him from his mount?

ASAHEL. No, his lordship fell of his own accord. We approached him entreating him to give us something to still our hunger with. He tried to strike and fell off. (*Bowing to* NABAL.) Oh, his lordship didn't hurt himself, did he? He didn't damage his limbs, did he?

ABIATHAR. Woe unto the ass that could not bear his master! We will stone it!

DAVID. Let him be!

ASAHEL. We ask no more than that his lordship give us something, or we shall die of hunger before his very eyes.

NABAL. You should have dropped dead long ago. You get nothing from me except cudgeling. Away, mongrels. Chew the earth, if you will.

ASAHEL AND THE OTHERS (*bowing*). Oh, have mercy!

NABAL (*striking at them with his staff*). With my stick! You'll soon feel Nabal's pity! Pity for thieves and robbers, ho-ho! I'll beat you one and all. (*They scatter with him in pursuit. He turns quickly and studies* DAVID.) So you're that David fellow? You're the head beggar? Would you like a few from my stick? You there, is my wife here? I was told she made off to you with a lot of food. They told me falsely. I'll have the tale-bearers' tongues cut out. They told me lies. Their accusations were false. You're as hungry as you were. As before, you beg on every road. Hungry dogs! Empty stomachs! But my wife. Where is my wife? She's not at home. I couldn't find her anywhere. Speak, slave, have you seen my wife? Wasn't she here? Hey, if I were to find her here! Before your very eyes I would strip her bare. You haven't seen my wife naked! Her flesh is sweet to kiss, ha-ha!

ABIGAIL (*from behind the stone*). Fie!

NABAL (*looks around*). Ha? (*Starts toward the stone.* DAVID *blocks his path.*) Ha-ha. I'd strip her naked and beat her bare body with this stick. I'll beat her anyway. She wasn't at home. The harlot! The wanton! Across her naked body with a stick and thongs!

(DAVID *seizes* NABAL *by the throat and starts to choke him.* ASAHEL, ABIATHAR, AHIMELECH *rush toward him with drawn swords.* ABIGAIL *rises cautiously from behind the stone, trying to see why it suddenly grew so quiet. Terrified by what she sees, she gasps, stifling an outcry with her hand.* DAVID *pushes* NABAL *away.* ABIGAIL, *her eyes fixed on* NABAL, *sinks slowly behind the stone.*)

NABAL (*falls full length upon the ground from* DAVID's *push but gets up at once, passing his hand across his face as though quite sobered. Then he looks at* DAVID *and works himself into a rage again, clenching his fists*) You do know my wife! She was here with you! Wife-chaser! Seducer! You slave that your master didn't beat enough!

(ASAHEL, ABIATHAR, AHIMELECH *rush forward with their swords.*)

DAVID. Back! Not a hair of his head shall be harmed! I swore it!

NABAL. Coward! Thief in the night! Runaway slave!

ABIGAIL (*jumps up*). Enough! Enough! Stop reviling him!

NABAL (*eyes popping*). She is here! She is here with you!

ABIGAIL (*steps slowly out from behind the stone*). He deserves your thanks and your blessing, not your abuse.

NABAL (*quite sobered*). She is here. She . . .

ABIGAIL. And stop insulting me and calling me vile names. I came here for your sake. I came here to save you from his vengeance, to save your possessions and the lives of all of us.

NABAL. Did you bring yourself as a gift to him?

(DAVID *stirs threateningly.*)

ABIGAIL. How can you say such things? You should be ashamed to speak such words to me!

NABAL. Did you come to placate him with empty hands and smooth words?

ABIGAIL. I brought him gifts.

NABAL. Gifts? Then it's true!

ABIGAIL. Calm yourself. There is no need for anger.

NABAL. Gifts!

ABIGAIL. A few. A trifling part of what you have.

NABAL. Gifts! Tell me which, what, how many!

ABIGAIL. Two hundred loaves of bread. . . .

NABAL. T-t-two hundred loaves? Go on!

ABIGAIL. Two pitchers of wine . . .

NABAL. Go on!

ABIGAIL. Five sheep . . .

NABAL. Sheep! Sheep! What else?

ABIGAIL. Five measures of meal . . .

NABAL. Ha! Five of everything! Five, eh? Maybe five times five?

ABIGAIL. As true as God lives . . .

NABAL. Go on! Go on! Give me the whole count. What else? How many oxen? How many cattle? How many goats? And milk? And butter?

ABIGAIL. Oh, no, no! None of these things. Only a hundred raisin cakes and two hundred . . .

NABAL. T-t-two h-h-hundred what?

ABIGAIL. Fig cakes.

NABAL. Fig cakes! Two hundred fig cakes! Fig cakes! Fig cakes! Two hundred of them! You . . . you . . . ! (ABIGAIL *moves to hide behind* DAVID.) You . . . ! (*He gasps, begins to choke, reaches for his throat.*)

ASAHEL, ABIATHAR, AHIMELECH (*surround him with bread and meat and cakes and wine in their hands. They thrust the food into his face, taunt him with it*). You see? We're eating your bread! We're drinking your wine! The meat is yours! Your cakes! Your fig cakes! Fig cakes!

(NABAL *suddenly collapses.*)

ABIGAIL (*cries out in fright and approaches him cautiously*). Nabal! (*He does not move. She bends over him.*) Nabal! (*She kneels and feels his heart.*) Nabal! (*With a terrified look toward* David.) He's dead!

DAVID (*bends over him*). He's dead. (*Softly, as if to himself.*) Blessed be the Lord who has pleaded the cause of my insult from Nabal and has kept me from evil. The wickedness of Nabal has fallen on his own head. (*To* ABIGAIL.) You, too, should praise the Lord.

ABIGAIL. He's dead.

DAVID. And you are free and delivered from the hand of the wicked.

ABIGAIL. God is my witness I did not wish his death.

DAVID. You kind and faithful soul!

ABIGAIL. But he reviled you so. . . . (DAVID *slowly puts his hand on her head and caresses her hair. She trembles and closes her eyes. Soon she opens them and looks at the corpse.*) I am ashamed that I cannot weep. . . . No, I can weep.

DAVID (*to* ASAHEL *and his comrades*). Take him away. Carry him back to his own earth near Carmel and bury him there with his forefathers.

AHIMELECH. To the dogs I'd . . .

DAVID. Silence!

ASAHEL. Pity the poor dogs. So hard a man. . . . (*They carry him off.*)

ABIGAIL (*arising, weeping*). Nabal!

DAVID. You have spoken his name for the last time.

ABIGAIL. No. He is my husband.

DAVID. Was. Now—I—want—

ABIGAIL (*raising her eyes to him*). Want what?

DAVID. To take his place.

ABIGAIL. Oh!

DAVID. Would you be my wife? If what I have read in your eyes is true. . . .

ABIGAIL (*bows her head, bends over slowly, and suddenly drops on her knees before him*). Let your handmaid be a servant to wash the feet of the servants of my Lord.

DAVID (*picks her up and takes her in his arms*). My dove! My pious dove!

BATHSHEBA

CHARACTERS
David
Bathsheba
Uriah the Hittite, her husband
The Prophet Nathan
A Servant
Guards

II Samuel 11–12

(The roof of the king's palace. Right foreground, the king's bed. A table set with wine stands before the bed. Several treetops are visible, some level with the roof, some higher. Far in the distance, the misty mountains of Judea. KING DAVID, right rear, is half-sitting on the balustrade that rings the roof. His arms are folded across his breast. Before him stands NATHAN THE PROPHET. Guards at the stairway leading to the roof.)

NATHAN. And he will not withdraw his favor from you as he withdrew it from Saul, whom he cleared from your path. *(DAVID leans over and scrutinizes something below among the trees.)* Your house and your kingdom will endure forever, your throne will . . . You are not listening to me, my King. What have your eyes perceived down there? *(DAVID slowly raises his hand left in a defensive gesture but remains as if transfixed. NATHAN looks down in the same direction and is suddenly horrified.)* A woman bathing! Do not look at her, my King!

DAVID *(without shifting his glance)*. How lovely she is!

NATHAN. My King, you must not look!

DAVID. Who is that beauty?

NATHAN. She is Bathsheba, the daughter of Eliam, the wife of Uriah the Hittite. She is a married woman. You must not behold her in her nakedness. You sin with your eyes.

DAVID. I accept that responsibility quite willingly.

NATHAN. Turn your eyes to me. I have come to you bearing God's word.

DAVID. But I have seen God's work. Do not disturb me now, Prophet. Let me admire God's handiwork.

NATHAN. King, you blaspheme!

DAVID. How glorious she is! Never have I seen such a figure, such a body!

NATHAN. Restrain yourself, my King. Avert your eyes and thoughts. . . .

DAVID. Should her husband be richer than I? I must be first in Judah and in Israel.

NATHAN. And now sinful desires are born in your breast. Close your eyes and. . . .

DAVID. I close my eyes and still I see her. Ho, guards, go fetch me Bathsheba, the daughter of Eliam, the wife of Uriah the Hittite. She is bathing in the river down below.

NATHAN (*springing up*). King!

DAVID (*to the guards*). Go do as I told you. (*To* NATHAN.) You may leave too.

NATHAN. Do not drive God away from you!

DAVID (*looking down, signals him with his hand*). Go, Nathan, go!

NATHAN. My King!

DAVID. You see I'm impatient.

NATHAN (*raises his voice*). My King, hear me out. Two men once lived in a city, one rich, the other poor. The rich man had sheep and cattle in great numbers and the poor man had only one little ewe, that he had bought and raised and that had grown up together with his children. It ate of his bread and drank of his cup and lay in his lap and was as a child to him. A visitor came to the rich man, who was loathe to take of his own sheep and cattle for the guest that had come to him. And he took the poor man's lamb and dressed it for his guest.

DAVID (*not removing his glance, angrily*). Fie on such a man! Fie on him! He must die!

NATHAN (*thundering*). You are that man!

DAVID (*gleefully*). They have her! They have taken her! How frightened she is! How she struggles! How quickly she covers herself. Ha-ha-ha. That covering will easily be ripped off. Ho-ho! They're bringing her! They're coming with her! (*Turns to* NATHAN.) Now go! Now go! (*Suddenly remembering.*) Wait. What were you telling me about that man? I believe I have sentenced myself to death!

NATHAN. And your sentence was just. Hear me! Thus saith the Lord God of Israel: I annointed thee king over Israel, and I delivered thee out of the hand of Saul. And I gave thee thy master's house and thy master's wives. . . .

DAVID (*raging*). I will hear no more! I know all that you can tell me and more than you can tell me. Spare yourself the effort.

NATHAN. Thus saith the Lord, I will raise up evil against thee out of thine own house. . . .

DAVID. Do not bring me to greater sin! Go!

NATHAN. And he will take your wives. . . .

DAVID. My sword! My sword! (*Rushes at* NATHAN *with clenched fists.*) Go!

NATHAN (*avoiding him*). So far have you forgotten yourself?

(*Covers his head with his cloak, wrings his hands over his head, and walks out with slow steps.*)

DAVID. Ahh, at last! Rid of him! (*Throws himself on his bed.*) Well, why don't they come? Why are they dragging their heels? Are they crawling? Have they forgotten how to walk? (*Listens.*) Come on! Ah, they're coming! They're coming!

(BATHSHEBA *is dragged in by the soldiers. She pulls free of them and runs half-way across the roof.* DAVID *signals the guard to leave.*)

DAVID (*scrutinizes her*). Ha-ha-ha! Head proudly erect, eyes full of hatred, not the slightest sign of fear. The beauty! Bathsheba, the king desires you.

BATHSHEBA. I am married.

DAVID. Ha-ha-ha!

BATHSHEBA. And I love my husband.

DAVID. What does that mean?

BATHSHEBA. I will not satisfy the king's desire.

DAVID. You will not yield?

BATHSHEBA. I will not yield.

DAVID. Your king?

BATHSHEBA. I kneel before my king and bow to him, but as a woman I belong only to the man I love.

DAVID. Oh, you rouse my blood as when I wrestled with the lion and the bear. Woman, you stand before the eternal conqueror!

BATHSHEBA. You slew when you conquered. Only through death will you conquer me too.

DAVID. I didn't conquer women so. Kings' daughters gave me their love with rejoicing.

BATHSHEBA. I love my husband. My love burns for him alone. For him my bosom breathes with passion. For him my soul melts in song.

DAVID. You must be mine.

BATHSHEBA. That I will never be.

DAVID. Woman, you forget you are in my power.

BATHSHEBA. You are used to having women offer you their love. You will not use force.

DAVID. Shall I teach you to love me? I am impatient. You have lit a fire within me. How shall I win your love quickly? Tell me, what virtues has Uriah that I do not. (BATHSHEBA *bursts out laughing, then, in fright, stifles her laugh with her hand.*) Well, is Uriah so much more than I?

BATHSHEBA (*trembling*). I do not know, my King.

DAVID. Then describe him to me.

BATHSHEBA. I can only sing of him. Tall is he like the cedar of Lebanon, and like the crown of the tree his black hair lies across the white of his neck. His eyes are brighter than stars. His face is woven of sunbeams. He is as young and as glorious as Adam in the Garden of Eden.

DAVID. Open your eyes and look upon your king.

BATHSHEBA. I see only Uriah.

DAVID. In all things I am like him, only I am not so young any more. Still, I am the king; I am David.

BATHSHEBA. Though you were much more, I would still love Uriah.

DAVID (*gesturing impatiently*). Don't say that to me again!

BATHSHEBA. My King, let me go.

DAVID. Go? Ha-ha! Come sit beside me. Here is wine; let's drink it. I am drunk with you and I want to get drunker still. And you, drink and fill yourself with a fire that will make you forget Uriah. Come, glorious woman! David, the strong shepherd and the stronger king, invites you! Come, my sweet, the poet and the singer languishes in his love for you! (*He drinks.*)

BATHSHEBA (*raises her eyes to heaven and joins her hands in prayer*). "The Lord is my rock, my fortress, my deliverer; my God, my strength in whom I trust; my buckler, and the horn of my salvation, and my high tower. I will call upon the Lord, who is worthy to be praised; so shall I be saved from mine enemies."

DAVID (*looks at her wide-eyed and astonished*). My words— my prayer—my psalm of praise to God—

BATHSHEBA. "The sorrows of death compassed me and the flood of ungodly men made me afraid. . . ."

DAVID. Stop, woman, stop! This will not help you. You want to remind me of God and of my gratitude to him, but it will do you no good. I am ready to break His word, His commandment, His law. I am drunk with you. Let Him punish me. Let His hand rest hard and heavy upon me. But I must have you. My blood boils. I want no master now. Come, glorious woman, come to my arms! For your sake King David has broken with his God. Do not tremble. Be proud! Cry out with rejoicing! (*He advances toward her.*)

BATHSHEBA. Uriah! Uriah!

(URIAH *enters. Grasping the situation, he looks thunder-struck. When he meets the king's glance, however, he falls to his knees before* DAVID.)

BATHSHEBA *(looks around, sees* URIAH *kneeling, and cries out)*. Oh, Uriah, my Uriah! My beloved! My deliverer!

DAVID. Is this Uriah? Stand up. *(Grasps his sword.)*

*(*URIAH *gets up.* BATHSHEBA *embraces him.* URIAH *frees himself from her arms and stands at attention before the king.)*

DAVID *(rebukes him)*. Who sent for you? Why did you come to me?

URIAH. Nathan sent me. He said you wanted me.

DAVID. Your blood be on his head.

URIAH. What does my lord want of me?

DAVID. What I want of you? What I—oh, yes. Wait here. I have a mission for you.

URIAH. Your servant will carry it out faithfully.

DAVID *(looks at him penetratingly and bursts out laughing)*. This is just a worm. *(Exits.)*

BATHSHEBA *(clings to* URIAH, *trembling and tearful)*. Uriah! *(*URIAH *stands motionless.)* You are angry with me. Your heart is turned to stone against me. But I have not sinned, neither against God nor against you, Uriah. I did not come here willingly. Uriah, do you hear me? The king's will brought me here. He saw me naked while I bathed, and his soldiers drove me, dragged me here. But I withstood him, and the king did not touch me. I spoke to him of my love for you and I called to God and to you. And you came in my greatest need. Uriah, believe me. I am telling you the truth. Uriah, why do you stand like that? Uriah, look at me! Uriah, save me and save yourself!

URIAH. The king desires you. Let the king's will be done.

BATHSHEBA *(cries out)*. Uriah! You cannot be serious! Recover your senses. Wake up! You are strong; you are powerful. You must help us both!

URIAH. Against the king?

BATHSHEBA. Kill the king!

URIAH. Bathsheba!

BATHSHEBA. You have your sword with you. Punish him.

URIAH. The king?

BATHSHEBA. The transgressor! The ravisher of your wife! The defiler of your name! The sinner against God! Oh, how could you have kept from punishing him before? How could you have fallen on your knees before him?

URIAH. He is my king!

BATHSHEBA. Uriah! How can you say that? Are you not man enough? The king wishes to take my love from you. Don't you care about my love? Don't you love me any more? Uriah, speak! Have I lost your love?

URIAH. I do love you, Bathsheba!

BATHSHEBA. You love me—you surrender me to the king without a battle?

URIAH. I cannot do battle with my king. (*Breaks out in a wild cry of pain.*) Oh, if it were another man—another man, even one of the king's best warriors! My fingers would coil around his throat like heavy rope and squeeze the breath of life from him. He would become a post, and with the iron of my fists I would hammer him into the earth. Oh, no one has yet died such a death as this defiler would die under the mighty hands of Uriah the Hittite, and long would people marvel at their strength—if it were another man.

BATHSHEBA. But you fear the king? You tremble at his strength? You feel weaker?

URIAH. My hand will never rise against my king.

BATHSHEBA. Uriah! Uriah! Listen! I spoke of God to this lust-king of yours. His own prayer that he sang when he was saved from Saul's hand I here sent up to God. Yet he did not restrain his lust and openly defied God and His commandments. Uriah! Uriah! In his sinful lust, the king forgot his fear of God. Cannot your honorable love raise you against the king?

URIAH. I cannot, Bathsheba!

BATHSHEBA. In the name of our great love, Uriah!

URIAH. I cannot, Bathsheba!

BATHSHEBA. If you cannot punish the sinner against your wife, against yourself, then punish the sinner against God! (URIAH *stands motionless.*) In the name of God, Uriah! Nathan sent you here so that you might punish the blasphemer and adulterer. (URIAH *remains silent.*) Are you so afraid of death? Then I'll die with you, Uriah. I would rather die than survive my shame. Take your sword and run me through. How sweet death will be at your hands! And if you die together with me, then death will be a dance to me! Why do you stand so? Have you turned to stone? Uriah, I want to die with you!

URIAH (*breathes heavily, starts to draw his sword, and suddenly thrusts it back*). My king needs me.

BATHSHEBA. What! Uriah! Uriah! Stop talking like that! You will be guilty of murder! You will kill my soul! You will kill my love! Has the king so robbed you of your will? Are you so much a slave? Uriah, you were my pride. Everything in me cried out in pride that I love you and am loved by you. And must all this be destroyed in me? I shall become a worm, Uriah! I shall despise myself, Uriah! Uriah, my soul implores you. Help yourself and help me! Help us both in our twofold trial! . . . You are silent, Uriah! You. . . .

A SERVANT (*enters with a letter in his hand and gives it to* URIAH). The king sends you back to embattled Joab with this and bids you leave at once. (*Exits.*)

URIAH (*takes the message, hides it in his clothing, and starts to leave. With a quiver in his voice*). Farewell, Bathsheba!

BATHSHEBA. You are going? You are going off, leaving me here in the hands of that ravisher? Is this the measure of your love for me?

URIAH. I can do nothing else, Bathsheba.

BATHSHEBA. You can do nothing else!

URIAH. I can die only one death—for my king.

BATHSHEBA. Am I nothing to you? Is the king so much dearer to you than I? Do you know where the king is sending you?

URIAH. To Joab, who is now besieging the city of Rabbah.

BATHSHEBA. Do you know why he is sending you there?

URIAH. I do not need to know why, nor do I care to know.

BATHSHEBA. He is sending you to your death! He wants to get rid of you! He wants to crush you like a worm! Don't you realize that? Can't you see that yourself?

URIAH. I must leave on the king's mission. Don't stand in my way.

BATHSHEBA (*struggles with him*). Uriah! Uriah! You will not go! You will not leave me alone! (*Tears the message away from him.*)

URIAH. How dare you! Give that message back to me!

BATHSHEBA (*escapes behind the bed, breaks open the king's seal, and panting reads the message as she continues to evade* URIAH). "Set Uriah in the forefront of the hottest battle and retire from him, that he may be smitten and die." Uriah!

(URIAH *stops. He is pale and breathing heavily. He shudders.*)

BATHSHEBA. Did you hear? Uriah, you are going to your death. Is it not far better to die here with me? Wake up, Uriah! Be brave! Rouse your fury! Become my champion again!

URIAH (*furious*). Give me that message!

BATHSHEBA. What? Are you turning on me? Are you venting your wrath on me? Oh! (*Tears the message.*)

URIAH. Bathsheba!

BATHSHEBA. (*throws the scraps into his face*). Go ahead! Fulfill the king's mission!

URIAH (*picks up the pieces*). I know it by heart. I am going into battle to die for my king, and dearly will the Ammonites pay for my death! (*Leaves.*)

BATHSHEBA. Uriah! He is leaving! He is gone! (*Furious.*) I spit on you! I send after you the venom of my scorn! I despise you! You dead worm! Ugh, to think that I once loved you! Out, out of my heart and my soul! Out, out! I will tear out my heart where love once nested! I will bite away the lips that once kissed him! And David asked to be compared with him, and I found David wanting! Ha-ha-ha! I laugh at myself in mockery! I loved a slave. Ha-ha-ha. Now I must go to the king. He shall cleanse me of my stain. He shall make me chaste. Oh, I loved a slave. Now I shall love a king! (*She walks toward the steps.*)

(DAVID *meets her triumphantly with open arms.*)

IN THE HAREM

CHARACTERS

David

Mikhal
Bathsheba
Abigail
Ahinoam
Maacah
Haggith } his wives
Abital
Eglah
Bathshua
Nine Others

Ten Concubines of David
Hushai
A Servant

(The great hall of the harem. On the left, under a canopy, is
DAVID's *throne, which is approached by a several carpeted steps.*
Arranged in a semicircle to the left and right, divans for his
wives. Opposite, a carpeted platform for the CONCUBINES. *The*
walls are hung with rich tapestries. Right rear, a tapestry over
a doorway is drawn and one after another there enter DAVID's
ten CONCUBINES *whom he left to guard the palace and who were*
ravished by Absolam. They enter sadly, heads bowed. Some
weep. They mount the platform and sink to their knees ex-
pectantly, facing the throne. Soon the wives enter, also in single
file, led by MIKHAL, BATHSHEBA, ABIGAIL, *eighteen in number.*
They take their seats on either side of the throne: to the right—
MIKHAL, ABIGAIL, MAACAH, ABITAL, BATHSHUA, *and four others;*
*to the left—*BATHSHEBA, AHINOAM, HAGGITH, EGLAH, *and five*
others. AHINOAM, *the mother of Amnon, who was slain by*
Absolam, and MAACAH, *the mother of Absolam, are clad in*
black.)

ABIGAIL. Sister Maacah and you, Sister Ahinoam, why have
you come dressed in black?

MAACAH. Need you ask?

AHINOAM. I shall never forget my dead son.

ABIGAIL. But our husband, the king, wishes to celebrate our
return to Jerusalem, and he will not want to see sorrow around
him.

MAACAH. His joy is my sorrow. I cannot rejoice at the return.
It cost me my son, my Absolam.

AHINOAM. It reopens my wounds too. I can see my Amnon
standing before me.

MAACAH (*laughing bitterly*). Is that a reason for wailing?

AHINOAM. A reason? He was the first-born son of King David,
and he was no defiant rebel against his father.

MAACAH. The ravisher of my daughter!

AHINOAM. He did that in the turbulence of passion, be-
witched by your daughter's beauty. He had it in his blood from
his royal father. But what his murderer, your Absolam, could do
in cold blood, driven by vengeance and rebellion, these ten

199

sorrowing women bear witness. (*The concubines crouch more humbly.*) If my son—

MAACAH. The cause of all our woes is your son. He was a scoundrel and he acted like a scoundrel.

AHINOAM (*rising, sternly*). You shall not call my dead son, the king's first-born, a scoundrel, do you hear!

MAACAH. He destroyed my two children. My Tamar still endures the bitter blackness of her life, but my Absolam, my Absolam—

AHINOAM (*sitting down again*). He destroyed himself, that rebel against king and father. His name will remain accursed forever.

MAACAH (*springs to her feet*). What did you say?

ABIGAIL. Peace, sisters. The king may arrive at any moment. Let the dead rest undisturbed in their graves. What has been done cannot be undone. The Lord's hand was in it too. And I say, you should not have come here in sorrow.

MAACAH (*sitting again*). My Absolam! My Absolam! My son! My only son! And his name will be cursed forever! The handsomest man he was in all of Israel. In his beauty there was none to equal him. From head to toe there was no blemish on him. Each of his limbs was a song of praise to God. His head of hair—when was the like of it ever seen? When it was shorn it weighed two hundred shekels on the king's scales. And he is dead!

AHINOAM. Then how must I mourn my Amnon? Had he lived, he would, as eldest, have inherited his father's throne, and he would have been king of Judah and Israel.

BATHSHEBA (*laughs*). Ha-ha!

MAACAH. My Absolam was king even while the king lived.

AHINOAM. That rebel! Why don't you boast of that to the king when he comes?

HAGGITH (*to* BATHSHEBA). You laughed, Sister Bathsheba. What is the meaning of your laughter? May I know?

BATHSHEBA. It was just a passing thought.

HAGGITH. You did not hide them well, those thoughts of yours. I know them.

BATHSHEBA. Then why do you ask, Sister Haggith?

HAGGITH. You think your Solomon will become king?

BATHSHEBA. I think what I think.

HAGGITH. You had better make no mistakes. My Adonijah is now next in succession to the king's throne.

ABIGAIL. You have completely forgotten my Chileab, Sister Haggith. After Amnon, he is the oldest. But why apportion the kingdom now? The king still lives. And remember this: he will himself choose his successor.

BATHSHEBA. That is what I think.

HAGGITH. My Adonijah is not less handsome than Absolam, and after Absolam, the throne should be his.

ABITAL. If crowns were handed out for beauty, then my Shephatiah would be king.

EGLAH. In that case, I think my Ithream should get the crown.

MIKHAL (*sadly*). Ha-ha, how they squabble over my father's kingdom, and I, being barren, must keep my mouth shut. (*To the other wives.*) Why are you silent? You have sons, too, and handsome ones at that. (*To a wife seated near* ABITAL.) You, Bathshua! Shemua must be king! (*To another next to* BATH-SHUA.) And you, call for Yibakhar! (*To a third.*) And you: Elishua, of course! (*Turns further to the left.*) And why not Nepheg or Japhia? Elishama? Eliada? Eliphalet? Mothers, stand up for the rights of your sons! You are all equally the king's wives, and your sons are the king's sons, the offspring of David's loins! Ha-ha!

BATHSHUA. Naturally, if Haggith will push the claim of Adonijah . . .

HAGGITH (*with proud contempt*). Your sons are but the slaves of my Adonijah.

THE WIVES (*except* MIKHAL, BATHSHEBA, ABIGAIL, AHINOAM, MAACAH *jump up with loud outcries and advance toward* HAG-GITH). Slaves? The king's sons? The impudence! She is mad! She talks like a market woman! The king should know of this!

ABIGAIL (*rises and tries to calm and separate the women*). Peace, sisters! Calm yourselves!

(DAVID *enters through a parted drapery in the rear, stops, and observes the screaming women. The concubines notice him and prostrate themselves. Sudden silence. The wives notice the king. Each retreats to her seat, sinks to her knees, and prostrates herself.* MIKHAL *and* BATHSHEBA *remain on their feet, bowing low.*)

DAVID (*advances slowly*). Arise! Be seated!

(*The wives rise and take their seats. Those who had quarreled loudly are ashamed, ill at ease, with bowed heads. The concubines remain kneeling.*)

DAVID (*ascends to his throne, sits down, and looks around*). Is this how you awaited me? Is this your reception of me? What was it that you were shouting about? What is it that I should know? You speak, Mikhal.

MIKHAL (*proudly*). You did not hear my voice. I was not among the screamers.

HAGGITH. She merely incited the outcries.

DAVID (*to* HAGGITH). I did not ask you to speak. (*To* ABIGAIL.) Will you not tell me what the shouting was about?

ABIGAIL. Oh, King, all is calm now. You, too, forget the clamor and let us rejoice at our return home.

DAVID. Still, I am curious. Shall I not satisfy my curiosity? Shall I not know what I must know?

ABIGAIL. Oh, King!

DAVID. You tell me, Bathsheba.

BATHSHEBA. Only a trifle, my King. A foolish word was spoken. You need not be displeased.

DAVID. That's a good beginning. Now I am eager for more. Was I the cause of the outcries? Did the foolish word concern me? (*Motions of objection from* BATHSHEBA, ABIGAIL, *and several others.*) Speak on, Bathsheba. You began splendidly.

BATHSHEBA. I was not among the shouters either—

DAVID (*impatiently*). Come, come! Abital, I heard your voice. Tell me, what is it that I must know?

ABITAL. Haggith called our sons the slaves of her Adonijah.

DAVID. That is most certainly an insult. How did you come to say that, Haggith? Are not their sons my sons? Are they less to me than Adonijah?

HAGGITH. To me he is much more.

EGLAH. She sees in him the heir to your throne.

DAVID. So? So. Now I know all. Now it all fits together. In your eyes I am as good as dead—

THE WIVES. Oh, no!

DAVID. And when you get together, you divide up my legacy.

ABIGAIL. You need not be bitter, King. This was the first time . . .

DAVID. Be still, Abigail. Make no excuses for anyone or any thing. Be quiet, my dove. I speak now. (*Contemplates the women with a bitter smile on his lips.*) Mothers! I see only old mothers before me. Where are my wives? Mothers! Mothers! What are you to me? What am I to you? I came to you and I forgot your years. And suddenly—so much old age! So much cold! Are you the ones who so rejoiced me and made my heart pound? Mikhal, how you look! So old and frozen into ice.

MIKHAL. I wish my death would come and free me from my degradation.

DAVID. Your degradation?

MIKHAL. To play a trifling part in David's life.

DAVID. And you wanted to be my everything?

MIKHAL. Mikhal, the daughter of King Saul, did not want to share her love even with God.

DAVID. Yes, yes. Yet you went off to Phalti, the son of Laish the Gallimite.

MIKHAL (*angrily*). You know very well that my father gave me to him. And besides . . .

DAVID. Besides?

MIKHAL. You had already taken up with two others. (*She points to* ABIGAIL *and* AHINOAM.)

DAVID. Both great beauties. How could I let them pass me by?

MIKHAL. It pleases you to be witty. That is your answer to me. And should I not . . .

DAVID. Despise me? Say it. (MIKHAL *turns her head away.*) Ha-ha! And she expected me to sacrifice so much beauty for her sake. Ah, how much I would have lost! Every one of you was the beginning of a new life for me; every new love, a new spring, full of song and renewal. Abigail, do you remember? At the first sight of you I lost my heart. Your very name had drawn me, and your eyes threw rays like ropes of fire to draw me and bind me to you. I could not tear myself free—and I did not want to. God had brought you and me together—how could Mikhal stand between? And how fair you were, Ahinoam, the loveliest flower in Jezreal. Could I leave you unpicked? It would have been a sin to do so. And you, Maacah, wondrously beautiful daughter of a king—you bore me the most beautiful son. (MAACAH *bursts into tears.*) Weep no more. Weep no more. Your son has been mourned enough. Why did you come here in sorrow? You, too, Ahinoam, why those old robes of mourning? Their age makes you older still. Oh, mothers! Mothers! Even you, Bathsheba, for whom my passion was so violent, even you are only a mother now.

BATHSHEBA. A grandmother, too, with many grandchildren. But let me tell you something: you have not grown younger either.

DAVID. Ha-ha! I am gray, quite gray. Gray beard, gray head, wrinkled face. Oh, no, I am no longer the young David, no more the blond hero. (*Rises.*) Yet! (*Draws himself to his full height, thrusts out his chest, and descends with firm step. With lithe and youthful movements he walks to his wives.*) Yet, I am still a man! Those gray hairs are not yet ice and snow. I am not yet stiff and frozen. My heart and blood still boil with flaming fires, and passions of all kinds still roar within me.

MIKHAL. Rejoice! King David will take unto himself new wives.

DAVID. As you said. These last years I have not grown any younger, and I begin to feel it. Absolam—he cost me much. Ha-ha, an enemy from my own house, as the prophet promised. That is the price I paid for you, Bathsheba.

BATHSHEBA. Am I not worth it?

DAVID. Ha-ha! You are! Indeed, you are! Oh, I thank you all for the great joys that you gave me, and I thank God, too, for having strewn you in my path—a glorious bouquet of flowers. Yet—like even the loveliest of flowers, you are all faded. But I have remained the picker. My hairs are gray; my face is lined, but I am still the plucker of flowers. Oh, I am still a man and I want passion and fire around me. Let joy regale the time of my manhood. My young concubines, I invite you to the dance. (*He runs back to his throne. Standing before it, he claps his hands as a signal. A servant enters through the curtained doorway rear and prostrates himself before the king.*) I want music. Let them play a dance—something wild and burning and passionate. I want to see a dance like a wildfire. (*The* SERVANT *arises and backs out. The* CONCUBINES *rise but are astonished and stand at a loss. Wild dance music is heard from behind the curtain.*)

DAVID (*to the* CONCUBINES). Well? Why so sad? Dance!

CONCUBINES. Oh, King!

DAVID. Dance, when I command yóu!

(*The* CONCUBINES *descend from their platform and begin to dance. At first they are undecided, but gradually they forget themselves and dance with fiery passion.*)

DAVID (*with hungry, devouring eyes, he watches their dance and the movements of their bodies. Suddenly he springs to his feet*). Stop! Stop! My head is in a whirl! Go! Absolam defiled you, and you are dead to me! Go. You have danced your last dance for the king.

CONCUBINES (*prostrate themselves*). Oh, King!

DAVID. I regret your loss, young wives, but it must be so. You shall have your separate quarters, but you shall never see me again. Go, you widows, go!

(*The* CONCUBINES *leave, right, with suppressed weeping.*)

DAVID. What a pity, so many young wives! Such glorious loveliness! Yes. Well, now I am left alone with you. Which of you has youth left in her body? Which of you would like to dazzle her husband! No! No! Go! Now I wish to be alone.

(*Bowing low, the wives start tó leave in reverse order from that in which they entered.* MIKHAL, *the last to leave, pauses at the curtain, shakes her head at* DAVID *and, laughing derisively, leaves.*)

DAVID (*sits a while, huddled in his throne, looking much older. Then he claps his hands. A* SERVANT *enters and prostrates himself*). Send Hushai in to me. (*The* SERVANT *arises and backs out.* DAVID *descends from the throne and walks to and fro as though he were very cold.*)

HUSHAI (*enters from the rear, bowing low*). Do you desire something, my King?

DAVID. Hushai, I feel cold.

(*With a merry smile on his lips and in his eyes,* HUSHAI *slowly raises his hand to his beard.*)

ABISHAG

(KING DAVID's *bedchamber. Night. Many lights illuminate the room. On a large chair, before a table laden with food and drink, sits the king, wrapped in layers of clothes, his eyes closed, as if asleep. Before him stands* HUSHAI THE ARCHITE. *Servants stand at the door and behind the chair.*

DAVID *finally opens his eyes and looks at the* ARCHITE. *The king is tired, spent, and sad.*)

HUSHAI (*bowing*). What is my King's command?

DAVID. Not here yet? Not one has been found? Is there no woman to bring me warmth?

HUSHAI. None of the messengers has yet returned.

DAVID. King David lives on only in the ballads of the maidens. In song and story I am still the hero and the champion: My feet are like the hind's. They carry me to high places. My hands are skilled in warfare and like bows of steel are my arms. My steps are large and broad under me, and my feet never slip—Ha-ha. It sounds good in the song, yet not one will lie in my bosom, as though it were the bosom of a corpse.

HUSHAI. I ordered them to find the most beautiful women, and that takes time.

DAVID. Ha-ha. The most beautiful—

HUSHAI. The better to warm you.

DAVID. Yes, yes. Your counsel was good, Archite, and your thought was wise, but before—before she is found, I will freeze.

HUSHAI. Let the thought of her warm you meanwhile.

DAVID. Yes. Yes. The thought. . . . Of the most beautiful. . . .

HUSHAI. Of the most beautiful women within the borders of Israel.

DAVID. Why not the most beautiful woman?

HUSHAI. That would not be wise of me.

DAVID. Not wise of you?

HUSHAI. Whom should I seek when the most beautiful woman of all ceased to warm the king?

DAVID. Ha-ha. Clever Hushai.

HUSHAI. Let her be but one of the most beautiful, and we can readily exchange her.

DAVID. Until at last the loveliest of all. . . .

HUSHAI. That one you shall never have.

DAVID. What?

HUSHAI. I shall use her only to arouse you. The excitement
will keep you warm and spur the force of life within you.

DAVID. Am I to die without having enjoyed the most beautiful woman?

HUSHAI. What will your life be to you after you have enjoyed
the most beautiful woman too?

DAVID. Yes, yes. You speak loyally, my faithful Hushai. Yet,
not wisely, ha-ha, not wisely at all. Don't you see, I shall never
believe you that I have already had the fairest. I shall think,
somewhere the fairest of the fair still lives, but your emissaries
have not found her yet. I shall think that the fairest has just
been born and that when she is grown, I shall be here no more.
You see, you may safely bring me the loveliest. I shall admire
her—and long for one lovelier still.

HUSHAI. Then let each be the loveliest in your eyes.

DAVID. How you squirm out of it, you wily Hushai! But
meanwhile you still don't have a single one. I am afraid they
will not come to the cold old king. They have hidden themselves, these fairest of yours, as from retribution or misfortune.
You—if your emissaries return alone, as they left, I shall punish
you. And I can tell you the sentence now: if they return without
one to warm me, you can go and choke yourself on a bone,
like your old foe Achitophel.

HUSHAI. I know my emissaries will fulfill their mission. Still,
just as a precaution, I now swear that from this moment on,
not a bite of meat shall cross my lips.

DAVID. Ha-ha. Tell me, how did you happen to think of this
device? Why didn't you drum up some war to rouse me and
keep me warm with its excitement? I would have pursued my
enemies and annihilated them. I would not have returned until
I had exterminated them. I would have destroyed them and
smashed them. They would have had to fall under my feet.
Why didn't you try to strengthen me through war, to renew
the vigor of my veins in battle?

HUSHAI. Peace reigns between you and the nations around
us, upon whom the fear of you has descended, and Judah and
Israel dwell in peace upon their soil. Would I not have sinned
against my people and my God had I contrived to lead you
to war? And besides, you have long been sending your captains
into battle.

DAVID. Why didn't you seek to warm me with God's word?

The Lord has always been my light. He has always illuminated my darkness. He has always been my strength. His word has always been the vital force of my life. Why didn't you seek warmth for me from Him who has always restored me and warmed me?

HUSHAI. The Lord has never left you, and you always bear His word within you, and still you grow cold and your limbs shiver with chills. And if you wanted to warm yourself with God's word, you should not have called me, but the prophets Gad and Nathan.

DAVID. You are a talented go-between. Your heart is drawn to women and your head is full of them.

HUSHAI. I am the best physician for your weakness. David the man is old and cold; therefore, David the man must be made young and warm.

DAVID. Then fetch me the remedy at once.

HUSHAI. Patience, my King!

DAVID. Patience! And my days may well be numbered. Death lurks at my shoulder. I don't want to die of weakness and old age!

(*A* SERVANT *enters and prostrates himself.*)

DAVID. What is it? What news do you bring?

SERVANT. Jehoida has arrived.

HUSHAI. Jehoida!

SERVANT. And he brought with him. . . .

HUSHAI (*rushing to the door*). The remedy—young and beautiful.

DAVID. Stop, Hushai! Wait! Don't bring her in yet. Remove these coats and coverings from me. (*With the aid of the servants he frees himself from the numerous coverings and rises.*) I want to move about unburdened and free my legs of their stiffness. I would not have my old age frighten her nor my weakness freeze the blood in her veins. Dress me in my royal robes. (*The servants rush for the clothes.*) Let a king greet her. Let her see that I am vigorous still and not a corpse awaiting burial. (*The servants begin to dress him.*) King David needs only the partnership of youth and he is David whole again, full of warmth and life, full of grace and song. Go tell Jehoida to come in alone. (*The servant leaves.*) I want to question him. Before I see her, let me imagine her and let him help me do that. I want to see whether reality can surpass the fancy. I want to see whether age has dimmed the power of my imagination. (JEHOIDA *enters and prostrates himself.*) Arise, Jehoida, and tell me what you have brought me. What is she like—her face, her figure? Wherein is she beautiful? (JEHOIDA, *who has risen, prostrates himself again.*) Get up and stay on your feet as I told you to, and speak. Reveal the richness of the treasure you have found for me.

JEHOIDA. Oh, King, I have no words!

DAVID. I tell you, describe her!

JEHOIDA. I ask your pardon, my King! Your slave does not want to blaspheme!

DAVID. Hushai, you go and have a look. Then come back and tell me.

HUSHAI. The suspense is getting me too! (*Goes to the door.*)

JEHOIDA (*to* HUSHAI, *as he leaves*). Oh, Hushai, you go to gaze upon the sun. Shield your eyes.

DAVID. You don't seem to have been blinded.

JEHOIDA. But I shall never be able to look upon my own wife again.

DAVID. You make me really curious. Where did you find her?

JEHOIDA. In Shunam.

DAVID. What is her name?

JEHOIDA. She is called Abishag.

DAVID. Young?

JEHOIDA. Spring itself was never so young.

DAVID. Her lips?

JEHOIDA. When you can tear your lips from hers you will know that you are really old.

DAVID. Tall? Short?

JEHOIDA. Oh, do not ask, my King! She is tall enough to block the whole world from your view, and small enough for you to take her in your arms and thank God that you have lived to behold her.

DAVID. Well, where is Hushai?

JEHOIDA. Do not take it amiss, my King, if he cannot tear himself away from her.

DAVID. I'll have his eyes. . . .

(HUSHAI *enters, leading* ABISHAG *before him.* DAVID *interrupts his angry threat, as if amazed and dazzled by the sight of* ABISHAG. ABISHAG *starts to prostrate herself.* HUSHAI *restrains her.*)

HUSHAI. I beg your pardon, my King, for having brought her in unbidden. I did not want you to hold up the poverty of my language for the mockery of children.

JEHOIDA. Now you see, my King!

DAVID (*after a brief silence, as though recovering from his amazement*). Now—I—see.

JEHOIDA. Did my silence exaggerate?

DAVID. I was not aware that my kingdom held such riches!

JEHOIDA. During the whole journey I sought words to clothe my admiration, but. . . .

HUSHAI. Enough. Let us leave the king to admire her alone. He will find the words, I'm sure, words most lovely and ecstatic. He may write a new song, a new psalm of praise. Go, Jehoida, you accomplished your mission with rare skill.

JEHOIDA. God showed me the way and guided my footsteps.

DAVID. And the king will royally reward God's grace to you.

JEHOIDA (*prostrates himself*). Blessings on you, my King! (*Arises and backs out.*)

HUSHAI (*to the servants*). You go too and stand guard before the door. (*The servants prostrate themselves, rise, and leave.*) Let me too wish you a good night, my King. I hope my wish comes true and the night is good to you. (*To* ABISHAG.) You know, sweet maid, what brought you here. . . .

DAVID (*as if awakening from his staring, impatiently*). Go, Hushai! Your tongue grows long and longer, and slips from one piece of foolishness to another. Farwell.

HUSHAI (*bowing*). I beg your pardon, my King. Good night and peace to you and peace to her who is with you. (*Leaves.*)

(DAVID *stares at* ABISHAG, *as before, and starts to walk toward her.* ABISHAG *sinks slowly to her knees and raises her hands as in prayer. Her countenance is thoughtful and ecstatic and her lips move silently.*)

DAVID (*astonished*). You are praying, Abishag! You are kneeling in prayer!

ABISHAG. I am thanking the Lord that He has brought me here to behold you with my own eyes.

DAVID. Truly? Does that make you so happy?

ABISHAG. Oh, King, need you ask that?

DAVID (*lifts her*). Come, arise and sit down beside me and tell me why it makes you so happy. (*He puts his arm around her and leads her to his chair. He sits down and seats her at his feet, pressing her close to his knees. He takes her head in his hands, turns her face upwards, and studies it.*) Well, tell me why you rejoiced.

ABISHAG. Who would not rejoice to behold King David?

DAVID (*releasing her head*). How good to hear! But I want to hear why *you* rejoiced.

ABISHAG. I grew up from childhood with your name in my ears, and your deeds filled my soul with wonder. I learned to babble "King David" almost as soon as I could call my mother or my father. And I was taught to love and fear you as I was taught to love and fear God.

DAVID. To fear?

ABISHAG. And to love.

DAVID. Which was greater?

ABISHAG. Love.

DAVID. You little flatterer, you're not telling me the truth.

ABISHAG. I am telling the truth, my King. You were my hero. You were my champion. At the dance I sang of your victories, and at play I told of your loves. I was your foe's greatest foe, and those who oppressed you first taught me to curse. When you ached, I wept, and when you were glad, I rejoiced. And, more joyful and exalted than anyone else, I could outshout everyone crying, "David, King of Israel, may he live forever!"

DAVID (*caresses her head a while*). How did you imagine me?

ABISHAG. As you are. . . . As I found you just now.

DAVID. With a full gray beard and bushy gray brows?

ABISHAG. My father saw you some years ago and he described you then, with pride and joy, to all his household and his friends. In wonder we fed on his tales of your greatness and beauty, and we envied him his fortune in having seen you. From his words I pressed you into my memory, and your portrait has lived unfaded within me.

DAVID. With my white hair and the lines in my face, old and cold—

ABISHAG. Old and cold?

DAVID. With the weight of seventy years on my shoulders?

ABISHAG. Who would count King David's years? King David is—King David! There is no braver man than he in all of Israel and there is none younger. Thirty mighty heroes are numbered in King David's army, yet none can compare with him. His feet are like the stag's. They carry him to great heights. His hands are skilled in war, and like bows of iron are his arms. . . .

DAVID. He-he— Do you know why you were brought here?

ABISHAG. To be a handmaiden to my king.

DAVID. Not a handmaiden but a wife.

ABISHAG (*ecstatically*). Oh! (*Covers her face.*)

DAVID. Are you glad? Are you frightened? (*Tries to remove her hands from her face.*)

ABISHAG (*herself lowering her hands*). Oh how I thank God that of all the daughters of Israel, I was chosen. Now I know why He made me so beautiful. Oh, to be King David's wife!

DAVID (*looks at her a while, breathing heavily, impassioned*). Kiss me, loveliest of daughters!

ABISHAG (*her eyes closed, she passionately bends her head and lips to him*). Oh! (*They unite in a long kiss.*)

DAVID. Soon I will believe it myself that King David is not old. Come. Now I want to celebrate my marriage to you. The wine is ready. Can you drink, my sweet?

ABISHAG. Should I get drunk, the bed is near.

DAVID. Ah—ha-ha! Drink, you flame, and make me blaze more fiercely!

ABISHAG. My King, how happy I am! My heart pounds and my pulses beat out a wild wedding dance! (*She drinks quickly.*)

DAVID (*passionately*). You! (*Seizes her, bends her head back, and quickly kisses her lips. Suddenly he stops.*) Tell me, has anyone else tasted your kisses?

ABISHAG. No. They have all been treasured for the king.

DAVID. And there is no longing in your heart?

ABISHAG. Longing?

DAVID. For someone who is handsome and young and glorious.

ABISHAG (*shyly*). Only for your embrace.

DAVID (*starts kissing her again, and with his lips on hers he lifts her in his arms*). King David is not old! King David has found his fire and his warmth! (*Carries her toward the bed. Suddenly he stops, closes his eyes, meditates, lowers her gently. He opens his eyes, gazes upon her, and, holding her by the arms, he pushes her gently away, and finally speaks.*) Yes, it shall be so.

ABISHAG (*frightened*). What is it, my King?

DAVID (*after a pause*). You shall not be my wife.

ABISHAG. Have I done anything wrong, my King? Have I acted unbecomingly? Will you send me away from you? Oh, where would I take my shame? Where could I hide my disgrace?

DAVID (*draws her passionately to himself and holds her close*). No, you shall not leave me. You shall stay with me. Day and night you shall be near me, to watch over me and to warm me. You shall be the sun whose rays will open my eyes in the morning, and you shall be the last that sleep will hide from my sight. Wherever my hand reaches out, let the velvet of your skin be as balm poured over my fingers. Let the fragrance of your hair be henceforth the only herbs to refresh my heart. And let the kiss of your lips be the key to mine. But you shall not be my wife.

ABISHAG. Am I then unworthy?

DAVID. Do not seek the cause in yourself, glorious woman. King David met you too late. Now he dares not drink the full measure of his happiness.

ABISHAG. I am too foolish, my King. I do not understand you.

DAVID. My whole life I have been fire and motion, and I thought I was like that bush that burned and was not consumed. Like you, I thought that I would never grow old, that I could not grow old, that my body would lightly bear the heavy weight of years. Yet look. Your hero is old and cold. King David's youth and strength have fled like the morning, like the spring. Now it is night and winter. They cover me with robes but I am not warmed, and my joy in life is gone. You were brought to warm me. Your young, splendid womanhood was to wake my manhood to renewed vigor. Your youth was to make me young. And it all happened. Yet suddenly I saw that only my *desire* for you could keep me warm.

ABISHAG. Only the desire for me? I don't understand.

DAVID. It is as though a difficult riddle had been put to you. You go about thinking and thinking, and you can find no rest in your search for the answer. You lose all desire for food, and at night sleep is driven from your eyes. You are all tense and you feel the strain in every limb. Yet when at last you solve the riddle, your head and heart grow light, the tension leaves, and your whole being grows relaxed.

ABISHAG. You have given me a difficult riddle indeed. What shall I make of it?

DAVID. You are my riddle. Desire for you will waken all my powers. It will heat my blood and make the hammer in my heart beat strong. The yearning for you will be the sharp goad that will neither let me sleep nor freeze. But if you were to be my wife, then you would become a riddle solved. What would then keep King David warm?

ABISHAG. I too wish, as your wife, to be your everlasting fire.

DAVID. That is what I meant. You must be my everlasting fire. But then you must remain my great longing, never to be fulfilled.

ABISHAG. Yearning, fulfillment—my King, I don't know what you mean.

DAVID (*kisses her passionately*). You guileless child!

ABISHAG. But you will not send me away from you?

DAVID. No. You heard me say so. I shall bind you to me and be bound to you.

ABISHAG. As a man is to his wife?

DAVID. As a man to his wife and more.

ABISHAG. Then I am your wife! Then I am your wife!

DAVID. My untouched and unstained! My fire that must never go out!

ABISHAG (*ecstatically*). Ahhh! Then I am King David's wife! (*Begins to dance wildly and passionately.*)

DAVID. Dance, you pure and glorious girl! Dance! Pour hot coals into me with the movement of your young limbs.

(ABISHAG's *dance grows wilder and more passionate, as she sings an accompaniment.*)

DAVID (*spreads his arms wide, thrusts out his chest, breathing deeply*). For this I thank Thee, God, and to Thy name do I sing praise!

THE GOLEM
A Dramatic Poem in Eight Scenes

H. Leivick
(1888–1962)

When H. Leivick[1] died in the early hours of December 23, 1962, days before his seventy-fourth birthday, Yiddish literature lost not only its greatest poet but its most revered personality. As the man was embodied in the art, so the art was embodied in the man. Slender, white-haired, a figure of austere simplicity, he had spent his life brooding over the problem of human suffering. It had haunted him from early childhood, and when he turned from his rabbinical studies in his middle teens, he had already begun to quarrel with God over the suffering he could neither understand nor justify.

At a conference of writers and intellectuals in Jerusalem in 1957 he spoke at some length on the problems of Jewish life. His concluding remarks pertaining to his own work as a writer provide as significant an insight into his art as anything in the large literature about him:

> And now, may I conclude by telling you something about myself as an individual and as a Jew, something that has followed me for a lifetime. It happened when I was no more than seven years old, and now, when I am on the

---

[1] Leivick began writing under his proper name, Leivick Halper, but changed it to its present form when his already established contemporary, Moyshe Leyb Halpern, protested the similarity in names, thinking the younger poet would be trading on the popularity of the older.

eve of seventy, it stands as fresh before me as if it had occurred today. . . .

Yes, I was about seven. One day, I went off to *kheder*. It was a bright, sunny winter day, cold and quiet, as often happens in the towns of White Russia. And I walked, in the early morning, to the *kheder* on the synagogue street. I passed a large market square and turned off into the street on which stood the Polish church. As I passed the church entrance a tall burly Pole bounded over to me, slammed his fist across my head, tore my hat off and threw both it and me to the frosty ground. He beat me, shouting, "Dirty Jew! When you pass our church you have to take your hat off! You dirty Jew!" I got up with difficulty, grabbed my hat from the ground, and ran off to *kheder* in tears. My heart cried out within me: Why did that big Pole beat me, a child of seven years? And why is it that when he, a gentile, passes a synagogue, no one makes him put on a hat?

I walked into the *kheder*, choked back the tears, and sat down to the study of the Pentateuch. The teacher began the lesson for the day, the verses about the sacrifice of Isaac. Isaac accompanies his father Abraham to Mount Moriah, and now Isaac lies bound upon the altar waiting to be slaughtered. Within me my heart weeps even harder. It weeps out of great pity for Isaac. And now Abraham raises the knife. My heart is nearly frozen with fear. Suddenly—the angel's voice: Abraham, do not raise your hand against your son; do not slay him. You have only been tested by God. And now I burst into tears. "Why are you crying now?" the teacher asked. "As you see, Isaac was not slaughtered." In my tears I replied, "But what would have happened had the angel *come one moment too late?*" The teacher tried to console me with the reassurance that an angel cannot be late. But the fear of coming too late stayed with me.

After *kheder* I went home. It was already evening. I walked past the spacious courtyard of Count Yassevitch. I stole inside. I had been told that in one of the rooms of the Count's palace his demented son was kept locked behind bars. I was filled with eagerness and with a strange fascination to see this unfortunate man behind bars. I wanted to see this man of pain and suffering. And then I saw him. I stood before his grated window and looked at him through the bars. He stood inside, near the window, and looked at me. Silent and motionless, he stood looking at me. Great terrifying eyes. The man himself—a giant, the black hair of his head and face—dishevelled, wild. I stared at him as if entranced, as if gazing into an abyss that drew me. Our eyes met. My knees began to buckle. To save myself, I thought up a trick. Near the window hung an iron pole with which they closed the shutters at night. The pole was frozen. I wanted to show this terrifying man that I wished to do something to make him joyous, to amuse him; I put my tongue against the frozen iron. The tip of my tongue stuck to the iron, froze to it. I tore my tongue away and it began to bleed. The blood filled my mouth and dripped down onto my clothes. I ran home in terror and came into the house spattered all over with blood. And soon after, I fell into a great fever.

As you see, four moments, four sharp experiences in one day in the life of a seven-year-old child. They would be too much even for an adult. How much more so for a child. But it seems there is no such thing as "too much" for a Jewish child! These four events of a single day left a permanent imprint upon my entire life and became the undertone of all my later poems and plays, the undertone of my existence as a Jew and of my fate as a Jew. . . .

Yes, I was seven years old at the time and now I am nearly seventy, and these four events are happening to me again today no less fatefully and no less tragically but also with no less decisiveness and no less honor.

I still feel afresh the pain of that Pole's—that gentile's—fist across my face, a blow for no wrong of mine. I still see the terrifying eyes of the man behind bars, bars behind which later on, in Czarist jails, I spent long years. Why? For wanting freedom. For wanting a world without bars. I see that incarcerated man, wildly unkempt, sunk in loneliness, in darkness—forlorn. I still bear within me the desire to test nature, that icy, frozen iron, the desire to place my tongue against nature's essence, to savor its taste, and savoring it, to feel my own warm blood dripping over me. But most of all I am pursued by Isaac's lying bound upon the altar, his looking at the raised knife till the angel of God announced that it was but a trial; and like a decree as well as a refrain my childish question still pursues me: "What would have happened had the angel come one moment too late?"

It pursues me because I have seen—we all have seen—

six million Isaacs lying under knives, under axes, in fires,
and in gas-chambers; and they were slaughtered. The angel
of God did come too late. Six million slaughtered Isaacs are
beyond my comprehension. But I can comprehend one
Isaac waiting to be slaughtered and thereby living through
the horrors of six million slaughtered, as though he were
himself slaughtered six million times. . . .

Have we not had enough of sacrificial altars? I ask, have
we not had enough? . . .

Leivick's talk, entitled "The Jew—The Individual," was intended to bear upon some of the problems of the individual
Jew in relation to Jewish life; but like all of Leivick's work it
penetrated to the individual man within the individual Jew.
Man—suffering, lonely, yearning for redemption, sometimes
purified by his sufferings to look with compassion on the sufferings of his fellows—man is at the center of his twenty-one
plays in prose and verse and his ten volumes of poetry. And
man is at the center of *The Golem,* his first published play
(1921), begun in his late twenties.

The materials of the play derive from legends, which became
popular in the Middle Ages, about various persons who were
credited with the power to create a *golem,* a creature of earth,
given life through the potency derived from the proper combi-
nation of letters of the divine Name. The most famous of such
creators was Rabbi Judah Loew of Prague (1512–1609), known
as the Maharal, who was said to have created a golem to defend
the Jewish community from those who were plotting to destroy
it. Numerous tales arose of the golem's prowess in frustrating
various plots, in this instance a plot to hide two bottles of
blood in the synagogue before Passover and then produce a
corpse, so that the Jews might be accused of using Christian
blood for baking matzohs. In all these tales, the golem remains
a robot, huge, crudely shaped, and clumsy, without a will of his
own, who acts under the direction of the Maharal.

To these materials, Leivick typically adds the motif of human
redemption and introduces the Man on the Cross as well as the
traditional figures of Jewish redemption. He introduces the
character of Elijah, the Prophet, forerunner of the Messiah of
the house of David, and the Messiah ben David himself, whose
advent is to inaugurate an era of peace and justice on earth. He

also suggests, in the person of Joseph the Golem, the figure of the Messiah ben Joseph, an obscure figure in Talmudic Haggadah, who will arrive during the cataclysmic days of Gog and Magog preceding the arrival of the Messiah ben David.

What emerges is far more than a play about an incident in Jewish history. It is a play in which the Jews become symbolic of a mankind suffering innocently, suffering in spite of its innocence, suffering because of its innocence. It is a play about mankind's yearning for redemption; and it is a play in which the Jews, as bearers of a redemption in peace and justice, suffer because that vision runs counter to the ways of the world. In the symbolic scene in the cave, the three redeemers meet in a brotherhood of suffering, outcasts from the world. But *The Golem* is not only a philosophical morality play; it is also a political parable about the relationship of ends and means in which the figure of Force, the Golem, reveals the dangers inherent in violence. And it is, finally, a play about the nature of man and about three figures caught up in conflict with one another.

The tragedy of the Maharal is the tragedy of the creator whose creation does not respond in accordance with his plan; the tragedy of the social dreamer whose dreams are frustrated, who discovers that force contaminates and consumes; the tragedy of a man who, grown impatient with the prospect of the eternal victim, grown weary of the sight of innocent suffering, learns that suffering is the inescapable lot of man, that endurance and the wisdom of endurance—compassion for the sufferers—are the only alternatives open to man as Man. From the very first he finds his vision of the ideal contaminated by reality, infected by life. Despite the intensity of his hopes and the mounting excitement of his vision of the impending miraculous liberation of man, the doubt and fear of failure never leave him. His is an error also of compassion. Knowing that suffering is the savior's lot, he drives off Elijah and the Messiah ben David. In an age of violence, their time has not yet come; it is still the time of Joseph, the Messiah of the Fist. But his is also an error of pride, of the delusion that he can control Force, that Force can really solve problems. He learns that it cannot, that the traditional wisdom of his people is rooted in the nature of reality, that whatever the temporary effect of the fist, it cannot solve the human condition. As Leivick remarks elsewhere, "Man lasts forever; redemption—for a while."

If the Maharal learns the limitations of hope, the Golem learns the pain of the individual's loneliness. Reluctant to leave the peace of nonbeing, he has life foisted upon him. And it is the only life possible. The Maharal cannot prevent the inevitable human qualities of fear and sorrow, pity and temptation, from imprinting themselves upon the Golem's heart. When the Golem comes to life, he learns not only to bend his head and chop wood; he learns the sorrow of loneliness, the need for love, the fear of death, the temptation to wield power and destroy. No sooner does he become a man than he begins to long for love—and to dream of his own redemption. He is drawn to the beggars—redeemers, filled with pity for their suffering. And like any man, like the nobleman's mad son, he is a prisoner of himself, of his body, of life. By the ironies that derive from the complex nature of man and life, the Golem, the principle of Force, yearns for peace and love, and the Maharal, the principle of Peace, creates force. And the Golem, the man that to his creator was a thing, is a thing become a man.

Opposed to the Maharal stands Thaddeus the Antagonist, the world. Thaddeus hates the Jews because he cannot stand the moral principle they represent, because they are a constant reproof to the principle of the fist, by which the world is governed, because the principle of the fist must always crucify the principle of compassion. It is the Thaddeuses who always crucify Christ. The conflict between Thaddeus and the Maharal is reminiscent of the conflict between John Claggart and Billy Budd. It is the conflict of moral opposites, of the principle of guilt and force with that of innocence and gentleness. Force cannot conceive the reality of gentleness, as guilt cannot conceive the viability of innocence and must subvert it to vindicate itself. As Claggart subverts Billy into violence and guilt, so Thaddeus subverts the Maharal. But the Maharal's innocence having been the outgrowth of morality, not of ignorance, like Billy's, he can see his error and pick up the burden of morality —and suffering—again.

THE GOLEM

Prague. Seventeenth Century

SCENE I. CLAY

(A deserted place on the bank of the river outside of Prague. Daybreak. All is dark and silent. Reb Levi Bar Bezalel, or THE MAHARAL, *an old man of seventy, stands over an outlined mound of clay, kneading the figure of a man. He finishes.* ABRAHAM THE SHAMMES *stands near him, helping with the work.* THE MAHARAL *straightens up from his work and addresses* THE SHAMMES.)

MAHARAL.
    It's done. All done. Now hurry to the synagogue,
    To Isaac and to Jacob and bid them come.
SHAMMES.
    And should I stay there, Rabbi?
MAHARAL.
    Stay in the synagogue. But Abraham,
    Remember, lock forever in your heart
    The secret you were privileged to know.
    Let no one ever hear of it from you.
SHAMMES.
    Forever, Rabbi.
MAHARAL.
    And do not tell them yet that all is done.
    They must see it for themselves.
    The day begins to dawn. Hurry.
    (Exit SHAMMES.)
MAHARAL *(bends over the figure)*.
    Yes, all is done and darkness covers all.
    The hour of wonder comes with the day,
    And as I look upon this great frame
    That has been shaped and kneaded by my hands,
    I can descry his shadow striding here,
    The shadow of a being breathing life.
    (Raises his head to the sky.)
    But who am I to say: "My hands have shaped?"
    Blind was I until You gave me sight—
    A puff from heaven's height upon my brows—
    And showed me where the slumbering body lay.

How many generations has he slept
While somewhere else his soul in longing wanders?
Or has the soul forgot, in age-long wandering,
The road's return to where the body sleeps?
Or does it, too, somewhere lonely slumber,
Waiting like its frame for You again
To free my eyes, reveal again . . .
I hear the rush of wings about my head.
The night around is filled with flutter.
Expectantly the figure lies outstretched.
His head, uncovered, looks aloft to heaven,
And from within his lips a prayer seeks release.
    (*He covers his face with his hands. Remains in this position
    a long while. Steps back in fright.*)
Who was it flew across my eyes?
Who touched my brow with something sharp?
Who pierced my ear with screeching shriek?
Whence comes the blunted echo that I hear?
    (*Looks around and listens.*)
I see no one. Silence. The river flows.
The stars go out, each after the other.
The eastern sky should have grown light,
And yet it darkens. O give me strength, Creator.
In the midst of joy and pride I saw
A second shadow of this great frame.
    (*A distant rustle is suddenly heard and something com-
    pletely black strides across the river, sways and revolves.*)
Who walks upon the surface of the river?
Approaches me yet comes no nearer;
Withdraws from me yet is no further?
    (*A* FIGURE *appears before* THE MAHARAL.)

MAHARAL.
    Who are you, dark presence?
FIGURE.
    You do not know me?
MAHARAL.
    I cannot see your face.
FIGURE.
    You do not recognize my voice?
MAHARAL.
    Your voice is like a cold wind
    That blows in a deep pit
    Without entrance, without exit.

FIGURE.

    I have a voice that is not yet a voice.

    I have a heart that is not yet a heart.

MAHARAL.

    Who are you? Speak. What is your name?

FIGURE.

    Not till later will I be known by name.

    I am not yet among mankind.

    I am as yet a shadow's shadow.

MAHARAL.

    Whence do you come?

FIGURE.

    I have come to warn you: create me not.

    Do not dislodge me from my rest.

MAHARAL.

    Vanish. I order you.

FIGURE.

    I tell you once again; again I warn:

    Create me not!

    You see: the stars go out, each one.

    So will the light go out

    In every eye that looks on me;

    And where my foot will tread,

    A blight will grow upon that place;

    And what my hand will touch,

    To dust and ashes will it crumble.

    Do not exchange my darkness and my stillness

    For the tumult of the streets and for the noise of men.

MAHARAL.

    O, help me in this heaviest hour, God.

FIGURE.

    I know you will not hear my plea.

    Therefore I come to give you warning—

    And let my warning be a plea.

    The whole night through you kneaded me;

    With coldness and with cruelty you shaped me.

    How good it was to be mere clay,

    To lie, lifeless and calm,

    Among the sands and stones of earth

    Between eternities.

MAHARAL.

    Now vanish to your refuge, Figure,

    And take your fear of life,

    Your sorrow, with you to your lair.

    When the hour of wonders comes

As soon as night retreats before the eastern sun,
Then, too, will your despair retreat.
For I was sent by God to knead you,
Disjoin you from the stony earth
And with the first ray that lights the sky
Breathe into you the breath of life.

FIGURE.

I do not want it.

MAHARAL.

Your days and nights and all your deeds
Have been decreed.
You are created for more than merely life.
In silence and concealment you will do
Great wonders, but your deeds will be in secret.
No one will know the hero. You will seem
A hewer of water, a cutter of wood.

FIGURE.

A Golem, a thing of clay.

MAHARAL.

A people's champion, a man of might.

FIGURE.

A servant—to be ruled, commanded.

MAHARAL.

A living man.

FIGURE.

A living man? Why do you stand and wait?
Where is the soul that will be breathed in me?
Why do you leave my eyes still shut?
Why is a heart not given me?
Where is the tongue, the teeth, where is the blood
That must be poured to flow in me?
How would you have me? Blind or mute?
Or lame? Or deaf, perhaps?
Or all at once? Speak. The night departs;
The day arrives. O darkness, darkness!
One moment more conceal me in your depths!
One moment more what I have been till now:
A lifeless mound of arid clay.
(*The figure dissolves into the darkness.*)

MAHARAL.

A darkness has invaded the desire
I strove so hard to render holy, pure.
With words of fear I have myself
Produced a flaw within the heart to be.

O, I did not surmount temptation
Nor did I guard my heart from sorrow,
From anguish and from pity. Great and greater
Grows the weight of every frightening word.
My own hands have turned his fate
Into the road of pain, confusion, and dismay.
How many weeks, how many days and nights
I strove to purify my heart and mind,
To shed entirely self and world
And be transformed into a single thought—Yours!
I saw but one within my mind, but one.
I saw him come and open wide his eyes,
A covert smile upon his lips,
And iron strength within his arms.
He sees, yet no one knows he sees;
He walks, yet no one knows his ways.
His life, his death—one silent breath,
One act of secret faith serene.
He comes to none; he speaks to none.
A corner somewhere is his waiting place
Until the moment that his summons comes.
What is there now to do? Doubt and fear,
The bitter and the angry loneliness
Have placed their taint upon the living word.
I see I am unworthy in Your eyes;
Perhaps I was ambitious, proud,
Too eager to descry what no man yet
Has seen before. I see, I see—
Before You what am I? A crawling worm,
A lump of earth, a grain of dust.

    (*A long silence.* The Figure of Thaddeus *the priest ap-
    pears. It approaches* The Maharal *at once.*)

Maharal.

    Thaddeus. Yes, it's he. He comes this way.
    My mind just spoke his name—
    Is this a second sign from God?

Figure (*collides with* The Maharal. *Steps back*).

    What brings you here this middle of the night?

Maharal.

    It is not night but break of day.

Figure.

    What brings you here at break of day?

Maharal.

    I do at break of day what God commands.

FIGURE.

And what did God command you do
That I should have to be there too?

MAHARAL.

You need not stay. Go freely on your way.

FIGURE.

That I can go my way is widely known.
Thaddeus can manage well.
But what causes that strange look within your eyes?
They flare with murder and black strength.
Murder in a rabbi's eyes? I have seen
In dungeons, at the stakes of holy courts
So many faces of so many Jews,
So many eyes of every sort, but I
Have never chanced to see two Jewish eyes
That looked upon me with true fury,
With murderous rage and hate, as yours do now.
They seem the eyes of some Golem run wild.
(THE MAHARAL *covers his face with his hands. His shoulders heave.*)

FIGURE.

Why have you suddenly concealed your face?
Grown silent? What is this? Who lies upon the ground?
A corpse? Or what? I've stood here all this while
And did not see it.
(*Bends down and looks at the clay figure.*)
What do my eyes discern?
What is this? A figure fashioned out of clay
Lies full length upon the ground!
(*Steps back and crosses himself.*)
O holy Jesus!

MAHARAL.

Until the time that he is fit for life,
To raise his arm, to stand upon his feet,
I bear the look that lives within his eyes.

FIGURE.

Protect me from the Evil One, from all
Who are unbaptised, cursed, and damned, O Christ.
(*Disappears.*)

MAHARAL (*is silent a long while. Awakens as from a trance. Looks around.*)

Is this a second sign that has been sent?
I see that it must be. The hand of God
Has ringed us round within a single ring

And paired me with this little mound of clay.
And all that I conceive, I see;
And everything I see, will be.
It will; it must!
And now my heart is light and glad. For I—
What am I? Your portents speak the truth.
It must be! And it will!

(*From the road leading to the city,* THE MAHARAL'S *two
students arrive,* ISAAC *the Kohen and* JACOB *the Levite.*
JACOB *carries a bundle of clothes in his hands. They come
quietly and seem scarcely to touch the ground.*)

MAHARAL (*going to meet them*).
      You come in time.

ISAAC.
      The day breaks, Rabbi.

MAHARAL.
      Did anyone observe you coming here?

JACOB.
      We walked beside the road and were concealed.

MAHARAL.
      Were you in synagogue till now?

ISAAC.
      Yes, Rabbi. Apart from one another
      We stood in prayer, and loud we prayed and lit
      No candle till the night was half-way gone.
      The dark surrounded us like a thick wall
      And cut off each from each. So far we seemed,
      We could not hear each other's prayer or speech.
      At first the distance frightened me, as though
      I sought a path in some dark wood
      And finding none, into its dark recesses
      I ran more swiftly. But suddenly I grew
      Quite calm, and felt the distance growing greater.

JACOB.
      And Rabbi, hear what happened after that:
      We stood, we thought, far from one another.
      It was so dark, and neither of us moved,
      As though we each were fastened to the floor,
      And each one thought that in the synagogue
      He stood alone. And then at midnight, as you
      Bid us, we lit the candles we had each
      Prepared, and when we did, behold the wonder:
      We stood together, side by side,
      And each one's candle lit the other's face.

ISAAC.

A great marvel, Rabbi.

MAHARAL.

A favorable sign. Your hearts
Have cleansed themselves in prayer
And grown worthy to speak the blessing
Which your lips must soon recite.

ISAAC.

Rabbi, may one look at him?

MAHARAL.

You may. Go close and look.
(Both bend over the figure and look at it.)

JACOB.

As yet there is not much to see. Clay.

ISAAC.

The clay is moving now; its eyes open.

JACOB.

It moves its legs.

ISAAC.

Its face contorts. It laughs.
(He recoils in fright.)

MAHARAL.

What ails you, Isaac?

ISAAC.

I looked at him and then was seized by fright,
Reminded of a dream that I once had.

MAHARAL.

A dream? When?

ISAAC.

Forgive me, Rabbi, I have sinned.
At midnight, when we lit the candles and took
A Torah Scroll out from the Ark as you
Instructed, and when to Genesis we rolled
It open, and each one called the other up
To read the Book, and seven times we each
Had read its early verses, no one disturbed
The reading. We returned the Torah to the Ark,
And silently we each began the Psalms.
And as I stood there, face to wall, reciting,
Suddenly my lids began to stick.
I struggled hard to keep from dozing, raised
My voice to chant aloud. All at once
I heard a clamor. Despairing cries came near
And nearer. Doors and windows then flew open.

The synagogue was filled with Jews in panic,
Who threw themselves in every corner, fell
And, breathless, crawled to hide beneath the tables.
And as they lay in silence, a man rushed in.
His face was strange, his head was large, his body
Tall, arms long, and eyes of piercing green.
He held a sword and thrust it everywhere.
Up and down he slashed and right and left.
And soon they all lay, gashed and slaughtered;
The darkness covering their bloody dying.
And then he raised his arm to me and would
Have brought it down upon my head—when you
Arrived, Rabbi.

MAHARAL.

I?

ISAAC.

As soon as he perceived you, he appeared
Discouraged. He dropped his sword and to the door
He rushed. But you were there to bar his way.
You seized the sword from him and aimed a blow
Across his face, but woe!
You failed.

MAHARAL (*beside himself*).

I failed?

ISAAC.

You struck the air.

MAHARAL.

He ran away?

ISAAC.

Like a shadow he dissolved and vanished.
That shape of clay reminded me of him.

MAHARAL (*to himself*).

So many signs! So many adverse omens!
Will not a single ray of hope shine through?
Lead me, O God, along whatever roads You choose,
But let your brightness gleam through all
That is concealed from me.

JACOB.

In synagogue they spoke of evil times
Of old and of the rumors that now thrive
In Prague about a savage tyrant who
Has slaughtered multitudes of Jewish folk—
And so he dreamt this dream, Rabbi.

MAHARAL.
>   Yes, my students, evil times will come,
>   And with evil times come great ones too.
>   We must be ready to receive those days.
>   As you see, God has brought us now
>   To the dawn of great and trying times.

ISAAC.
>   My hands are trembling with fear, Rabbi,
>   Shall I lay the bundle down?

MAHARAL.
>   Is everything contained in it?

ISAAC.
>   Everything, Rabbi.

JACOB.
>   Where will he stay? In the synagogue?

MAHARAL.
>   An end to questions now. Contain your fears.
>   Secrete them in your hearts, and with your fears
>   Hide all that you will see and hear.
>   And now come to the water. We wash our hands.
>   (*They go to the river.*)

SCENE II. WALLS

(The Maharal's *study.* The Maharal *enters.* The Golem *remains standing outside the door. He is taller than the doorway and he does not know enough to bend.*)

MAHARAL.
> Now bend your head. The door is low and you
> Are tall. Remember that, when one is tall
> And wishes to come through a door that's low,
> He must incline his head. You see—like this.
> (*Shows how one bends his head.* The Golem *comes in stooping and remains so.*)

MAHARAL.
> Now raise your head and stand up straight.
> (The Golem *straightens up. Remains silent. He is powerfully built—a giant. Large eyes. There is something heavy and dull about them and at the same time something childlike. Rather heavy lips with deep indentations at the corners. They are frozen into a smile that smiles at— nothing. And yet it seems a smile that is on the verge of tears. The hair of his head, mustache, and beard is black and curly. His eyes open ever wider as he stares at everything.*)

MAHARAL.
> Your eyes are open. You have seen the sky
> Above, the sun that rises in the east;
> You have met Jews upon the streets, in courtyards;
> I have spoken to you; I speak now.
> (The Golem *is silent.*)

MAHARAL.
> You have a mouth and teeth, a tongue to speak,
> Why are you silent?
> (The Golem *is dumb.*)

MAHARAL.
> Speak. I command you, speak.
> Joseph is your name.

GOLEM (*terrified*).
> Joseph?

234

MAHARAL.

You are a man.

GOLEM.

A man.

MAHARAL.

You have a heart to live.

GOLEM.

To live.

MAHARAL.

You need not be discouraged.
You do recall your name—
(THE GOLEM *is silent.*)

MAHARAL.

Have you forgotten? Joseph is your name.
Remember it.

GOLEM.

Joseph.

MAHARAL.

And do you know what I am called?

GOLEM.

Rabbi.
(*Begins to stride around the room, climbing over benches,
tables, knocking them over. Presses against the wall,
pushes it. The windows rattle.*)

MAHARAL.

What are you doing? Stop. You will awaken
Everyone.

GOLEM.

I want to leave this place.
(*Strikes the wall.*)

MAHARAL.

I tell you—stop. Walk around a bench, a table.
One passes them. One does not knock them over.
And neither can one penetrate a wall.
I tell you—stop. Don't strike the wall.

GOLEM.

I want to leave this place.

MAHARAL.

I told you on the way here, did I not,
That you should carry out what I command.

GOLEM (*seats himself on the floor, helpless*).

I will obey, Rabbi.

MAHARAL.

Always you must hear

My words and not forget them.
Do you recall your name?

GOLEM.

I know. My name is Joseph.

MAHARAL.

Get off the floor and sit upon a bench.
(*Takes him by the hand, helps him get up, and seats
him on a bench.*)
I see that you are tired. You come from far.
But do not fear. You are a welcome guest.

GOLEM.

A welcome guest.
(*Looks around and smiles.*)

MAHARAL.

Why do you smile?

GOLEM.

I do not know, Rabbi.
Something is burning on the windows.
I do not know, Rabbi.

MAHARAL.

The sun is rising yonder.

GOLEM.

Your beard is long and white. And mine is black.

MAHARAL.

I found you on the outskirts of the town
You were asleep.

GOLEM.

I do not know, Rabbi.
Fire from somewhere to the windows comes,
And keeps on getting redder. And the walls—
They start to burn. And look, your face burns too.
(*Jumps up and strides about again.*)

MAHARAL.

Where to?

GOLEM.

There. To the fire. I am afraid to stay.

MAHARAL.

You may not go.

GOLEM.

I want to go. I do.
You are so small compared to me, so old.
How small a head you have. You speak to me
And tremble. Your hands
Tremble.

MAHARAL.

Have you once more forgotten who I am?

GOLEM.

I do not know.

MAHARAL.

You are to be my servant.
And therefore you have come into my house.
You will be wholly under my command.

GOLEM.

What must I do?

MAHARAL.

Nothing yet.
You live here—or somewhere else, perhaps.
You wish to live with me?

GOLEM.

No.

MAHARAL.

You cannot go away. You are a stranger.
In my house you will feel at home.

GOLEM.

Something within me rises up and chokes me.
A ringing in my ears.
Before my eyes—both red and green.
My legs—they rise. They wish to go.
My hands—how easily they seize your throat
And carry you away. What is there here?
I want to run, and yet I cannot go.
(*Shouting.*)
I want to strike my hand upon your head
And yet I cannot move. Look, I stagger,
The walls are spinning round.
The fire within the windows flames up higher;
The walls conspire with the door
To hurl themselves upon me. Let me go.
I want to smash, destroy. I want to twist
My head from off my shoulders, twist my arms and legs.
Put out the fire around me.
Take away the walls.
(*He hurls himself wildly against the wall, smashes it with his fists. The walls shake.*)

MAHARAL.

Be calm, I say.
The mighty powers now begin to surge within you.

They cleanse themselves a path into your soul.
The black darkness of your other being
Has not released your head and heart
And from within you speaks its unclean curses.
  (*He puts his hands on* THE GOLEM's *head, caresses him,
  and calms him.*)
Your shoulders tremble. Sit down. Catch your breath.
I foresaw this outbreak of your hatred.
Until that hour arrives of joy unstained,
Of weeping purified, of gleaming calm—
Let blind fear meanwhile cease!
My first blessing, let it fall upon your heart,
My first comfort, on your dishevelled thoughts.
You know not who you are and, fearful, are
Astonished at yourself, your arms, your legs.
Something has befallen you which has wiped
Wholly clean remembrance of your life.
You start anew.
You are my guest. A welcome guest.
Let that alone suffice to let you see
The first reflection of your first hope.
Do not so stubbornly resist.
Someone comes.
You have awakened everyone. Say nothing.
You are a guest and come from foreign parts.
Let that be your reply.

GOLEM.

I am a guest and come from foreign parts.
Whatever once occurred, I have forgot.
  (THE REBBETSIN *and* DEVORALE *enter, frightened, startled
  from their sleep.*)

REBBETSIN.

What's wrong? What was it shook the house?

DEVORALE.

Such terrifying cries, Grandfather.

MAHARAL.

You had a dream.

REBBETSIN.

But I was thrown from bed. Such cries they were!
Who is this? Who sits here, Arye Levi?

DEVORALE.

Oh, how strange he looks.

MAHARAL.

Why are you both so startled?

A stranger, our guest. Coming back from bathing,
I saw him lying on the bare ground,
Exhausted from his travels. Who is he?
Whence does he come? I cannot yet discover.
His speech is so unclear and very strange,
It would be better not to question him.
A poor man, it seems.

DEVORALE.

He looks unfortunate.

REBBETSIN.

He does not seem a Jew. Such hands,
Such shoulders this man has.
I feel uneasy, Arye Levi.

MAHARAL.

No need to fear.
The dust of roads is still upon him.

DEVORALE.

Oh, Grandma, look. See how he stares at me!
What does he want, Grandfather? Ask him.

MAHARAL.

He is a silent man. He does not answer.

DEVORALE.

Again he lifts his head to gape.
Such shining, melancholy eyes.

REBBETSIN.

Don't stare at him. Come, child, let us go.
A poor man. He should be pitied. And yet—
He makes me feel uneasy. Stranger, what is your name?

GOLEM.

Joseph.
(He smiles. He rises and looks intently and marvellingly at
DEVORALE.*)*
Rabbi, who is she?
Why is she fearful? Why does she run away?

DEVORALE.

Oh, hide me, Grandma. Let us leave.
He stares at me. He frightens me.

REBBETSIN.

You see,
The child is frightened. Is he mad or what?
To gape so at another.

MAHARAL.

Why do you stare so, Joseph?

GOLEM.

Who is she, Rabbi? Why does she run away?

MAHARAL.

>She is my daughter, do you hear?
>Remember not to speak to her.

GOLEM.

>Her long hair
>Hangs down over her shoulders.

DEVORALE.

>What is he saying, Grandma? Come, I'm frightened.

REBBETSIN.

>It is disgraceful for him to speak so.

MAHARAL.

>He does not really know what he is saying.
>Confused, it seems. His mind is not quite clear.

GOLEM (*suddenly*).

>Food.

MAHARAL.

>Food? Yes, bring him some.

REBBETSIN.

>Before his morning prayers?

MAHARAL.

>You see who he is.

REBBETSIN.

>Go, child, back to sleep awhile,
>And I will bring a bite for him myself.
>(THE REBBETSIN *and* DEVORALE *leave*.)

GOLEM.

>Where did she go?

MAHARAL.

>To bring you food.

GOLEM.

>And then she will not leave me any more?

MAHARAL.

>I have already told you once. She is
>My daughter; do not speak or think of her.
>(*Sharply*.)
>I see a startling change came over you.
>As though in sudden terror you leaped up.

GOLEM.

>I felt so good each time she looked at me.

MAHARAL.

>Be still!

GOLEM.

>May I not take her by the hand?

MAHARAL.

> You may not even look at her. Remember,
> A wholly different life is yours to live,
> A different air to breathe, a different speech.
> In time you too will come to see it, feel it.
> Till then, be mute. Be locked within your muteness.
> You hear—be mute.

GOLEM.

> To speak to no one?

MAHARAL.

> Just answer when you're spoken to. No more.
> And keep yourself aloof from people. When you
> Come into the synagogue or elsewhere,
> Take your place unnoticed, in some corner.
> If one approaches you to ask a question,
> Answer without anger. To be set
> Apart, is neither punishment nor grief—
> It is the road that you must take
> To wonders and to joy.

GOLEM (*sits down. Turns his head away*).

> It suddenly grows dark for me.
> I can no longer see at all. Hold me,
> Rabbi, I am falling.

MAHARAL.

> You are not falling, merely hungry.
> (THE REBBETSIN *comes in followed by* DEVORALE. THE
> REBBETSIN *brings milk and bread and a pitcher of water.*
> THE GOLEM *sits hunched over the table.*)

REBBETSIN.

> Will not our guest wash?
> (THE GOLEM *sits motionless.*)

REBBETSIN.

> What ails him, Arye Levi? Look,
> He does not raise his head.

DEVORALE.

> Is he asleep?

REBBETSIN.

> Honored guest, wash for eating. Here is water.
> Why is he silent, Arye Levi? Ask him.
> (THE GOLEM *raises his eyes but says nothing.*)

REBBETSIN.

> You want to eat—then wash.

MAHARAL.

> Wash, Joseph.

(THE GOLEM *pours water over his hands, wipes them clumsily in the towel* THE REBBETSIN *holds out for him. He says nothing, begins eating hungrily.*)

REBBETSIN.
No blessing for the bread—how hungrily
He gulps his food. A pity to behold.

MAHARAL.
Should I invite him to remain?

REBBETSIN.
With us?

MAHARAL.
I need a servant, and the synagogue must have
Someone to carry water, cut the wood.

REBBETSIN.
He gave the child a fright. God knows—
May we be spared misfortune—who he is.

MAHARAL.
He is a man—an honest, lonely man.

REBBETSIN.
If you think so. You are a better judge.
But I—

MAHARAL.
You are afraid?

REBBETSIN.
May God not punish me.

MAHARAL.
You need not be afraid. Fortunate was the hour
That God led him across my path.

REBBETSIN.
What do you mean, Arye Levi?

MAHARAL.
I have long
Needed a servant, a man of strength like him.

REBBETSIN.
You know best, I guess. I must go.
(*To* THE GOLEM.)
Should I bring you something more to eat?
(THE GOLEM *shakes his head—no.*)

REBBETSIN (*to* DEVORALE).
Why do you keep following me?

DEVORALE.
Because 1 am afraid, Grandma.

REBBETSIN.
Are you a child?

MAHARAL *(putting his hand on* DEVORALE'S *head)*.
    There is no need to fear, child.
DEVORALE.
    Will he remain here always?
MAHARAL.
    I do not know as yet.
DEVORALE.
    And still his eyes are glued to me.
    (She and THE REBBETSIN *both leave.)*
MAHARAL.
    Well, have you had your fill?
GOLEM.
    My eyes feel heavy, Rabbi.
MAHARAL.
    Your eyes feel heavy? Good. You will sleep
    And when you wake, the world will seem quite different.
GOLEM *(nods, dozing. Awakes with a start)*.
    I must leave! Something urges me to go.
MAHARAL.
    You may not leave this place.
GOLEM.
    And where is Devorale?
MAHARAL.
    Did I not warn you about that?
GOLEM.
    She looked at me.
    Why did she go away, Rabbi?
    Why are you angry with me, Rabbi?
MAHARAL.
    I am not angry. You merely fancy that.
    But never mention Devorale again.
    *(*THE GOLEM *is silent.)*
MAHARAL.
    Well, do you hear my warning?
GOLEM.
    I hear, Rabbi.
    I will obey you. See, my eyes
    Grow heavy once again.
    (Falls asleep sitting up.)
MAHARAL.
    He sleeps.
    (He sits down opposite THE GOLEM *and watches him sleep.
    He rises, stands over him, does not take his eyes away from
    his sleeping face.)*

So much mute anguish in his countenance.
(*Shudders.*)
Is this he? The man I dreamt into existence?
The champion? The hero? He? Such hands,
Such shoulders, legs. So much body?
So much still sorrow?
(*Stands with his face to the wall, deep in sorrow.* THE
REBBETSIN *comes in quietly, is surprised.*)

REBBETSIN.

Oh, why is it so quiet here? Arye Levi!
(THE MAHARAL *turns around and motions with his hand
for her to be quiet and to leave.*)

MAHARAL.

Say nothing. He is asleep.

REBBETSIN.

Sitting up?

MAHARAL.

It does not matter. He should sleep. He must.
(THE REBBETSIN *leaves on tip toe.*)
I will be with you soon.
(*Stands over* THE GOLEM, *listens to his deep and heavy
breathing.*)

SCENE III. THROUGH DARKNESS

(THE MAHARAL's *study. Evening.* THE MAHARAL *sits dozing over an open book.* DEVORALE *stands next to him in fright and tries to wake him.*)

DEVORALE.
    Grandpa, wake up.
MAHARAL (*awakens*).
    What? What is it?
DEVORALE.
    You cried out in your sleep. Such outcries, Grandpa!
MAHARAL.
    I merely dozed. A little nap.
    A dream, child.
DEVORALE.
    "Fire! Blood!" you shouted,
    And words about the Fifth Tower.
MAHARAL.
    Yes, a dream,
    A nightmare. Go, my child,
    It's nothing. Just a dream.
    (DEVORALE *exits.*)
    (THE MAHARAL *sits leaning over the table, his face resting on his hands, which cover it.* THE GOLEM *enters softly and stands near the door. He holds an axe in his hand. He scrutinizes* THE MAHARAL. *The more he looks, the more Golem-like the expression on his face becomes. First, he breaks out suddenly into a broad smile that reveals his white teeth. And then his face contracts into a stiff, frozen expression. He walks softly over to the table where* THE MAHARAL *sits deep in thought. He sits down on the other bench directly opposite* THE MAHARAL *and assumes* THE MAHARAL's *position and facial expression. For some moments they sit opposite each other in this fashion.* THE MAHARAL *suddenly looks up with a start, sees* THE GOLEM *and is frightened.*)
MAHARAL.
    Good heavens! Is it you? How did you come here?

And who sat you at the table?

GOLEM.

I do not know, Rabbi. I saw you sleeping, sitting.

MAHARAL.

You need not imitate all that I do.

Why did you come here now?

GOLEM.

You called me.

MAHARAL.

When?

GOLEM.

For quite a while.

I heard you calling: "Joseph! Joseph!"

MAHARAL (*looking at him sternly*).

I did not call you. No.

Go back to work.

Have you split all the rails?

GOLEM.

They do not let me work.

MAHARAL.

Who?

GOLEM.

They taunt me.

MAHARAL.

I asked you—who?

GOLEM.

The boys. And grown-ups too.

They stand around and look and look,

And everyone asks what my name is. Everyone.

And where I came from.

MAHARAL.

Just do not answer them.

GOLEM.

I do not answer. I keep quiet.

You told me to keep quiet.

MAHARAL.

They will not harm you.

GOLEM.

I hate them.

MAHARAL.

You must live peaceably with everyone.

GOLEM.

I look at no one and I speak to no one.

You see, they stare in through the window.

MAHARAL (*goes over to the window and looks out*).

Don't be afraid. Go back to work. I will
Myself go out and tell them all to stop.

GOLEM.

They do not fear you either. I say:
The Rabbi will come out and scold you,
And when I say that, they only laugh the harder.

MAHARAL.

Well, go back. Soon I will come out.

GOLEM.

I would have let one have it with my axe—

MAHARAL.

What are you saying? You?

GOLEM.

Oh, take them from me.
Drive them away. Why do they talk and stare?
Such talk, such eyes. All and each.
The axe runs lightly in my hands. Up
And down, by itself, and I'm so tall.
The tallest. And the axe runs higher, higher.
Why do you say one may not raise an axe,
When, of itself, my axe flies from my hands?

MAHARAL.

Itself? I see now. It will no longer flee.
I gave your arms their strength
And gave you work to fill your loneliness.
"Let the axe be a feather in your hand"—
Such was my blessing to you.
But now I see it must be otherwise.
Let every axe-lift be heavy toil—
Great strain and sweaty work.
And every time it sinks into the wood,
Let your breath sink, too, like a heavy weight.
I do not punish you. It is a favor,
To keep the lightness of your arm from tempting you.

GOLEM.

I hate them all. You, too.

MAHARAL.

Me, too?

GOLEM.

I fear your glance, your every word.
And always I think I hear your voice:
"Where are you? Come here." I thump the axe

Into the wood and answer: "Here I am."
And all begin to laugh and mimic: "Here I am."

MAHARAL.

Go back to work and pay no heed to anyone.

GOLEM.

But I ignore them now. My eyes are down.
The people are the ones who make me raise
My head and look them in the eyes.

MAHARAL.

Did I not place a charm around your neck
To draw your eyes in friendship to men's faces?

GOLEM.

It worked for but a moment. The first time
I straightened up from splitting logs and saw
So many eyes and faces circled round me
It seemed to me that they all smiled in kindness.
They spoke no words; they merely watched me idly.
And suddenly they all began to speak,
To scamper back and forth and toss their arms;
They shouted curious words and started laughing,
And running in and backing off. And then
I heard your laughter too.

MAHARAL.

Mine?

GOLEM.

As though you had concealed yourself behind them
And set them all to shouting: "Golem!"
I left my work undone
And came to you.

MAHARAL.

Do you feel easier now?

GOLEM.

I feel good with you.
If you were always with me, never left me,
I would not be afraid of any eyes;
I would not be afraid to hear my name.
Do not send me away from you.

MAHARAL.

I am not sending you away. You see me
So many times each day. And when you need me,
Why, you can always seek me out.

GOLEM.

I want always to be with you, always.
When they're all watching as I chop,

Why aren't you among them? Why don't you, too,
Like all the others, always stand and watch?

MAHARAL (*smiles to himself*).

Stand always? Does he understand the words
His lips are speaking? He reasons like a child,
With no perception and no sense. But from his reasons
A great fear stares,
A fear that is no child's.
(*To* THE GOLEM.)
And do you know where you will sleep? In the Fifth Tower.
There even Jews sleep. The shammes will
Conduct you there and make a sleeping place for you.
You surely would not want me there to sleep near you.

GOLEM.

Why not? Is there not sleeping place enough for two?
(THE MAHARAL *smiles. His face grows sad. He walks to the
wall and stops thoughtfully.* THE GOLEM *watches and places
himself at the wall too.*)

MAHARAL (*turning away from the wall*).

I cannot always be with you. Know
That you came here to be alone.
And so I say to you: Go do the work you do.
When you have finished—go to sleep where you
Are told to sleep. You must be with yourself
And not with me. It is hard for you
And dark. Yours is the darkness, and it will
Pursue you step by step until it rises into light.
I took you for a servant not that I
Might follow you and watch you as you eat and sleep.
I'll call you when I need you. Go.
(*Exit* GOLEM, *axe in hand.*)

MAHARAL (*alone*).

Impatience grows more tense within me, fed
By every evil rumor, restless dream.
Who will make plain the meaning of my dream?
You show me signs that follow one another:
Great dangers threaten us.
They come. They stand before us—
False accusations, blood and fire, destruction.
I know that rescue steps upon misfortune's heels,
That comfort, too, sits upon the sword,
That light for us lies hidden in the blackest flame.
But still impatience tosses in my heart,
Impatience with myself—my greatest sin before You.

You sent me him—the helpless servant.
Helpless himself—he must bring help to us.
Himself in darkness—he must bring us light.
At the chasm's brim we hang, suspended by a single hair,
And he who is to save us is the first to cry for help.
I sent him out in anger; yet he did no wrong.
(*He looks out of the window.*)
I am myself, it seems, still fearful of his glance.
You stamped the sorrow of a feeble mind upon him,
Of strangeness and cold loneliness,
So that we might not know the greatness
That is his. No doubt it should be so.
I will wait. I tear impatience from my heart
So that the fear which threatens us may not confuse
My thoughts nor cloud my aged vision;
So that I may perceive the truth of what he is.
His being's light must surely be revealed,
For he is—Yours.
(*He stands leaning against the window.* REB BASSEVI *enters, an elderly Jew, richly dressed.*)

REB BASSEVI.
Good evening, Rabbi.

MAHARAL.
A guest; indeed, a guest.
A good year to you, Reb Bassevi. Sit down.

REB BASSEVI.
I beg forgiveness, Rabbi, that, unasked, I . . .

MAHARAL.
What kind of talk is that, Reb Bassevi.
A welcome guest, indeed.

REB BASSEVI.
I crossed the courtyard of the synagogue;
Behold, knots of men in earnest talk.
They wonder and they worry,
And rumors rush from mouth to mouth.
And I myself, Rabbi—I hope my words
Are no transgression—am not without uneasy thoughts.

MAHARAL.
Be seated, Reb Bassevi.

REB BASSEVI (*sits down*).
Am I, perhaps, intruding, Rabbi?

MAHARAL.
Not at all, Reb Bassevi.

REB BASSEVI.

    I thought: it might be wise
    To step in briefly at the Rabbi's for a chat.

MAHARAL.

    A good idea, Reb Bassevi. Very kind of you.
    But you seem troubled, not yourself.
    Could it be something else that brought you here?

REB BASSEVI.

    Something else? No—I hardly know, myself, Rabbi.
    You should have seen the turmoil in the courtyard.
    Hardly the usual noise at all. That Tankhum,
    Lugubrious man, clad in tatters and in gloom,
    Was spewing words—he got them God knows where—
    Denouncing, cursing, knots of men around him.
    He threw his hands and talked and talked.
    On top of all, that other came along, that woodcutter.
    He is enough to scare one half to death.

MAHARAL.

    You, too, like all the others, Reb Bassevi? A man
    At work, chopping wood. What cause is there for fear?
    We have been seeking long an able woodman,
    Reb Bassevi. You know that.

REB BASSEVI.

    Yes, but this man
    Has not, it seems, found favor in anybody's eyes.
    You should have been there to see how all,
    Came pouring, Rabbi, young and old,
    From every house. To the court they ran
    To gape at some marvel. Rabbi, to tell
    The truth, when I just saw the man, I could
    Not help stopping to stare, entranced at how
    He raised the axe. Never have I seen a man like that.

    (THE MAHARAL *sits, thoughtful and alarmed.*)

REB BASSEVI.

    Who is he, Rabbi? Do you know?

MAHARAL.

    Of course I know. He is not native here.
    He comes from foreign parts, but that's no matter.

REB BASSEVI.

    We have no reason, then, to fear—
    As long as you know him.

MAHARAL.

    Tell everyone—
    There is no cause for fear.

REB BASSEVI.

I'll tell them, Rabbi.

MAHARAL.

But you are still uneasy, Reb Bassevi.
I see it in your face.

REB BASSEVI.

Forgive me, Rabbi.
Perhaps I am at fault. Uneasiness
Has welled within me these last few days,
And this uneasiness, most of all,
Has brought me to you now, Rabbi.

MAHARAL.

God is our Father, Reb Bassevi.

REB BASSEVI.

These are the words I long to hear from you,
Rabbi, the words of comfort, hope, and faith.
My hairs are gray—time for my heart itself
To carry always the words of solace, calm,
And not be frightened nor succumb to fear.
How can we help it? We are sinful, Rabbi,
And times are evil. May God have mercy on us.
Last night, I could not close my eyes till dawn.

MAHARAL.

I did not think to hear these words from you.

REB BASSEVI.

I confess my hope—
That talk would ease the burden of my fears.

MAHARAL.

Do we ourselves not magnify the danger?

REB BASSEVI.

You may be right. We may exaggerate.
But what if the opposite is true? What
If danger far exceeds our fears? Who knows,
Who knows what they prepare behind our backs?
Who knows what traps are daily set for us?
Who knows whose hands will bring catastrophe?
What do they want of us, Rabbi? Tell me,
I mean quite simply, I wish to understand:
What do they want of us?

MAHARAL.

They want so much of us, so very much.
But we can give them nothing.
Or—it may be we can. Indeed, we can;
We do not want to. *We do not want to.*
With but one fingertip

We touched the world and everything it holds.
Standing at the side, we merely breathed upon it,
And all the world and everything it holds
Will bear forever the imprint of our touch,
And storms, great raging whirlwinds, will erupt
From our gentle puff of air.
Then why should we seek causes,
Or ask questions what they want of us?
If cause be needed—let them find a cause!
And seek they do. They seek and find.
And yet, what does it profit them,
This frenzied searching and discovering?
And we—we stand aside from all the causes.
We are both hard and easy, near and far.
If we desire, we turn our face in greeting to the world.
If not, we turn our backs upon it.
The world is but a passageway, an anteroom
For us. Perhaps that passage is too long,
Too littered and cluttered with spears and axes.
But who will undertake to clear away those axes
If, with the axes, he must clean away
Our touch as well, our crimson step?

REB BASSEVI.

Must the road stretch into eternity?

MAHARAL.

And we—beyond that; we can liberate the world—
We can, but we refuse.

REB BASSEVI.

Refuse?

MAHARAL.

For this, precisely, is what *they* would want.
To free the world as they desire
Means: to free the world of *us*.

REB BASSEVI.

I hear and every word lashes
The anguish of my heart.

MAHARAL.

Anguish? What is anguish, Reb Bassevi?
We have grown into it, grown part of it,
Wrapped it around us, set the torch to it
And scattered its light through all the worlds.
Go see yourself now, Reb Bassevi—
Your face glows with anguish. But an hour
Of impatience greater than this pain may come,

An hour of stubbornness still greater, and I
Or you or any in the street, even Tankhum,
Instead of brushing one fingertip against the world
May raise his hand up whole, with all its fingers—
What do you think, Reb Bassevi, would happen then?

REB BASSEVI.

Catastrophe. Catastrophe for us.

MAHARAL.

Catastrophe? What if it were not I alone,
Or you or someone else somewhere,
But he, that very woodman in the yard,
Should raise his whole hand with all its fingers,
Then would they still want us to—
(Stops abruptly, frightened by something.)

REB BASSEVI.

What ails you, Rabbi? You have grown so pale!

MAHARAL.

A noise, I think, Reb Bassevi. Do you hear it?

REB BASSEVI.

A noise? No, I hear no noise.

MAHARAL.

I must have fancied it.
(Looks out of the window.)
Yes, it was imagination. The court grows empty.

REB BASSEVI.

What should I say now, Rabbi, when I see
The fear aglow on your face too?

MAHARAL.

What should you say? Nothing, Reb Bassevi. Nothing.
There is a time for silence. You know, Reb Bassevi,
The Jews now in synagogue will finish praying
And all go home and quietly as always
Go to bed; but, perhaps, like you
They will not close their eyes all night;
And yet, not one of them will rise from bed
And yield to fear.

REB BASSEVI.

Is that intended as reproof, Rabbi?

MAHARAL.

No, not reproof. You miss my meaning, Reb Bassevi.

REB BASSEVI.

To hear your words of comfort was my hope.

MAHARAL.

And words of comfort still are here,

For all fears are needless, Reb Bassevi.

REB BASSEVI.

Needless?

MAHARAL.

Yes, fears without foundation.

REB BASSEVI.

I want to understand you clearly, Rabbi.
You say there is a time for silence,
And yet, I feel, your terror is not silent,
Your. . . . Forgive me, Rabbi, for these words.

MAHARAL.

Forgiven, Reb Bassevi.
But bear my words in mind:
No longer lie awake the whole night through.
A Jew must never keep himself from sleep.
We are old men both, Reb Bassevi,
But one must never grow too old
To apprehend all wonders.
Do you perceive my meaning? *All* wonders.

REB BASSEVI.

Your words are wise, Rabbi; perhaps, along with you,
I, too, will merit living long enough for that. . . .
(*A commotion is heard outside the door.* MAHARAL *opens
the door and looks out.*)

MAHARAL.

What's going on there? Tankhum? Let him, child.
He may come in.

REB BASSEVI.

Tankhum? That's too much!

MAHARAL.

It doesn't matter, Reb Bassevi.
(TANKHUM *comes in dishevelled and tattered. One of his
lapels is deeply rent in sign of mourning.*)

TANKHUM.

Such impudence! Tankhum wants to see the Rabbi,
And they won't let him.

MAHARAL.

Sit down, Reb Tankhum.

TANKHUM.

No time to sit, Rabbi.
I have to hurry, hurry.
My flaming chariot awaits me.

REB BASSEVI.

And will there be no limit to your mourning?

TANKHUM.

    A limit? No, there is no limit.
    For every garment waits
    For me to touch it,
    To rend its edge in mourning.
    Had it not been for our great festival of Pesach
    My son Jochanon still would be alive;
    Should we therefore wash our hands of Pesach?
    You do not answer. Do you want to cast off Pesach?
    I send my fiery chariot upon you.

REB BASSEVI.

    I've heard all that, Reb Tankhum.

TANKHUM.

    You've heard it?
    Though you heard a thousand times
    You've still not heard.
    How can the deaf hear?
    How can the blind see?
    Do you see my face in the middle of the night?
    Do you hear my voice?
    With arms spread out wide
    And eyes turned inside
    I stretch my throat to the sky;
    Over the roof of the tower,
    Through each of its shattered windows,
    I hurry and scurry and fly.
    Five is the number of towers—
    Five.
    One for the east and one for the west,
    One for the north and one for the south.
    The fifth one—for me.
    Who suffers the grief of the towers?
    I do!
    I am the Lord of the ruins.

MAHARAL.

    Sit down, Reb Tankhum, rest yourself.
    (TANKHUM *sits down, panting wearily.*)
    Reb Tankhum, the courtyard seems to be deserted.

TANKHUM.

    Deserted. All have gone
    Into the synagogue for evening prayers
    Leaving Tankhum alone with him—that cut-throat.
    But Tankhum has no fear of cut-throats.
    And this is what I came to tell you,

That Tankhum has no fear of axes.

REB BASSEVI.

Do you hear that, Rabbi?

MAHARAL.

Why do you speak such words as these, Reb Tankhum?

TANKHUM.

Why such words?
Do *you* ask that, Rabbi?
Darkness is coming upon us, darkness
From all sides,
And no one can stop my fiery chariot,
Not even you.
For no one will dare;
For no one has yet sat in it,
Or roasted in its fire,
Or rolled under its wheels.
Let hands reach out for me,
Let axes lift,
Voices shout—
Hands grow tired,
Axes rust,
Throats get silent,
And if not silent—slit.
(*Runs over to* THE MAHARAL.)
And who is master here?
You, Rabbi, or is it Thaddeus?

MAHARAL.

Thaddeus?

TANKHUM.

You do not know who Thaddeus is?
He's one whom you should know. And did you know
That Thaddeus came to see the Fifth Tower;
Did you know that, Rabbi?

MAHARAL.

I know, Reb Tankhum.

TANKHUM.

The Rabbi knows?
(*He rests his head on the table.*)

REB BASSEVI.

Is that really true, Rabbi?

MAHARAL.

He wants to drive the paupers out.

TANKHUM.

But who is master here? Am I or you?

Or is it the woodcutter, perhaps?
(Jumps up again.)
Expel us? What is he waiting for?
I have more ruins than I need,
The whole world's ruins wait for me,
Have waited long for me;
Through gaping holes they scan the world,
They breathe to me,
Call me to come and rule.
Should I but come,
What joy for them,
What song
And dance.
Then should I turn my face, ignore
That plea?
Who will hear it, if not I?
I will—
Because my heart is filled with pity for the world.
(He stops throwing his arms around and stands as though congealed.)
The world's great eyes
Are filled with longing.
Who sees the great eyes of the world?
I do.
Who can assuage the longing of the world?
I can.
Because my heart is filled with pity for the world.
In my fiery chariot I soar
Round and round the towers
Every middle of the night.
In my fiery chariot
Lies my son,
Festive for the Passover.
His left eye, run through by a spear,
His right one—closed.
His right arm lopped off at the shoulder,
His left one—at the elbow.
Each first Passover night I tell my son:
Arise and be alive.
Regain your eyes and arms,
For the world thirsts with lust
And hungers with longing.
And he rises up,
And he waits,
Until we hear footsteps:

They. . . .
Again they stab his left eye through,
Hack his right arm at the elbow,
Hack his left one at the shoulder.
I lay him back into the chariot,
And I say:
Until next year. . . .
Because my heart is filled with pity for the world.

(TANKHUM *runs out in haste.* THE MAHARAL *and* REB
BASSEVI *sit in amazement. A long silence.*)

REB BASSEVI.

Such words, such words.

(THE MAHARAL *starts to pace the room. Stops at the window and looks out.*)

REB BASSEVI (*standing up*).

The evening prayers will soon begin.
Good day, Rabbi. (*Exits.*)

MAHARAL.

A good year. I too will be there soon.

(*He paces back and forth. Stops at the window again.
He puts his head out and looks anxiously. From the courtyard uneasy voices of men and women are heard. They
run past the Rabbi's window, crying:* "Where is the Rabbi?
Rabbi, please come out." *Women's voices:* "Heaven help
us! Such grief upon us!" THE MAHARAL *starts towards the
door.* THE REBBETSIN *enters, leading* DEVORALE *by the
hand. Both are terrified.* DEVORALE *weeps.*)

MAHARAL.

What happened?

REBBETSIN.

The new man, that woodman, heaven help us.

MAHARAL.

What has he done?

REBBETSIN.

A new misfortune come upon us, Arye Levi!
He frightened Devorale to death.
She went outside to get a pail of water.
Well, he ran over and would not let her near the well.

DEVORALE (*weeping*).

He said that *he* must carry water.

MAHARAL.

And what did he do then?

REBBETSIN.

It is disgraceful just to speak of it.

In everybody's sight he grabbed her, kissed her.
If people had not been around he might have choked her.

MAHARAL.

What is he doing now?

REBBETSIN.

What should he do? A golem, not a man!
He stands immobile, as if turned to stone.

DEVORALE.

Drive him away! Don't let him stay!

(THE MAHARAL *and both women leave. A commotion is
heard from the courtyard, then subsides.* THE MAHARAL
returns followed by THE GOLEM *carrying his axe. He
stands in the middle of the room, curiously rigid, his hands
hanging at his sides.* THE MAHARAL *studies him a while,
takes the axe from his hand.* THE GOLEM *does not move.
He looks as though he is asleep standing.*)

MAHARAL.

You stand like stone
And do not see me come towards you.

(THE GOLEM *stands rigid.*)

Lift up your head and raise your eyes.
Let me look into them.
The cries you wakened still re-echo. Fear
Still lurks behind you, staring
Over your shoulder, ready to attack.

(THE GOLEM *does not move.*)

For you, I prayed to God for wonders—
My prayers of tears and pain were answered:
That you might see where no one saw,
And hear all things that no one heard;
That you might feel beneath your step
The doings nine ells in the deep;
That fire might not consume your flesh;
That in water you might not drown;
Aromas borne by farthest winds
Your nostrils might perceive and know;
And if need be, your body might
Become transparent as the air
Or to another be transformed;
That you might see and not be seen.
I give you glory for your life,
And for your hands, a blessed strength.
And you—you stand as stiff as wood;
Your eyes are dull, your mouth, distorted.

Upon your shoulders, massive walls,
Still lies the lifeless woe of clay;
Primordial, dust-encrusted worms
Upon your arms are crawling still,
And from your breath, for miles around,
Erupts the stench of rotting rock.
Your life is old a single day,
And yet how soon the man in you
Has hurried to reveal himself
In hatred, passion, and misfortune.
Did I convey you here among us
That you might be like other men?
Well, let us say there fell upon you
The heavy weight of fear and darkness,
Despair and dread that each one feels,
But where is there upon your face
The gleaming light, the radiant glow
Of our common trust and faith?
Why are you dumb? Reply, reply!
Before I raise my staff against you!
(THE GOLEM *comes to, stretches out his hand in joy to*
THE MAHARAL.)

GOLEM.

Where am I? Rabbi, where am I?
And where did everybody go?
Everyone was shouting so
And crying, milling round about me;
I could not understand the reason.
When suddenly it grew so still;
My eyelids to each other stuck.
Rabbi, I was asleep.

MAHARAL.

You were asleep?

GOLEM.

I am uncertain, Rabbi. Under me
The earth began to move and sway.
A hand reached out and drew me off,
And flung me high into the air
And then it hurled me down again.
I fell. Whereupon the earth
Was in an instant split apart
And broken into separate halves.
I flew into the deep abyss
But had no place to fall upon,

And as I flew I noticed: You
Were riding on my back and urging,
Driving me deep into the void.

MAHARAL.

Speak on.

GOLEM.

Your face I saw in double image:
One half was large—as large as mine,
The other—smaller still than yours;
Your eyes were four—and all were dead.
In one alone a speck of red,
And from it burning blood was dripping.
Then suddenly I saw your head
Begin to bob and toss about,
To beat itself against my own,
And with the eye that dripped hot blood,
It burnt its way into my brow,
And bit by bit into my brain
It sank until it reached your neck;
And as you sank, I saw,
Your neck was long and white and lithe.
I threw my hands around your throat
And fiercely I began to choke you.

MAHARAL.

Let words your hatred dissipate.

GOLEM.

Am I asleep? I can see nothing more;
I cannot see your face or eyes.
It was *my* throat that someone's hands were choking.
I thought at first that it was yours.
Oh, stay with me and do not leave me.
(*He stretches full length upon the floor at the* RABBI's *feet.*)
Oh, stay with me, or else—drive me away.

MAHARAL.

Get up. I see your grief,
And I forgive you.

GOLEM.

Do not leave me.

MAHARAL.

Stand up.

GOLEM.

A little longer, Rabbi,
Let me lie here at your feet.

MAHARAL.

 Stand up.

GOLEM.

 One moment longer, Rabbi.

 I feel so good, so much at ease.

 It grows so bright.

MAHARAL (*overjoyed*).

 Did you say bright? What do you see?

GOLEM.

 You.

MAHARAL.

 And now?

GOLEM.

 You touch me with your hands.

MAHARAL.

 I bless you. Now what do you see?

GOLEM.

 Fire! Fire!

 A great flame spins and churns.

 It tries to set me blazing but it cannot.

MAHARAL.

 And now?

GOLEM.

 A mass of water streams and whirls.

 I sink and yet I do not drown,

 And stones hail down upon my head

 And bound away.

MAHARAL.

 What else?

GOLEM.

 And vicious dogs attack me

 But my flesh remains unharmed.

MAHARAL.

 What do you hear?

GOLEM.

 Deep beneath the ground,

 I hear muffled voices;

 I hear the talk of stones and roots;

 I hear the steps of feet that hurry;

 I hear a wind. It whirls about.

 It calls me by my name,

 And I am not afraid of it.

 And, Rabbi, see the face that stares at me,

 A face entirely made of light,

A body huge, like mine;
He flutters over me
And soars as though on wings.
He grows out of my shoulders
And spreads out of my arms.

MAHARAL.

Stand up.
   (THE GOLEM *stands up.*)
And now what do you see?

GOLEM.

I see a man attired in black;
He comes this way with silent steps,
With steps that lurk for theft.

MAHARAL.

Now open wide your eyes again.
Again behold the light,
The wings of one invisible
That grow from you.
Go forth unto the Fifth Tower,
And there you stay, and there you sleep.
(THE GOLEM *bounds out of the room with a leap. THE
MAHARAL, himself astounded, leans his face against the
wall. His shoulders heave.*)

SCENE IV. BEGGARS

(In the Fifth Tower. A large room, a shambles. On both sides, entrances to other rooms. One wall has been broken through. The others are blackened, covered with cobwebs, soaked by the rains. No doors, shaky thresholds, broken windows. Here and there an unbroken pane of stained glass. In various places there are signs of former murals. They are all smeared and covered with stains and careless scratches. In one corner there still hang the chains of sacred lamps.

Paupers and beggars live in the room. On the floor, where they sleep, old rags, bundles, torn pillows lie about. Beggars' bags hang on the walls.

The night has just begun. A cold spring wind howls through the windows. It is dark.

A sick pauper, feverish, lies in a corner in a tangle of rags. The rest have not yet arrived.)

SICK MAN.
  My bones ache, all of them.
  Were I to die, no one would know.
  How cold it is.
  (Sits up.)
  Is no one here?
  If I could only have a little warm water.
  I've had no food at all today.
  Oh, my bones, my bones.
  (Lies down again.)
  Why do they take so long to come?
  Is not the day sufficient for them?
  They would devour the whole world.
  And what would they have then? There hangs
  My bag stuffed full of bread. . . . Oh, my bones.
  (Sits up again.)
  So deep the dark. I have no strength
  To stand and light the lamp
  Or stuff the gaping windows.
  (Stands up, shuffles in the dark, falls again.)

265

Oh God of Abraham, of Isaac and of Jacob.
(*Covers himself with the rags lying near him, huddles under them and shivers. Silence. THE GOLEM enters. Stops in
the middle of the room. Does not know which way to turn.
Says nothing.*)

SICK MAN (*raising his head*).
Has someone come, thank God?
(THE GOLEM *says nothing.*)
Have you no tongue to answer one who ails?
Why are you silent, eh? Who are you?
(THE GOLEM *says nothing.*)

SICK MAN (*with growing fear*).
Who are you?
(*Jumps up and looks at THE GOLEM. Starts to shout.*)
Fire! Fire!
Who are you? Answer. Wait a bit
And I will light the lamp.
(*Lights a smoky lamp. His fright increases.*)
What do you want? Why don't you speak?
A pauper?
(THE GOLEM *does not reply. Sits down on the ground.*)
A place to sleep, is that what you want here?

GOLEM.
Don't speak to me.

SICK MAN.
Where do you come from? Don't you carry any bag?
Is this the first time you have been to Prague?

GOLEM.
Don't speak to me.
(THE SICK MAN *sinks back onto his bed and looks at THE
GOLEM with eyes of terror. THE GOLEM stands up, walks
into the next room, sits down near a wall facing the doorway. He can scarcely be seen in the darkness. THE REDHEAD
and THE BLIND MAN enter.*)

REDHEAD.
You understand?

BLIND MAN.
But are you sure?

REDHEAD.
You can't mistake a priest.

BLIND MAN.
Then it is true.

REDHEAD.
If all are talking, then it must be true.

BLIND MAN.

You say he walked behind us?

REDHEAD.

No more than twenty paces,
With staff in hand, bent over, silent,
Then suddenly he turned off to a side.

BLIND MAN.

And God has punished me. I cannot see
The steps of him who follows after us.

REDHEAD.

Punished you say? Perhaps it is a blessing.
You know that I'm not one to tremble;
Still, there was a shortness to my breath.

BLIND MAN.

The foot of one who was no beggar has never
Yet walked the road that leads to Tower Five.

REDHEAD.

Just try and get someone to come here.
Your only answer will be gaping eyes.
Everybody is afraid of ruins.

BLIND MAN.

And we—are we ourselves quite unafraid?
We come to spend the night here—and no more.
Sleep hides and covers us with its protection.

REDHEAD.

And if you hear a stranger's footsteps
Behind you, suddenly—
You see my point? What brings a stranger here?

BLIND MAN.

What brings him here? God only knows,
The living God, our Father.
(*Suddenly.*)
Are we alone?

REDHEAD.

The sick one's here. Asleep.

BLIND MAN.

Besides the sick one?

REDHEAD.

I told you; he alone.

BLIND MAN.

Do I imagine? Look around with care.

REDHEAD.

What do you mean?
(THE BLIND MAN *feels around with his hands. Touches*

THE SICK MAN, *who awakens*.)

SICK MAN.

A little water. Bring a little water.

REDHEAD.

There is no water here.

SICK MAN.

In the other room there is. Oh, no,

Do not go in. Some stranger is in there.

REDHEAD.

A stranger?

BLIND MAN.

You hear? I told you. . . .

(*He feels his way to the threshold of the other room.*)

A stranger? Who's the stranger, eh?

REDHEAD (*looks in and jumps back*).

It's him, that woodcutter, the one—

BLIND MAN.

The one that grabbed at Devorale?

He's here? What is he doing here?

REDHEAD.

Some kind of clown.

BLIND MAN.

Don't shout. Speak softly.

The Rabbi warned us not to tease him.

REDHEAD.

I wasn't teasing him—just talking.

But how did he get here? Who brought him?

SICK MAN.

He came himself.

And scared me half to death.

REDHEAD.

Someone like him can really frighten you.

BLIND MAN.

Keep quiet. Don't be smart.

GOLEM (*appearing in the doorway*).

I hear my name was mentioned.

REDHEAD.

Your name? No. I only said—

I only meant—

GOLEM.

Don't mention it again.

(*Goes back.*)

REDHEAD.

You understand? You can thank God

That you are blind and cannot see him.

BLIND MAN.

The Rabbi has himself befriended him.

REDHEAD.

There's something queer about this. Mark my word.

SICK MAN.

Stuff up the windows.

REDHEAD.

The holes, you mean.

SICK MAN.

Stuff them before I freeze.

REDHEAD.

Our rags are few; the holes are many.

What shall I stuff them with?

SICK MAN.

Oh, God of Abraham, of Isaac and of Jacob.

(THE BLIND MAN *sits down on the ground, takes some coins out of his breast pocket and ties them into a knotted rag.*)

REDHEAD (*takes a bag from the wall, shakes a few crumbs out of it. To* THE BLIND MAN).

You made a lot, did you? I didn't get a farthing.

BLIND MAN (*wraps up the rag and puts it back into his breast pocket*).

A lot. And how would I know whether it's a lot?

You ask these sightless eyes of mine.

They are the ones that get the coins—not I.

If day and night are one for me,

Then let me have a knot of coins, at least.

Well, yes, you ask these sightless eyes of mine.

REDHEAD.

The bread's all gone. Tomorrow's Friday.

Tomorrow there will be fresh Sabbath bread.

(*Packs rags into his bag and ties it.*)

Let the bag be ready, packed.

BLIND MAN.

What are you saying? I can't hear you.

REDHEAD.

Just talking. What have I to say?

I say, the bag should be all packed and ready.

BLIND MAN.

What do you think of that?

Forgot to say the evening prayer.

(*He stands facing the wall and begins to pray softly. In come* THE HUNCHBACK, PEG LEG, THE TALL MAN, THE

SHORT MAN. *All have full bags.* THE REDHEAD *goes to meet them.*)

REDHEAD.

We have a guest, a guest,
The one that in the courtyard . . .

ALL.

What guest?

REDHEAD.

Where do you come from that you haven't heard?
The woodman from the prayer-house yard.

TALL MAN.

Is that the truth? Has he come here?
The whole of Prague is buzzing about him.

REDHEAD.

Well, there he sits. He's hiding in the dark
And sitting there with gaping eyes.
(*All look in.*)

SHORT MAN.

What a size!

REDHEAD.

Stop shouting. He might hear you. It's not safe.

PEG LEG.

Why, does he fight?

REDHEAD.

He doesn't have to fight.
A look of his can set your heart to pounding.

TALL MAN.

What is his name?

REDHEAD (*whispering*).

They say his name is Joseph.
(THE GOLEM *strides in. All back away to a side.*)

GOLEM.

My name was mentioned here.
Say it no more.
(*Goes back again.*)

REDHEAD.

The second time today.
And twice to me. He must be mad!
I thought I whispered.

SICK MAN.

What's wrong?
Is there a law against pronouncing the man's name?
(*They look at one another in amazement.*)

TALL MAN.
> And every good-for-nothing lands up here.

REDHEAD.
> The Rabbi sent him here himself.

ALL.
> The Rabbi himself?
> *(They sit down and untie their bags.)*

REDHEAD.
> You met nobody on the way?
> The priest . . .

ALL.
> Who? Thaddeus?

BLIND MAN *(saying his prayers, he signals with his hand for them not to talk)*.
> Well, well. Sh sh.
> *(All stop talking. Take out what they have begged.)*

REDHEAD.
> My bag's all packed,
> And you are just unpacking yours?
> A waste of time and trouble, just a waste.

TALL MAN.
> What is he saying?

REDHEAD.
> I told you. Or don't you hear me well?
> They want to drive us out of here.

BLIND MAN.
> Sh, oh, sh . . .

TALL MAN.
> Expel us? From this place? From this ruin?
> And all of Prague is envious of us.
> Wherever you pass by these days, they ask:
> Is there not room for more in Tower Five?
> You see it now? The whole of Tower Five
> Will be packed tight with Jews
> Expelled from all the houses.
> You see, you can be driven from a house,
> But who can drive you from a ruin?
> Do you see now why Tower Five
> Will be packed tight with Jews?

BLIND MAN.
> Akh, well, shsh. . . .

HUNCHBACK.
> Supposing, God forbid, they come
> To drive us from this place too?

TALL MAN.

> We'll open all these bags of ours:
> "Take everything away; it's yours."
> And when they take it all away,
> Well, then, they've taken everything:
> The crumbs and the chunks of bread,
> Our clothing and—what else? What else?
> Well, then they've taken everything.

BLIND MAN (*finishes praying, remains standing against the wall*).

> There is a God in heaven, Jews.

SICK MAN (*sits up*).

> Of course there is a God in heaven—and He watches
> As beggars sit after a day of begging
> And complain about the bread.
> And when they drop with weariness
> And close their eyes and fall asleep,
> The bread is unguarded.
> And anyone can come and take it;
> It need not be a foe—just any passerby.
> For he who passes by—he does not sleep.
> He sits in silent gloom and does not sleep,
> And beggars are exhausted and they sleep.
> There is a God in heaven—and He watches.

TALL MAN.

> What's wrong with him? What is he saying?

SICK MAN.

> I have not begged for two whole days. So what?
> My bag stays tied up tight, untouched.
> And anyone who wanted to could long ago
> Have opened it and emptied it and gone away.
> But no one came. So what?
> They still can come tomorrow or the next day:
> Because it never is too late.
> They might still come today.
> There is a God in heaven—and He watches.

BLIND MAN.

> What is he saying, eh?

SICK MAN.

> I have been lying here the long day through;
> I saw and heard all things.
> And he who hears and sees all things
> Must lie in one location.
> The one I loudly called upon,
> Was not the one who came.

The one I did not call upon,
He was the one who came.
The last spoonful of water for my tongue
There was no one to give.
I lit a flame because of fear
And fell face down upon the earth—
My thirst was still unstilled;
For he, the one I did not call,
He was the one who came.

ALL.

Whatever ails the man? What is he saying?

SICK MAN.

I'll speak no more; I'll speak no more.
Let him speak whom I did not call.
There is a God in heaven—and He watches.

(Lies down again, burrowing his way into the rags. THE GOLEM comes out and remains standing near the doorway. All are motionless with fear. Suddenly TANKHUM comes in. His eyes scan everyone. He sees THE GOLEM and stands frozen.)

REDHEAD.

The place will soon be jumping.

(TANKHUM throws him an angry look but says nothing. Walks up close to THE GOLEM and bursts out laughing.)

TALL MAN.

What are you laughing at, you crazy loon?

TANKHUM *(to THE GOLEM).*

Do you know them?
(Points to all of them.)
Do you know who they are? Do you know what they do?
Your hands are large—go beat them up;
Your feet are large—go trample them;
You had an axe, I saw—where is it?
You see that hunchback? See that redbeard?
You see the peg leg—split it;
You surely know how wood is split.

(THE GOLEM says nothing. Goes back into the darkness. TANKHUM sits down on the ground and takes his head in his hands.)

REDHEAD.

A loon, I tell you.

TALL MAN.

And all you have to do is get him started.
(All are quiet.)

TANKHUM.

Remember, meanwhile I am master here!
The sills are mine.
The broken windows all are mine.
And I'm the one who let you in.
I am!
I am!
In seven days and seven nights,
He will arise.
From the flaming chariot he'll come;
Then all of you will have to leave.
For Tower Five belongs to him,
To him—my heir.
Do you not hear these ruins shouting,
These windows calling:
"Oh, when will he be here?"
Pick up your rags,
Tie up your bags,
Make clean this house that is
My heir's.

(*Enter two wandering paupers, strangers,* THE OLD BEGGAR *and* THE YOUNG BEGGAR—ELIJAH THE PROPHET *and* THE MESSIAH. *They come with bags on their backs and staff in hand, dusty from their long journey and very tired.*)

BOTH BEGGARS.

Good evening, Jews.
(*All reply:* "A good year.")

OLD BEGGAR.

We are in luck. You see—Jews everywhere.
And can we spend the night here?
What do you say?

TALL MAN.

Of course, Grandpa.
(*He greets both with a handshake and a "sholem aleichem."
All the others except* TANKHUM *and* THE SICK MAN *do the same.*)

OLD BEGGAR.

Aleichem sholem, Jews, aleichem sholem.
You sleep upon the bare floor, do you not?
Then we will also take our rest that way.
We'll only spend the night here, just tonight.

REDHEAD.

Grandfather, you can even sleep here many nights.
These ruins can accommodate us all.

OLD BEGGAR.

    We need to spend just *one* night here, no more,

    And with the day we must be on our way again.

    We are fatigued. He—even more.

    He is still young and unaccustomed to the road.

    His feet, moreover, are. . . .

    (*They throw down their bags and prepare to seat themselves.*)

TALL MAN.

    I see—he really limps.

OLD BEGGAR.

    From the long road

    His feet have broken out in sores

    He really needs to rest—

    But the time for that has not arrived.

TALL MAN.

    You seem in a hurry.

OLD BEGGAR.

    No, not in a hurry any more.

    We drove ourselves to come here. These last days

    Both day and night we walked.

    From here on we will no longer hurry.

TALL MAN.

    You need something in Prague?

OLD BEGGAR.

    We need, yes, we need. . . .

    What's new in this big town of yours?

TALL MAN.

    Not good, Grandfather.

OLD BEGGAR.

    That so? Not good?

    (*Silence.* THE YOUNG BEGGAR *sits down, begins to unbind his wounds. He unwinds the rags from his feet and winds them on again.*)

HUNCHBACK.

    You know, he doesn't look like any beggar.

    His face is so refined.

TALL MAN.

    You've come from far off, Grandfather?

OLD BEGGAR.

    From far, from very far. Already it was night.

    We walked—and there before us stood a castle.

    We looked: vacant windows, open doors;

    And so we figured we could enter.

Tonight, at least, we'll sleep and rest
The whole night through.

YOUNG BEGGAR.

So weary. I'm so weary.

OLD BEGGAR (*pointing to* TANKHUM).

Why does he sit like one in mourning?

TALL MAN.

His wits are somewhat addled.

(*All watch* THE YOUNGER BEGGAR *bind his wounds.*)

YOUNG BEGGAR.

They keep on spreading and they open.
They come up to my knees. How tired I am.
My eyelids are so heavy.

(*Slumps to the ground and falls asleep.*)

OLD BEGGAR (*places a bag under* THE YOUNG BEGGAR's *head.*)

Sleep well; sleep well.

TANKHUM (*jumps up*).

Guests come to spend the night here,
And no one asks for permission!
I'm still the master here!

REDHEAD.

Be quiet. Can't you see this man is sleeping?

TANKHUM.

Asleep? How does he come to be asleep?
He must wake up.
Let him pry his eyelids open.
This is a place for wakefulness,
For trembling,
For fevering,
For lurking. . . .
The dead will soon arise,
And he—he sleeps!

REDHEAD.

You madman! Shut your mouth.

(*He pushes him and* TANKHUM *falls down.*)

OLD BEGGAR.

Don't hit him. Please.

REDHEAD.

I tell you, it's impossible to stand him;
We have enough to bear without him.

TANKHUM (*lies on the ground shouting*).

The dead will soon arise,
And should he sleep?

(THE MAHARAL *enters hurriedly. His eyes look stern and angry.*)

ALL (*surprised*).

The Rabbi! The Rabbi!

MAHARAL (*looks at* THE OLD BEGGAR. THE OLD BEGGAR *looks at him. A long silence*).

Why are you here? Why have you both come here?

Who sent for you?

Who ordered you to come?

OLD BEGGAR.

Only to spend the night.

One night to rest on our long road.

MAHARAL.

You came yourselves? To come at no one's bidding!

Pick up your bags at once

And—go.

I order so.

OLD BEGGAR.

We are exhausted from our journey.

Our haste was great—

MAHARAL.

You hurried here?

Then hurry back again. I order it.

OLD BEGGAR.

He sleeps so soundly. Do not waken him.

MAHARAL.

Are there no ruins elsewhere in the world?

You like it only here? Awaken him.

(*Pounds with his staff.*)

To come unbidden! To come unbidden!

(THE GOLEM *enters. When* THE OLD BEGGAR *sees him, he changes completely. He grows pale, begins to tremble, and quickly starts to wake* THE YOUNG BEGGAR.)

OLD BEGGAR.

Wake up! Wake up! Be quick!

We have to leave. We have to leave.

(*Starts to gather his things together.*)

YOUNG BEGGAR. A little longer. Let me sleep a little more!

(*He sees* THE GOLEM *and also starts to tremble and hurry.*)

Come quickly. Let us leave.

(*They grab their things and hurriedly run out.* THE GOLEM *starts after them.*)

MAHARAL (*restrains him*).

Where to?

GOLEM.

>   With them. I want to be with them.

MAHARAL.

>   Stay here. I order you. *Their* time
>   Has not yet come. This is *your* time.
>   (*To the others.*)
>   Thaddeus is coming here.
>   (*A frightened commotion.*)

ALL THE BEGGARS.

>   Thaddeus? What does he want to do?

MAHARAL.

>   He wants to drive you out of here.
>   The Fifth Tower does not belong to us.
>   (*All start to fill their bags.* THE SICK MAN *and* TANKHUM
>   *remain as before.*)

MAHARAL (*to* THE GOLEM).

>   Will you know what you have to do?

GOLEM.

>   I'll know, Rabbi.

MAHARAL.

>   But not to death.

GOLEM.

>   I'll know, Rabbi.

MAHARAL.

>   Your power to be unseen—let it awake!
>   Now go in there and wait.
>   (THE GOLEM *returns to his former place.* THE MAHARAL
>   *exits. The beggars, busy with their packing and their fear,
>   have noticed nothing.* THADDEUS *enters, accompanied by a*
>   MONK.)

THADDEUS.

>   You see these beggars? Pretenders every one.
>   Believe me, they are wealthier than both of us.
>   You see that hump? That hump is false—
>   A pack of rags, no more.

MONK.

>   Then he is quite an artist.

THADDEUS.

>   And he—that blind one—isn't blind at all.
>   We know them well, those eyes that are kept shut.

MONK (*pointing to* PEG LEG).

>   Well, there's one, Father, that you can't suspect.
>   That leg is wood, all right.

THADDEUS.

>   Don't you believe it.

Not even if you touch the wood.
His kind can amputate a leg
And keep it hidden in a bag
And when they need it, take it out again.
They live up here like lords,
As though they owned the place.
The walls are filthy, hammered full of nails;
The air so foul it takes your breath away.
To think that here once lived in glory
Our heroes, gentlemen, and nobles!
That these louse-ridden, littered floors
Once felt the step of royal feet.
Do you not hear them shouting from the walls—
Those murals, smirched and spat on?
And there still hanging in the corner, are the chains
Of holy lamps. Their rays once lit *His* glance of love,
The tears that dripped in sorrow from His crown of thorns,
Which they, grim unbelievers, stuck into his brow.
Now all is ruin. He has been cast out,
The flame—extinguished; just the chains remain
To dangle mockingly, and—those bags. Those bags!
(*To the paupers.*)
Why do you gape and stand around in silence?
You live among us, angry and embittered,
And wear your anger as he wears his hump.
Have we not tortured you enough,
Oppressed you, burnt you, led you out to slaughter?
We have grown weary of our hatred,
Of our cruelty and fury.
Yet you parade your zealotry before us
And clench your teeth in obstinate tenacity,
And all the more, you smash our dreams of peace,
And all the more, you stoke in us the fires of hate.
No peace can ever be between us,
For you haunt us like an evil dream.
We cannot share one Earth with you,
Warmed by the same sun, breathing the same air.
The air your lungs inhale
Becomes noxious to our hearts;
And our hearts yearn for *peace and calm*,
For respite and release from you.
You sit upon our conscience and our brain,
Like black spiders in a knot
And weave and weave the nets of nightmare.

Though we have hounded you so much
We will yet hound you more.
We long for love and virtue, peace and calm,
But only in your blood will that desire be stilled,
In dance around the faggots of the stake;
And we will light them more and more
Until you free us from yourselves!
You say that we accuse you falsely,
And you scurry and you work to prove us liars.
You defend yourselves.
Why do you lack the courage to proclaim it
To the world, with dignity and pride,
And say: Yes, we do drink blood for Passover;
We have always drunk it, always will!
We burn you at the stake, though innocent—
Why do you go to burn as though to dance?
Why do you not attack us
As we do you, with torch and axe?
And even now, this moment, as I speak,
Why do you hear my words and do not answer?
Where is there one among you with the courage
To step forward, seize my staff,
And break it on my skull. You say nothing.
Already you await my shout: Get out!
Always, always you are ready to depart—
Then go!
(*All the beggars leave in silence with their bags upon their
backs.* THE SICK MAN *and* TANKHUM *remain to the last,
then they too jump up and run as if from a fire.*)
Such dogs. Give them a command—they run.
(*Frightened.*)
Do you hear that? Steps.
Is one of them still left?

MONK.

No one is here, Father.

THADDEUS (*looks into the next room*).

No one. But don't you hear the footsteps?

MONK.

It is your fancy only.

THADDEUS.

I do hear steps. What's going on?
I feel a movement in the air.

MONK.

My knees give way.

THADDEUS.

Holy Saviour, protect us!

(*They cross themselves. There is a whistling and a whirling in the air about them, as though someone were whipping long, wet rods about. Steps of great, unseen feet are heard. Terrible blows begin to descend on the heads of* THADDEUS *and* THE MONK. *They dodge about in wild terror, duck down to the floor, run to the doors, but wherever they go the blows of unseen hands pursue them.*)

THADDEUS.

The place is haunted! Evil spirits! Run!

(*But they are stopped at every door and thrown back. And the blows do not stop falling on their heads. Their noses begin to bleed. They fall to the ground moaning with pain and fear. Suddenly they are lifted off the ground and tossed out of the windows. The thump of their bodies hitting the ground outside can be heard. Silence. The flame of the lamp stops quivering and burns upright.* THE GOLEM *strides in from the side room. He is very excited. His face is pale, his eyes aflame. His nostrils flare from his deep breathing. He leans against a wall, his head turned to the side.*)

GOLEM.

Where are you, Rabbi? Where are you?

MAHARAL (*hurries in*).

I'm here. I'm here.

GOLEM.

Oh, Rabbi, Rabbi.

MAHARAL.

Speak, I hear you.

GOLEM.

Don't leave me. Take me by the hand.

MAHARAL.

What troubles you?

GOLEM.

It's dark, Rabbi, dark.
Don't go away.

MAHARAL.

I have to leave. Now go to sleep.

GOLEM.

Don't go. Don't go.

MAHARAL.

There is still much for you to do. Go to sleep.
(*Exits.*)

GOLEM.

> Oh, Rabbi, stay with me, with me.
> (*Looks around.*)
> Gone.
> Why has it suddenly grown quiet?
> How dark it is, how dark. Where are you, Rabbi?
> (*Stretches out on the ground, calling.*)
> Where are you, Rabbi? It's so dark, so dark.

SCENE V. UNBIDDEN

(A field outside of Prague. Night. Chunks of cloud in the sky. THE OLD BEGGAR *and* THE YOUNG BEGGAR *sit beside a road leading off into the distance.)*

YOUNG BEGGAR.
No one wants to hear my summons;
I'm a stranger in these lands.
And my weary feet are ailing;
Ailing are my outstretched hands.

Dark and cold, with dying tears
Tomorrow hurries on his way.
No one will prevent his progress
Or his steps to Prague delay.

There is no one come to greet me,
None with joy and none with tears.
On all roads that lead to Prague
Night has fallen, hiding fears.

Six long days and nights have passed.
Now the seventh faded yonder.
All, in breathless fever panting,
Wait to see the Golem's wonder.

From the man who wears the cross,
To the beggar with his sacks,
Comes the savior, the Golem,
With his fist and with his axe.
OLD BEGGAR.
Hold your bitter words, my son,
This, it seems, is for the best.
God-defended, God-protected—
Go to sleep, to sleep and rest.
YOUNG BEGGAR.
Let us leave this place of horror.

See, the smoke is rising high
From the burning stakes of Prague
Upward to the evening sky.

Mine is not to help the victim,
Neither can I die with him.
Now the victim has expired
And the fire is growing dim.

OLD BEGGAR.
Why this talk of victims dying?
Where are horrors such as these?
There is but the floating moon
And the gentle springtime breeze.

YOUNG BEGGAR.
Can't you hear a stifled outcry
Carried towards us from somewhere?
Many feet are treading softly
In a cave. Those feet are *theirs*.

OLD BEGGAR.
Whose feet are they?

YOUNG BEGGAR.
The feet of foes.
Men who know their mission well.
And a masked, grimacing visage
Cries from far-off: Do not tell . . .

Silence me; make dumb my tongue.
Close my eyes and shut off sight.
Terror like a pall has fallen:
Fear of pogroms Pesach night.

OLD BEGGAR.
Lie and rest and fall asleep.
This will be our last night here.
There, you see, a gleam flew by
Bringing consolation, cheer.

Yours forever is this gleam,
As you journey, as you plod,
For it knows your heart is faithful,
Chosen by almighty God.

Your despair grows out of sorrow,
Out of love, your anguished plight;
Your impatience is duration,
And your darkness is the light.

No one, no one is to blame
That we sit here at a side,
If we were no longer patient
And we came before our tide.

(*They both sit in silence.*)

OLD BEGGAR.

Let my knees provide your pillow.
Go to sleep and slumber there
Till the early drops of dew
Tell us that the morning's fair.

In the silence I will guard you,
Guard your harried, fretful sleep.
Do not think you have been punished
Though your anguish has been deep.

Not correction but a hidden,
Secret sign of Heaven's choice.
If not soon or the day after—
Some day you will hear the voice.

YOUNG BEGGAR.

Do not speak but quickly come.
As the night grows still and clear,
Take me back into the desert,
For in stillness grows my fear.

Hands and more hands I see wrung;
Lopped off heads and limbs like stubble.
Eyes are bursting and run out;
Fire and flame and smoking rubble.

In the doorways of the houses
Two stand still while others die.
Both are studying the clock-hands
Slowly dragging—you and I.

All the throats have long been cut.
Still we two, expectant, wait
In the rubble, blood and ashes,
Watchful lest we come too late.

For we are the mute observers
Of the murder, death and cark.
Silent witness, spread your news,
Tell blind secrets to the dark.

(Clasps the knees of THE OLD BEGGAR.)

Oh, forgive me that I open
Unhealed wounds that cannot heal,
And forgive me that I bite
Bleeding lips to make them feel.

And forgive me that I wait
For the words that will bring gladness.
I have fooled and gulled myself
With a joy that turns to sadness.

YOUNG BEGGAR *(lying with his head sunk).*
On my chain
Rock and sway,
Old and blind
Eternity.

Take my steps,
Circled rings,
Twist them tight
Into links.

From the headlong, mad
Stampede
Gather up
The hours you need.

Wind, to death
Rock in slumber,
On my links
Without number.

In disguise,
Myself I stay
On the chain
To rock and sway.

(He falls asleep. THE OLD BEGGAR *sits watching over him.
Starts to doze himself.* THE MAHARAL *enters in a hurry, impatient. He is trembling with rage.)*

MAHARAL.
Are you still here?
Must you be ordered more than once?

OLD BEGGAR *(awakens with a start).*
Do not be angry. One last night
We stay—no more.

MAHARAL.

    Begone at once!
    A single second is too long!

OLD BEGGAR.

    The road is long and dark.

MAHARAL.

    You need not speak to me of darkness
    Nor wake compassion in my heart.
    Whom do you beg for mercy, and for whom?
    For him? Let it suffice
    That I choke back some weeping of my own,
    That I restrain my knees from bending,
    From falling down before him while I cry: have pity.
    Woe would be to me and woe to him
    Were I to drive my hardness from me,
    To open wide my heart to mercy.
    No need to speak to me of darkness.
    Why did you have to bring him here?
    To let him see the face of death and danger?
    What can he do for us? What should he do?
    The world has not exhausted yet
    Its store of cruelty, on us.
    Has *each* of us in every land felt
    The butcher's knife against his throat?
    Has he yet heard the final groan?
    Or seen the last of lifted swords?
    How could he say he saw or heard,
    If my throat stands unslaughtered here,
    If my body is unburned!

OLD BEGGAR.

    Oh, Levi, Levi.

MAHARAL.

    Take him away. Escape.
    Do not contaminate his heart with our dread.
    By what way shall we go to greet him
    If every road is strewn with corpses
    And each one walks on pointed spears?
    And who should sing his praises—
    The throat that has been half cut through?
    And who should open doors for him—
    The butcher's blood-smeared hands?
    And what should light and shine above him—

Possessions flaming in the night?
He must go. He must not stay in this domain.
Can his fingers coil into fists of iron
And murderously smash in skulls?
Can he stand the smell of blood?
Can he spill it? Can he exact a tooth for tooth,
And eye for eye and head for head?
Can those gentle hands scratch in the filth
Of pits, digging for limbs, for bones, for ashes?
He cannot. And should he want to, I
Would stand opposed. He must be *the last*. . . .
And woe to him if he should try
To intercede for us against our will.

OLD BEGGAR.
We merely came to look;
His heart was full of longing for you.

MAHARAL.
Let him muffle deep his longing.
There is another one to do my bidding,
The only one permitted to be dark,
Permitted to spill blood for blood.
The world deserves no other to chastise it,
And we, as yet, no better to defend us.

OLD BEGGAR.
Wake up. We must depart.

YOUNG BEGGAR (*stands up*).
You come once more to drive us?
(THE MAHARAL *is silent*.)
Why do you hound us?

MAHARAL.
I must.

YOUNG BEGGAR.
Why do you not allow me this night's sleep?

MAHARAL.
This night will be a night of blood.

YOUNG BEGGAR.
My eyes are eager to observe the crimson night.

MAHARAL.
Let them rather be struck blind.

YOUNG BEGGAR.
My ear longs for helpless lamentations.

MAHARAL.
Let your ear instead be stricken deaf.

YOUNG BEGGAR.

> My lips are thirsting to recite
> The Confession with the dying.

MAHARAL.

> Better for them to be mute.

YOUNG BEGGAR.

> Have you no warmer words for me?
> (THE MAHARAL *does not reply.*)
> Your words to me are hard and stern.
> I take them as the speech of love. I came
> Myself, awaiting no one's call. I came
> I wanted to walk through the world,
> Myself to hear the echoes of my steps.
> Perhaps, perhaps I also hoped
> That everyone would hear their echo too.
> I looked into so many eyes;
> I saw so many steps on all the roads;
> But all the eyes were looking somewhere else.
> My glances were left hanging in the air,
> And my footsteps. . . .
> And now the only thing I want is rest,
> To stop my eyes from looking at the world
> And turn them back into myself as always
> And rock upon my sleeping restlessness.
> Who knows—perhaps I came one moment late.
> Perhaps it was one stroke of time too soon.
> Who knows? Since it was I who chose to come,
> To stroll about and see the world,
> How can the world be held accountable?
> Is it, for that, obliged to stop
> Its murders, put an end to hate,
> And halt the wars of nations and of brothers?
> For after all, I came myself,
> Merely to stroll about and see the world.
> And now I go. In the desert I
> Shall find the sleep I lost on hounded nights
> And—joy to you and all of you.
> (*Exits with* THE OLD BEGGAR.)

MAHARAL (*impulsively he reaches out his hands to them and remains standing, bent over his staff*).

> Not with honor,
> As should be,

Did we greet
Our guest—nor glee.

Not the comfort
Of a bed;
Not with water,
Not with bread

Not a rag
His wounds to bind;
Not a blessing:
Fate be kind.

On he hastens,
Walk and run.
Back again
He must not come.

Far and further,
Plod and pant,
The world sees but
A mendicant.

Tightly shut
His lips are both.
One is laughing,
One is wroth.

Brows are arching,
Eyes are glaring,
One is gaping,
One is staring.

In his ears,
Songs of hailing
Follow after
Sounds of wailing.

Neither young
Nor yet the old
Ever will
His face behold.

*(Stands leaning on his staff in deep sorrow. The sky has
become completely overcast. A strong wind begins to blow.
A storm is brewing.)*

Alas, alas.
They are no more.
(His head bowed, he starts back to Prague. The wind rips at his clothing.)
No more, no more, no more.
(His figure is lost in the darkness. The storm breaks.)

SCENE VI. REVELATIONS

(In Tower Five. THE GOLEM is lying face down, asleep. The rain whips in through the windows. An echo of a distant, tremulous voice is heard: "No more, no more, no more." As though the voice were calling him in his sleep, THE GOLEM starts to toss, murmuring unintelligibly, and then again lies motionless. TANKHUM, drenched by the rain, appears at the door, pokes his head in, enters on tip-toes, shakes off the rain. He does not notice THE GOLEM.)

TANKHUM.
> Cowards!
> Nowhere do they let me in.
> Every threshold barred.
> Doors and windows closed and shuttered.
> Tankhum knocks and no one answers.
> Cowards—
> They think I seek a lodging for the night.
> *(Laughs and clamps his hands over his mouth as he does.)*
> Everybody's dead.
> They think I do not know.
> Did I not knock at every door,
> Stride through every street,
> Banging on the shutters, shouting:
> "Prepare a welcome! Come!"
> Prague is dead.
> Without rhyme or reason, all at once,
> Prague is dead.
> *(Sound of thunder.)*
> Should I change to festive dress
> And wait?
> Well, there is time to sit and rest,
> While all the ruins are made ready,
> Swept clean and polished bright.
> My order was as follows:
> Remove those coffers with the carvings
> From their secret hiding places. Take

From them the vessels, gold and silver,
The polished cups and ornamented trays,
The candelabra with the seven branches.
Now open chests; take out the cushions,
The embroidered coverlets, the robes,
And bring them all to me.
On the tables, spread the cloths,
And set out cups and candelabra.
In purest white
Let every couch be covered.
The candles I have brought myself.
I have them here.
And he will bring the wine, he who is
The last of all my heirs,
The reddest wine with deepest glow,
With brightest gleam, brighter far than blood.
The candles I have brought myself.
I have them here.
 (*Takes some candles from his bosom.*)
Did I, perhaps, forget to order something?
I think not.
Attendants stand at all the doors;
In darkness and in storm,
Faithfully they stand,
Vigilant and patient,
Alert to do their duty.
Is there not some command that needs repeating?
My servants, hear. I tell you once again:
In purest white let every couch be covered,
In *purest white*.
(*He lights a candle, sees* THE GOLEM, *edges toward the door.*)
The very one.
The only one.
The last one.
Since all the Jews are dead,
Since no one comes here to rejoice,
He has come.
He sleeps. But soon he will awaken
And be a witness,
The one and only,
For all of Prague is dead,   .
And he is left asleep,
The last,

Alone,

Eternal.

(*He is about to go into the other rooms, when* THE GOLEM *begins again to toss about, moaning weirdly in his sleep, tossing feverishly and murmuring* "No more, no more, no more.")

Who is no more? What is no more?

GOLEM (*awakens. Sits up*).

No more, no more, no more.

He drove them both away,

And—stands alone and grieves:

"No more, no more, no more."

(TANKHUM *is about to run out, when* THE GOLEM *leaps up and blocks his way.*)

GOLEM.

Don't run away. Stay here. I want to talk.

Now I arise, you see. Now I grow large;

And now I spread my wings;

And now I stand before you,

From my darkness quite distinct.

Now I stretch my hands to you;

Now I withdraw them.

Now I clasp my hands together.

I must not speak, but I am speaking.

TANKHUM.

Who are you?

GOLEM.

You do not know? I am he, who, sunk

In sleep, yet heard the outcry:

No more, no more, no more.

And if you wish, I'll throw myself again

Still deeper into sleep,

Still deeper.

TANKHUM.

Be wakeful. It's my wish. I'm not afraid.

And who you are, I do not know.

If all are dead,

One must remain.

Let that be you.

GOLEM.

I am the one. I am.

TANKHUM.

And when you will be asked to be a witness,

And—one to share my feast—

Do you know of my approaching feast?
And if you do not know, you will;
For you must join me at my feast.
No music makers will be there;
So you will make the music.
No dancers have been asked to come;
So you will do the dancing.
Say, can you caper at a feast?
Or play the cymbals? Dance a round?
Do you know how a bridegroom is received?
How he is circled round with candles,
At his head and at his foot—lighted candles?
(*Spins around.*)
Now do you see the way to dance?
(*Falls to the ground, dizzy.*)

GOLEM.

You do not know me? I will become another.
Beware to look upon my face.
I am condemned to suffer here.
I do not want to any more.
I am revolted by my flesh,
By my staring, glassy eyes,
By the muteness that I hate.
My days and nights grow dusty here;
A longing drives me on to flee myself,
To fly into the distance.
The time has come. See how
I spurn myself
As I would spurn a worm.

TANKHUM (*lying on the ground, afraid to raise his head*).

Who are you? Tell me who you are.
Through the long nights I spent here in the tower
The darkness has revealed
Its deepest secrets.
Are you one of those mysteries?

GOLEM.

I am the secret, not of darkness, but of light,
Not always, but now.
Your staring at me will discover nothing
Though you burst your eyes with gaping.
For all obscurities are plain to me
And dark to you.
Voices from afar I hear

And singing
And tremulous breathing
And soaring steps.
I go. Whereto?
To stride upon the surfaces of waters,
To rest upon the openings of chasms,
To follow hard the footsteps of the banished beggars.

TANKHUM (*raises himself to look at* THE GOLEM *but falls back in mortal terror*).
Another, yes another, not the same.
A luminous, a glowing,
Gleaming countenance.

GOLEM (*the brightness of invisibility begins to glow around him*).
I warned you not to look at me.
If you raise your eyes to me a second time,
You die.
Now terror seizes you; again I say,
You are not dreaming.
Do you not know that I am everlasting
And not from here,
And not the fiddler at your feast
Nor the dancer
Nor the witness?
I turn away from you,
For I am everlasting.

TANKHUM.
One sole survivor,
One was left,
And now he too is going.
Then I must be the one who's left,
I myself.
Myself—the father,
Myself—the fiddler,
Myself—the dancer,
Myself—the witness,
Myself—the mourner.

GOLEM.
I go where meadows roll,
Where sorrow's outcry: "No more, no more, no more,"
Has not yet reached.
I go to the east,
And from the west I hear a voice

And from the north and from the south.
I go to all the corners of the world,
For all are calling me at once,
And all pursue the fleeing beggars,
Calling, "Come back, come back, come back."

(He flies through a door and disappears. TANKHUM stands with the candle in his hand as the rain whips through the windows and the wind blows the flame of the candle. TANKHUM huddles against a wall. Suddenly he breaks out into mad laughter.)

TANKHUM.

Tankhum fooled, Tankhum fooled,
And Tankhum let himself be fooled.
And who was it that did the fooling?
A fool, a Golem did the fooling, Tankhum.

(From a remote part of the tower a woman's voice is heard weeping and calling for help. "Help! Help!" re-echoes through the ruins and then is cut off abruptly.)

TANKHUM.

Help. Who should help?

THE CALL *(again)*.

Help!

TANKHUM.

Who can help? Who?
Who wants to help? Eh?
Who should help? Who?

(Runs out hastily and disappears. DEVORALE and THE REBBETSIN run in from one of the remote rooms. They can scarcely catch their breath and in fright they cling to each other to keep from falling.)

REBBETSIN.

The evil ones have brought us here.
We cannot leave—who knows the way?
Oh, we are lost, my child!

DEVORALE.

So many doors and caves; where do they lead?

REBBETSIN.

I scarcely feel my head, so bruised
Is it from bumping into walls.
And who's to blame? You are. Such folly
To come here in the middle of the night.

DEVORALE.

Who would have thought it?

REBBETSIN.

> Such madness! I've never heard the likes.
> To come here looking for your grandfather!
> And what would he be doing in these ruins?

DEVORALE.

> Who would have thought it? Now you scold me,
> But did not you yourself say we should go?

REBBETSIN.

> I did. Of course I did—since all
> Are hiding behind barred and bolted doors.
> It's midnight and your grandfather
> Is still not home from evening prayers.

DEVORALE.

> My whole dress torn to tatters in the darkness.

REBBETSIN.

> My hands are raw. The walls
> Are full of nails. It's thundering again.

DEVORALE.

> If only *he* would answer: this is where he sleeps.

REBBETSIN.

> Be still! We have enough of trouble now.
> O God of Abraham, of Isaac and of Jacob,
> Take pity and be merciful to us.

DEVORALE.

> Come, let us look again.
> Somewhere there is a door that leads outside.
> (*They go over to the various doors, feeling their way in the
> dark. They search and turn back again.*)

REBBETSIN.

> Oh, what shall we do, child?
> Such a misfortune!

DEVORALE.

> Don't weep; don't weep.
> (*She breaks into tears herself.*)

REBBETSIN.

> We must do something; try to call again.

DEVORALE (*in a tearful voice*).

> Help!

REBBETSIN.

> Arye Levi! Arye Levi!

DEVORALE.

> Stop shouting, please.

REBBETSIN.

> Hush, I hear an answer.

TANKHUM'S VOICE *(from a distance).*

> Who should help?
> Who can help?
> Who ought to help?
> Who? Ha-ha-ha.

> *(Both women huddle together in a corner with bated breath.)*

REBBETSIN.

> Let us be quiet. Let us pray to God.

DEVORALE.

> I feel dizzy. I think I'm falling.

REBBETSIN.

> Hold on to me, dear child.

> *(THE GOLEM bolts in, with the glow of invisibility hovering over him. Both women cover their faces with their hands and let out a scream of terror.)*

GOLEM.

> Why do you shriek in terror when I come
> To liberate, to save, to lead you out?
> Your cries for help were carried by the wind,
> And from afar I spied you in this place.
> One stride—and every road is clear for me.
> The darkness dissipates and all is light,
> And everything I touch becomes transparent;
> I stretch my arms—they reach across the world
> From end to end.

BOTH WOMEN.

> Oh, leave us. Go away.

GOLEM.

> You tell me "Leave"? I came to free you,
> And yet you are afraid. Where shall I go?
> And who else, do you think, will come to save you?
> Do you believe that he—that beggar—will yet come?
> You hope in vain, I tell you. I myself
> Leaped up from slumber when I heard
> That sad outcry: "No more, no more, no more";
> And I started after it to turn it back.
> In vain my springing up, in vain my haste,
> In vain the shattering of sleep!
> If I returned with nothing,
> Can you still hope that he will come?
> I am the only one who can deliver you,
> I alone.

BOTH WOMEN.

    Do go away! Are you not he who is called Joseph?

GOLEM.

    Joseph is not my name today; there is
    Another Joseph now, one who no longer
    Lies, flung full length, upon the floor, no longer
    Sleeps in prodigious sleep of darkness.
    In silence I arose; in silence, left.
    I knew the Rabbi would have kept me back,
    And so I did not ask for his permission.
    Long have I dreamt about myself.
    Why do you look at me in deathly fright?
    You did not think to see me? It is true
    That nobody must see or hear me,
    That I must not reveal myself,
    Must ever be the one unseen, enshrouded,
    Till he who holds my fortune's reins
    Shall say: "Go, conquer, hear and see."
    And do you know who holds my fortune's reins?

BOTH WOMEN.

    Please go away. You frighten us. Please leave.

GOLEM.

    You do not know who holds my fortune's reins?
    Then I will tell you, if you wish; and do not fear,
    This is the first time and this is the last
    That I reveal myself or speak
    To anyone or look into his eyes
    Or step across a threshold to come in,
    An unexpected midnight visitor,
    Or speak such words or hear such silence.
    This is the first time and this is the last.
    Pray, do you know who follows me and calls
    And forces me to come back here? And do you know
    What "first and last time" means? You do not.
    And if you wish, I'll tell the secret.
    I was asleep. It seemed so strange:
    I did not even see the light
    Within my dream, and were my eyes to open
    I would not see myself, and should I shout
    I would not hear the outcry of my voice.
    And then I heard and saw a thousand miles.
    I saw with eyes shut tight; I heard
    With deafened ears, and called and shouted
    With a tongue grown mute. Do you not hear.

As I do, a moaning in the ruins?
That is my call. I thought I would not care,
That I would leave these ruins and their call
And let the moaning die in the tower's void.
I thought this. But, you see, within my heart
A love awoke, a longing,
And a shiver shook my frame.
I am impatient for the moment when
Again, I can fling myself, and stretch and lie,
Pressing against the floors in empty darkness.
You know, I love this Tower Five.
(*He sits down on the ground.*)
I'll sit a while, a little while.
I'm weary. I will rest. The dark, the void
Will wait. May I sit down?

DEVORALE.
What is he asking us? What does he want?

GOLEM.
No need to fear.
I will not harm you—look at me.
Why do you tremble so—your hands, your lips—
Since you will never see me more, never?
I am so luminous now, the very brightest,
Brighter than he, the young wanderer,
And brighter than the Rabbi. Should I tell
You where the young man's feet are treading now?
And where—the Rabbi's?

REBBETSIN.
Have you seen the Rabbi?

GOLEM.
Have I seen him? I see him always.
The steps of the wanderer disappear,
The thunder that rolls down from heaven swallows them.
You think the thunder's coming now is aimless?
The Rabbi comes. He is returning now.

REBBETSIN.
Where is he coming from?

GOLEM.
From the field beyond the city.
I too come from there, where all the roads
Were closed to both the wanderers.
I saw the Rabbi standing there in sorrow,
His head bowed—and he, the wanderer,
Went plodding on his wounded feet, step

By step where all the roads were driving him.
And oh, how much I longed to follow him,
To run before him and be with him,
And lie down at his feet and be his shadow.
And yet, how could I if my heart began
To burn with yearning for my tower of ruins?
Oh, yes, the Rabbi is coming home.
If I must come, then he must surely come.
The Rabbi tarries, for his steps are heavy
And his head sinks beneath the weight of sorrow.
The road back was but a step for me,
The darkness—but a single wink.
The Rabbi walks in shrouds of lightning, blasts of thunder.
The whirlwind was the first to seize him.
It tosses him from side to side, and plucks his clothes.
You hear, the rain is whipping in through every hole.

REBBETSIN.

Oh, God, be merciful, be merciful.

DEVORALE.

Escape. We must escape.

GOLEM.

Please do not go.
No one must see me at this moment,
No one hear my words except those
For whom I freely have unveiled myself.
Do you know who it is that sits with you?
My face is known to you, as is my name,
But you have never seen me yet.
You would be blinded in a single instant
Were you to look at me against my will;
For death and dazzling blasts and fiery flames
And everlasting dying—these are my eyes.
I live, and do not know myself how long,
With people and with beasts and with the worms,
In water and in fire and in stone
And I can never see the start nor end
Of me and of my everlasting dying.
I plead: relieve me of my fate of wonder;
But no one hears my plea. Just now, as I
Was flying hither from the field, all at once
I heard a curious ringing in my ears,
And in my eyes strange fires began to burn.
Perhaps— No, what am I saying?— I
Would enter any house, what matters which,

For every house would look at me in fear,
And every house would drive me off in terror.
  (*His head sinks as he sits. Thunder and lightning.*)

DEVORALE.
  Be merciful to us; be merciful.

GOLEM.
  And still you are afraid? The Rabbi soon will come.
  I see him near. The rain pours down
  But has no power over him.
  The lightning lights his path. He comes. He comes.
  He must not know what I have said before you.
  I see a special terror in your face.
  You look into my eyes, and I recall the moment
  When I embraced you, pressed you close to me.
  I still can feel your warmth upon my fingers,
  And at my breast I still can feel your trembling.
  But then I could not speak; I could not catch
  My breath. It is different now.
  I do not even want to touch you.
  It is enough for me to sit, face
  To face with you, as I sit now, and speak
  In words that nimbly dance, that dance and dazzle.
  If I should wish, frozen as you are with fear,
  I could grab you and hurl you high into the air
  Then fling you down onto the ground and pick you up
      again
  And spin you round my head with dizzy speed
  And spin and spin so long and fast
  Until your hands would grapple round my neck
  And your lips, aflame with hurt and locked in pain,
  Would suck themselves into my own.
  (*Both women, in despair, hide their faces and wring their
  hands.*)
  And more:
  I would toss you on my shoulders,
  And through the stormy, flashing dark
  I'd carry you into another of the towers,
  And we would twine together into one
  And huddle in the covering of emptiness.
  And I would open up my eyes and see
  The winds shredding your garments into tatters,
  The lightning laying bare the whiteness of your skin,
  And the emptiness overflowing with your warmth.
  And I would bite into your limbs

And suck your white flesh into myself.
Then stillness once again.
The rain whips in through every hole.
The shafts of lightning twist together and unravel,
And one after another bricks fall and sink.
(*He stands up.*)
Come, let me lead you out. I am revolted
By your fear and still more by my revelation
Of myself. I am shamed enough
That I could not pass you by
Without remembering your warmth upon my fingers,
That I revealed to you so many secrets;
To you—two lost and frightened women.
(*Goes to the door and stops.*)
The moaning in the ruins has grown silent.
One step of mine and peace descends
On every room and cavern, for every step
Of mine is joy and every gesture
Of my hands is peace. See how you quake,
And your faces—ashen, drowsy, dreaming.
Like you, I forget my words and feel my lids descending.
I could lie down and fall asleep. But I do not.
I can remove my sleep to other places,
But you can go nowhere, nowhere at all.
From every side the long-expected comes upon you
With sharpened axes and with fires prepared.
And now into the heart of night flow,
Still warm, still freshly dripping from the sword,
The first red drops. One by one. And suddenly
The drops storm up in streams, a stream
For every door, a stream for your door too.
And the red streams bear you off, far and further.
Houses burn and fall in dying fires,
And with the houses, heads—burnt and after drowned.
They ring you round and float upon the streams.
The bells of monasteries ring. The crosses glow.
And mouths still red with flame catch up the bell-sounds,
And swallow them, and hurl them back again
Like long and snaking tongues. They turn you round.
They drown you, pull you out—to drown you once again.
And you—you sit as you do now, dreaming
And slumbering in peace—my peace.
You see before you only fear and sorrow.

I say to you:
Raise up your eyes and see how far and high
I spread my arms, how light my breath.
I raise my feet and float above the floor.
My strides have wings.
Arise and go. I lead the way.
(*Both women, having grown faint with fear, have sunk to the floor and sit with faces covered. They do not move.*)
Awake. I'll show the way for you to leave.
You lost, bewildered women, follow me.
(*He takes them by the hands and helps them stand up. Both women follow him as if in a trance.*)
You need not fear because I touch you.
I only lead you, merely show the way.
(*He leads them out. He returns in a moment, sits down in a corner, and rocks with his hands crossed over his heart.*)
No more, no more, no more.
Walls, my walls,
Why are you dumb?
Caves, my caves,
Why do you sleep?
Why don't you ask
Whence do I come?

Risen up and brightly shining,
I unbound my pack of words,
Spoke them into emptiness.
Now—as then—
The rain is pounding
On the ramparts of my tower.

Was there any
One who told me—
Go and chase after the shadow
Of the two?

No one, no one, no one.

When they called
For help and rescue,
Was it me
They called upon?
Were they hoping
I would come?

Walls, my walls,
Why are you dumb?
Why are you silent,
Caves, my caves?

TANKHUM (*gliding in*).
Who should save? Who?
Who can save? Who?

GOLEM.
I can.

TANKHUM (*with a ringing laugh*).
Ha, ha, ha, you!
Who are you? Who?
(*Astounded.*)
You have come back? How fast.
The very same.
Not long ago he was another,
And now he is the same again.
(*Angrily.*)
You fooled old Tankhum; you fooled Tankhum.
(THE GOLEM *grows darker and darker.*)
From all the corners of the world
He has come back.
Ha, ha, ha.
What's going on in all the corners of the world?

GOLEM.
Be quiet. Do you hear?

TANKHUM.
I hear. Of course, I hear.

GOLEM.
Move over close to me. Nearer.
(TANKHUM *moves up against* THE GOLEM. *They both sit.*)
Well, here I am again, you see.
A moment earlier or later, in a night
Of ceaseless thunder and of rainstorm,
Of distant places unattained,
What does a moment late or early matter?

TANKHUM.
Of course. What does it matter?

GOLEM.
How much at home I feel here. You too?

TANKHUM.
Yes. Of course.

GOLEM.

> Even there I felt its warmth,
> Rushing through the field and forest,
> Seeing all and hearing all.
> I knew that somewhere there are walls—
> You know that too?

TANKHUM.

> Yes, of course I know.

GOLEM.

> And what if these four walls
> Were also light, transparent?
> Where could I go to flee the all-perceived?
> And where would I find hardness for my skin
> And icy shivers, thorny darkness,
> And desolation, fenced and bounded?
> I spoke to you with angry words
> When I departed. But even in my anger,
> You must have heard the augury of my return,
> The portent of my longing and my love.

TANKHUM.

> I heard. Of course, I heard.

GOLEM.

> My brightness has corroded my own vision;
> And all those that I met throughout the night
> Were scattered in its gleam.
> But they will each be found. Each one of them
> Has somewhere a corner of his own,
> A place to rest his head and press his brow
> And burrow into with his eyes and lie in silence.
> Reb Levi has his room, and the young wanderer—
> His desert nest of stones. One night and then another
> He hurries there and he will come to it,
> As I have come to this; and like me, he too
> Will fall with joy to kiss the pointed stones
> That will embrace him with their sharpness,
> Caress him with their hardness and their desolation.
> Reb Levi is at home and sees
> The wonders and the terrors both revealed.
> And now he slumps across the table, lying silent,
> Like me, happy in his stoniness.
> And now he rises up and walks. He comes this way,
> Like me, to seek the warmth of these four walls,
> Where he is always certain to find one—me—
> Who waits for him and is forever his.

TANKHUM.
>His?

GOLEM.
>Do not ask. Move closer still to me.

TANKHUM.
>Are you asleep?

GOLEM.
>Neither ask nor speak. Let light be darkened.
>Let the bright be hidden from my eyes.
>Press close to me, you rain-washed floors,
>And send your chill through all my limbs.
>The breath of thunder let me hear,
>And let the wind lash the pouring rain.
>Move off and stay away.
>
>*(He falls to the ground and lies prone in the same position
>as in the very beginning. TANKHUM, in great fear, carefully
>tip-toes away from him. He comes to a door and quickly
>disappears through it. His rapidly retreating footsteps echo
>through the distant rooms of the tower. They grow fainter
>and then are heard no more. Utter darkness. THE MAHARAL
>enters carrying a lantern.)*

MAHARAL *(illuminates* THE GOLEM *with his lantern).*
>No change. Still the same.
>*(Silence.)*
>The rain pours in upon him.
>Get up. It's time. Get up.
>*(THE GOLEM sits up.)*
>You've slept enough.

GOLEM.
>Rabbi.

MAHARAL.
>You've been asleep for two whole days.

GOLEM.
>I wanted to awaken long before.
>So many times I sat up, yet I could not
>Open up my eyes. I feel cold and wet.

MAHARAL.
>It has been raining in upon you all the while.

GOLEM.
>I did not feel the rain when I was sleeping.
>Where am I, Rabbi?

MAHARAL.
>You do not know? In Tower Five.

GOLEM.

> And I kept dreaming that I was out
> Somewhere beyond the city far, that I
> Was striding, striding over great, shadowy fields.
> Some people came in my direction.
> I started walking towards them. They came nearer.
> I ran to them so I might see their faces.
> Yet no matter how I turned nor where I stood.
> I saw no faces, only napes.
> No eyes, nor foreheads, noses—only napes.
> No mouths—and yet I heard them speak.
> I asked: Who are you? They replied: "You."
> Where do you come from? They replied: "From you."
> I asked: Where are you going? They replied: "To you."
> And as they spoke these words, they quickly wheeled about
> And one after another started rushing here
> To Tower Five. I followed. And as I ran
> I noticed: they were five in number,
> Two women and three men. At last I caught them
> And grabbed one with both hands. I looked
> And I saw—you.

MAHARAL.

> Me?

GOLEM.

> You were drenched and chilled.
> Your clothes were sticking to your skin, your beard
>   dishevelled;
> Your hands seemed palsied as they swung in all directions,
> And where your face should be were two great gashes.
> The one ran from your forehead down; the other ran
>   across.
> And both were glowing red as flame.
> They glowed, they died, and they turned black.
> You fell upon your knees before me, pleading,
> "Oh, save me, Joseph, from the cross.
> Oh, save me, Joseph, from these gashes.
> A thousand years I bear them on my face;
> No flesh has ever healed upon them."

MAHARAL.

> And then?

GOLEM.

> The others, when they saw
> You kneeling and in tears, attacked me.

They threw me to the ground and spit into my face.
And one, with swollen wounds upon his feet,
A young beggar, stepped upon me, crying: "Golem!"
I jumped from under them and seized the shouter
By both his hands and flung him high into the air
And thought to smash him to the ground and finish him,
When unexpectedly you slashed your staff
Across my head and stammered out:
"Do you know whom you are about to beat? Golem!"
A blackness came upon me. I fell.
All five of you began to carry me
And drag me by my arms and legs
Until you dragged me to a pit. You threw
Me in and, shovelling earth by handfuls, buried me.
But half my head stuck out. Suddenly
I heard one of the women, Devorale—

MAHARAL.

Who?

GOLEM.

I recognized her voice. She was seized with sobbing.
She fell upon my half a head, embraced it,
And with both hands she pressed me to her heart and wept.
She wept. The others shovelled earth and shovelled.
Then I heard you cry in the self-same voice:
"Do you know whom you weep for?
A golem is not mourned."

MAHARAL.

Enough. You hear? I am alone. Alone.
I come to you at midnight as you see.
I bring you rest and peace. For two whole days
You slept. I came here many times
To summon you to eat and drink.
You did not hear me.

GOLEM.

I am not hungry yet.
My limbs were chilled before. They are not now,
Since you are here.

MAHARAL (*placing his hands on* THE GOLEM's *shoulders*).

Now come with me. I need you.

GOLEM.

Now I am ready, Rabbi. Summon me.

MAHARAL.

The midnight must not be encountered here
But in the depths of Tower Five, deeper far

Than all the depths you gazed at in your dreams.
Now hear the word that I reveal to you
And grasp it well. See its redness;
Perceive its warmth, its trembling and its sharpness.
The word is—blood.

GOLEM.

Blood.

MAHARAL.

Repeat again but louder.

GOLEM.

Blood.

MAHARAL.

Again but softer.

GOLEM.

Blood.

MAHARAL.

I call you. Come.

(*They both go to the door leading deeper into the tower.*
TANKHUM *glides across the stage with lighted candles in
his hands.*)

TANKHUM (*breathless, in a fit of coughing*).

Res-cue us!
Who will rescue? Who?
Who can rescue? Eh?
Wh-o c-a-n res-cue? Wh-o?

SCENE VII.   IN THE CAVE

*(In the subterranean caverns of Tower Five. One can almost
touch the darkness. THADDEUS, accompanied by THE MONK,
emerges from the depths of the cave. THE MONK carries a small
torch. They are both panting from their long journey under-
ground.)*

THADDEUS.

    Your hand here. Steady now.
    Were not the air so stifling and the dark so dense,
    We would have long ago fulfilled the mission
    That was ordained for us by God and Jesus.
    You see, the cave is long deserted and untrodden;
    And yet our hearts refused to fear,
    And our hands disdained to tremble. To the synagogue
    Our steps by God Himself were guided.

MONK.

    I'm falling. Help me, Father.

THADDEUS.

    Straighten up
    And catch your breath. The air is lighter here.

MONK.

    All was done just as you instructed me.
    I was not frightened, firmly held the knife
    In my right hand, my left clamped hard
    About the throat. Not an outcry, not a shudder.
    I corked the bottles well and placed them right.
    I still can feel the warmth upon my hand.
    Oh, catch me! My head spins again.

THADDEUS.

    Are you afraid? Coward. Do you not see who leads you?
    You see my gray beard, my staff of age,
    And in my eyes the nights I lay awake?
    For whose sake did I lie awake? For mine?
    Who basks in the reflected glory of the cross?
    Do I alone? Or do you more than I?
    And who did more to make the knife-edge sharp?

And who inhaled more of that warmth
Although I stood aside; did I or you?
What was done I did, not you, and I
Should be the one to totter, for you did nothing—
A mere whisk along the edge.

MONK.

Forgive me, Father.

(*He kisses* THADDEUS's *hands.*)

THADDEUS.

I forgive you. I am kind.
Go calmly to your cell and sleep.
And I am more than calm. I am exultant,
For watching you fill those flasks with blood,
I saw before my eyes such visions
As no one but Him ever could have seen.
And He, while He still hung, nailed to the cross,
He saw the same visions that I beheld
And raised one corner of his brow
And softly, lovingly dispatched a glance here;
For even then this cave stood ready for the deed,
And this knife too. Glittering, gleaming, sharp,
The knife shone upon Him from within the cave.
It shone, caressed His opened lid;
And glittering, gleaming, His eyelid closed.
You think: revenge? No. Love alone.
For blood is—love. Blood of children,
Since He also was a child. And every knife
From that time on is blessed.
Those crucifiers never will deprive
Or rob us of the sanctity of knives;
For never must there be an end to flowing
Of the blood of those who could not see
The gentle gleam His closing eyelid cast.

MONK.

Oh, Father, someone comes, I think.

THADDEUS.

You fancy fears of every kind. You coward! Who
Would come here? Who knows the secret entrance?
I say again, have no fear.
You hear the sound of steps? Of course. Those steps are
His.
Softly, lovingly he hovers over us
And breathes in deep the crimson scent.
He comes to life not only up above

But here with us as well. He comes!
His pale cheeks flush,
And from His eyes the joy of love flows,
And childlike tenderness and pity.
He bears the cross upon His shoulders. He dances with it;
He sings with it, lives with it, plays with it.
He is here—Jesus Christ, our Lord!
He is here! Do you not see Him? Raise your eyes!

MONK (*crosses himself in terror and falls to the ground*).

Oh, come, I am afraid, afraid.

THADDEUS.

And now do you see?

MONK.

Oh, merciful Jesus, have pity!
Oh, holy Father, take me from this place!

THADDEUS.

Away! Away from my eyes!
I tell you: see—and you are deaf and blind.
Away!

(THE MONK *starts to run.* THADDEUS *follows. Both disappear. From the opposite side* THE MAHARAL *and* THE GOLEM *enter.* THE MAHARAL *carries a lantern,* THE GOLEM —*an axe and a spade.*)

MAHARAL.

Stop here and peer ahead! What do you see?

GOLEM.

I see the cave's full length from end to end.
To the right—a narrow path, to the left—a broad one.
A hundred paces in, a third,
Most difficult to follow, forks away.

MAHARAL.

Where do the first two end?

GOLEM.

The narrow one leads to the synagogue;
The broad one—to the priest.

MAHARAL.

Now listen well and tell me what you hear.

GOLEM.

I hear the last breath of one already dead.

MAHARAL.

What do you smell?

GOLEM (*shudders*).

The word! The word you gave me secretly!

The word is red and sharp and warm and still.
I feel it and I hear it and I see it.

MAHARAL.

Restrain your shuddering. Pronounce it.

GOLEM.

Blood.

MAHARAL.

From which side?

GOLEM.

From the right, along the narrow path.

MAHARAL.

Come, let us go to it.
We must not speak to one another,
But to ourselves keep on repeating:
"Through death and blood and dying breath."
We walk ahead but must not look behind.
Begin the journey and say with me:
"Through death and blood and dying breath."

GOLEM.

"Through death and blood and dying breath."
(*They start walking, but suddenly an unseen being pushes*
THE MAHARAL *back and blocks his path.*)

MAHARAL.

You must go alone. The evil spirits
Of the cave are barring me. Go on alone,
For you are not within their power.
You need no torch, but take the spade and axe.
Seek out the place beneath the synagogue
And take whatever you will find
To him to whom it rightfully belongs.
Your stride is long; your eye is bright.

GOLEM.

Will you now leave me, Rabbi?

MAHARAL.

Are you afraid?

GOLEM.

Oh, no, but come with me.
You'll see, should anyone attempt to bar
Your way again!

MAHARAL.

I must not go.
With a thousand eyes, peril seeks a pretext.
I bid you go alone.

GOLEM.

> Always, no sooner do you come
> To me than you must leave again.
> In the tower above us, day and night I lay
> Waiting for you to come and stay with me.
> I thought that every rustle was a herald
> Of your coming. You had bidden me
> To speak to no one and to go nowhere.
> I spoke to no one; but every passing instant
> I heard within me such outcries, such words
> As I had never heard before. I had
> To clamp my teeth to keep from crying out.
> I had to bind my legs and bend them double
> To keep them from arising by themselves
> And running off, so driving was my urge to leave.
> Yet you—no sooner have you looked at me
> Or briefly spoken than you turn upon your heel
> And leave me once again alone. Do not leave.
> I see this blackness as if brightly lit.
> I see these caves from end to end and side to side.
> I hear the rocks converse and move; from every crack
> Like snakes the shadows start to crawl and slither.
> And nearer come the sounds of barking,
> Of howling and of grinding teeth.
> Though I am not afraid, yet stay with me.
> I want your nearness, Rabbi, just your nearness.

MAHARAL.

> The tracks we follow lie upon such roads
> As rule themselves. They seek out every means
> To heap confusion on us and mislead us.
> On you they will unleash still greater terrors;
> But, though you are alone, you must pass through.
> You must, for you are sent. You have no choice.
> Whatever you may see or hear
> Must not distract your eyes and ears.
> Pierce through the seen and heard; see and hear
> That other, in the distance, that you *must* discover.
> Remain alone.

GOLEM.

> One moment longer, Rabbi.

MAHARAL.

> The danger grows with every instant. And you—
> What are you in its sight that for your sake

Should be delayed for even half an instant
The redemption of a people?

GOLEM.

How often has it happened,
When you must send me somewhere, that you come
And wake me from my lethargy and silence
And change me wholly to a different being?
You think I do not know this?

MAHARAL.

Your entire life is but an expectation
Of those moments when I need you.
And now that one has come, you still do not perceive
How great the meaning has become of each day
Of yours that had the honor to await all this.
The accidental, the superfluous
Of your life depart. Deeds and prowess call.
Grace descends upon you, and over you
The protecting wings of Providence unfold.

(THE MAHARAL *leaves. Darkness. Slowly a soft light begins to surround* THE GOLEM. *His eyes grow large and bright, his face—sharp, his entire body—supple, like a tiger set to spring.*)

GOLEM.

This distance and this depth—one stride,
One leap, one glance, one flutter
Through blood and death and dying breath.

(*He is about to leap when suddenly a great commotion breaks out in the cave. Fierce roaring winds arise. From above and from below a hail of rocks pours over* THE GOLEM's *head. He shakes them off and steps back. As he retreats the storm subsides. He waits several moments and then strides forward again with a wild outcry.*)

Through blood and death and dying breath.

(*A fearsome barking arises and a thumping of dogs' paws on the earth. The cave is filled with moaning and commotion.* THE GOLEM *strikes out in all directions with his axe. The barking ceases. Flames and clouds of smoke appear; they coil about him and surround him. His clothes begin to burn. He tosses about like a madman, uttering suppressed cries. He falls to the ground. The flames disappear. He lies on the ground panting. He gets up furiously. His clothes are charred but he is himself unharmed.*)

GOLEM.

Where are you, Rabbi? Where are you? Come here!
*(He sinks to his knees. Shadows of all sorts, spirits of the
cave begin to move about in the light that surrounds him.
They dance and spin and twist about over his head.)*
Where are you? Come and see how everything
Awakes in wrath against me.
The fire is quelled; the storm has stilled; but now
The silent terrors start to crawl from their seclusion.
They twist, they turn, and they embrace
And dance in rings about me. They trick my eyes
And dazzle them with double fires.
They trick my ears with double sounds.
The very cave turns double too.
The glow about my head begins to dim.
*(He wants to start walking but he does not know which
way to go. He keeps turning around in the same place as a
wild circle of spirits whirls about him.)*

CAVE SPIRITS.

Round about,
Round about.
Who is he whom we surround?
Who is it that leads him round?
Whose protection has he found?
None at all.
None at all.

He is not within our power;
On this night before the Seder,
Who has brought him at this hour
In our midst,
In our midst?

Round about,
Round about.
He himself awakened us,
From our dark has shaken us;
Who is he who dared do thus?
No one, surely,
None at all.

Turn and twist and form a chain;
Sing the song of death and pain;
Spin him dizzy, then again
In our midst,
In our midst.

GOLEM (*stands as if chained to the spot*).
>The fire did not consume me;
>The stones were powerless to fell me;
>Now break asunder, whirling wheel,
>And tear apart the double dance.
>I have been sent to go
>And not to loiter in your midst.

CAVE SPIRITS.
>Dance in double ranks,
>Form a triple column,
>Play your fiendish pranks;
>Cast a dizzy spell,
>Twist it, weave it well;
>Raise your fiendish shanks,
>Kick them gay and solemn.

>He is lost forever.
>Seize him, choke and tear.
>Half from half then sever;
>Let this severed thing
>Lie within our ring.
>Whom must he deliver?
>Who dispatched him here?

>Since you wield an axe,
>Let your own blood flow,
>Before he comes back
>Who issues these commands
>And you to us remands,
>Who grabs, himself, the axe
>And holds it for a blow.

>Make a path. We hear
>His footsteps pound the ground.
>Pallid tapers flare,
>Blaze as red as blood,
>In a fiery flood.
>Let him know and fear
>Whom we dance around.

>Stand apart in pairs.
>The dancing chain be broken.
>Make your columns fair.
>Stand like silent dead,
>Drenched in bloody red.

Let him dance on air
Whose death has now been spoken.

(*The dance of the spirits stops. A blood-red light suffuses
the cave. Silence.* THE GOLEM *falls to the ground terrified
by what he suddenly sees: from the path he was to have
taken, a figure appears entirely like* THE MAHARAL. *A cold
fury on his face, his eyes—piercing, his lips pressed together. He walks with short, stiff steps and is drenched in
a red glow. With every step he pounds his staff on the
ground and each blow re-echoes through the cave.*)

FIGURE.
You summoned me before?

GOLEM (*raising his head*).
Who are you?

FIGURE.
You ask me who I am? You do not know?

GOLEM.
Oh, no! Oh, no! You are not the Rabbi.
You are another; you are not he.

FIGURE.
Not he?
(*Laughs angrily.*)
How impudent you are! Do you not know
Whose hands control your fate? My hands!
Why did you call? I ask again.

GOLEM.
Oh, go away from me. I am afraid.
You are another, not the Rabbi.

FIGURE.
Again your speech is impudent. Speak so
To me once more and you shall feel my stick!

GOLEM.
Have pity.

FIGURE.
I am the Rabbi.

GOLEM.
Have pity. Someone
Misled me here—the Rabbi. You.

FIGURE.
Does that concern me? I shall never
Let you escape. You shall stay here
Forever.

(THE GOLEM *starts to run;* THE FIGURE *bars his way.*)
Do not run. Stand still. All is lost.
No one can ever leave this place.

GOLEM.

Let me go. You hear me? Let me go!

FIGURE.

Contain your impudence—you see this stick?
Or shall I pluck your hairs out one by one?
Or knock your teeth out of your mouth,
A tooth for every word?

GOLEM.

Away from me! Away!
(*He swings his fists and then jumps back.*)

FIGURE.

You raise your fist to me? To me, your Rabbi?
Hey, all of you, come here, come here!
Tear out his tongue and leave him dumb;
Splinter his legs, that he may never run.
Throw him to the ground and rend his flesh
And slit his throat.

GOLEM.

Stop your calling! Whom are you calling? Stop!

FIGURE.

Silence! Do you see now
That I am Rabbi?

GOLEM.

Yes, I see.

FIGURE.

Now you know
That it was I who brought you here.

GOLEM.

You, you.

FIGURE.

Then hear in silence. I am master. I
Can do with you whatever I please to do.
I do not harm you because I toy with you,
With you and with your fears and with your sorrows.
Beyond that, I have no need of you.
Stop staring, golem, dimwit, hunk of meat!
Shut tight your gaping eyes,
Fall to the ground and lie there. Fall, I say.
(THE GOLEM *sinks to the ground.*)
Well done. Your head down. Lower, lower.

Your head still closer to the ground. Dig deeper.
Bend over double and stay seated so
By day and night, by day and night.

(THE GOLEM *forces his head between his knees.* THE FIG-
URE *vanishes.* THE CAVE SPIRITS *come creeping out, form
into ranks. They move lightly, scarcely touching the
ground.*)

CAVE SPIRITS.
>   With howling winds
>   Put out the flame.
>   Set the dogs
>   The winds to tame.
>
>   Hurl the rocks
>   Upon the dogs.
>   Fling the child
>   Against the rocks.
>
>   In a sack
>   The child doth lie.
>   Take the cord—
>   The sack untie.
>
>   In the sack
>   Search with care.
>   Wine-red flasks
>   Are lying there.
>
>   From the flasks
>   We'll drink our fill
>   When the furor
>   Has grown still.
>
>   He will sit there,
>   Sit and sway
>   In his stupor
>   Night and day.

(*They leave.* THE GOLEM *remains seated alone. He raises
his head and looks around.*)

GOLEM.
>   Where am I? What has happened here?
>   How did I come into these depths?
>   Who were my partners in a whirling dance?
>   I must go somewhere. Where? And to what end?
>   Why has it grown so quiet all at once?

And what is this? An axe? A spade?
Where am I? Who has brought me here?
(*He lets out a weird yell, which he continues until he is breathless.*)
I shout—no one replies. Should I not shout?
Should I lie down and call no more?
Something is glowing there, before my eyes.
(*He huddles close to the ground and lies still.* THE IN-VISIBLE *appears above him. It grasps him by the shoulders and shakes him.*)

INVISIBLE.

Behold me. This once and for all time,
Behold me.
(THE GOLEM *leaps up gaping.*)
Do not run. Wherever you may go
I follow. Behold me and rejoice.
Your fear before confused you;
Your dancing dizzied you; I saw it.
Now you can see it too.

GOLEM.

Who are you? Tell me!
How can it be?

INVISIBLE.

Do not inquire. Behold. Let that suffice.

GOLEM.

Your face is bright—like mine before.
But all is darkness for me now.

INVISIBLE.

It had to be that once you might behold
Yourself—once and never more again.

GOLEM.

Why am I here? I do not know. Do you?

INVISIBLE.

You came to see the dance of madness,
And what you saw was the beginning;
Let me reveal the end to you,
The full measure of Unreason.
You hold an axe, a spade—you have no need
Of them. The flasks are ready. Stretch your arm.

GOLEM.

Ah, now I know. I can remember now.

INVISIBLE.

Why trouble to remember?
What if you have forgotten? It is all one.

You will fulfill your mission either way.
For what else can an emissary do
Except what he must do? Here or there,
Sooner or later—when it's done,
It's done. It may be late for someone else,
But for yourself, how can it be too late?
Stretch out your hand, no more than that
It hardly pays to move a step.

GOLEM.
From here?

INVISIBLE.
Yes, from here. What is distance? Nothing.
And buried secrets become plain
From always to forever; and every road
Is but a step. And obstacles
Are merely toys for those who wish to leave
Unreason even if but for one moment.
And what are blood and death and dying breath?

GOLEM.
Ah, now I can remember all.

INVISIBLE.
And how are you alone? Am I not like yourself?
No blood nor death nor dying breath.
You understand? Not even dying breath.
Reach out your hand. If anything lies hidden
Anywhere, of itself it will arise
And grasp your fingers. For what is buried deep
Within this cave has long revealed itself
To every eye. There it lies.
You see? Bend over. Pick it up.

GOLEM (*looks down and sees a bundle near his feet*).
How is it that I did not notice it before?

INVISIBLE.
But neither did you see yourself before.

GOLEM.
Am I to pick it up?

INVISIBLE.
What for? Just let it lie.

GOLEM.
You scoff at me. You look like me
And yet you scoff at me.

INVISIBLE.
Then should I leave?

GOLEM.

Yes, I am afraid.

The cave begins to spin once more.

Oh, no. Stay here.

INVISIBLE.

Untie the sack,

And then I go.

(THE GOLEM *unties the sack and removes two bottles of red liquid.*)

Now do you see?

GOLEM (*cries out*).

Blood! Blood!

INVISIBLE.

Why shout? Just put them down and let them stand.

(*Disappears. A waxen-yellow light suffuses the cave. The ground opens and the SUBTERRANEANS emerge. They carry tall lit candles in their long, scrawny hands. After so long a sleep in their graves, their clothes are rotted and tattered. They dance a very quiet round around the bottles, scarcely moving. The hands holding the candles are stretched in front of them. THE GOLEM presses back against a wall, watching the proceedings with great anxiety.*)

FIRST SUBTERRANEAN.

With a voice that clearly rings

For the first time each one sings.

Risen are we from repose

To bring the end of all things close.

Joy we breathe with every breath,

In the very face of death.

ALL THE OTHERS.

Long the readied candles wait

For the sleeping dead to wake,

Till they burn down and are spent

In our outstretched hands.

Neither do we weep nor worry,

We but carry, carry, carry

Candles that are slowly spent

In our outstretched hands.

When we sing our final song

We lie down where we belong,

With our candles, if not spent,
In our outstretched hands.

FIRST SUBTERRANEAN.
Count the steps with careful count,
For this place is chosen ground.

Seven times we make a ring
With death's eternal signet string.

Guests are coming from afar.
Surely you know who they are.

ALL.
Yes, we know who is expected.
That is why we have collected
Candles that will all be spent
In our outstretched hands.

When we hear their steps about,
Let the candles be burnt out;
Let them all be wholly spent
In our outstretched hands.

For we speak not, only tarry,
And we carry, carry, carry
Candles that are wholly spent
In our outstretched hands.

FIRST SUBTERRANEAN.
For the last time bend your head
To the circling, bounding thread.

Then return to sleep at last,
For the end approaches fast.

ALL.
Now we end the seventh turn,
Holding stiffly, as they burn,
Candles not entirely spent
In our outstretched hands.

FIRST SUBTERRANEAN.
Near and nearer, very near,
Whispers of their names I hear

Names that flutter fleetingly,
Since they number one in three.

One has been here all along.
He has heard our soaring song.

There he stands with gaping eye,
Knowing neither what nor why.

Someone did the clothing sear
Of him who is a stranger here.

ALL.

Let the standing stranger stay,
See the candles as they sway,
Candles that are slowly spent
In our outstretched hands.

For we swear upon his head
He will soon be dying, dead.
Snuff the candles, though unspent,
In our outstretched hands.

(*They snuff the candles and sink back into the places from which they appeared.*)

GOLEM.

If I must remain forever,
Let me sit within the round
Circled by the counted paces
Measuring the chosen ground.

No more spirits do I hear,
Only one—that lit this place.
Death lies heavy on my hands
And my hands—upon my face.

(*He sits down inside the marked-off circle. An invisible hand pushes* THE YOUNG BEGGAR *into the cave. He is fettered to a long chain. He has been pushed so hard that he falls to the ground. He lies a while and then arises.*)

YOUNG BEGGAR.

Here I am at last,
And at last set free.
In the final hour,
I am one of three.

Trip my stumbling feet,
Chain that circles round.
Closer comes my death
With each opened wound.

Hither have I come
Nevermore to leave.
I my own consoler
As I sit and grieve.

Eat into the stone,
Flesh-tormenting pain.
To console myself
I remain, remain.

(*Feeling about in the darkness.*)

Where are you? Answer me.
We must renew old friendship,
We three who must be here, yes, three, three,
Three.
And sit here hip to hip.

The world goes its way; we go ours.
No one is between us.
The madness of the final, final, final
Wonders
Will itself protect us.

Attend to what I say,
Oh nailed-one on your cross.
We shape a peace, a peace, a peace
Forever from today.
You, Golem, are you lost?

(*He stumbles into* THE GOLEM.)

GOLEM.
　　Go! I sit within the circle,
　　Since I must forever stay.

YOUNG BEGGAR.
　　Take me too within the circle;
　　I will stay forever too.

GOLEM.
　　Then sit. But tell me, where is he,
　　He who is to be the third?

YOUNG BEGGAR.
　　Soon he will be with us too,
　　He who is to be the third.

GOLEM.
　　You repeat the words I say
　　As I say them, word for word.

YOUNG BEGGAR.

    The words you say are my words too;

    So I say them, word for word.

GOLEM.

    Still you bandage your old wounds.

YOUNG BEGGAR.

    Yes, I bandage still my wounds.

GOLEM.

    You exude the smell of rot.

YOUNG BEGGAR.

    Yes, it is the smell of rot.

GOLEM (*shouting*).

    Silence!

    (*Both sit in silence.*)

YOUNG BEGGAR.

    Two whole days my parching gums

    Have not felt the taste of water.

GOLEM.

    Drink. Bottles two,

    Filled and brimming, wait for you.

YOUNG BEGGAR (*takes a bottle, opens it, puts it to his lips and cries out in alarm*).

    Blood!

GOLEM.

    Why the shouting and the outcry?

    Put it back and let it stay.

    (*An invisible hand pushes in* THE MAN WITH THE CROSS *on his shoulders. He is bowed down under the weight of the cross.*)

MAN WITH THE CROSS.

    Here I am at last

    And at last set free.

    In my final hour

    I am one of three.

    Press me to the dust

    As I have always been.

    I already know

    What it is I must.

    Seeking my redemption

    Along the wall I grope,

    In pain await the end.

    I have no other hope.

    Nails that pierce my hands,

Thorns that are my crown—
Scrape along the walls,
Till I wear you down.

(*He gropes in the dark, calling.*)
Where are you? I am lost;
I am alone, alone, alone—
Rejected.
I do not dare put down the cross.
My Master bade me wear it.

Oh, blessed be His mouth that gave;
I can but bless, forgive and bless,
And understand.
My master is my former slave;
My kingdom is at hand.
(*He comes upon the two who are seated.*)

GOLEM.
Stop. We sit within the circle,
Since we must forever stay.

MAN WITH THE CROSS.
Take me too into the circle;
I will stay forever too.

GOLEM.
Then sit. Now that we are three,
All are here that should be here.

YOUNG BEGGAR.
All are here that should be here.

MAN WITH THE CROSS.
Now that we are all three here,
All are here that should be here.

GOLEM.
You, too, speak the way he does,
Saying over, word for word.

MAN WITH THE CROSS.
The words you say are my words, too,
So I say them, word for word.

GOLEM.
Do you carry still the cross?

MAN WITH THE CROSS.
Yes, I carry still the cross.

GOLEM.
You exude the smell of death.

MAN WITH THE CROSS.
Yes, it is the smell of death.

GOLEM.
　Silence. Do not speak.
MAN WITH THE CROSS.
　I am thirsty.
GOLEM.
　Drink. Bottles two,
　Filled and brimming, wait for you.
MAN WITH THE CROSS (*puts a bottle to his mouth and cries out*).
　Blood!
GOLEM.
　Why the shouting? Can't you drink?
　Put it back and let it stay.

　(THE CAVE SPIRITS *return and dance around them again.*)
CAVE SPIRITS.
　Once again
　And yet again—
　Now the threesome is complete;
　Here the final hour they meet;
　They await no more to greet,
　None at all,
　None at all.

　On the cross there lies the axe;
　On the sack the chain lies lax;
　Let their friendship slowly wax,
　In the ring,
　In the ring.

　Round and round,
　Round and round,
　Keep on whirling, dancing so;
　We shall dance away your woe;
　Who we are, you surely know—
　None at all,
　None at all.

　Well protected you will be,
　Your protecting spirits—we.
　Sit embracing each, you three,
　In the ring,
　In the ring.

　(*They whirl more and more madly.*)

　Oh, redeemers, you redeemers,
　Be redeemed.

Harken to our stern decree:
Not to wring your hands in bliss,
Nor to stab your eyes in glee.
Let your solace be remiss.

Finally you found your way here.
Rest instead:
You have borne your burdens well.
Is there more that you can tell?
See how ably we can spread,
We can cover, we can smear
Blood that's dead.

Your rule is acknowledged here
Where you reign.
Loyal subjects that we are,
We obey you near and far.
We protect you, we amuse you
Without gain.

Anoint your heads, redeemed brothers,
Each the others'.
Your exalted brows bow down.
Press your temples till it dazes,
Till the raging fire that blazes
Is your crown.

(CAVE SPIRITS *leave.* THE SUBTERRANEANS *return with the
unconsumed candles in their hands. As softly as before
they dance around the three.*)

FIRST SUBTERRANEAN.

With a voice that clearly rings
For the first time each one sings.

Risen are we from repose
To bring the end of all things close.

Three together, see them sit;
Neither speak nor move a whit.

Who they are you surely know.
Sing the story of their woe.

ALL.

There is nothing more to sing.
There's the cross—but not to carry;
There's the chain—but not to ring;
There's the axe—but not to harry.

So we sing the song of nothing.

No one's lids are locked by us;
They are locked without our help.
No one's tears are caused by us;
They are shed without our help.

So we sing the song of nothing.

We leave steps on no one's road.
Neither do we rouse nor kill.
No one journeys forth to greet us.
No one bids us warm farewell.

So we sing the song of nothing.

There's no need for us to hurry;
So we softly dance and turn,
And we carry, carry, carry
Candles that will never burn.

And we sing the song of nothing.

FIRST SUBTERRANEAN.

Not an outcry, not a moan—
Sitting there like chiselled stone.

Dead worms creep and crawl and hurry
In the heart of all their glory.

No surcease they brought, but snares
To him who waited with his cares.

Chastisement they brought, not calm
To him who waited for their balm.

Just a pretext, just a hoax
For the fool who likes his jokes.

ALL.

Since they sit there in their muteness,
Our tongues can only babble.
We would point in some direction,
But our fingers are like stubble.

So we sing the song of madness.

Everything that had beginning
Long ago came to an end.
Footsteps printed in the road
Long are covered by the wind.

So we sing the song of madness.

Hands that wring themselves in wrath
Ever in their wrath stay wrung;
Long ago there was fulfilled
Every promise ever sung.

So we sing the song of madness.

FIRST SUBTERRANEAN.
Slowly, slowly, rein your pace.
Each of you, conceal his face.

No more will we come or stay;
No more will we dance or sway.

Keep your voices soft and slow;
No more come we from below.

On these candles let us spit—
Leave these silent three to sit.

ALL.
There is hardly need to spit,
For the flames themselves expire.
Let us throw upon this threesome
Wicks that will no more show fire.

So we go back to the grave.

Brush your hands off, brush them well,
Take a step and turn around.
For eternity grow silent
As you sink into the ground.

So we go back to the grave.

(*The candles go out in their hands. Darkness. Everything
disappears. Several moments elapse. Steps are heard and
a light appears. THE MAHARAL hurries in carrying a lantern. THE GOLEM is sitting along guarding the bottles. His
eyes are gaping and his face is like a madman's. He does not
move a muscle.*)

MAHARAL.
Great God, why are you sitting here?
Why are you silent?
(*He sees the bottles.*)
You found it? Quickly, now, remove it.
Why do you sit?

(THE GOLEM *does not move his head. Says nothing.*)
Answer, speak.
What happened?
(THE GOLEM *does not reply.*)
Do you not see who speaks to you?
(*Shakes him by the shoulders.*)
I tell you, speak.
Do you not know me? Have you grown mute?

GOLEM (*looks at* THE MAHARAL. *Lowers his head again*).
Who are you? Go away.

MAHARAL.
You do not know me?

GOLEM.
I do not. Nothing. Leave.
(*He jumps up crying.*)
Have you come back to torture me? Away! Away!

MAHARAL.
What happened to you? You are scorched and blackened.
What are you doing now?

GOLEM (*sinking to ground*).
Let me. Let me.
Say nothing. I do not know. Something burned
And barked and stormed and danced
And sang and died. Remove this blood!
Remove it! Take it far away!

MAHARAL (*takes him by the hand*).
Be calm and look at me. And be yourself again.
(THE GOLEM *sinks back into rigidity.*)
You do not recognize me yet?

GOLEM.
Who are you?

MAHARAL.
I am the Rabbi.

GOLEM.
The Rabbi? Who is this Rabbi? You wish to sit?
It is forbidden. Do not come to me nor touch me.
This spot is marked and bounded and surrounded
For me alone and no one else.

MAHARAL.
If madness so contorts your face,
Let madness leave you. Hear and understand.
Your life is now at stake. Your mission still
Is not fulfilled and yet how deeply sunk
You are in fear and madness! Poor being,

What have you done with all your brightness and your joy?
Where did you scatter them and lose them?
Darkness and wild terror have possessed you.
Awaken! If your eyes are blinded,
Then seek with blinded eyes; but bring back
The brightness that I gave you.
Wake up!

GOLEM.

Oh, do not waken me. I am happy so.
I will lie down and rest. There. You see?

(*He lies down and curls up.*)

MAHARAL.

I bid you rise and be as once you were.
Let this bewilderment be taken from your eyes
And your distorted features take their proper shape.

GOLEM.

Whoever you may be, desist from torment.

MAHARAL.

Go quickly. End your mission.

GOLEM.

What mission do I have?
You are a stranger here. What can I do for you?
You see, now all is spinning once again.
And now I'm well and all is bright,
And I am unafraid. I know all now.
My well of breath runs dry.

MAHARAL.

You must fulfill your mission. You must!

GOLEM.

Call no more. Leave me here. Forever.

MAHARAL.

You must fulfill your mission. You must!

GOLEM.

Be quiet. Here they come. They come to me.
To me alone.

MAHARAL.

Who comes?

GOLEM.

Do you not see? Do you not hear?
Be quiet, quiet, quiet.

(*Suddenly he arises, opens his eyes wide, and embraces* THE
MAHARAL.)

Oh, Rabbi, Rabbi! Are you here? My Rabbi!

SCENE VIII. THE LAST MISSION

(The anteroom of the old synagogue. It is Friday evening and the Sabbath is being welcomed. Through the open door opposite, a part of the synagogue can be seen: the Holy Ark, chandeliers, and the gathered worshippers. At left, a door to the courtyard. THE GOLEM is stretched out on a bench. He looks shabby, unkempt, lean and sleepy. He is wearing only one shoe. The other foot is bare and its torn shoe lies where it was dropped.

THE GOLEM leaps up with all his strength, closes the door to the synagogue, and falls back on his bench.)

SHAMMES *(coming in)*.
>   Did you hear that slam? Where do you think you are?
>   Why should it vex you if the door is open?

GOLEM.
>   If I shut it, let it stay shut. And they—
>   They constantly come by and open it.
>   If it is shut, let it stay shut.

SHAMMES.
>   Indeed! If he shuts it! And who are you?
>   That's impudence for you!

GOLEM *(muttering)*.
>   If it is shut, then leave it shut. Leave it shut.

SHAMMES.
>   What are you muttering about? Speak louder.

GOLEM.
>   It's no concern of theirs.
>   *(Turns with his face to the wall.)*

SHAMMES.
>   And how long will you lie there?
>   Near time to say the prayers of Sabbath welcome.
>   The Rabbi too will soon be here;
>   And you have not yet even put your shoes on.

GOLEM.
>   What shoes?

337

SHAMMES.

What do you mean "what shoes?" Your shoes, not mine.

GOLEM.

I wear one, can't you see?

SHAMMES.

A waste of words to talk with you, a waste.

GOLEM.

Well, hand it over and I'll put it on.

SHAMMES.

I hand it over?

GOLEM.

If you don't want to, don't. Away from me!

SHAMMES.

It is forbidden to walk barefoot
In a synagogue.

(THE GOLEM *does not reply*.)

Can you not hear what you are told? Are you deaf?
The prayers will soon begin.

GOLEM.

I don't know how to pray.

SHAMMES.

You are a savage. You should be sent away.

GOLEM.

The Rabbi hasn't come? He isn't here?

SHAMMES.

Why do you ask?

GOLEM.

No reason. Tell him that I want him.
Go tell him to hand me my shoe.

SHAMMES.

Your shoe? The Rabbi?

GOLEM.

And why do you repeat? Can't you hear?
(*Jumping up*.)

Go tell him that I want him; Joseph wants him.

SHAMMES.

Such impudence! I've never heard the likes! Madman!

GOLEM.

I told you: go.
(*He springs toward him*.)

SHAMMES (*runs to the door, shouting*).

Come quickly everyone; come quickly.
(THE GOLEM *flops back onto his bench*.)

SHAMMES (*at the door*).
>This man has surely lost his mind,
>He rotted there so long in Tower Five.
>He was supposed to chop our wood and carry water.
>A fine state I would be in if I had
>To wait for him to bring me wood and water.
>He has been put up in the anteroom,
>Given a bench to sleep on, food and drink.
>Cared for, and he—has no regard.
>Either he sleeps for two whole days on end
>Or wakes, as now, for three nights in succession.
>A riddle, on my word.

GOLEM.
>Tonight I will not shout.
>I will be quiet.

SHAMMES.
>You will be quiet? Sure. You said that yesterday,
>And still you bellowed all night long.
>No one closed an eye. The yard was crowded.

GOLEM.
>Tonight I will be still. I will be still.

SHAMMES.
>Why don't you wash yourself? Put on your shoes.
>The Sabbath comes into the world,
>And what a Sabbath this one is.

GOLEM.
>Away from me.

SHAMMES.
>Did you not hear about the miracle?

GOLEM.
>What miracle? What miracle? Oh, let me be.
>(*Stretches out face down on the bench.*)

SHAMMES.
>He's really mad.
>(*He opens the door to leave.*)

GOLEM (*calls*).
>You send the Rabbi here. I want Reb Levi.

SHAMMES.
>Get up and come into the synagogue
>And wash your face.

GOLEM.
>When he arrives then I'll get up and wash.
>When he arrives.

SHAMMES.

Have you ever heard the like?

GOLEM.

A week has passed since I first came;
Not once has he been here to see me.

SHAMMES.

And he should come to you?

GOLEM.

He cast me utterly aside;
Put me in here and now he does not come.
I pleaded with him so:
Don't take me from the cave and from the darkness.

SHAMMES.

What cave?

GOLEM.

You do not know? That cave.

SHAMMES.

I don't know what you're saying.

GOLEM.

I may not speak of it or tell. I must be mute.
Away from me. I may not speak. I must be mute.

(THE SHAMMES *leaves quietly. He leaves the door open.
Men poke their heads in, look around, and disappear.
THE TALL MAN and THE REDHEAD come in and stand
near the door.*)

TALL MAN.

I tell you, he is—he. The same Joseph.

REDHEAD.

Hush, do not mention him by name.

TALL MAN.

No matter. See? He doesn't even move.

REDHEAD.

Do you recall how there he bounded in
Whenever we would speak his name?

TALL MAN.

Do I recall? Of course I do.

REDHEAD.

Is he asleep?
He might decide to pounce on us.

TALL MAN.

They say he sleeps from sun to sun.

REDHEAD.

You mark my words: there's something curious
In this, more by far than meets the eye.

TALL MAN.

No mystery at all. A clod, a golem.

REDHEAD.

> Do you recall those two—the wandering beggars?

TALL MAN.

> Of course I do.

REDHEAD.

> And how they were afraid of him?
> As soon as they laid eyes on him,
> Without a word they ran, like men possessed.

TALL MAN.

> Who can tell?
> The Rabbi himself ordered them to leave.
> He must have known them from before and was
> Unwilling for them to remain in Prague.

REDHEAD.

> You know what I will tell you? It was he
> Who pummeled Thaddeus. He was the one.

TALL MAN.

> He?
> But he left Tower Five with us.

REDHEAD.

> If I say it was he, then it was he.

TALL MAN.

> How do you know?

REDHEAD.

> I know; for that night really opened up
> My eyes, though how and who I cannot tell.
> I only know: something strange occurred
> In Prague the night we left, driven out
> Of Tower Five, our bundles on our backs,
> And mutely trudged from street to silent street
> Not knowing where to knock for shelter, and he
> Behind us, huge and heavy, empty-handed,
> Arms dangling, feet like hammers. In my heart
> I felt each step of his. And then we looked
> Around and saw him standing still behind us.
> Remember that?

TALL MAN.

> I felt relieved when he fell back and stopped.

REDHEAD.

> And no one even thought of calling him.
> I can still see him standing there, in the middle
> Of the street, his long arms hanging limp,
> Stock still as he descried and heard something
> That was happening in Prague.

TALL MAN.

A night that was, a night indeed!

REDHEAD.

And he went back to Tower Five
And stayed there. Did you know?

TALL MAN.

Yes, I heard them say so.
(THE SHAMMES *enters.*)

SHAMMES.

The service is about to start.
The Rabbi has arrived.

GOLEM (*having been lying with his face to the wall throughout, he now jumps up*).

Arrived, has he? Is he here?

SHAMMES.

He is. Why do you ask?

TALL MAN (*frightened*).

He's not the same at all. How changed he is.

REDHEAD.

How lean and how unkempt! He doesn't see us.
Or do you think he doesn't recognize us?

GOLEM.

I must get dressed! Quickly! My shoes!
(*He finds his shoe, starts to put it on, and then hurls it
away.*)
Let him come here—and then I'll put it on.
You send the Rabbi here. I'm waiting.

SHAMMES.

But this is utter madness!

REDHEAD.

Perhaps he needs him? Who can tell?

GOLEM.

I want to see him.

REDHEAD.

Are you afraid to go into the synagogue?

GOLEM.

He told me to remain here always. Penned
Me up in here and doesn't come to see me.
(*He sits with his head hanging.*)

TALL MAN.

You probably did something wrong.
(THE GOLEM *bellows incomprehensibly.*)

REDHEAD.

Should I hand you your shoe?

GOLEM.

Away from me!

REDHEAD.

But we are in the synagogue, not in the tower.

GOLEM *(stands up, his eyes directed towards* THE REDHEAD*)*.

The·tower?

TALL MAN.

The same eyes, don't you see? Come away.

REDHEAD.

Again he stands as he stood in the street:
His arms hang limp; he stands and listens
To something happening in Prague.

SHAMMES.

Why do you tease him?

REDHEAD.

I am not teasing him. I only want
To tell him that the tower stands vacant.

GOLEM.

Vacant?

REDHEAD.

And all the doors are boarded up,
And all the windows too.

GOLEM.

Then I'll go rip them off.

REDHEAD.

Someone will only nail them back aagin.
Besides, nobody sleeps there any more.

GOLEM.

I'm going back. I will not stay here.

REDHEAD.

Who stops you?

GOLEM.

The Rabbi stops me.
(Screaming.)
Go get the Rabbi!
(Hammering on the wall.)
Get the Rabbi!
You, what do you want here? Who are you?
(Surprised.)
You came from there? You boarded up the doors
And left? And Tower Five is left alone?
Alone? And he who sits there, he who waits
For me can never leave and come to meet me?

REDHEAD.

> Who is the man that waits there for you?

GOLEM.

> What do you mean—who?
> If I am here then *he* is there alone.
> And all along I heard him calling me.
> He called in such a choking voice
> As though someone were strangling him.
> Now I know why. The doors are boarded up.
> Away from me! Get out of here!
> (*He rushes toward them with fists flying, just as* THE
> MAHARAL *comes in.*)

MAHARAL.

> Do not raise your hand!

GOLEM (*recoils. He senses* THE MAHARAL'S *eyes upon him and
he hangs his head. Suddenly, with joy, he cries*).

> Oh, Rabbi.

MAHARAL.

> Against whom do you raise up your hand?

GOLEM (*stammering*).

> Forgive me, Rabbi.

MAHARAL (*to the assembled Jews*).

> Go to the synagogue.
> (*They leave.*)
> The Shammes says you want to see me.
> (THE GOLEM *does not reply.*)
> Why are you silent? Speak. What do you want?

GOLEM.

> What should I want?

MAHARAL.

> You called me, did you not?
> And you are barefoot!

GOLEM.

> You want me to get dressed, Rabbi?

MAHARAL.

> Do I want?

GOLEM.

> But you deserted me.

MAHARAL.

> So shabby and unkempt and dirty too.
> The Shammes says you lie awake all night.

GOLEM.

> I cannot sleep. I am afraid.

MAHARAL.

Of whom?

GOLEM.

All of last night I lay in fear
Of my right shoulder.

MAHARAL.

Why of the right one?

GOLEM.

I do not know, Rabbi. I turned to look
With both eyes at my left one. Suddenly
I saw the right one start to rise and rise
And, growing large, crawl over to the other side.
I fell upon the ground, face down, and hid
My eyes and lay there. Then once again I heard
Someone yank back my head from where it lay
And force me once again to see my shoulder.

MAHARAL.

And after that?

GOLEM.

I saw I could not hide.
My shoulder suddenly tore off and turned
Into an arm that reached from here to Tower Five.
The fingers curled themselves about my neck
As if someone wanted to embrace and kiss me.
And then the arm stretched out to beckon me,
And all the fingers winked and cracked,
And all began to weep and moan,
And the weeping reached from here up to the tower.

MAHARAL.

And yet you wanted to remain there.

GOLEM.

Because you wanted to be far from me.

MAHARAL.

How do you know?

GOLEM.

You do not need me any more.

MAHARAL.

And how do you know that?

GOLEM.

I have fulfilled your every mission.

MAHARAL.

But are you sure there are no more?

GOLEM.

> You neither come nor call me any more.
> Stay here with me.

MAHARAL.

> I am with you.

GOLEM.

> Stay with me always. Do not go to them.

MAHARAL.

> Do you quite understand the things you say?

GOLEM (*jumping up*).

> I do!

MAHARAL.

> Why do you jump? Stand still.

GOLEM.

> Why do you torture me?

MAHARAL.

> I gave you freedom and I bade you go
> Wherever you desired.

GOLEM.

> You put me here.

MAHARAL.

> When I permitted you to go
> You chose to stay.

GOLEM.

> And where should I have gone
> Since you hold fast my life within your grasp?

MAHARAL.

> How is *that* known to you?

GOLEM.

> I know all now. Your hand
> Lies over me but you are not with me.

MAHARAL.

> How should I be with you?

GOLEM.

> Stay here with me forever in the anteroom.
> I wil give up my sleeping bench to you
> And I will lie at your feet upon the floor.

MAHARAL.

> So much unrest in your heart and so much hate;
> So much dark passion and cold anger
> And helplessness flow in your veins.
> How can the fault be yours? No mother's breath
> In childhood hovered over you;

No angel's pinion brushed your crib.
And I was certain you would save yourself,
Find peace and start to live as all live,
As Jews live.

GOLEM.

Rabbi, Rabbi.

MAHARAL.

You cannot free yourself of helplessness;
There is no hindrance you can overcome,
And least of all yourself. What does it matter
That you did perceive some faint glimmer,
If everything that was revealed to you
Did not enlarge your life or calm unrest
Or let a smile be born upon your lips?
You ask me to discard the world, to leave it
And here remain with you. And if I do?

GOLEM.

My restlessness will leave me.

MAHARAL.

Your unrest is your fate. You fashioned it
Yourself when first you looked upon God's world:
You did not smile.
Is it enough for you to drag about
Half barefoot and half shod while Jews are praying?
Is that enough?
(THE GOLEM *stands covering his face.*)
You are unhappy. I know. But once or twice
Try going to the synagogue with all
The worshippers and try to understand.
I bade you to be quiet, to stand aside
But not to be estranged. You just as soon
As you appeared among the people there,
You took so strange a stance and looked so wild,
That all ran off in terror. How everything
Would warm to you if only once you smiled.
(THE GOLEM *stands very sad.*)
Why don't you answer?

GOLEM.

Do not forsake me.

MAHARAL.

The congregation waits to pray with me;
Should I sit here with you?

GOLEM.

Then let me go to Tower Five again.

MAHARAL.

    The tower is closed.

GOLEM.

    Forever?

MAHARAL.

    Forever.

    (He walks toward the synagogue door.)

GOLEM.

    Don't go away from me.

    (He seizes THE MAHARAL *by the arm.)*

MAHARAL.

    Be still. Enough.

GOLEM *(demandingly)*.

    I say, remain!

MAHARAL.

    So? You command?

GOLEM.

    I command.

MAHARAL.

    Do *your* lips speak these words?

GOLEM.

    Yes, mine.

MAHARAL.

    So? Yours?

GOLEM.

    Yes, mine. You see this hand?

    It, too, is mine!

    (He holds his fist threateningly over THE MAHARAL's *head.*
    THE MAHARAL *does not flinch. He pierces* THE GOLEM
    with his eyes. THE GOLEM *remains poised with his fist in*
    the air as though frozen.)

MAHARAL.

    Why do you stand unmoving? Lower your arm.

    (He goes into the synagogue, closing the door behind him.
    THE GOLEM *sinks to the floor. He falls and throws his arms*
    around his head. Then he starts to tear his hair and his
    clothes. He stretches out with his face to the floor and loses
    his breath in a long, drawn-out moan. Silence. The prayers
    of Sabbath welcome are heard through the door. The
    candles on the reading stand in the anteroom begin to
    flicker and sputter. THE GOLEM *gets up on all fours, crawls*
    over to his sleeping bench, and throws himself upon it.
    The door opens from time to time, heads look in and dis-
    appear again. THE GOLEM *stands up, takes his shoe, tries*

*to put it on, but his hands shake. He throws his shoe away.
He finds some pieces of bread and takes several bites. As
he chews he grimaces. He drinks some water and splashes
it over his face.*

*All at once he takes an axe from under his pillow, the
axe with which he used to chop wood. He stations himself
near the door, opens it slowly, and looks into the synagogue. He opens the door and closes it. It is obvious that
he is contemplating some terrifying act. He raises the axe
high. Suddenly he runs from the door to the window,
smashes the glass with the axe and jumps through the
window into the street.*

*Every word of the cantor's is now heard clearly. He be-
gins to recite the words "mizmor shir lyom hashabbos,"
and the congregation follows him, when suddenly screams
of terror, wailing of women and children are heard from
the street. Then the crash of shattered glass and collapsing
walls. The crowd in the synagogue is heard stamping toward the door to the anteroom. The door bursts open and
people pour in. No one knows what has happened. They
all start for the street.)*

MAHARAL *(runs in, deathly pale, claps his hands together).*
He is gone! He is gone!
*(He starts to run out when he is met by the returning
crowd of men, women, and children wringing their hands
and moaning.)*
What happened?

ALL.
—The servant! The Golem! With his axe!
—Out there are two with bloodied heads!
—He is destroying Prague!
—He ruins houses!
(All follow THE MAHARAL *out. The doors are open. The
sounds of running and shouting.)*

TANKHUM.
My head! My head!
Who will save, eh?
*(He runs into the synagogue. The commotion in the street
comes closer and closer.* THE MAHARAL *leads* THE GOLEM
in by the hand in which THE GOLEM *holds a bloodied axe.
The crowd bursts in and presses toward* THE GOLEM.
Women moan. With one hand THE MAHARAL *restrains*
THE GOLEM; *with the other he protects him from the
crowd.)*

MAHARAL.

I bid you all: go into the synagogue.

THE CROWD.

—He has spilled blood!

—Jewish blood!

—Stone him!

MAHARAL.

I bid you all to go to the synagogue.

(The crowd goes into the synagogue. THE MAHARAL closes both doors. THE GOLEM stands in the middle of the room. The axe, as if frozen to his hand, descends slowly.)

MAHARAL.

What have you done? Does your mind grasp that? Tell me.

GOLEM.

I have spilled blood.

MAHARAL.

Are you aware whose blood it was you spilled?

GOLEM.

Jewish blood.

MAHARAL *(buries his face on the reading stand where the Sabbath candles are burning).*

On my head falls the blood. On my head.

He came to save and yet he shed our blood.

Are we thus punished for our joy, Oh Lord?

Are we chastised because we wished to save ourselves?

Did You not grant approval?

Was not this done through You?

Why, then, such castigation?

(Silence.)

Or did You only wish to try me?

Did You reveal to me the more than human,

Allow me to create, to rule, command,

Only that I might see at last

My insignificance, my massive sin?

And more than that—my sin against all Jews?

That, in impatience and despair, I wished

To turn my back on those ways of Your people

That are eternal, gentle, patient, full of faith?

My sin in wanting what the foe lays claim to?

The foe demanded what was his.

The blood that I desired to save—I shed.

(Pause.)

I quite forgot the axe.

Why are you silent? Speak. You found the axe
So useful. Let me also bend my head.
Now split it. Let the axe taste my blood too.

GOLEM.

Rabbi.

MAHARAL.

Oh, quiet! Do you still say "Rabbi," you Golem you!

GOLEM.

Rabbi.

MAHARAL.

How great and just is Your chastisement, Lord.
And he—can he be even charged with guilt?
Since he has mighty fists—he raises them.
You opened wide my eyes to see that I
Lack wholly any power over fists.
And now? What will be now?

GOLEM.

You will be with me.

MAHARAL.

The prisoner of your large fists.

GOLEM.

You will stay with me.

MAHARAL.

In a net of blood and muddied madness.
And should I leave you—

GOLEM.

Then I will again—

MAHARAL.

You planned it all; you planned it well.

GOLEM.

For longing.

MAHARAL.

So? For longing? You have taken me
And keep me captive from all the Jews and all the world.
Without you I will not be free to move.
I will sit here, sleep here. Ingenious plan.

GOLEM (*joyfully*).

You'll always stay with me?
And never leave? Why do you look so angry?
What harm have I done you? Sit down, Rabbi.
Or would you like to rest? You're tired.
No one will come in here.

MAHARAL.

> No one will come in here. And there
> The congregation stands and waits.
> *(He sits down on the bench and rests his head wearily on his hand. THE GOLEM stands near him, grateful and contented.)*

GOLEM.

> You will not go away, Rabbi?

MAHARAL.

> With you. With you. I will not leave.
> I will stay here. Sleep here, eat here.
> With one foot shod and face unwashed.
> And there the flock will stand and wait
> To sing its psalm of Sabbath welcome.
> And I will not appear before the worshippers.

GOLEM.

> What are you saying, Rabbi? Careful, you nearly fell.
> What ails you, Rabbi?

MAHARAL.

> They will grow tired of waiting, and they will
> Finish the prayers without me and go home.
> And I will stay here just with you, with you.
> The candles will soon burn their last.
> It will be dark—so unlike the Sabbath.
> What do you say, Joseph? Anything?

GOLEM.

> I have not said a word, Rabbi.

MAHARAL.

> It will be dark, and we will sit together,
> As we do now, you with your bloodied axe
> And I—
> *(He sinks down without finishing. A commotion is heard from the synagogue. Someone is struggling to get to the door. It bursts open and DEVORALE runs in. Someone from inside the synagogue closes the door again.)*

DEVORALE.

> Grandfather, Grandfather!
> *(She weeps.)*

GOLEM *(joyfully)*.

> Oh, Rabbi, look! It's Devorale.

MAHARAL *(raises his head)*.

> What is it, child?

DEVORALE.

> I am afraid, Grandfather. Come out of here.

Grandmother is crying; all are crying. Come.
What ails you, Grandfather?

GOLEM.

The Rabbi will remain with me. Don't cry.
You have come too? You will stay too, Devorale?

DEVORALE.

What is he saying, Grandfather? Speak to me?

MAHARAL.

Don't cry, my child.

GOLEM.

You will be mine! You will be mine!

DEVORALE.

What is he saying, Grandfather?
(*She throws her arms around* THE MAHARAL.)

MAHARAL.

I'm weary and I'm resting. Stop your tears.

DEVORALE (*charges at* THE GOLEM).

Murderer!

GOLEM (*grasps her by the arm*).

No need for shouting. Do not fear. The Rabbi rests.
Do not awaken him. And do not cry.
I will not harm you. Will you stay?

DEVORALE (*struggles to tear her arm out of his grasp*).

Don't touch me! Go away!

GOLEM.

You should not shout. The Rabbi doesn't shout.
And I am happy; I am overjoyed.
(*He draws close to her.*)
How sweet is the aroma of your hair.
How warm your hands. Why do you run from me?
I hold you firmly. You are mine. Mine.
You came to me.

DEVORALE.

Why are you silent, Grandfather? Look at him!
(THE MAHARAL *sits in utter dejection.*)

GOLEM.

Yes, you are mine! You are! And you are good.
Where were you all this time? Oh, Devorale!
(*He hugs her tight.* DEVORALE'S *weeping is muffled by his
embrace.*)

MAHARAL (*stands up, wringing his hands*).

Is she your captive too?
(*With regained strength.*)
Joseph! You Golem, you!

(THE GOLEM *releases* DEVORALE.)

DEVORALE *(throws her arms about* THE MAHARAL).
>   Hide me! Take me away!

MAHARAL *(firmly)*.
>   Go tell them in the synagogue I'm coming.

DEVORALE.
>   Come now. I am afraid.

MAHARAL.
>   I bade you go.
>   Be reassured, my child, and go.
>   (DEVORALE *leaves fearfully.*)

GOLEM.
>   Where did she go? Where to? And why?

MAHARAL.
>   No one must witness the fulfillment of your mission.

GOLEM.
>   Mission? What mission? Have I not
>   Performed your every task?

MAHARAL.
>   The final task. You see, the candles all
>   Are dying down. A single light,
>   The last, still flickers. Soon it too
>   Will die. You must make haste.

GOLEM.
>   Where shall I hasten, Rabbi?

MAHARAL.
>   To leave the darkness. The seconds that remain
>   Are few, a very few. When all is dark,
>   The moment will have passed for your last labor.
>   I tell you, hurry.

GOLEM.
>   What must I do?

MAHARAL.
>   Do not inquire. All has been locked
>   And sealed; all is forgiven.
>   I am restored and rested.

GOLEM.
>   I obey, Rabbi. Send me and I go.

MAHARAL.
>   You need not go. Here, before my eyes,
>   You will perform the final task. Lie on the ground.

GOLEM.
>   As then? To press my ear and listen?

MAHARAL.
> You will hear nothing now. The earth is dumb.
> She rests. It is the Sabbath. You will also rest.

GOLEM.
> What will you do with me?

MAHARAL.
> You heard my words. I give you Sabbath rest.
> Your whole life cries for rest.
> Now lie upon the ground.

GOLEM (*lies down on the floor*).
> I'm lying, Rabbi.

MAHARAL.
> Stretch out your legs.

GOLEM.
> I have stretched out.

MAHARAL.
> Stretch out your arms.

GOLEM (*sits up trembling*).
> What will you do with me? What will you do?

MAHARAL.
> Do not inquire.

GOLEM (*stretches his hands pleadingly to* THE MAHARAL).
> Do not command me, Rabbi, to lie down.
> What will you do with me?

MAHARAL.
> There is no answer. Stretch out a second time.

GOLEM.
> I am stretched out full-length, Rabbi.
> You will not leave me, will you, Rabbi?

MAHARAL.
> Close your eyes.

GOLEM.
> You will remain here always, will you not?
> They are already closed.

MAHARAL.
> I issue this decree: Let hands and feet
> And body with its limbs and sinews
> Return unto their rest.
> Breathe out your final breath. Amen.
> (THE GOLEM *no longer moves. The flickering candle on
> the reading stand dies out.*)

MAHARAL (*stands over the dead* GOLEM *a long while. Finally he
stirs. He goes to the synagogue door, opens it, and calls in*).
> Call the Shammes here.

(THE SHAMMES *comes to the door.*)

MAHARAL *(to* THE SHAMMES*).*

    Let no one enter here till after Sabbath.

    And now call everyone to sing again

    From the beginning the Psalm of Sabbath praise.

    (He goes out, closing the door firmly.)